College of St Mark and St John
006162

Max Weber and the dispute over reason and value

International Library of Sociology

Founded by Karl Mannheim

Editor: John Rex, University of
Aston in Birmingham

Arbor Scientiae
Arbor Vitae

A catalogue of books available in the *International Library of Sociology* and other series of Social Science books published by Routledge & Kegan Paul will be found at the end of this volume.

Max Weber and the dispute over reason and value:

A study in philosophy, ethics, and politics

Stephen P. Turner

Regis A. Factor

University of South Florida

Routledge & Kegan Paul

London, Boston, Melbourne and Henley

First published in 1984
by Routledge & Kegan Paul plc
39 Store Street, London WC1E 7DD, England
9 Park Street, Boston, Mass. 02108, USA
464 St Kilda Road, Melbourne,
Victoria 3004, Australia and
Broadway House, Newtown Road,
Henley-on-Thames, Oxon RG9 1EN, England
Set in Times 10/11pt by Columns of Reading
and printed in Great Britain by
Redwood Burn Ltd, Trowbridge, Wiltshire

Library of Congress Cataloging in Publication Data

Turner, Stephen P., 1951-
Max Weber and the dispute over reason and value.
(International library of sociology)
Bibliography: p.
Includes index.
1. Weber, Max, 1864-1920 – Addresses, essays, lectures.
I. Factor, Regis A., 1937-   . II. Title.
III. Series.
B3361.Z7T87 1983   301'.092'4   83-9642

ISBN 0-7100-9889-8

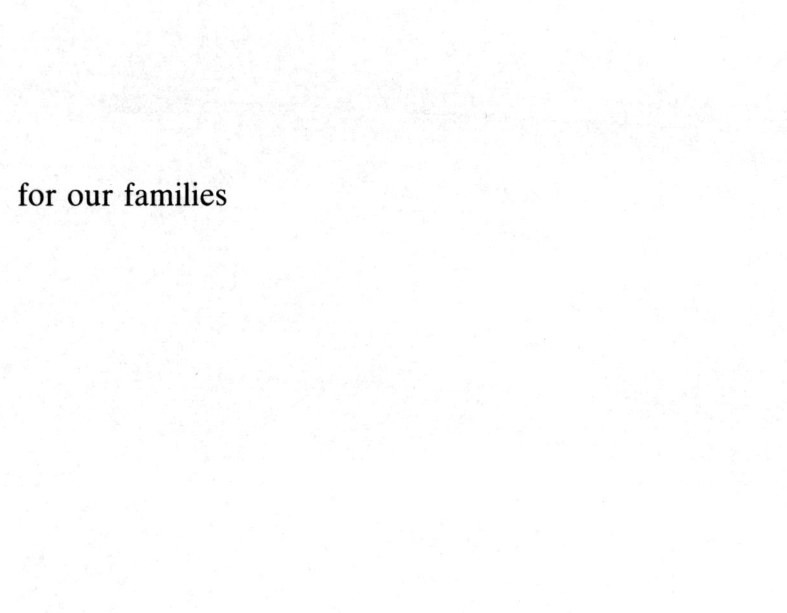

for our families

Contents

Acknowledgments

Portions of Chapter 2 are reprinted, in much modified form, from our article 'The Limits of Reason and Some Limitations of Weber's Morality,' in *Human Studies*, vol. 2 (1979), pp. 301-34, by permission of Ablex Publishing Corporation. Portions of Chapter 9 are reprinted, in modified form, from our article 'The Critique of Positivist Social Science in Leo Strauss and Jürgen Habermas,' published in *Sociological Analysis and Theory*, vol. 7 (1977), pp. 185-206, by permission of Arun Sahay. Quotations in Chapter 7, in the section that discusses the Dewey-Hutchins dispute, are reprinted from *Foundations of the Unity of Sciences: toward an international encyclopedia of unified science*, edited by Otto Neurath, Rudolf Carnap, and Charles Morris, vol. II, pt 4, John Dewey, 'Theory of Valuation,' pages 413-45, originally published as John Dewey, *Theory of Valuation*, vol. II, pt 4 of *International Encyclopedia of Unified Science*, Copyright 1939 by The University of Chicago. Material from the Frank Knight papers is quoted by permission of The University of Chicago Library. We have been helped in this project by many scholars. Robert Eden, Georg Kleine, J. P. Mayer, Guy Oakes, and others have read portions of the manuscript at earlier stages and have made valuable suggestions. The final version was typed by Becky Cox, of The Center for the Study of Science in Society, Virginia Polytechnic Institute and State University, where Turner was Visiting Professor in the fall of 1982. Mrs Cox's integrity, accuracy, and helpfulness made the final typing and revision a pleasure. The library staff of the University of South Florida at St Petersburg, especially Susan Dillinger and Tina Neville, were helpful in tracking down elusive texts. Summer Turner assisted in editing the manuscript. Her encouragement and that of Deborah Factor greatly facilitated completion of this study.

St Petersburg, Florida

Stephen P. Turner
Regis A. Factor

Introduction

Why should anyone care about the history of the arguments for and against Max Weber's conception of the relation of reason, or, more broadly, rational and cognitive knowledge, and values? According to the conventional story, the dispute is uninteresting. Weber was a heroic defender of reason and science against ideological attack; he did not himself hold any unusual views about science or ethics, but defended widely accepted and evident distinctions between science and ideology. Although his views have suffered various politically motivated attacks, by Marxist ideologues, moralistic liberals, Nazis, and, more recently, criticisms by Germans educated after the Second World War under the influence of American natural rights propaganda, Weber's position has prevailed, particularly among social scientists in the United States, primarily because of the similarity between his views and the canons of academic 'liberalism' in the best sense, i.e., the canons of tolerance, fairness, and disinterestedness.

In spite of the plausibility of certain of its elements, this is a fairy tale. No one author or school is responsible for it. It was built up bit by bit and for the most part innocently – such as when Reinhard Bendix, in his influential study of Weber, omitted a discussion of his methodological views, which had been the main subject of Weber discussion in Weimar Germany, and when later interpreters, such as Anthony Giddens, credited Lukács's *Destruction of Reason*, completed in 1952, as the origin of the Frankfurt critique of Weber, neglecting the earlier formulations of these arguments.

Some of what will be said in this book will come into direct conflict with the conventional story. Weber's arguments are quite distinctive both in structure and in their practical moral and political implications. The distinctive structure of connected arguments consists of a version of the fact-value distinction based on the claim that the world is a meaningless chaos, a strategy of argument that uses examples of antinomic values, whose conflict is claimed to be rationally irreconcilable, a 'decisionistic' view of the value choices one must make in life, and a rejection of the 'rationality' claimed for various moral and political ideals and views, which are held to be based on concealed irrational value choices.

These were very convincing ideas, for at their center was an apparently simple fact of logic: if choices between ends must be justified in a deductive way, by reference to a 'higher' end, one is faced with a difficulty over the justification of the 'ultimate' end; it cannot itself be 'justified' in this same way (for nothing can justify an end without the same problem of justification arising for this 'more ultimate' end). So ultimate value choices must be non-rational. It is a short step from this to the idea that various value disputes are the result of conflicting decisions of this rationally irresolvable sort, and a short additional step to other Weberian ideas, such as the view that making a choice and carrying it through consistently is itself a virtue, and that moral sentimentality, when it takes the form of a failure to carry through a choice, is a vice, for it defeats the choice.

The political implications of these ideas were never far away. The world of politics, according to Weber, is a world of struggle between the bearers of various rationally irreconcilable values, and the possibility of the achievement of any value depends on the reality of power. He believed that the achievable values in the present are few and do not include the values of socialism or traditional liberalism, which are, respectively, naive and outdated. The only achievable values are national power and perhaps the preservation of the freedom of personality for the few, though even this, he thought, was increasingly threatened by the historical trend toward bureaucratic forms of social organization.

Some of Weber's friends and admirers restated these and related arguments and adapted them to other domains. Gustav Radbruch did this for the philosophy of law, and Hans J. Morgenthau later did it for international politics. However, flaws in the core arguments were evident by the 1920s, and a long process of adaptation and fragmentation ensued. Much of the process occurred in the course of the emigration, during which many political implications were shed or reformulated. Some writers abandoned or ignored the philosophical value doctrine but preserved Weber's political analyses. Joseph Schumpeter, for example, presented Weber's nonnormative theory of democracy apart from any appeal to Weber's rejection of natural law justifications for democracy.

In the process of adaptation and selection, the distinctiveness of Weber's conception was lost, as was its intellectual unity. Some of its central political implications were suppressed or deemphasized, to the point that Weber's views came to appear to be liberal and democratic. The particular doctrines of value and the limits of science were assimilated to superficially similar Logical Positivist arguments and superficially similar ideas about the need for an unbiased sociology and professoriate. These were distortions of Weber's views.

The selective and distorted use of Weber's ideas and their appearance of being 'just common sense' or 'reason against ideology' go together. Those ideas that were deemphasized because they were easily discredited or had unpleasant associations did not become part of any conventional wisdom; other ideas fit with the parts of the previously received conventional wisdom, such as the deductivist notion of rationality; other ideas, such as the doctrine of value-free science, could be, and were, applied to immediate and significant issues. One might add to this the peculiar circumstances of the emigration, where authors who relied heavily on Weber's ideas, such as Schumpeter and Morgenthau, minimized the extent to which their ideas had origins in Weber's work. Thus the ideas surfaced and sometimes became influential, independent of Weber's name and independently of other distinctively Weberian ideas. Doubtless the sequence of translations of Weber's work also abetted the fragmentation, though the sequence was itself influenced by consideration of audience appeal and by the consideration that particular arguments had already become familiar through the efforts of such modernizers and adapters as Schumpeter and Morgenthau. Weber's later critics also contributed distortions, particularly in the course of generalizing arguments established in the Weimar era critique of Weber to such movements as positivism and positivist social science, thus lumping together distinct arguments. Yet the core Weberian ideas proved extraordinarily resilient, in spite of their being obscured in these ways. In the case of Weber's argument on the relation of rationality and values, certain elements of the argument have come to be routine, taken-for-granted elements of discourse, both in academic disciplines, particularly political science and sociology, and, to a certain extent, in the political culture itself.

The difference between these two versions of the history of the Weber dispute is telling. The conventional account depends on treating much of the Weberian legacy as unquestionably true and unproblematic. Much of our sense of what has been achieved in this century by sociology, political science, and by social and political theory, depends, implicitly, on our reliance on standards akin to Weber's. Similarly for our sense of the development of the university as an institutional form: the professionalization of the universities and university education and the technicization of discourse in the human sciences may be regarded as good only from a perspective informed by distinctive assumptions. More subtly, the difference challenges our ideas on the political education and political culture of contemporary democracy. Relativism and the idea that values are matters of opinion, not fact, have become visible features of contemporary moral culture to which the social sciences have made a contribution. Any question about the intellectual adequacy of this relativism and the fact-value distinction also raises the question of whether this cultural development is an achievement or a threat.

In this book we shall retrace the development of the dispute and show how the participants in the dispute have used, revised, and adapted the arguments to new contexts. Our primary concern will not be historical, however. Our deeper purpose in retracing the steps by which this entrenchment occurred is to make a beginning for a rethinking of the arguments. Accordingly, our emphasis throughout will be on explicating arguments and counterarguments, and on providing, for an Anglo-American audience, enough historical and intellectual context to make the development of the dispute, and the arguments on both sides, intelligible. Our hope is that by explicating the arguments we shall restore these routine, taken-for-granted elements to the level of discourse and enable them to be questioned anew: to use the history of the dispute as a means of showing the problematic character of much that appears unproblematic.

The very fact of the taken-for-granted character of some of these ideas necessitates this approach. A 'simple history' could not be other than a partisan history, because, as we shall see, virtually all the standard terms that the historian would use to characterize the dispute, such as ideology, science, liberalism, positivism, and rationality, are implicated in the dispute itself. Similarly, the question of the political significance of Weber's words and actions lies close to the heart of broader questions about the meaning of the political history of his era, and in particular about imperialism. To answer questions about Weber by reference to the historical circumstances necessarily embroils one in the disputes about the meaning of the historical circumstances which parallel interpretations of Weber's role.

This book, then, is not a rethinking of the Weberian legacy as much as a preparation for a reconsideration, and not so much a history as prolegomena to a history. Similarly, it is not a reinterpretation of Weber so much as an attempt to provide, through comparison and explication, enough intellectual distance between Weber and present commonplaces so that a serious rethinking is possible.

These are, so to say, limitations of intent. There are also some important limitations of content. We will ignore, for the most part, the dispute over the possibility of a value-free sociology, save as it enters incidentally into the dispute over the core arguments on value. Weber's argument for a value-free sociology, after all, depends on the core arguments, which are logically prior to and independent of the methodological argument.

Similarly, there are many interpretive questions and historical issues that we shall not pursue. For example, we shall make no attempt to assay Weber's influence in producing various common present-day ideas. The present-day common notions about values derive from many sources, including the idea of truth as consensus, which tends to support a contrast between consensual science and nonconsensual morals, and the contrast between morals as subjective feelings or 'inner decisions' and the world, which is not private. There are obviously many other sources for these ideas in the culture itself. In the case of the latter, one might cite the Puritan distinction between the profane world and the inner soul, or Descartes's doctrine of intention. These ideas, which have also become commonplaces, obviously lend plausibility to Weber's arguments, and they went a long way in the preparation for their acceptance. But we have no means of disentangling them.

We have necessarily been selective in the texts we have chosen to explicate. We have made a variety of assumptions about how much context and explanation is needed for our audience. Because, for example, most of this audience will already have some familiarity with the Frankfurt School and with the political, social, and academic life of Britain and the United States, these will not be discussed at length. Moreover, rather than attempting to analyze each variant of a frequent claim, such as, 'Weber's great concern was human freedom,' a task that would be endless, we have considered in detail only the early literature (in the case of this particular claim, Karl Jaspers) and the most significant later departures and innovations. Where particular claims are repeated as often as is this one, we have simply recorded the fact. In short, we have tried to discuss important departures, but not mere variations on the standard themes.

We have also kept in mind the nature of the extant Weber literature and have tried to complement it rather than repeat it. The exegetic literature on Weber's texts is vast, and we have made no attempt to add to it. Nor have we attempted to deal with the question of the sources of Weber's ideas. Our thought is that one weakness of recent discussion of Weber is that the forest has been sacrificed for the trees. So we have attempted to locate the Weber discussion in the broader cultural and philosophical environments of the various traditions it has touched.

1 Problems of context and interpretation

Weber worked in a political context unlike our own; thus, to understand some of the subsequent disputes it is essential that we understand this context and, beyond this, understand the broader historical disputes over the interpretation of this political world and Weber's place in it. In this chapter we shall give a brief account of the relevant political facts of the Wilhelminian era and notice some major problems of historical interpretation that bear on Weber's views. We shall discuss the parliamentary situation and the politics of the extraparliamentary movements. As it happens, these constituted only a small portion of German political life. Parliament had little to do with such central matters as the affairs of the Prussian monarchy, the army (which remained the creature of the monarch, not the parliament) and the bureaucracy and judiciary, which retained traditional independence and deference. Parliament and the political potential of parliamentary life, were, however, Weber's primary concern.

The main lines of conflict in German parliamentary politics in the late nineteenth century were class and interest lines, and this fact was certainly recognized by the participants in it, who knew it as *Interessenpolitik*. This obvious class character doomed politics to a standoff, because the parties could not hope to expand their electoral appeal significantly. And, because the political powers of the parliament were for the most part limited to the approval of the budget (Barkin, 1970, p. 16), there was little incentive for programmatic innovation. This made for rather staid political parties; they were more concerned with proving their fidelity to their constituents' interests than with handling broader questions of policy.

The parties in effect ceded political initiative to figures in the bureaucracy, especially those around the Kaiser, in matters traditionally associated with party politics, especially in the development of public support for programs. The government group produced policy and advanced it by attacking public opinion and the parliament (cf. Böhme, 1967, p. 236). The state, as the Hegelian formula goes, stood above particular interests, and in the atmosphere of *Interessenpolitik* it alone could credibly speak for the nation as a whole. In consequence, 'loyalty to the state' became an explicit part of the *program* of certain parties (Anderson, 1939, p. 60). Of course, the government group did not speak for the nation, but for the established order. Their political strategy followed Bismarck's teachings that the best means of preserving the established order was a healthy national pride, and that the man in the street is uninterested in politics if he is employed and given order, as well as a sense of national prestige.

The politics of the parties

The Social Democrats symbolized the internal tensions, and fear of social democracy and revolution was the great theme of the politics of both the government group and the other major parties. The Social Democrats knew that one point of the government group's imperialist politics was to create internal unity, and they objected that 'the social question . . . could not be exported' (Anderson, 1939, p. 120). Questions of reform and the policy of imperialism were thus closely linked in the minds of the politicians of the time. This is a link that is crucial to the understanding of Weber's views, for his own innovation in the debate over German policy was his attempt to treat reform as a requirement, albeit a subordinate requirement, of a serious imperialist policy.

The Social Democrats were committed to a diverse set of nonmilitarist, democratic, and revolutionary ideals – ideals which could coexist only in a situation of permanent parliamentary opposition. The nominally revolutionary outlook of the party was the pretext of much repressive legislation, which eased gradually after 1890 as a consequence of the emperor's failure to strengthen the penal code against 'revolutionary activity.' So excessive were his proposals that they failed (though on close votes) because of a public reaction that showed a fear of a return to absolutism. The Social Democratic party, in any case, gradually accommodated more and more to the political requirements of parliamentary compromise (Barkin, 1970, pp. 276-7; see also Schorske, 1955).

The remaining parties each had peculiarities. The large 'Center' party was Catholic and, consequently, could not hope to expand significantly. It performed a balancing act among the well-defined economic interests of the Social Democrats, representing the proletariat; the Conservatives represented the Junkers and agrarian interests; and the representatives of the industrial bourgeoisie, who formed a variety of parties, spread across the political spectrum between the New Conservatives and the Progressive People's party. By the 1890s, National Liberalism was a dead letter, 'more a reminiscence than a political factor,' as Theodor Mommsen put it. Bismarck was largely responsible for this. In the 1880s and at the time of unification he outmaneuvered the Liberals, coming up with a grip on the electoral machinery and the bureaucracy that effectively precluded Liberal control. To retain their position as the dominant party, the Liberals acceded to Bismarck's policies of power politics and finally stood for nothing, declining as a parliamentary factor, though retaining substantial influence in the newspapers.

The Conservative parties for the most part represented the interests of the Junkers, a class whose position is without close analogues in Western Europe. The maintenance of this unique position was itself the object of Conservative *Interessenpolitik*, and because these interests ran counter to Weber's stance, they are of special concern here. As a class, it was at the top of a Prussian social order based on large estates, which produced grain as a cash crop. The social order was patriarchal and oriented to the pursuit of the military virtues. Military noble classes had declined during the nineteenth century throughout the rest of the European world. The persistence of the Junkers was a result of the special political arrangements they had made. The Liberals of 1848 had unsuccessfully attempted a national revolution whose aim was to unify Germany. Where the Liberals had failed, Bismarck, the chancellor of Wilhelm I, king of Prussia, succeeded. So when the political structure of the Reich was worked out, the Junker class, the dominant class in the kingdom that had brought about unification and the class that had supplied the military and political leadership in the struggle for unification, was in a position to write the rules to preserve its position, which it did.

The rule that was the main prop of this order was the three-tiered voting system that existed in Prussia but not elsewhere in Germany. The rule divided taxpayers in each electoral district into three groups according to tax payments. The group paying the top third of the total taxes was entitled to cast one-third of the votes in the district, and so on down. The effect of this was that 15 percent of the population controlled two-thirds of the votes. This system was a source of great inflexibility in the parliament, especially in combination with the effects of population shifts, for there was no reapportionment. By 1907, Conservative deputies required an average of 18,000 votes for election while Socialists required an average of 70,000 (Barkin, 1970, pp. 18-20). Thus, although the Social Democrats were the largest vote-getters in the nation for many years, they were grossly underrepresented in the Reichstag itself.

The economic foundations of this order were threatened by the development of the world agricultural market in the late nineteenth century, and especially by competition with American grain. The apparent solution to this threat was simple. To support the system of large estates in the East Elbian region grain prices needed to be high, and anticompetitive tariffs needed to be imposed. This necessity became acute in the early 1890s, which saw a drastic fall in world grain prices. The emergence of the tariff as the focus of political conflict was new. Before the 1880s, under more favorable world market conditions, the Junkers had been supporters of free trade (Barkin, 1970, p. 34). But from 1879 on, tariff protection was the key issue for the Junkers, for it was the condition of their survival as a class. The issue itself was bound to create a particular alignment of political interests. The main losers in the face of high grain tariffs would be the proletariat: one socialist deputy estimated that the increased tariffs of 1902 would cost the ordinary worker twelve extra days of work a year in food costs (Anderson, 1939, p. 60). But tariff politics have some peculiar characteristics. Policies may be tailored to create support, by creating a package of tariffs that satisfies the right combination of political interests. The successful political combination, pioneered by Bismarck, turned out to be the combination of agricultural tariffs and heavy industry tariffs (Barkin, 1970, p. 35).

One's assessment of the Junkers and the Conservative parties depends on one's assessment of the social order they upheld. Weber's assessment was based on his nationalism. He regarded this social order as an obstacle to the development of the imperialist power-state he desired. As the Prussian ruling class, the Junkers had great influence in the court and in the bureaucracy. They also dominated the military, which, under the unification agreement, was under crown control and therefore retained a significant degree of independence from the parliamentary system (Barkin, 1970, p. 17). The culture of the Prussian ruling class, *Preussentum*, was the subject of considerable debate at the time. One of Weber's themes was that it was out of place in the modern economic and political order, and he was furious at businessmen who imitated the nobility (ibid., p. 202). Yet *Preussentum* had virtues as a cultural tradition. The excellent civil service, which largely consisted 'of impecunious Junkers – many of whom had no other means of subsistence than their truly Spartan salaries,' was 'entirely devoted to its duty, well-educated and informed,' but also 'highly critical of the capitalist bourgeoisie' (Schumpeter, 1950, p. 341). It was also largely indifferent to the geopolitical ambitions and anxieties of bourgeois figures like Weber (Anderson, 1939, pp. 64-5; Kennedy, 1980, pp. 30-1, 350-1). It was this indifference, and the Junkers' concern with preserving the traditional economic order of great estates east of the Elbe, that infuriated Weber.

The debate over *Preussentum* was not a reflection of a typical struggle between a rising bourgeoisie and a declining rural elite. In Germany, industrialization was carried out in large part from the top, under the paternal direction of the bureaucracy rather than by independent entrepreneurs operating under *laissez-faire*. Industrialization involved the state in the provision of interest-free loans, the protection and encouragement of cartels and virtual monopolies, and, by the 1890s, protectionist tariff arrangements. This was a 'mixed economy' from the start, and neither the great industrialists nor their protectors and beneficiaries had any interest in having it otherwise. In a true *laissez-faire* economy, as Adam Smith predicted, the state would naturally fall into an antagonistic relation to business, especially in breaking up combinations and suppressing or limiting fraud and other such means of making money by subverting market processes. The fact of control by state finance and state ownership of various railroads and mines made German relations between business and the state a much more gentlemanly affair, in which connections (and therefore demeanor suitable to the tastes of the Junker-dominated bureaucracy and the court) counted for more than the virtues celebrated by Samuel Smiles.

The effect of industrialization on the social structure of the nation was that it expanded the class of nonnoble possessors of great wealth and created a large industrial proletariat out of a small one. The industrialists, for the most part, came from the older bourgeoisie in western Germany; but in contrast to western European regimes in which the bourgeoisie had struggled against the royal state and the aristocracy from a position of economic independence, the great German industrialists, having made their fortunes in the context of state support, had not developed a taste for *laissez-faire* or antipathy to state power as such. To be sure, they were opposed to costly social legislation, and this too was a theme of the politics of the imperial era (Barkin, 1970, pp. 166-7); nevertheless they tended to regard state action as an essential element of a successful national economy.

The political consequence of the influence of the state on industrialization was that a wedge was driven between the great industrialists and the petty bourgeoisie. Their interests ceased to coincide when the state promoted heavy industry as a matter of policy, because the petty bourgeoisie, as consumers, paid higher prices for industrial products and paid indirectly for the financial arrangements the state used to support heavy industry. The differences in interests were matched by differences in cultural style: the great industrialists took to mimicry of the nobility and eagerly sought titles and estates.

The extraparliamentary movements

If tariff policy was the main consideration on the agenda of the political parties at the turn of the century, it was by no means the main concern of the regime or of political discussion. The government group had launched a campaign to make Germany a great military power, and the details of this pursuit occupied the court and the bureaucracy. The nature of the government's initiative and motives here is open to dispute. In the 1880s, according to Hans-Ulrich Wehler's *Bismarck und der Imperialismus*, the political strategy of the government and Bismarck was 'social imperialism' (Wehler, 1968), 'a sham policy intended to make German business interests and the German middle-class believe that the state could advance the interests of German commerce abroad (and also help to repress working-class socialism at home) without changing its basic constitutional structure and social composition' (Smith, 1978, p. 239). Bismarck's geopolitical intentions, on this view, were never serious. His main concern was preserving the existing domestic order, and he used such developments as 'colonialist agitation among groups representing depression-plagued industries' as a framework in which to co-opt business interests (ibid).

Whatever the origins of the policies, a lively group of movements developed that were not parties but pressure groups. Ultimately they grew to such significance that the court and the bureaucracy felt constrained by them. The extraparliamentary movements were in a position, as was the state, to claim to speak for the nation and ideals as distinct from mere interests. The claims were not always true, for two reasons. First, the movements were often closely associated with parties. Second, once they had announced a program, the pressure groups gained support from those whose interests coincided with it as well as from those who simply agreed with the movements' ideals. But they did manage, in virtue of the fact that they were not associated with parliamentary compromise in a situation where 'compromise' meant betrayal of the interest of one's constituency, to make believable propaganda of a noninterest politics sort. Indeed, there was considerable incentive, given the parliamentary standoff, to avoid interest-based appeals. More important, they were able to form broader coalitions than could the parties.

The major extraparliamentary movements were the Pan-German League, the Navy League, the Colonial Society, the Commercial Treaties Association, the Agrarian League, and the Central Union of German Industrialists. Tariff policy was the original *raison d'être* for the Agrarian League, which supported high tariffs, and for the Commercial Treaties Association, which opposed them. Although these movements all involved relatively specific sets of policies, they engaged in general propaganda for policy and appealed to 'national' considerations.[1]

In the light of later history, the Pan-German and Navy Leagues were the most significant of these groups. The aim of the Pan-German League, according to its initial pronouncements, was to

> bring together the nationally-minded citizens without consideration of party in the thought that the accomplished fact of the unification of the German race is only the beginning of a larger national development, that is, the development of the German people into a cultural and political world power, as the British people already are and the Russian people doubtless will become (Anderson, 1939, p. 200).

These were precisely the goals Weber espoused all his life, and Weber was an early member of the League. He soon resigned, however, on the grounds that the League did not truly serve the national interest but promoted the interests of the Junkers, even when these conflicted with the geopolitical needs of the power-state. The charge of interest politics was more often, and justly, leveled at the Navy League, which was supported by industrialists who saw the building of a German navy as an excellent means for making money.

The peculiar interplay between interest politics and the 'higher' goals of national power can be seen in an incident in 1899. The year-old Navy League, encouraged by Pan-German anti-English agitation, pressed for new naval expenditures. Tirpitz toured the ship-building yards, and *Die Post* began a mild agitation. The Social Democrats acquired and reprinted a circular letter that had been addressed to the local branches of the League and that urged naval expansion as a means of assisting industry. This caused such a scandal that the League was forced to put itself through a much publicized, albeit fake, 'purge of its undesirable elements' and to pledge that there would be no politics in their 'educational' efforts on behalf of the navy (Anderson, 1939, pp. 170-1).

Yet the 'unpolitical' character of the extraparliamentary movements was not all sham. Each group had a nucleus of idealistic believers in its cause. The Colonial Society, whose aim was to promote the establishment of German colonies, was organized by geographers and explorers, ex-military and naval officers, and a few merchants (Anderson, 1939, p. 179). The Pan-German League was also composed primarily of persons acting on ideals. The ideals were of a particular sort. As Pauline Anderson put it, they 'found the greatest common denominator in nationalism and imperialism' (ibid., p. 224). But the ideals were themselves the essence of unpoliticality. They certainly were not an extension of Conservativism. The Conservatives wished to preserve the claim that the Junkers were the truly patriotic Germans and thus were deserving of special state consideration, but they generally pooh-poohed the idea of a navy and colonies and got caught up in these movements only once they had been established, and then only to a limited extent (ibid., pp. 64-5; Barkin, 1970, p. 154).

If there is an 'ideological root' to the nationalism and imperialism established in the 1890s, it is perhaps to be found in the liberal doctrines of national freedom. The geopolitical tactic associated with nationalism, namely power-politics, was rooted in Prussian traditions of statecraft, and this gave the movement a conservative ring (although the liberals, such as Weber and Meinecke, soon made this tactic their own) (Anderson, 1939, p. 65). But the point of these movements and of the appeal to the ideal of national greatness was that these aims were above 'mere politics.' So each interest sought to attach itself to these ideals, in the expectation that this association would legitimate the interest. The free use of this rhetorical device ultimately created a situation in foreign policy in which the cooler heads in the government could not effectively resist the internal pressures of the more aggressive members of the bureaucracy and the military. At the moment of decision over war in 1914, the chancellor, Bethmann-Hollweg, felt compelled to go along with the war aims of these aggressive elements because of what he perceived to be the demands of imperialist and nationalist public opinion (Gordon, 1974, p. 218).

Nationalism or liberalism?

One political lesson to be drawn from the effusion of nationalist sentiment in the 1890s was that the parliamentary standoff might be broken by the creation of a party devoted to nationalist ideals with a mass following. This lesson was drawn by Weber in the late 1890s for Freidrich Naumann, then head of the small Evangelical-Social party. Naumann changed political direction under Weber's influence, becoming the sort of archnationalist and imperialist Weber had proclaimed himself in his *Antrittsrede*, his inaugural academic speech, 'Der Nationalstaat und die Volkswirtschaftspolitik.'

There are a number of difficulties in interpreting Weber's nationalism and in locating his political stance among the political positions of the era. These difficulties derive not so much from a dearth of explicit political action or speech on Weber's part, for Weber was an active and aggressive public figure, but from the problem of interpreting the other stances he opposed and of separating the ritually required nationalist utterances from his genuine political message, and, more generally, of separating tactical positions from sincere expressions of his convictions.

Such problems are presented by all political figures. They are, however, especially significant in connection with Weber, because it is sometimes denied that Weber's actual statements were sincere and therefore denied that they indicate Weber's true position. Roth, Beetham, and Kocka all argue that Weber's political utterances were instrumental, and that he was led to leave out points that would have qualified his position but that would have either served no polemical purposes or would have led to the defeat of his real purposes (Roth, 1971a, p. 68; Beetham, 1974, p. 31; Kocka, 1976, p. 300). These arguments raise troubling questions of historical methodology.

It is difficult to imagine, much less provide, evidence that would warrant the claim that any large class of Weber's statements was insincere. To do so, it would be minimally necessary to show that Weber had some underlying purpose that he believed would be served by making false or misleading utterances. The usual places to search for evidence of such a purpose would be in Weber's private statements or in his other writings. Yet Weber's private statements about, for instance, the meaning of democracy, were often stronger than his public ones. In conversations with friends, Weber recounted a statement on the meaning of democracy that he had made to Ludendorff:

> In a democracy the people choose a leader whom they trust. Then the chosen man says, 'Now shut your mouths and obey me.' The people and the parties are no longer free to interfere in the leader's business (Weber, 1975, p. 653).

When he explained his advocacy of parliamentary forms in a private letter, he remarked, 'To me, forms of government are something technical, like any other machinery. I would equally strike out against the parliament and for the monarch if he were a politician or showed promise of becoming one' (ibid., p. 585). These statements are by no means exceptional, though they are doubtless exaggerated for effect. We shall return in Chapter 3 to this interpretive problem, for it connects to the more general problem of Weber's intentions.

The problem of locating Weber's stance among the political positions of the era raises different issues. It is a commonplace that Weber's nationalist sentiments 'were at the time in the mainstream of German liberalism, placed between the conservatives to the right (to the right of whom also stood the popular anti-Semite parties) and the socialists to the left' (Tribe, 1979, p. 175). That commonplace is seriously misleading. The anti-Semitic parties were insignificant during Weber's life, not 'popular' in the sense of being 'large.' The German political spectrum from conservative to socialist had little to do with the right-to-left spectrum in such nations as France, England, and the United States. The two largest parties, from the 1890s to the present, with the sole exception of the Hitler era, were the Socialists and the Catholic Center party, which was to form the core of the Christian Democratic party of the present (which became large enough to form a majority in parliament by extending its base to include Protestant elements from North Germany). The Conservative party was never large. In the imperial era, as we have noted, it owed its significance largely to the Prussian voting system and the lack of a secret ballot in Prussia. With the exception of the National Liberals, the remaining parties were splinter parties, which behaved as such. The National Liberal party had degenerated into a splinter party by the 1890s, and was distinguished only by the fact that it was the largest of these parties and by its special influence in the newspapers (a medium that was open to the adherents of other bourgeois parties as well).

The parliamentary relations between the dominant parties consisted for the most part in the making of tactical coalitions in which each party made concessions on issues that were tangential to their main concerns. The Center party was mainly concerned with the prevention of a repetition of Bismarck's anti-Catholic *Kulturkampf* and therefore found that it had a great many tangential issues on which to make tradeoffs (Ross, 1979). Yet it was also the only party with a responsibility to a wide social base of supporters. It naturally assumed the parliamentary role of balancing between conflicting interests. The Social Democrats refused to take a stand on foreign policy issues and consistently opposed the nationalist and imperialist program. They worked for the amelioration of the lot of the workers but, recognizing their 'minority' status, did not attempt to provide a comprehensive national program. The Conservatives had a national program but were powerless to put it into effect on their own parliamentary strength, so they were reduced to compromising in order to defend what they took to be the vital issue of grain tariffs.

Weber, Naumann, and others opposed these parties. But 'opposition' in this context was not an especially strenuous intellectual act. All that it required was an articulation of the popular prejudices against ignoble politics. Weber went beyond this prejudice by analyzing the social and structural reasons for the triviality of parliamentary politics and by attempting to create the political means for overcoming it. But the intellectual basis of this effort was never far removed from the popular revulsion against politicians, and Weber relied on this theme repeatedly in his political writings. For this reason alone it is difficult to locate Weber's political ideals in any standard scheme of categorization.

In short, German liberalism consisted in leftovers: the ideas and impulses not absorbed by the Center, the Conservatives, and the Socialists. This lack of coherence is understandable. The practice of liberal party politics reflected the anomaly that the class that liberalism largely represented, the bourgeoisie, flourished under the protective hand of a state over which it had little direct control, and had entered into an alliance with the state on terms that assured both its prosperity and its powerlessness. The dominant liberal ideas, such as they were, accommodated the dilemma without facing it.

German liberalism is connected to the liberal tradition as a whole at two points: in the idea of individual freedom, and in the idea of a government of laws, not men, which is explicitly opposed to absolutism. Yet even at these points of connection, the German tradition differs. In the next few chapters, we shall have something to say about freedom, for this is a central category to Weber's own thought. The other point of connection is through the idea of the *Rechtsstaat*, which played a different role in the German liberal tradition and was of less significance as an ideal by the time of Weber's maturity, though it also played a role (a negative one) in Weber's thought. One way of understanding this intellectual background is developed by F. A. Hayek, in his *The Constitution of Liberty* (1960).

Hayek's own view is that a free society requires a genuine reverence for grown institutions, customs and habits, and, as he quotes Joseph Butler, for 'all those securities of liberty which arise from regulation of long prescription and ancient ways' (Hayek, 1960, p. 61; Butler, 1896-7, p. 329). 'Paradoxical as it may appear,' Hayek remarks, 'it is probably true that a successful free society will always in a large measure be a tradition-bound society' (1960, p. 61). Not all liberals, however, have held this opinion, and Hayek points out that the whole question of the place of custom or convention and moral tradition really separates two basic forms of liberalism, what he calls the 'French,' or rationalist, conception and what he calls the 'British,' or antirationalist, view. The labels French and British reflect only the dominant sources of the two traditions, and not the nationalities of the adherents. Tocqueville, Hayek says, is more a part of the British tradition (ibid., p. 56), John Stuart Mill more a part of the rationalist (ibid., p. 61). The French tradition, he says, 'arose largely from an attempt to interpret British institutions' (ibid., p. 55). The two traditions proceed differently. The rationalist tradition derives an absolutely valid pattern from human nature. The 'British,' or antirationalist, view is that the 'human nature' of the rationalists 'is very largely the result of those moral conceptions which every individual learns with language and thinking' (ibid., p. 65). For the antirationalist tradition, and for Hayek, we must always work inside a framework of morals and values not of our own making (ibid., p. 63). When Weber described the doctrine of the rights of man as an 'extreme rationalist fantasy,' he clearly had in mind 'rationalist,' 'French' liberalism.

Hayek sees German liberalism as forming a third and distinct liberal tradition, whose greatest idea was the idea of a *Rechtsstaat*, or 'the rule of law.' The main aim of this doctrine, he suggests, was the limitation of administrative discretion (ibid., p. 199), in contrast to such aims as limiting a legislature or monarch. The idea was put into practice in the 1860s and 1870s in Germany, under the influence of Gneist, a student of English law, by the creation of a system of separate administrative courts with powers of review (ibid., p. 201). But the idea was never fully realized, for no sooner had this cornerstone of the *Rechtsstaat* been laid than a change of intellectual climate took place. The changed climate led to the creation of the welfare state and 'monarchical socialism.' The detailed implementation of the idea of the *Rechtsstaat* was not possible in the new climate. The *Rechtsstaat* required not only an administrative judicial structure but the construction of a detailed set of specific rules governing the actions of the bureaucracy to which legal appeal could be made. The new tendency was to widen the loopholes and expand the sphere of discretionary authority to deal with the new tasks of government.

Hayek's view of the doctrine of the *Rechtsstaat* is perhaps too generous, as well as a bit idiosyncratic. The doctrine always threatened to serve as a formalistic principle that could legitimate tyrannical authority as readily as it could limit administrative discretion. But it was a genuine and distinctive political idea. By Weber's time, however, it was not the core idea of what came to be called 'liberalism' in Germany. The term 'liberalism,' as a political label, lived on apart from the idea and apart from the impulses behind the idea. The history of the term is itself revealing.

The term was at first associated with the liberal ideas that the 1848 revolutionaries shared with the West, ideas which were in significant part gone from the German scene as early as 1860. The later generation of liberals that included Lujo Brentano and Theodor Mommsen was committed to free trade, to world peace, to partnership with England, and in some sense to the English model of democracy. They accepted the label 'liberal' and for them it distinguished a set of ideas that stood above interests and particular parties. The next generation, that of Weber and Naumann, did not adhere to these notions. Naumann's party labels 'Evangelical-Social' and 'National-Social' reflected their abandonment of the attitudes that had gone with 'liberalism,' which, in any case, no longer had much popular currency.

Naumann and Weber were political allies of Mommsen and Brentano for a period, so there is a sense in which the former were the 'successors' of the older liberals. But the alliance failed in the face of serious differences that had to do with the core ideas to which Mommsen and Brentano were committed. For them, the younger generation had turned away from liberal ideals. Theodor Mommsen provided an extraordinary affirmation of this gulf and of the despair with which the old liberal viewed the German realities, in these remarks, in a codicil to his will written in 1899:

> I have never had political position and political influence, nor aimed at it. But in my inmost self, and I believe with what is best in me, I have always been an *animal politicum*, and wished to be a citizen. That is not possible in our nation; even the best among us never rises above doing his duty in the ranks and treating political authority like a fetish [*politischen Fetishismus*]. This rift between my inner self and the people to whom I belong has firmly and consistently determined me to appear as little as possible as a person before the German public, for which I have no respect (Mommsen, 1952, p.71).

Perhaps it was Weber and Naumann whom he thought of as 'the best among us' who could not rise above treating political authority like a fetish. In any case, his was a sensibility very different from theirs.

Attitudes toward the English are the crucial *differentia* of the positions of the two generations. Naumann was bitterly anti-English. 'If anything in world history is certain,' Naumann wrote in 1900, after coming under Weber's influence, 'it is the future world war, that is, the war of those who seek to save themselves from England' (quoted in Sheehan, 1966, p. 184). Such sentiments were a constant source of friction during the brief time of Brentano's political cooperation with Naumann. In 1907, Naumann told Brentano, 'I want to remain in harmony with you but there are things about which almost the entire younger generation thinks differently.' These disagreements marked the effective end of influence of key portions of the Western liberal tradition in Germany.

In their place was the doctrine of world struggle, the idea of national glory and the idea that war was justified by the cultural threat of the English and the 'Russian threat.' Yet these too were 'liberal' ideas. One might say that Treitschke, the liberal who advanced these ideas years earlier, was the spiritual godfather of the new generation, but this would be unfair, for Brentano, too, expressed fear of the 'transfer of the center of culture to the United States and the hegemony of Russia in Europe' (ibid., p. 187). Such fears were part and parcel of the German liberal tradition, and the history of the movement is perhaps understandable as the triumph of these ideas over the ideas shared with the Western tradition. The triumph is understandable enough: while the Western ideas had little popular appeal, the nationalist ideas had great appeal. The shift in emphasis was not, however, a matter of expedience. The Western principles became increasingly 'unrealistic' in the eyes of people like Weber and Naumann. Naumann pressed the Weberian idea that 'the old pure theory of rational humanitarian morality' had to yield to the realization of the inevitability of international struggle (ibid., p. 185).

The younger generation abandoned the label 'liberalism' in stages. They still spoke of the parties opposed to the Junkers but allied with the 'Bülow bloc' against the Center and SPD as 'liberal,' and they still spoke of 'liberal unity.' But the fact that they sought new labels signaled that the old one had lost its appeal. The change coincided roughly with the development of anti-English feeling, especially during the Boer war. The war put German Anglophiles, Brentano included, in an awkward position. But it put the younger generation in an equally awkward situation, because despite all their vociferous anti-English views it was clear to all that the political reforms they proposed resembled the British parliamentary system. Thus, their enemies could easily associate these views with the hated English. The value of this rhetorical weapon increased after the war. In Weimar, Spengler accused the regime of succumbing to the British model.

By this time, the term 'liberal' was largely an epithet, which signified to those who used it the discreditable notions of parliamentarism in its Weimar form, the *laissez-faire* economics of Weimar, the collapse of order, and the degenerate mass-societies of England and America. Early Nazi ideology stressed this last aspect, typically equating liberalism with 'the false belief in the equality of man' (Strasser, 1978, p. 90). Jaspers, it may be noted, did not use the term liberal in his defense of Weber or in his 'diagnosis of the time'; rather he preferred 'freedom' (Jaspers, 1933). 'Freedom' is thought of in terms of the freely developing personality, which is an older German liberal idea, and without being associated with the political freedom of 'liberalism.' The politicians and thinkers spoken of as 'liberal' in this period, such as Meinecke, were liberal in little more than the sense that they were supporters of the Weimar system, albeit half-hearted ones. Thus, in Weimar liberalism meant parliamentarism. When writers like Heidegger attacked liberalism, these were the only present political embodiments of liberalism they had in mind, though they also had in mind the associations of parliamentarism with the English and with mass-society – things of which contemporary admirers of Weber, like Jaspers, were equally fearful. Heidegger himself, in his famous posthumously published interview on politics, said that he would have preferred Naumann to Hitler, a preference that reflects this underlying similarity in outlook on the historical situation.

It should be pointed out that liberalism in the sense of economic *laissez-faire* was never a prominent part of the German liberal tradition, although some figures, notably Brentano, were more sympathetic to 'Manchesterism,' as it was called, than others. Hayek makes the salient point that economic liberalism had not been the order of the day in Germany from the time of Bismarck's adoption of protectionism and policies favoring industrial concentration and cartelization. The interventionist policies of Bismarck and his successors Hayek simply described as socialist, as did many contemporary American and British observers. He points out the connection between this form of socialism and nationalism, and remarks that Naumann's views are 'as characteristic of the German combination of socialism and nationalism as any' (Hayek, 1944, p. 174). The connection was simple: economic policy needed to be strictly subordinated to the task of attaining national and world political goals. Weber endorsed this theme in his inaugural speech. The subordination not only was a matter of practice by the time Weber emerged as an influential figure but had been consented to by the 'liberal' economists in Germany. Even Brentano publicly supported the cartel movement, which by 1888 he had recognized to amount to 'the planned allocation of production' (Sheehan, 1966, pp. 111-12). Weber's 'economic liberalism' was weaker than Brentano's, for his sense of the ultimate significance of national struggle was greater. One should notice that when later writers, such as Mannheim and the Marxists, referred to the period of the *Kaiserreich*, or for that matter the Weimar period, as a period of *laissez-faire* capitalism or economic liberalism, they relied on an implied contrast to a fully-planned socialist economy and not on an economic liberal's idea of *laissez-faire*.

All this discussion of the political ideals and the practical political situation of the liberal parties may be summarized briefly. By the early 1890s, these parties were characterized primarily by their opposition to the Socialists. They longed to recapture the glory they had once had as major participants in the struggle for unification. Nationalism *cum* imperialism was both a substitute for the great goal of unification and a filler for the political vacuity of the parties. Some 'liberals' believed that these 'ideals' might contain the right political formula for defeating the other parties. This hope was not as forlorn as the experience of the imperial era might have led one to believe. Hitler found the right formula here; and when he did, he confounded the Conservatives and weakened the Center and the Socialists sufficiently to seize power.

First and second-order problems of interpretation

To notice the similarities, even the structural similarities in the tactical political situations, between the nationalistic liberals and Hitler embroils us in interpretive difficulties over 'continuity.' These difficulties relate to the problem of interpreting Weber in this way: the first-order controversies in which Weber was engaged 'double back' on the second-order controversies about his work. This 'doubling back' is a recurrent, even characteristic, feature of the Weber controversy. It can be best understood through examples. The first-order controversy, in this case, involves the interpretation of such things as Weber's attacks on his immediate political opponents, the opponents of his brand of imperialism and nationalism. Weber's attacks on his opponents, and his positive articulation of his own position, involved a conception of world history and the place of Germany in world history. Ideas similar to his were used by the Nazis, as well as many other European political writers. For Weber, the 'demand of the day' was national struggle, which he believed necessitated political and social reforms and industrialization. In his view, the need for national struggle was built into the world political and economic situation, a situation that was structured by the fact that the world markets had been divided up by the other great powers, especially by British colonization. This was a common notion at the time. From the 1890s to 1914 dozens of books appeared, both in German and

English, devoted to the idea that Germany and England were in a state of commercial war that threatened and perhaps necessitated actual war.

One second-order controversy that is relevant to the interpretation of these views is the historical dispute over German war aims in the 1914 war. If one regards the German position in the First World War as at least partially justified by its 'defensive' character, for example, one will regard Weber's insistence on the necessity for struggle as correct political analysis, and one will credit his unwillingness to succumb to the war hysteria that gripped many intellectuals as evidence that he was a moderating force. If one does not take this position but regards the war, as for example Fritz Fischer does, as a planned aggressive bid for the goal of geopolitical greatness, one will regard Weber as a minor propagandist for the policy and viewpoint of the regime. Fischer, indeed, has treated him in exactly this way (1967, 1975).

A related second-order controversy that bears on the problem of interpreting Weber is the question of the class character of modern imperialism generally and German imperialism in particular. After the First World War, it was common to blame one's opponents for the war or the failures of the war, and during this period of recrimination Joseph Schumpeter, a close friend and associate of Weber in the editing of the *Archiv für Sozialwissenschaft und Sozialpolitik*, published a study of imperialism that developed the argument that the bourgeoisie was not the source of modern imperialism. Schumpeter minimized the influence of German commercial interests in the war and in an aggressive international stance. A quite different view was developed by the Weimar historian Eckart Kehr, who studied the interests behind the building of a great navy – the crucial element to the German challenge to Britain – and showed the dominant role of bourgeois elites in the Navy League, the mass pressure group that agitated for the navy. The Junkers, according to Kehr's analysis, were originally opposed to naval expansion and were the last group to become supporters of the navy, which they did with little enthusiasm (Kehr, 1930).

The positions Weber himself took present the first-order interpretive and evaluative problems. Disputes like the Fischer controversy or the dispute over the class character of German imperialism are second-order problems – in this case, problems over the historical context to which interpretations and evaluations refer. The 'doubling back' happens because Weber also took positions on the question of the character of the historical situation of the time. Those of Fischer's critics who take the position that Germany was justified in the war take a position that coincides with Weber's own analysis and helps justify his actions. The doubling back goes beyond this, for Weber's defenders have sometimes given their own historical interpretations, as Guenther Roth does in his *Social Democrats in Imperial Germany*, which support, or simply recapitulate as fact, opinions that Weber himself held, in this case the opinion that the Social Democrats destroyed their political effectiveness through their idealism (Roth, 1963).[2]

An analogous 'doubling back' of first-order interpretive questions onto second-order questions arises in connection with the empirical or historical question of the character of modern democracies. If one holds, with Weber, that modern democracy is generally either a matter of rule by a clique or of leaders competing for followings (rather than, say, rule through the representation of constituencies whose interests are articulated in more or less rational and free public discourse), one will assess his proposals to maximize the plebiscitarian and dictatorial features of the German state as a 'realistic' stance for democracy rather than as a repudiation of democracy.

A similar but radically more complex and consequential 'doubling-back' problem arises with Weber's account of the relation of reason and values. For a person convinced by Weber's account of the dictates of 'logic' and of the ultimate nonrationality of value choices, Weber himself must appear to be bowing to rational necessity in many of his writings on values, and his critics must appear as failing to bow, i.e., as irrational. This problem runs through the Weber literature. It can be seen in a particularly clear way in Guenther Roth's article 'Political Critiques of Max Weber,' in which Weber's critics are labeled as 'ideologists' (1965, p. 222).

The difficulty with such labels should be evident. Part of the issue between several of the critics and Weber is the adequacy of the distinction between 'value-committed' (or 'ideological') and 'scientific' discourse that is presupposed by Roth. In order to evaluate these critiques and Weber's position one must treat the validity of Weber's doctrine of values and rationality as an open question. The 'ideological' criticisms have often specifically proceeded from this question. Leo Strauss's critique, for example, proceeds from an examination of Weber's doctrine of the irreconcilability of value conflicts (Strauss, 1953, pp. 64-70; cf. Wegener, 1962, pp. 266-9; Lukács, 1962, pp. 534-5; Habermas, 1973, pp. 265-6). Weber himself considered the doctrines Strauss has examined to be on the 'fact' side of the fact-value boundary (Weber, 1975, p. 321; Bruun, 1972, p. 162), as he must, because they are crucially presupposed by his own account of sociological methodology. Weber's account of methodology, and especially his discussion of the problem of *Wertbeziehung*, amounts to the claim that descriptions of the facts of interest to the historian are value relevant, and that no single true value position may be discovered on which a uniquely valid standpoint could be based, because value positions are subject to rationally irreconcilable conflicts (see esp. Wegener, 1962, pp. 269-79). Weber's argument for this conception, as the critics point out, itself has 'political' implications, in that it directly implies certain things about the possibility of political philosophy and ethics as these disciplines have been traditionally understood. They also figure in Weber's own arguments for particular practical policies, both university policies and national policies. Some of the implications of these conceptions are drawn by Weber himself; others are left unstated. It is logically appropriate to criticize Weber both on grounds of his premises and on grounds of that which is implied by these premises. So Weber is exposed to criticisms *qua* scholar if his scholarly position has such implications. If Weber's view of values is right, Roth is right in saying that Strauss is a political critic and ideologist. If Weber is wrong about values, Roth is wrong about Strauss and is wrong in his historical discussion of the nature of these criticisms, for critiques that examine the political implications of the doctrine of values are neither 'ideological' nor 'political' in any illegitimate sense.

An analogous problem arises over the factual question of the nature of value conflict in the present historical situation. Consider Wolfgang Schluchter's *The Rise of Western Rationalism*, which argues that it was Weber's intent, in providing an account of the process of Western rationalization, to explain the development of Western morality. This means that Weber had to describe the present state of moral life. Schluchter concedes that Weber believed that a 'modern ethic would . . . be possible only as a kind of existentialist ethic of personality' (1981, p. 58). Weber's own philosophy was 'a kind of existential ethic of personality,' and he held this to be the only serious *philosophical* possibility. What are we to make of this? Is Weber like a Hegel or a Nietzsche who identifies his own opinions with the fate of mankind? Does his description depend on his philosophy?

Less sophisticated followers of Weber have sometimes made the mistake of thinking that such questions may be resolved by treating the philosophical claims as sociological observations. Weber, according to one such view, had no 'philosophy' of value; he was merely reasoning from 'the natural, historical, and empirical fact' that there is no rational basis for the reconciliation of conflicting values in the modern world: he was not a philosopher interested in advancing ethical claims but was simply facing up to the historical reality of the present situation, the reality of conflicting values. His political advice, his attacks on professorial prophets, and his advocacy of value-free sociology were all based on the evident historical fact of value conflict, something that no philosophical argument can wish away.

The difficulties with this account of Weber's views are elementary: in the first place, this account has Weber deriving various 'oughts' about politics, professorial ethics, and the like from the 'is' of value conflict – a kind of derivation he would have rejected in principle. Beyond this, usages like 'historical fact' and 'natural fact' are a faulty imposition on Weber. His methodological writings teach that there are no such things; there are merely facts described and interpreted in our own 'value-related' vocabularies.

Whatever one might think of this doctrine, the claim that the modern world is an arena of radically distinct value stances with equally valid claims to rationality seems to be a good example, not of a natural fact, but of an interpretation. One might describe the factual situation differently by suggesting that our daily affairs rest on a great many largely unspoken ideas of fair play and obligation. One might point out that when these break down, there are serious and visible consequences. Indeed, one might say, were all morals to break down into the universal and dramatic 'rationally irreconcilable conflicts' spoken of as a natural fact of modern life, little of what we think of as modern life would continue.[3]

Schluchter does not fall into the trap of speaking about value conflict as a 'natural, empirical, and historical fact,' for he is acutely aware that Weber's concept of the ideal-type precludes this. But there is a problem in treating Weber's description as 'merely an ideal-type.' The philosophical conception that allowed for Weber's particular description of the moral situation of modern man, i.e., as the realization in historical fact of the philosophical problem of the rational irreconcilability of ultimate value choices, was, for Weber, not 'just another conception.' He took it to be metaphysically or logically true. Indeed, the methodological argument that informs Weber's use of the concept of ideal-type depends on the philosophical argument; so it is impossible to abandon the philosophical argument without abandoning or changing the use of the notion of ideal-types as well.

Schluchter realizes all this, so he tries to evade the question of whether Weber considered his description of contemporary morality to be merely an ideal-typical construction of historical facts or a philosophically true description of the nature of values as such (1981, pp. 18-24). In the context of Schluchter's own inquiry, this evasion is perhaps justified. In other contexts, unavoidable problems occur. If Weber was right about the philosophy of values and about the empirical state of contemporary moral life, his denunciations of other moralists as, e.g., 'big boys in university chairs' and his remark on 'that part of Nietzsche's work which is of lasting value . . . the "morality of superiority" ' (Weber, 1978b, pp. 387-8), can be seen as facing up to reality and seeking a new, more appropriate, moral sensibility. If Weber was wrong about the empirical situation, he may be considered culpable for worsening it. His advocacy of a particular philosophic view of the nature of morality, if it is wrong, becomes not 'facing up to reality' but stance-taking.

Stances on these subjects have implications for questions about the meaning of the university and the vocation of scholarship, and these issues have also been tied to the Weber controversy throughout its history. These secondary disputes also 'double back' on the problem of interpretation and evaluation, in two ways. One relates to the matter of the culpability of various elements in the German academic community in the collapse of the Weimar regime and the rise of Nazism, a question on which there are various possible views, some coinciding with the views of Weber's defenders, and some coinciding with the view of his critics. There is also the question of the proper function of the university in modern society, on which there is a similar conflict. Certain of Weber's defenders have been closely associated with the defense of a particular view of the university which reflects Weber's ideas (e.g., Bendix, 1970). The issues and the range of alternative viewpoints on the latter issue defy easy description. The ideal of a liberal education as opposed to a professional one, the notion that an education ought to be an introduction to the Western cultural tradition, and the idea that 'professors ought to profess something' all are in conflict in one way or another with the Weberian notion of the vocation of scholarship, and both the issue of the proper relation between the scholar and the state and the scholar's place in the political community of discourse may be intelligently approached on other than Weberian grounds. So here again a second-order decision on one side or another on these questions bears on one's first-order interpretation and evaluation of Weber's conception and conduct.

Professors and politics in Weber's era

It should be borne in mind that the German professoriate of Weber's time had enormous public influence and participated in public affairs to a greater extent than academics in the United States ever have. Treitschke, the Berlin historian, for example, was a National Liberal deputy for eleven years (Barkin, 1970, p.

7). Analogous public roles have been played by academics in American life, but it must be noted that the list is filled almost entirely by former university presidents, rather than ordinary scholars. This was not the case in Germany, where contact between academics and the public was continuous. In Berlin, for example, professors gave well-attended weekly public lectures (ibid., p. 10). The professoriate was expected to provide political leadership, and it was responsive to these expectations.

At the moment of the beginning of the war in 1914, even the eighty-two year old Wilhelm Wundt, who had never been a political man, indeed had never spoken at a public gathering, took himself from his study to speak at a rally in Leipzig. The setting, with the organ playing a Bach *Präludium* and the crowds streaming in from the street, shouting for victory and waiting for the great scholars to explain the meaning of the crisis (Schwabe, 1961, p. 604), reflects an underlying relation between scholarship and politics that is different from present-day Germany, and radically different from the situation in the United States. At the time, there was enormous faith in learning, and scholarly expertise was not distinguished from political expertise in the public mind. The influence of 'liberal' professors, who were for the most part not at Berlin, was especially great. Although the Liberal parties had declined in influence by the 1890s, the newspapers, in which the professoriate often wrote, were disproportionately liberal. An indication of the influence of these newspaper writings is given in Weber's account of his postwar meeting with Ludendorff, who had been, with Hindenburg, military dictator of Germany during the last part of the war. 'There you have your highly praised democracy,' Ludendorff said. 'You and the *Frankfurter Zeitung* are to blame for it' (Weber, 1975, p. 653).

It is difficult to gauge 'influence' that is exerted by words, so it is difficult to assess the influence of the professoriate. But the political gestures of the professoriate were well publicized and well understood. The 1914 prowar proclamation of the 'Ninety-three German Intellectuals' was widely read throughout the world. Stefan Zweig has described his horror at the document, which he called an 'inane manifesto,' but he did not underestimate its influence, and his remark on it reflects the peculiar significance of such gestures. 'This,' he said, 'was the favorable difference between the First World War and the second: in the first the word still had power' (Zweig, 1964, p. 240). Nor, of course, was the political involvement of the professoriate limited to the war era. Admiral Tirpitz wrote in his memoirs that he had first been awakened to Germany's need for a great navy by Treitschke's lectures, which he had heard as a student many years earlier

(Tirpitz, 1919, p. 144).

The professoriate's political involvement was of a very special sort, geared more to the preservation of personal dignity than to the demands of politics (Barkin, 1970, pp. 7-10). But this perhaps, in an era of *Interessenpolitik*, lent it special authority. Weber's own attempts at political leadership, which were quintessentially attempts to retain dignity within the political realm, exploited both this special authority and the air of freedom from the dirtiness of politics. The *Interessenpolitiker*, who used professors as speakers and placed them on advocacy committees of all kinds, had exploited the dignity of the professoriate for years (ibid., pp. 173, 203-4; Anderson, 1939, pp. 171-2). Weber's most conspicuous public battle of the 1890s was with one Professor Wagner, an economist who spoke for agrarian causes (Barkin, 1970, pp. 205-6; Mommsen, 1959, p. 78). The antinomy between the dignity of the professor and the crassness of the party politician was a significant element in the political semiotic of the day. On the side of the electorate, the touch of the professoriate elevated politics. On the side of the professoriate, which for the most part took a position similar to that taken in Thomas Mann's 'Letters from an Unpolitical Man,' politics, at least party politics, degraded the professoriate (1956). This has some bearing on our judgment of Weber's political writings for public audiences. It suggests that they were seriously formulated and seriously intended, and not merely the momentary tactical utterances of a casual politician. For a professor, entry into the political arena, especially in print, was too fraught with significance for it to be done casually or for it to be governed by expedience. This must have been especially so for Weber, who nurtured political ambitions until the end of his life. Indeed, he must have felt doubly constrained in his political writings: first, by the need not to compromise his dignity, and second, by the need not to make statements that would return to haunt him politically.

2 Reason and decision: Weber's core doctrine and value choices

Weber wrote a great deal on the subject of values, value choice, the place of rationality in relation to values, and on substantive value choices. It has been said of Veblen that he thought systematically, but wrote unsystematically. The same may be said of Weber on values. There is no simple rendering of his 'position' and no attempt to directly engage standard philosophical claims about values or morals. Instead, one finds the repeated application of certain ideas and devices. Yet these applications make up a relatively coherent whole, and readers have been accustomed to treating the Weberian *corpus* accordingly. In this chapter we shall present the basic Weberian ideas on values and their substantive applications, with an eye to the later disputes and to the problem of Weber's distinctiveness in the philosophical tradition and in comparison to the neo-Kantianism of his time.

THE NATURE OF VALUE CHOICE

In the important paper Weber wrote in the value-judgment dispute with the *Verein für Sozialpolitik* (Social Policy Association), he referred the reader to another source, his friend Gustav Radbruch's *Einführung in die Rechtswissenschaft*, for its discussion 'on the "irreconcilability" of certain ultimate evaluations in a certain sphere of problems.' Weber qualified the reference by saying, 'I diverge from him on certain points,' but then added that 'these are of no significance for the problem discussed here' (Weber, 1949, p. 11). Radbruch later gave a succinct characterization of his own philosophy of law in an article directed to an Anglo-American audience. The philosophy of law suitable for the present social conditions, he told them,

> must do justice to the paradoxes, antinomies and relativities of life. It must be *antinomic*, that is to say, it must not cloud the irremovable contradictions between the highest legal values, such as justice, expediency, legal security; on the contrary it must fearlessly state them as such. It must be *relativistic*, that is to say, it must present the various conflicting concepts of law and life, such as the authoritarian, the liberal, the democratic and the socialist concept side by side, without one-sidedly identifying itself with the one or the other. And it must be *decisionistic*, that is to say, it must vigorously appeal to responsible decision of the individual legislation between such antinomies and relativities (Radbruch, 1936, p. 544).

Mutatis mutandis, this also is a good description of Weber's ethical theory.

'Paradoxes, antinomies, and relativities' are the hard core of Weber's argument on ethics, and of his successors. The central place they are given in their writings is their distinctively 'Weberian' feature. Most of the other elements of Weber's and his successors' arguments are more widely shared, or are philosophical usages with a long history of their own, such as the fact-value distinction and the concepts of rationality, spheres, and ultimate values. These ancillary devices and notions are essential to the arguments, and many of them were contested in later years. Weber used or assumed various standard philosophical notions without giving an articulated defense of them or showing that he was aware that they were contestable. We shall examine some of these devices and notions shortly. But their role in Weber's own position is more readily understood by considering the 'antinomies' they serve to explicate.

Weber gave only a few examples of antinomies, which fall in two categories. One kind was political: 'whether one should, e.g., in the name of justice . . . accord great opportunities to those with eminent talents or whether on the contrary (like Babeuf) one should attempt to equalize the injustice of the unequal distribution of mental capacities. . .' (Weber, 1949, pp. 15-16). Such questions, Weber said, 'cannot be definitely answered' (ibid., p. 16), and he suggested that analogous antinomies are widespread in politics. Yet the category of antinomies that impressed him most, and that recur in such later texts as 'Politics as a Vocation' and 'Science as a Vocation,' were matters of individual choice. He focused on a particular type of conflict, one that arises between two types of evaluations of action, those made on the basis of the actual consequences of the action and those made on the basis of the actors' intentions (ibid., p. 16; cf. Jaspers, 1946, p. 44). All

Realpolitik, Weber told us, takes the 'consequentialist' alternative as its point of departure (1949, p. 16), while Christian ethics, especially those of the Sermon on the Mount, he thought of as 'intentional.' Between these, he believed, we must simply choose: there is no rationally justified middle path between these alternatives. 'It is really a question not only of alternatives between values, but of an irreconcilable death-struggle, like that between "God" and "Devil" ' (ibid., p. 17). Indeed, it does amount to a choice between 'God' and the 'Devil,' since, as Weber emphasized,

> In numerous instances the attainment of 'good' ends is bound to the fact that one must be willing to pay the price of using morally dubious means or at least dangerous ones – and facing the possibility or even the probability of evil ramifications (Weber, 1946, p. 121).

These are superficially persuasive examples. To give 'consequences' as grounds against an act that is justified solely by its good intentions is apparently pointless, and to give bad intentions as a consideration against a choice that is ultimately justified by its consequences seems equally pointless: the person devoted to producing the consequences will not be concerned with intention, and the person whose actions are ultimately justified by the purity of his intentions in the eyes of God will treat this as the definitive test of the act – not its consequences. But the simplicity of the examples is deceptive.

To see how they work, we need to notice several features of their construction. The distinctive feature of the examples used by Weber and Radbruch is a particular kind of confusion of two kinds of choices, substantive moral choices and choices between ethical theories. The point can be more readily seen in the work of Radbruch, where the claim that there exists a set of 'irreconcilable conflicts' is instantiated with some different examples, all of which have the same peculiarity as Weber's examples. The distinctive feature of the examples is that, in each case, the conflicts between the viewpoints are not so much substantive first-order conflicts as conflicts between theories of the nature of morality, or law, i.e., second-order theories. When Radbruch described the 'idea of legal certainty' as one of the antinomic poles of legal philosophy, he had in mind a second-order theory of the nature of law, namely, 'legal positivism.' The antinomic pole he described as 'justice' he equated with the doctrine of natural law, another second-order concept of the nature of law. The third antinomic pole, which he described as 'expediency,' is the doctrine of *Polizeistaat*, a Continental legal theory which construes the ultimate basis of law as *raison d'état*. This too is a second-order doctrine. When he discussed first-order conflicts between individual, transindividual, and transpersonal values, the conflicts involved the same peculiarity. The conflicts were, at the same time, substantive conflicts at the first order and second-order conflicts about the reality or nature of 'transindividual' and 'transpersonal' entities; that is, they were conflicts about the metaphysical status of 'the nation' or of *Kultur* (Radbruch, 1950, pp. 94, 111). Weber's account of the nature of the conflict between ethics of intention and ethics of responsibility works in the same way. It is dependent upon a conflict between theories of the nature of morality, specifically, between the theory that the moral validity of an act must ultimately be judged on the basis of the intentions of the actor apart from consideration of consequences and the theory that validity is ultimately a matter of consequences.

As a construction of the problem, this leaves a great deal to be desired. Because the dilemmas are not merely first-order, substantive dilemmas but also, properly speaking, second-order dilemmas between alternative ethical theories, i.e., theories of the nature of moral justification, a gap exists between the dilemmas and the conclusions drawn from them. To show that one cannot choose between an intentionalist and a consequentialist account of the nature of ethical choice is not to say that one must choose between 'God' and the 'Devil.' The existence of alternative second-order ethical theories, in contrast to the existence of alternative substantive prescriptions, does *not* imply that one must choose between the alternatives, for there is no contradiction in claiming, for example, that an act is good by virtue of conscience *and* by virtue of its good consequences. Nor is it inconsistent to be, as G. E. Moore was, an intuitionist with respect to ultimate ends and a utilitarian with respect to means and to subordinate ends.

Nor is it clear that there are substantive contradictions that force one to choose between alternative ethical theories or alternative metaphysics claiming higher reality for 'the state' or for 'culture,' or between alternative theories of legal justification. On the contrary. One cannot easily imagine a coherent *substantive* desire for a *Kultur* whose political values led to the annihilation of all its other values, or a goal of 'the nation' in which the 'nation' was merely a prison or a horde. Similarly, it is by no means evident that there are necessarily any substantive implications of a choice between modes of justification based on consequences and those based on, for instance, Christian doctrine. Luther notwithstanding, it is difficult to see how a person who understood that his actions are to have largely evil consequences and nevertheless performed the actions could be said to have 'good intentions'; for this reason a consideration of consequences does bear on the choices of an 'intentionalist,' contrary to what Weber suggested. Weber's own formulations of the substantive aspects of the dilemmas he described reflect this difficulty in his argument. He was forced to appeal to descriptions of individuals, such as the anarchistic socialist who has no concern over the question of whether his actions might succeed, that are rather contrived.[1]

Weber constructed these examples to serve a particular purpose in the structure of his general methodological argument. It is a form of a more general problem, which was a central concern of the neo-Kantian epistemology of his time, the problem of the justification of ultimate premises. The neo-Kantians reasoned that our knowledge of anything – e.g., moral facts, such as obligation or duty, or historical facts – is founded on presuppositions. They believed that we must accept these presuppositions because it is only by virtue of making them that we can know these 'facts.' Yet, when we inquire into the matter of the most fundamental presuppositions, we discover that there exist alternative possible presuppositions even at this most fundamental level. To decide between these alternatives on the basis of the 'facts' or the 'truth' of the alternatives is impossible, simply because to speak of 'facts' or 'truth' involves presuppositions: in attempting to base a decision on some particular 'truths' or 'facts,' we have already decided to accept certain presuppositions. One way to cut this Gordian knot is to accept that one must make these decisions about fundamental presuppositions nonrationally. This was the way out that Nietzsche took for all presuppositions and that Weber took specifically with respect to valuative presuppositions.

Most of the neo-Kantians sought some means of avoiding the consequences of the conclusion that 'basic presuppositions' are rationally baseless, and Weber was no exception to this. But where some other neo-Kantians aimed to preserve certain moral categories, Weber's specific concern was to avoid the consequence that causal knowledge of the world was rationally baseless. This meant that he was compelled to give an account of the nature of causal explanation that avoided the result that causal reasoning was itself based on rationally baseless presuppositions. He did this by using the term 'logic' to include, among other things (Bruun, 1972, p. 162), the specific features of causal reasoning he wished to preserve. This usage, it may be noted, is contrary both to later usages of the term 'logic' and to traditional logic (Weber, 1949, p. 166). We need not consider the details of this account here, other than to notice that to formulate it Weber needed to restate the problem of presuppositional choice in terms of values alone, for to construct it in terms of presuppositions in general would have raised the question – later raised, as we shall see, by his Weimar-era critics – of the rationality of his own presuppositions about the possibility of causal knowledge. A formulation strictly in terms of values would not raise these questions directly, and this is what Weber presented. The basic structure of the problem of knowledge, in short, is shared by Weber and the neo-Kantians. The examples are distinctively Weber's, because Weber had a specific set of things he wished to save from the claim that presuppositional choices were rationally baseless.

Rationality and 'ultimate values'

Consider an objection made by Leo Strauss to Weber's 'Babeuf' antinomy. 'Even if,' Strauss said, 'one would grant that Babeuf's view, as stated by Weber, is as defensible as the first view [i.e., that one should grant great opportunities to great talent], what would follow? That we have to make a blind choice?' Strauss suggested that we do not merely 'choose' in this case, but that 'if, as Weber contends, no solution is morally superior to the other, the reasonable consequence would be that the decision has to be transferred from the tribunal of ethics to that of convenience or expediency' (1953, pp. 68-9). Thus we can settle the dispute, rationally, on prudential grounds. Strauss's argument raises several questions. What is the 'rational' status of the consideration of expedience? Is it a genuine reason? What is its ultimate basis? Is it ultimately based on a value choice?

A Weberian would reply to Strauss's argument by saying that if one makes the choice on the prudential grounds of expedience, this proves that one's ultimate value was really 'expedience.' Radbruch, in discussing 'expediency' as a polar antinomy in legal thought, treated it precisely in this way. What makes this treatment so plausible is that it seems to follow from the notion of 'ultimate values': the value that 'decides' between conflicting values is, by definition, 'more ultimate.' Yet prudence and the various other practical means of deciding between alternatives are not, in any obvious sense, more ultimate, nor are they values. So 'more ultimate value' is strange terminology for describing such considerations.

This raises some questions. One difficulty flows from the term value. By Weber's time the word 'value' had become, as it is now, a portmanteau term for any sort of moral, evaluative, or aesthetic good or aim. Heidegger complained about this usage, as have many others, such as Phillip Rieff, who has remarked, that 'When I hear the word "value" I reach for my wallet' (1972, p. 7). The term itself suggests both subjectivity – value as 'having value for a particular person' – and choice, because what one values, in contrast to, for example, what one is obliged to do, sounds like the sort of thing that can change according to one's will or thought. As it happens, part of what is contested in ethics is precisely the question of whether morals is a matter of 'subjective choice.' So to use the term values is to state the problem in a way that lends support to Weber's account.

A similar difficulty arises with terms in the 'reason' family. Notice Strauss's term 'reasonable.' His use of it reflects a view of the nature of rationality or reason that is sharply at variance with Weber's own, and consequently the Weberian argument and Strauss's objection pass each other by. For Weber, the consideration Strauss offers is not 'rational.' At best, he would say, such 'reasonable' considerations conceal a valuative commitment (e.g., to expedience) that is irrational at base. And this is more than a dispute over terminology. A great deal – including a large part of the history of philosophy – is at stake in the question of what counts as rational or as a reason.

Begin with some dictionary definitions. Rational and reason have the same root: beliefs and actions that are reasonable are simply those for which there are good reasons or warrants. A rational person is one who exercises his faculty for reasoning; an irrational one does not exercise this faculty and thus does not have good reasons. 'Irrational' expresses the negation or privation of rationality and is used in contrast to 'rational' to mean 'absurd,' or 'not guided by reason.'[2] In their original uses the terms 'reasons,' 'rational,' and 'irrational' marked contrasts between types of beliefs or, less frequently, actions or desires. However, there is a tradition, which we might call 'deductivism,' that identifies reasoning with deductive reasoning from principles, or with calculation. In this tradition the question Is it rational? is answered quite differently than are questions involving reasons in our ordinary usage, such as Is it reasonable? or Is it warranted? Such questions are ordinarily answered without explicit appeals to more general principles. For the deductivist, in contrast, to lack a general principle is to lack a genuine rational warrant. So to accept a deductivist conception of rationality is to accept a problem over the reasons for the first premise: either one accepts that it must be justified by a nondeductive type of reason, or that it cannot be justified.

A full explanation of the various solutions to this problem in the history of philosophy would be an enormous undertaking in itself. For our purposes only a few of the major variations need be identified. One line of variation involves the notion of 'knowledge' and proceeds by accrediting various nondeductive means of knowledge as sufficient for warranting the acceptance of principles.

Principles warranted in these ways can then be used in a deductive way to warrant other principles, choices, or particular claims. Among the many such nondeductive methods or forms are knowledge by induction, intuition, connaturality, revelation, and dialectical ascent. The effect of these 'epistemological' variations is to preserve the identification of reason with reasoning from principles by expanding the notion of 'knowledge.' The point of the expansion is to permit such things as deductive axiologies, theologies, aesthetics, and the like to be considered to be 'knowledge.'

Another line of variation involves the concept of 'reasons.' 'Variation' is perhaps a misleading term here, for the usual argument is that the deductivist notion of reasons as 'warrants by deduction from principles' is itself a variation, an artificial and misleading restriction on the ordinary sense of 'reasons.' This line of attack is often conjoined with arguments for a broader sense of the term 'knowledge,' but it stands apart from and does not depend on these arguments. When Strauss said that 'reasonable' considerations can be brought to bear on the 'antinomic' conflict Weber formulated, he meant 'reason' in this prosaic, prescientific or pretheoretical sense of 'good reason.'

Weber's construction of some of his examples of antinomic choices, such as the Babeuf example, depends on denying that 'reasons' of this sort are 'rational' in the full sense. It should be noted that certain antinomic choices in the 'personal' category can be plausibly claimed to be irresolvable in terms of ordinary 'good reasons' or prudential reasons. Strauss, for example, conceded that a choice between salvation and a worldly good of some sort cannot be reconciled in this way. But there are, as we have noted, other objections to the interpretation of the theology of 'intention' these particular antinomies presuppose. We shall return to this matter shortly, in connection with the Two Kingdoms argument. It will suffice to say that the antinomies in this set, involving intentionality, would be substantive moral problems only for believers in a rather peculiar theology of the divine will.

Weber's central arguments, then, depend on his restrictive, or as we shall say, 'deductivist,' model of rationality. This model, together with his account of value choice, determines his account of the relevance of reason to evaluation. He claimed that the functions of reason in evaluation are limited to three: the formulation of internally consistent end-choices or 'value axioms,' the deduction of implications of ultimate choices for action in specific situations, and the determination of means. Reason retains a substantial role as a critical tool, for Weber believed that one can give rational grounds against decisions for ends that purport to be attainable but that in fact are not attainable by any available or known means.[3] Moreover, he believed that many frequently sought political ends were unattainable and that one could rationally demonstrate their unattainability (Weber, 1949, pp. 20-1). But reasons – and this is the crucial reservation for Weber – cannot show us *what* to choose.

The refutation of previous philosophy

These claims place Weber in a specific relation to previous philosophy and ethics. They exclude, as involving an inherent confusion, doctrines that purport to rationally warrant 'evaluations' or 'value judgments.' Such doctrines are falsely understood by their adherents, because they confuse value choices and genuinely rational considerations and are therefore based on concealed value choices (cf. Radbruch, 1936, pp. 536-7). The full significance of this thesis cannot be grasped until one realizes how sweeping the exclusions are. Not only Schmoller and his immediate predecessors and Weber's sociological contemporaries, but the bulk of the philosophic tradition, from Socrates to Mill, are 'confused' according to this criterion (Voegelin, 1952, p. 20). Yet as Strauss has pointed out, the elaboration of the philosophic basis of this wholesale denial of the rationality of the philosophic tradition occupies hardly more than thirty pages of Weber's voluminous writings (Strauss, 1953, p. 64). Similarly for Weber's defenders: they have taken the conception for granted, and no serious defense of it can be found in their writings. This raises some interesting questions. Did Weber believe that he had refuted all previous philosophy? The fact that he devoted so little writing to the problem suggests that he did not. Instead, Weber seems to have taken the refutation of previous philosophy for granted.

It is an interesting historical question as to why he might have proceeded from such an assumption and why he believed it needed so little rational support. The answer seems to be that he accepted the neo-Kantian dilemma of the impossibility of rationally justifying 'ultimate presuppositions' as definitive of the possibilities of philosophy. The acceptance of the dilemma in these terms in itself constitutes the refutation of all previous philosophy, and this acceptance formed Weber's point of departure. He did not need to do more than give it a schematic formulation (cf. Wegener, 1962, p. 279). It also spared him the necessity of formulating any serious metaphilosophical views. He did not, for example, give accounts of where previous philosophies had gone wrong. As we shall see later, this left a gap which had to be filled in a different, nonphilosophical, way.

Weber did not approach the neo-Kantian philosophical framework as a philosopher; that is, he did not attempt to replace it, solve it, show it to be false, or to transcend it, as Husserl and Heidegger did (cf. Grab, 1927). Rather, he attempted to understand his own activities in terms of the framework (Bruun, 1972, p. 8). The intellectual force of his writings on philosophical and methodological matters comes from his insistence on, and rigor in, taking the dilemma through to its consequences for the possibility and character of sociology and the possibilities of valuative choice in politics.

The rigor and drive is philosophical, in some sense. This suggests that when Weber declined to speak as a philosopher, we are to understand this to mean that he declined to make original philosophic contributions. We are not to understand him to mean that he ignored philosophy or thought it to be irrelevant or inconsequential for his work. On the contrary, the evidence of personal testimony is that Weber took epistemology very seriously and that he regarded scholars whose work lacked a firm basis in epistemology to be irresponsible, or worse (cf. Honigsheim, 1968, pp. 28-9). Rickert's critical discussion of Weber also suggests that Weber possessed the 'Platonic mania' for philosophy, even though Weber denied that this mania is the proper motive for science, in his speech 'Science as a Vocation,' which emphasizes the motives of the specialist (Rickert, 1926, p. 234).

It should be noted parenthetically that the dispute over the question of whether Weber 'was a philosopher' (Bruun, 1972, pp. 10-14) has little bearing on the question of his adherence to the doctrines discussed in this chapter. The dispute has generally proceeded on anachronistic premises. To say that Weber was a sociologist, and not a philosopher, is to fail to understand that in Weber's era there was no social category 'sociologist' in our sense; rather, 'sociology' was a task which had to be invented and defined. The discourse Weber was engaged in, and his self-assigned task in this discourse, was to invent sociology as a discipline having a mode of social description that met certain epistemological criteria – criteria which were themselves drawn from a particular, neo-Kantian philosophical tradition and which Weber understood to be opposed to other philosophies, especially those which involved 'absolute' ethics and teleological philosophies of history. The task of the definition and invention of sociology as a particular kind of science, then, was motivated by a specific philosophy of values and is unintelligible apart from it.

Nihilism, decisionism, and relativism

Formal relativism in ethics is sometimes the preliminary to a *de facto* denial of practical moral relativism. One may claim, for example, that the life of a Teutonic knight is philosophically or ethically neither better nor worse than the life of a utilitarian but deny that the life of a Teutonic knight is a practical present-day possibility. Weber went beyond formal relativism in this way, by denying the historical appropriateness or possibility of certain apparent alternatives. But he put the idea of appropriateness more grandiloquently as 'the fate of the times,' which one can accept like a man or evade.

Weber went beyond formal value relativism in some other ways as well. Significantly, he specifically disavowed the label 'relativist,' and Marianne Weber remarked that 'Weber rejects the interpretation of this standpoint as "relativism" as a "gross misunderstanding" ' (Weber, 1949, p. 18; Weber, 1975, p. 325). Part of the reason for this disavowal involves the issue of tolerance. 'Relativism' frequently is understood to conjoin with the categorical imperative to imply that certain rights that a person claims for himself extend to the adherents of viewpoints he rejects. If one claimed, for example, that a member of the community should not be excluded from electoral participation because of his political affiliation on the grounds that every viewpoint deserves an equal minimum of access to the political process regardless of its content, one would be adopting a relativist standpoint, at least with respect to political participation.[4] Thus relativism as a philosophy of values demands tolerance in the execution of practices that are value-sensitive. Weber evidently took relativism to have such implications, for he remarked that relativism can be adhered to only by those who accept a very special type of 'organic' metaphysics (Weber, 1949, p. 18). He would say that one could be an adherent of tolerance only on the basis of a metaphysical belief that the best outcome could be achieved by tolerance. He did not hold such a metaphysical conviction.[5] On the contrary, he believed that 'the highest and most stirring ideals can become effective for all times only in a struggle with other ideals that are just as sacred to others as our ideals are to us' (Weber, 1975, p. 325; cf. Wegener, 1962, p. 262).

Because of remarks such as these, some writers (Strauss, 1953, pp. 42-8; Aron, 1954, pp. 42-3) have characterized Weber's position not as relativism but as 'nihilism' or 'disguised negative value absolutism' (Wegener, 1962, pp. 249-52). Strauss argued that Weber's value position amounts to nihilism, because when Weber denied that one can give a rational justification for pursuing science, *eo ipso* he was denying that there is any ground for pursuing science as Weber understood 'science' or for listening to his results, which presuppose an unjustifiable commitment to the 'value' of the pursuit of science conceived in the Weberian fashion (Strauss, 1953, p. 76; cf. Bruun, 1972, pp. 72-5; Albert, 1972, pp. 48-51, 68-71). Nihilism is a kind of self-refuting or self-negating position. Thus when one interprets someone as a nihilist, the issue is usually not whether the person is in fact a nihilist, but whether the philosophical devices he uses to avoid self-refutation are successful. Weber's means of avoiding a self-refuting nihilism was the distinction between philosophic truth and value choices. His 'nihilistic' denial of the rationality of value choices occurred at the level of philosophic and universal truth or 'logic' (cf. Bruun, 1972, p. 162) and is therefore, he would argue, not itself a choice without a rational defense or a 'baseless preference.' It is problematic whether this metaphilosophical distinction is defensible. If it is not, Weber's position collapses into 'Protagorean' or vicious relativism, nihilism of the self-refuting kind (cf. Oakes, 1982).

There is another sense in which Weber was not a relativist. Weber believed that a recognition of the nature of value choices has 'substantive indications' (Weber, 1949, p. 16). The crucial substantive indication is that if one is to guide his life consciously and not merely let it 'run on as an event in nature,' one must choose his own fate, that is, the meaning of his activity and existence, through 'a series of ultimate decisions' (ibid., p. 18). Here Weber goes beyond formal relativism to the position Radbruch called 'decisionism.' The connection between Weber's rhetoric of 'fate' and 'ultimate decisions' and his understanding of the nature of values is not made explicitly by Weber himself, but his remarks can be intelligibly integrated. To say that ultimate value choices are rationally irreconcilable is to say that an attempt to honor more than one value may produce conflicts in which the individual is faced with betraying one value or another. Once a person makes the essentially arbitrary value choice that gives meaning to his life, the decision imposes a responsibility to follow this choice through to its limit, to realize it completely (cf. Strauss, 1953, pp. 44-5; Löwith, 1927, pp. 98-9). A corollary of the doctrine of the irreconcilability of value choices is that consistency is the only universal value, because sooner or later every end will be betrayed by the inconsistent person (cf. Henrich, 1952, pp. 122-3).

The requirement of intellectual integrity plays a rhetorical role in Weber's discussions of the present-day possibilities of choice. In 'Science as a Vocation,' Weber's strategy was to describe the conditions of scientific work and true scientific achievement in modern times and to ask what possible valuative choices an individual may make today as a basis for his own decision to become a scientist. He began by rejecting previous philosophical justifications for science, from Plato to the Utilitarians. Weber went beyond saying that his value choice merely differed from those of Plato and other previous philosophers (Rickert, 1926, pp. 233-6). Rather, the positions taken by these philosophers are, in Weber's terms, 'former illusions' that have now been 'dispelled' (Weber, 1946, p. 143).

As he presented the problem in this essay, the value choices that can now be made involving science are sharply limited and exclude these 'illusory' ones. Weber's own choices emerge through this process of elimination and are revealed only at the rhetorical point where the illusory choices have been identified, so that those choices not based on illusion, which therefore can be held by a man of intellectual integrity, remain. The final nonillusory choices for the intellectual turn out to be limited to three: to return to the old churches, to 'tarry for new prophets,' or to meet the 'demands of the day' in a vocation (1946, p. 156). The first two of these are hardly appealing. The first is described as suited 'to the person who cannot bear the fate of the times like a man' (ibid., p. 155). Those who are tempted by the second are invited to contemplate the fate of the Jews, who have 'enquired and tarried for more than two millennia' and whose experience teaches us that 'nothing is gained by yearning and tarrying alone' (ibid., p. 156).

A formally analogous argument is presented in 'Politics as a Vocation,' where the actual conditions of political life in modern times are depicted so that the alternatives can be examined within a specifically limited framework. The choice we are faced with if we choose within this framework is between leaderless democracy, or rule of the clique, and leadership democracy, i.e., rule of a charismatic leader with a party machine (Weber, 1946, p. 113). The other choices are illusory. Weber dismissed the worship of power as a choice by saying that the sort of penny-ante power politics of the politician who worships power *per se* 'leads nowhere and is senseless' (ibid., p. 116). He was even more critical of 'ethical' ideals of political action, such as the demand to act in accordance with Christian ethics, demands which he said are based on confusions over the nature of politics. To act in accordance with the gospels or absolute ethics is commonly to opt for the actual worldly defeat of the ends valued by these ethics. For example, to act in accordance with the ethical demand for peace by laying down arms in the face of an enemy serves to make war profitable for the attacker and therefore discredits peace and encourages war. Similarly, truthfulness, if it is truthfulness about documents suggesting the war guilt of one's country, might unleash passions that would preclude balanced investigation and therefore would defeat the goal of truth (ibid., p. 120). The conflict inheres in political action as such, for to achieve any worldly political end one must use the means of politics, namely, state violence; and to do so 'contracts with diabolical powers' (ibid., p. 123).

Of the many ends of which politicians and intellectuals speak, few are actually achievable in this world: to be a 'this-worldly' socialist, for example, is impossible, because one cannot act to obtain socialist ends (e.g., by fomenting a revolution) without risking a reaction that would put one's goals out of reach for generations. The upshot of this argument is that one end in whose service one *can* responsibly act today is 'the fatherland' (Weber, 1946, p. 126).

Three devices: historical appropriateness, illusoriness, and 'spheres'

The character of these arguments against historically inappropriate and illusory choices is unclear. Consider the way in which Radbruch argues for the historical appropriateness of his own philosophy of law:

> When shattered social conditions press for quick regulation through the Legislature general theories about the aims and instruments of law, a legal philosophy and a legal policy must be ready to hand. . . . On the other hand, a country which is in the midst of a yet uncertain development is bound to be reluctant to tie itself to all too rigid natural law principles (Radbruch, 1936, pp. 543-4).

For Radbruch, a legal philosophy is a practical requirement, but the philosophy must suit the historical situation. This presupposes a rejection of a legal philosophy of 'eternal values.' But the force of the argument is unclear. What sort of compulsion is expressed by the 'must' and the 'bound' in the formulation? Similar questions may be raised about Weber. One gloss of Weber's own discussion of the place of Christian ethics in politics is this: it used to be possible to act in the world and in concord with the law of love without finding any radical practical conflicts in doing so. Today that is no longer the case, since to follow the law of love means earthly defeat, and the law of *Realpolitik* means sin; so one must choose. Again this presupposes value-relativism, for the moral absolutist would say, 'One must still do the right thing, even if it is painful and involves the sacrifice of inferior values, like the nation.' But Weber seems to have meant something more than that it is painful to do the right thing, or that there are practical difficulties in acting justly.

To see what he did mean, we must take a roundabout route. One may think of such concepts as justice, just consent, and fairness in various ways: as parts of natural law, or, if one is a pragmatist, as parts of hypotheses of political practice that have been well tested by political experience, or one can simply treat them as parts of a *prima facie* valid moral and political tradition, which should not be rejected without good reason. Weber's position depended on the rejection of all these construals, insofar as they legitimated the concepts as 'rational.' Yet he could not refute these construals directly, for they were alternatives to his own doctrine of the relation of reason and value: to refute them would require some sort of metaphilosophical criterion to decide between construals, and Weber had no such criterion.

Perhaps the strongest alternative to his own account of the relation of reason and value was natural law theory, and his handling of this doctrine is illustrative of his use of the categories 'dispelled illusion' and 'historically inappropriate.' The texts are too vague and poorly argued to yield a very satisfactory reading of Weber's thoughts on the matter. The difficulty arises from the device of constructing antinomies that are simultaneously first-order moral conflicts and second-order conflicts over ethical theory, which conceals metaphilosophical questions from Weber: alternatives appear as alternative value choices, not as philosophical alternatives. Weber cannot have escaped being aware that there are philosophical alternatives, of which natural law is a conspicuous example, that cannot be readily placed in the category of 'value choice.' The category of 'dispelled illusions,' and the category of historical inappropriateness served him as residual categories into which such views could be placed.

In the case of natural law, Weber faced particular difficulties. The language of natural law doctrine, far from being dead, was ubiquitous, so much so that Weber himself did not always avoid slipping into it. He gave a rather strained historical account of natural law which supported the idea that these were mere survivals, and that the historical time of natural law has passed:

> Legal positivism has, at least for the time being, advanced irresistibly. The disappearance of the old natural law conceptions has destroyed all possibility of providing the law with a metaphysical dignity by virtue of its immanent qualities. In the great majority of its most important provisions, it has been unmasked all too visibly, indeed, as the product or the technical means of a compromise between conflicting interests (1978a, pp. 874-5).

Such ideas as a sense of natural justice also had to be dismissed, so Weber claimed that 'so-called "public opinion" ' was 'concerted action born of irrational "sentiments" and usually staged or directed by party bosses or the press' and spoke of an 'ethos' as an emotional impulse that 'takes hold of the masses' (ibid., p. 980).

These arguments are presented in 'sociological' texts, and their significance in connection with Weber's account of values might be questioned. Nevertheless, a great deal of the persuasive power of Weber's account of values and of present-day practical choices rests on assent to such ideas of what is and is not historically appropriate in ethics and legal thought. Indeed, some readers have taken Weber to be giving a kind of factual proof of the historical inevitability of 'rationalism' – making him into a historicist after the fashion of Comte and his law of the three stages. This is not what Weber intended to do. He explicitly rejected such 'laws' in his discussions of historical ideal-types. Nevertheless the historical appropriateness arguments fill some important gaps. Unless one attempts to reduce such philosophies as natural law to concealed value choices, and then shows them to be faced with equally valid antinomic alternatives, it is necessary to provide a metaphilosophical argument against them. So the historical claims serve as a kind of nonphilosophical substitute for an argument.

The idea that such a substitution is proper itself amounts to historicism. But Weber seems to have thought of it differently. He wrote as though he were simply addressing his intellectually serious contemporaries, who, in common with him, recognized the illusory character or inappropriateness of the 'alternatives' (Oakes, 1982, pp. 602-8). He saw himself as speaking to what we might call the community of those without illusions.[6] He gave no 'philosophical' justification of the belief that he was in the historical position of speaking to such a community, but proceeded as though the 'illusions' were also rejected by his audience, which at most needed to be reminded of their illusory character. Such an interpretation certainly fits the tone of 'Science as a Vocation' (1946, pp. 141-3). His followers were impressed by the device, for in the later dispute the historical appropriateness claim frequently appears. Arthur Salz, in his defense of Weber, gave the idea a central place.

Another device is also important for Weber. When Weber discussed choices, he assumed that one could speak of 'political' choices separately from other kinds of ethical considerations – that there is a 'sphere' of politics. Thus, he said that in the political sphere the fatherland is his ultimate value. But he also said that the various moral spheres 'interpenetrate.' This notion of spheres is never further justified or explained, but it is central to making

Weber's whole analysis plausible. Consider what one would think if told by someone, 'My ultimate value in the sphere of desserts is chocolate pudding, and my ultimate value in the sphere of body shape is thinness.' The real decisions here have yet to be made. Thus if one defines spheres in this way one might readily assent to a value choice that in practice is meaningless, for – as any dieter knows – valuing chocolate pudding and eating it are two different things, because of the consequences of the act for other values. Similarly, to concede that national greatness is one's goal in the sphere of politics means nothing until we ask such questions as How is this to be balanced against the consequence of my mother suffering – or my son dying in war? It should be noticed that Utilitarianism and natural law are about such questions. Weber's ethics does not deal with them and is thus not properly commensurate with these 'alternative values.' Yet without the 'spheres' device Weber's argument simply collapses into existentialism – as Jaspers's did.

Criticisms of this interpretation

The cruder alternatives to the general line of interpretation developed here take the line that the value conflicts that Weber discussed were not disputable philosophical matters, but simply the brute givens of the immediate historical situation, and that the features of his views stigmatized as decisionist were not a 'philosophy' at all but merely the articulation of some elementary principles of reasoning for the benefit of an audience neglectful of the demands of rationality. One such elementary principle should now be familiar: if there are different, conflicting, starting points or 'ultimate' principles or values available, they cannot be reconciled by rational argument. In Weber's time such alternatives were in fact available, though they had not – and here the historical claim becomes relevant – been available in the past, when natural law doctrines dominated. One flaw in this defense of Weber should now also be familiar: it assumes without argument what we have called a 'deductivist' view of rationality, as well as the view that premises may not be 'known' by any means other than deductive inference, both of which are philosophically controversial. In short, it presupposes part of what is in dispute between Weber and those who disagree with him.

The list of those who disagree on these points is long. Mill, in *Utilitarianism*, denied that the utilitarian principle may be subject to 'proof, in the ordinary acceptation of the term' but did *not* admit that there are no sufficiently compelling grounds for accepting it. G. E. Moore's intuitionism supposed, roughly, that one arrives at this principle by intuition, not by decision, and that 'the good' is the same for everyone. Contemporary Aristotelians and Platonists similarly supposed that different arguments from those Weber counted as rational suffice to warrant normative results. What is at stake between Weber and his opponents here, then, is not the claim that there can be a 'scientific ethics,' but the question of what sort of reasoning is admissible and required in ethics and metaphysics. Put a little differently, the problem of providing rational justification for one's ultimate premises confounds everyone who supposes that rationality is solely a matter of reasoning deductively from premises, a point that later critics made repeatedly. Issues over rational adequacy tend to turn into such questions as What else must count as rational in order to establish these allegedly ultimate premises? or How can the questioning of certain ultimate premises be blocked? Weber took what amounted to a hard line on these issues by denying the 'rational reconcilability' of moral claims. But the hard line was not against persons who supposed that ethics could be, in some crude sense, scientific, but against those who had a different view of the nature of ethical and philosophical reason or truth.

As a matter of historical interpretation one must keep in mind that Weber's views were not far removed from conventional German philosophy of the time, so the question Did Weber have a philosophic view that was distinctive in the more limited context of contemporary German philosophy? must be answered differently. His conception of the 'demands of reason' was not distinctive in this limited context; here Weber is distinguished primarily by his device of constructing antinomic pairs of 'rationally irresolvable' value conflicts. So the original interpretive argument – which says that Weber cannot be claimed to be the adherent of a distinctive philosophical or cultural stance – can be saved by reformulating it. Weber was not submitting to genuine constraints so much as following the conventional philosophy of his contemporaries in Germany: he did not go very far in seeking alternatives and was rather naive in thinking of this local philosophic consensus, which was even then beginning to dissolve, as a crucial world-historical moment in which past illusions had been dispelled and defeated.

Radbruch used the term 'decisionism' in a straightforward way to designate the view that it is an obligation to decide responsibly between antinomic alternatives. The term decisionism has a more confusing lineage, however, and is later used in a number of mixed senses. A mixed sense is central to an important account of Weber that rejects the interpretation of Weber as a decisionist, developed by Wolfgang Schluchter. Schluchter adopts Habermas's categories of decisionist, technocratic, and pragmatic, and argues that Weber was not a decisionist but conformed to the 'pragmatic model' (Schluchter, 1979b, pp. 74-6). In addition, he argues for an alternative interpretation of Weber's views of the relation between *Gesinnungsethik*, or ethics of intention, and consequentialisms, or ethics of responsibility, in opposition to the usual interpretation, which holds that Weber's approach devalues ethics of intention.[7]

Weber, Schluchter says, was concerned with *informed* choice, and science has a role in enabling informed choice. Part of making an informed choice involves not merely selecting means to a preselected end but selecting the ends themselves, particularly in light of, as Schluchter quotes Weber, 'the inescapable "factualness of our historical situation", the "fate of our culture" ' (Schluchter, 1979b, p. 80). These things, as Schluchter points out, are not merely matters of subjective opinion. They fit Habermas's pragmatic model in the sense that Weber allows the expert to participate in discussion of the selection of ends, in the making of 'informed choices,' and not merely in the selection of means, as in the decisionistic model.

Making an informed choice, however, does not exclude 'commitment' of the sort characteristic of *Gesinnungsethik*. Indeed, Schluchter argues, even though Weber argued for the contrariety of ethics of intention and of responsibility, he also affirmed that the person has a calling for politics only if he considers both maxims at the same time (Schluchter, 1979a, p. 55). The implications of this claim in Weber's text are not entirely clear. It is not paradoxical to say that the responsible politician needs to feel a serious commitment to his goals, even to the extent of saying in some situations, 'I can do nothing else, here I stand.' But to say that the politician must *respect* two kinds of ethical imperatives – arrive at an ethical life-style that lies, as Schluchter puts it, '*between* the two ethics' – is something quite different (ibid.). Schluchter acknowledges that 'this would be logically unsatisfactory, and would besides be at odds with his own premises' (ibid.). Yet Weber, he points out, seems to be describing someone like this when he says that 'an ethic of ultimate ends and an ethic of responsibility are not absolute contrasts but rather complements, which only in unison constitute a genuine man – a man who can have the "calling for politics" ' (ibid.).

Schluchter argues that statements like this reflect Weber's rejection of reliance solely on the ethic of responsibility, and his embrace of something 'between.' So the issue with this part of Schluchter's interpretation comes down to the question of whether Weber's statements reflect merely a recognition of the need for commitment within the framework of an ethic of responsibility, or the logically problematic position 'between.'

During the war a large theological literature in liberal Protestantism developed on the subject of the relation between the demands of this world and the demands of Christianity, and Weber's speeches probably reflected this background. The controversy bears on the issue over Schluchter's interpretation. One thesis, known as the Two Kingdoms argument, argued by Weber's relative Otto Baumgarten, held that 'in the Sermon on the Mount . . . Jesus was speaking solely in terms of the individual soul,' but 'where international life was concerned . . . Germans were bound to live as "disciples of Bismarck," acting in accord with realities, not ideals' (Gordon, 1981, p. 47). In this view, 'the Kingdom of God was an ideal which Jesus never expected to come about as a product of earthly development' (ibid.). Other liberal theologians rejected this and held that war was ultimately justified only if it could lead to lasting peace and a better future (ibid., p. 48), an optimistic hope that Weber would, of course, have rejected. One of these theologians used the phrase 'Watchmen, is the night almost over?' to refer to 'the night of barbarism, when one believed in the calling of the sword to decide in questions of right' (ibid., p. 54).

The second view, opposed to the Two Kingdoms argument, would be a 'between the two ethics' interpretation. But Weber, writing in this period, attacked those who supposed that Christian ethics could inform political action, even in a modest, tempering way and denounced as un-Christian those who take this path *between* the demands of politics and of Jesus, praising instead those Florentines mentioned by Machiavelli 'to whom the greatness of their native city is more important than the salvation of their souls' (Weber, 1978b, p. 223). So Weber's view seems closer to Otto Baumgarten's, in which the separation of the two types of demands is the dominant theme.

Schluchter's dispute with Habermas over the term decisionism is more straightforwardly a terminological rather than a textual problem. When Habermas uses the term pragmatism he alludes to Dewey's discussion of the relation between value formation and the empirical recognition of the consequences of various desires and valuations. Part of Dewey's claim is that in discussing consequences we do give 'factual' reasons for and against value choices, so value choice is not 'irrational' or 'nonempirical.' The concept of 'informed decision,' to which Schluchter appeals, fits this nicely. All that is at stake between Schluchter and Habermas here is the question of whether Weber is a decisionist or a pragmatist in the sense of regarding this sort of discourse as an important or a minor part of political discourse and of the activities of the expert. This is a matter of emphasis. But one should note that the question of whether Weber is a decisionist or a pragmatist in his ethical theory *per se* is an entirely different question. As we shall see in a later chapter, Dewey's broader argument is that the fact-value, means-ends, and theory-practice distinctions are *themselves* undermined by an adequate understanding of the way in which desires and valuations arise, and he rejects the distinctions. Weber is of course not a pragmatist in this sense – his position is, after all, based on these distinctions. And Schluchter's argument does nothing to challenge the idea that Weber is a decisionist rather than a pragmatist in the sense of supposing that valuation is ultimately a matter of nonrational choice.[8]

Choice and commitment remain central to any interpretation of Weber's explicit account of values. One may perhaps, as Habermas and Schluchter do, vary the emphasis on the role of 'responsibility' as against 'decision' in the concept of 'responsible decision' (to use Radbruch's term) but it remains the case that Weber's is a doctrine of values that forces explicit decision and also forces the consideration of the consequences of alternative decisions. 'Forcing' is as characteristic of the rhetorical structure of Weber's discussions of valuative questions as it is of the formal structure of his philosophy of values.

This suggests that Weber's own values should be comprehensible as matters of 'responsible decision' – that we can apply these standards to his own valuative thought, as he applied these same standards to that of others. As it turns out, matters are not so simple. In the next chapter, we shall see that there is a great deal of confusing evidence that suggests that there are conflicts and complexities in Weber's political values which he never fully resolved. In this chapter we shall pursue the matter of Weber's choice from the narrower perspective of his own account of values. We shall learn what this account excludes – and this turns out to be a great deal. We shall also see how these exclusions bear on and create problems of interpretation. This narrower perspective will serve to show in more substantive detail why there is a 'Weber problem' and how serious a challenge to many received moral and political ideas Weber's account of values presents.

WEBER'S 'SCHOLARLY' VALUE CHOICE

In ' "Objectivity" in Social Science,' Weber remarked that all sciences originate in technical, practical pursuits (Weber, 1949, p. 51). The scientist differs from the pragmatic user of scientific, technical means by virtue of his interest in the subject, which is not 'utilitarian' but 'for its own sake.' In 'Science as a Vocation' this interest is treated as a value choice. Each specialty, we are told, presupposes the value of the particular kind of knowledge it seeks: the physical sciences 'presuppose . . . that it is worth while to know the ultimate laws of cosmic events as far as science can construe them' (Weber, 1946, p. 144); medical studies presuppose the task of maintaining life; aesthetics presupposes that there are works of art and does not ask whether there should be works of art; jurisprudence asks what is valid according to the rules of juristic thought and does not ask whether there should be law; finally, the cultural sciences do not ask whether it is worth the effort to attain an understanding of social, political, and artistic phenomena – they presuppose this (ibid., pp. 144-5). It is not clear whether Weber wished to say that these are the only possible presuppositions for science, but this is clearly the drift of his remarks. He stated as a fact that modern science is specialized and that excellence occurs only within specialties (ibid., p. 134), and he revealed that his own value choice is the choice of a specialist. But he did not defend this choice or urge it upon his listeners, because, as a value choice, it was nonrational. This is a rhetorical strategy that, as we shall see, recurs in several of these discussions of scholarly and political value choice.

The 'Ethical Neutrality' argument

In 'The Meaning of "Ethical Neutrality." ' Weber 'rationally' examined two 'polar' alternatives: the standpoint that accepts the fact-value distinction and that, furthermore, considers that both fact and value are suitable matters for instruction; and the standpoint that holds that even where the distinction between facts and values cannot be easily followed, evaluations should be kept to a minimum. In this discussion, Weber made the familiar distinction between that which is warranted by reason and that which must be based on personal value choices. His strategy was to use reason to show certain positions he opposed to be confused. Only after attacking these positions and showing the genuine alternatives to be more limited than might be supposed did he present an explication of his own value choice (Weber, 1949, p. 4). Weber drew a sharp line between the two steps. Because the question of university policy was a practical one, it involved evaluations; so he did not attempt to advance any policy recommendations on the basis of reason alone. However, the positions that Weber rejected implicitly or explicitly on the basis of reason alone turn out to include the positions of his opponents, and the value choices he presented as admissible turn out not to be real choices at all.

Weber began by rejecting the alternative of minimizing evaluation. Along with it, he rejected the distinction between 'partisan' and 'nonpartisan' value judgments. He argued that one cannot avoid suggesting preferences by merely abstaining from valuative discourse on matters of practical concern, for preferences are implicitly suggested to the audience by empirical analyses. Thus abstention achieves an end opposite to its intent and is therefore excluded as a rational alternative. The alternatives now come down to a choice between advancing one's own evaluations, while distinguishing them from fact, and examining consequences of various evaluations, distinguishing these evaluations from fact without advancing one's own evaluations. Reason cannot decide between these alternatives, because the former is based on the idea that the university's aim is to mold human beings by inculcating certain valuative attitudes (education, not just instruction, as T. S. Eliot put it); and this idea is a value choice. Weber's personal value choice was the latter, for he believed that 'the academic lecture hall achieves a really valuable influence only through specialized training.' Specialized training, he held, does not involve a person's general moral outlook; the only moral quality required for this training is intellectual integrity (1949, pp. 1-12).

In a sense this text formulates a 'liberal' conception of the university, because it allows all valuative viewpoints to be examined and allows all scholars, if they live up to the standard of intellectual integrity and excellence in their work, to participate in the university. Weber was famous for his remark that an anarchist could make a good professor of law (if he did not profess anarchism!) (1949, p. 7), and for his defense of Michels, who had been excluded from habilitation on grounds of his socialism (Weber, 1974, pp. 14-18; see Weber, 1975, p. 359). The defense is warranted by his conception of the university. Roth, reading the 1960s into Weber, identifies Weber's position with 'the ineradicable conflict between the liberal scholar and the radical student,' and takes him to be concerned with eliminating indoctrination and ideological harangues (Roth, 1971b, p. 53). But the parallelism is false: the exclusions Weber envisioned are much more sweeping than 'indoctrination and ideological harangues,' as Weber himself recognized in his allusion to the doctrine that the university has the task of the transmission of values and the development of character. As Marianne Weber remarked, 'to Weber, suggesting life philosophies (*Weltanschauungen*) inside the lecture room was just as undesirable as deliberate political indoctrination' (Weber, 1975, p. 231). Thus, he rejected precisely what certain university traditions have taken to be their central concern (Lilge, 1948, p. 142). So by taking a position that warrants a policy of excluding persons devoted to these tasks from teaching, Weber was taking a step beyond the 'liberal' university.[9]

Weber's views can be illuminated by considering his statement of the editorial policy of the *Archiv für Sozialwissenschaft und Sozialpolitik* on his assumption of the editorship. He suggested that the *Archiv* should not be a place where polemics against certain currents in social policy are carried on, or where struggles are waged for or against different ideals.

> It excludes no one from its circle of contributors who is willing to place himself within the framework of scientific discussion. It cannot be an arena for 'objections,' replies and rebuttals, but in its pages no one will be protected, neither its contributors nor its editors, from being subjected to the sharpest factual, scientific criticism. Whoever cannot bear this or who takes the viewpoint that he does not wish to work, in the service of scientific knowledge, with persons whose other ideals are different from his own, is free not to participate (Weber, 1949, p. 61).

This is essentially what his personal value judgment told him should be excluded from the university. But there is a curious difficulty in knowing just what policy he would adopt were he empowered to act, and this difficulty is increased by a curious feature of his rhetorical strategy in the 'Ethical Neutrality' text.

The text begins by carefully distinguishing what Weber took to be value choices from what is given by reason. Yet he also wished to make some claims that sound more like assertions about obligations that flow from the moral nature of things than mere explications of his own preferences. He suggested, for example, that 'every professional task has its own "inherent norms" and should be fulfilled accordingly,' and proceeded to describe the inherent norms of the task of the university professor (1949, p. 5). The notion of 'inherent norms' has obvious affinities with the sociological concept of 'role,' and some sociologists have characterized Weber's formulation as a claim that the sociologist who acts politically, as Weber himself did, must strive to keep the roles of scientist and politician separate.

What is mysterious here is the provenance of the norms governing these roles. Weber used the phrase *eigenen Gesetzen* to describe them, a phrase which recalls natural law, and this notion of norms is inconsistent with his own value theory, which implies that value choices cannot be based on the nature of things. But if these norms do not inhere in the nature of some 'thing' apart from individual preference, whence do they derive? If they can derive only from Weber's personal preferences, decisions, or commitments, how could they impose an *obligation* on anyone other than Weber himself and those who make a decision for the same value?

In this text, Weber was not merely advocating a personal moral choice. The question he was addressing was, in part, a question of university *policy*, i.e., a question of how the power of the university to exclude should be used. There is no portion of Weber's philosophical conception that would preclude his enforcing exclusions of his academic opponents on the theory of values, if he had the power. Moreover, his support of Michels's cause and his argument for the restriction of academic personnel decisions to questions of competence would have been consistent with the exclusion of persons who disagreed with his conception of values; persons 'mixing' fact and value would *ipso facto*, for Weber, be persons who lacked intellectual competence or integrity. In fact, in some situations, he did explicitly use these methodological doctrines to exclude his opponents. At one meeting of the German Sociological Society, where he could appeal to an exclusionary rule, he intervened in the discussion, which drew this response from the discussant, Hermann Kantorowicz:

> I would very much like to address a modest heartfelt proposal to the chairman. That a methodological-philosophical principle, namely the exclusion of value-judgments, can be reduced to a point of order, is clearly a piece of play-acting of the most remarkable sort (quoted in Käsler, 1983, p. 233).

Such exclusions are very much in contrast to such classic documents of the liberal university as the AAUP Declaration of Principles of 1915, written, as it happens, by a committee that included several social scientists. According to this declaration, in value-sensitive 'domains of knowledge, the first condition of progress is complete and unlimited freedom to pursue inquiry and publish its results' (AAUP, 1922, p. 496). The obligations of the lecturer fit with this: on controversial matters, 'while he is under no obligation to hide his own opinion under a mountain of equivocal verbiage, [he] should, if he is fit for his position, be a person of a fair and judicial mind; he should, in dealing with such subjects, set forth justly, without suppression or innuendo, the divergent opinions of other investigators' (ibid.). The questions of the validity of the fact-value separation and the denial of the possibility of rational morality are questions that were not settled in Weber's time, and they are not closed today. Accordingly, they fall into the category governed and protected by these principles.

To mark this contrast is not to say what Weber would have done were he empowered to act. It is simply to indicate what *sort* of argument he made and the grounds he chose and did not choose. In short, Weber did defend university autonomy, but he did not do so on specifically 'liberal' grounds. His argument was based directly on a particular idea of the task of the university and the norms appropriate to the activities that fulfill this task. He was not committed to dialogue in the classical sense or in the liberal sense elaborated in such texts as Mill's *On Liberty*. These notions both involve some form of the 'metaphysics' of tolerance Weber specifically rejected (Weber, 1949, p. 18).

The aims of the argument

We are left, then, with questions of Weber's intent in advancing this reform of discourse, and here it becomes necessary to look at his opposition. Weber's remarks on Treitschke have been stressed by some interpreters because, on a certain interpretation of Weber's intent, Treitschke can be regarded as the primary representative of what Weber opposed. He was a professorial 'prophet,' in that he lectured with great passion and little respect for any distinction between fact and value. Treitschke's name also has some unpleasant associations; his ardent nationalism and anti-Semitism are, in various ways, in the lineage of Hitlerian ideas. By stressing Weber's criticisms of Treitschke, one suggests differences between Weber's views and this lineage. Roth suggests such an interpretation when he speaks of Weber's opposition to 'Treitschke and similar professors of ideological creeds' (Roth, 1971a, p. 68).

Three distinct issues have become confused in this simple picture. One issue is the question of Weber's view of Treitschke and his ideas. Another is the specific issue of lecturing style. A third is the problem of mixing fact and value. The task of separating these issues is complicated by the fact that Weber himself often ran the second two issues together. Weber was not unclear on the question of the rights and duties of the occupant of a professorial chair; he spoke to this question in some detail. But we are faced with a kind of unclarity on the problem of fact and value, for his views underwent something of an evolution, at least with respect to the ways in which he applied the distinction. A certain amount of context must be filled in to make all this intelligible.

The part of the context relating to Treitschke himself is the most straightforward. Although Weber's black-sheep uncle, Hermann Baumgarten, who influenced Weber, had been a critic of Treitschke's (Weber, 1975, pp. 81-2), Weber was personally friendly toward Treitschke, and he adopted many of his social and political ideas. He admired Treitschke's call to commitment and followed his political conception in certain important respects. He echoed Treitschke's call for a German *Weltmachtpolitik*, or world-power politics, in his own inaugural lecture (Weber, 1971, p. 23; idem, 1980, p. 446; cf. idem, 1978b, p. 266). Mommsen's and Treitschke's judgment of Switzerland, that neutrality is self-mutilation, became Weber's position, and Treitschke's analysis of the American caucus system and spoils system found a place in Weber's later analysis of the American party system. Weber parted from Treitschke's theory that there was an 'irrational residuum' in human nature and from Treitschke's one-sided glorification of power. Weber was impressed with the ethical price that those who seek power must pay, in a way that Treitschke was not.[10] Nevertheless, Weber adopted Treitschke's commitment to the glory of the nation as his own and insisted that this commitment is ultimately not rationally defensible. This, and Weber's later emphasis on the basis of the political power of a great leader in his charismatic, irrational appeal, and his attempt to devise a constitution in which this force could be maximized all seem to be a kind of backhanded tribute to Treitschke's own glorification of the irrational. One might summarize the philosophical relationship to Treitschke by saying that Weber made what he recognized to be a nonrational commitment to the same ends as Treitschke, but differed in that he emphasized that these ends must be pursued rationally, in an intellectually self-disciplined manner. For Weber, this meant a devotion to *Realpolitik* and to the task of attaining a realistic grasp of the world historical situation. Neither a politics with a place for sentimentality and extraneous moral considerations nor a conception of the place of the German nation in the world that was based on myth or romance would be acceptable to Weber.

It was Treitschke's style of lecturing that Weber thought most objectionable, for he thought it tended to interfere with the student's task of obtaining political maturity, especially by undermining scientific objectivity (Dorpalen, 1957, p. 239). Weber was disturbed at the 'frenetic jubilation' of students listening to Treitschke's lectures. Treitschke's lecturing style was based on oratorical talents that were almost unique to Treitschke. His personal magnetism was such that even foreign and Jewish students, whose countries and peoples were regularly subjected to Treitschke's contumely, could not help being fascinated by him (ibid., p. 240). Yet his style was well within the limits of the academic customs of the times. The liberal Lujo Brentano, Schumpeter reported,

> addressed his classes as he would have political meetings, and they responded with cheers and countercheers. Adolf Wagner shouted and stamped and shook his fists at imaginary opponents, at least before the lethargy of old age quieted him down. Others were less spirited and effective but not less hortatory in intent (Schumpeter, 1954, p. 802).

So one theme of Weber's argument is a critique of these customs and of the persons who lectured in this way. However, this was not Weber's central concern. Schmoller, Weber's opponent in the *Methodenstreit*, is discussed at much greater length than is Treitschke. But with Schmoller the issues are much more complex. Someone who presents values *as* facts is not merely undermining the objectivity of his hearers but is committing a kind of fraud upon them. Weber suggested that Schmoller was doing this. But this suggestion is much less plausible than the claim that Treitschke undermined his students' objectivity.

The history of Weber's use of this argument is extremely involved. In his inaugural lecture, Weber specifically advanced two doctrines, the doctrine that science is incapable of deducing ultimate values from its findings and the doctrine that 'the interests of the nation-state ought to have absolute priority over all other considerations; not only in practical politics, but also in those scholarly disciplines which took an active part in the actual processes of legislation and political decision-making' (Mommsen, 1974a, pp. 28-9; Weber, 1971, pp. 12-18). In this context the argument that science had no business deducing ultimate values was 'meant explicitly to clear the way for the unrestricted application of the principle of nation-state interests' in such disciplines as economics (Mommsen, 1974a, p. 29). This was an extreme viewpoint, which Weber formulated in militantly nationalistic language that, we are told, shocked his listeners.

In Weber's later writings he departed neither from the doctrine of the separation of fact and value, nor from his militant nationalism. But he combined these doctrines with the idea that the scientist should abstain from evaluations in the classroom and when speaking with the authority of science. The setting in which this demand for abstention surfaced was a meeting of the *Verein für Sozialpolitik*. If we are to understand Weber's doctrine of value-freedom as an attempt to free science *from* values and valuative considerations, we are hard pressed to explain what Weber was doing at these particular meetings in the first place. The association was founded as a forum for the discussion of opinions on policy by scholars. T. S. Simey has told us that the general trend of the association's work was to 'present a businesslike and unemotional treatment of troublesome problems' (Simey, 1966, p. 310). Weber knew all this as well as anyone. By advancing his attack in these meetings, he purposely plunged the association into the open political controversy it had tried to avoid.

According to Simey, the attack began with a provocation by Weber, which was taken as such. The acrimony increased at each meeting: one member wrote to Schmoller, president of the association, that the Webers' 'shrill quarreling' had turned the association into a 'comic opera.' He suggested that the solution to this problem was to concentrate on practical issues, to keep away from theoretical and political matters unless they were unavoidable. Schmoller replied that he, too, was surprised by Weber's tone (Simey, 1966, p. 311). In their eyes it was Weber who was engaging in politics and harangues.

Though the manifest content of Weber's later methodological attacks against his opponents in the 'value-judgment discussion' involved the idea that his opponents confused fact and value, the discussion started very differently, with an attack by Weber on the 'passion for bureaucracy' of the dominant 'conservatives' in the association (Weber, 1956, p. 127). Only after he had to face the uproar that his remarks caused did he shift the course of the argument by complaining that fact and value were being confused. In short, the association had sided against him (as he knew they would) in a political dispute, and only then did he complain about their failure to separate fact and value. This step was, as Simey has pointed out, 'highly illogical,' for Weber had spoken as a scholar about social policy in the association in the past with equal casualness about mixing fact and value, and certainly without any abstention from value judgments, and was therefore no less guilty of 'confusion' than his opponents. Moreover, it was Weber, not his opponents, who had introduced political and valuative controversy into discussions that were oriented to practical problems and strove for impartiality and objectivity (Simey, 1966, pp. 312-17).

Weber's targets in the value-judgment controversy were not radical students or 'ideologists' like Treitschke, but staid members of the establishment oriented to moderate reform. Weber's other writings on these issues, such as 'The Meaning of "Ethical Neutrality,"' show that those who search for a middle road between opposed values and those who wish to avoid value disputes are subject to much harsher criticisms than was Treitschke (Weber, 1949, pp. 6-7, 10). The general aim of Weber's attack, accordingly, was much more radical than mere disapproval of the abuse of the lectern by extremists, and it was in no simple sense a defense of reasoned discourse against unreason.

But what was his aim? Some light may be shed on this question by asking who would benefit by the imposition of the Weberian strictures. Because Weber's attack was initially political, it is appropriate to ask which political value positions would be served and which would be harmed by being restated and advanced under the new procedures of discourse. It is reasonable to suppose that Weber believed that his own extreme nationalistic position would be best served by the new ground rules, for he believed that a good scientific case could be made to show that the power interests of the nation were ultimately not served by the policies supported by the *Verein*. Weber made his case against bureaucracy before the association by showing that bureaucratization did not lead to international power (Weber, 1956, p. 130; cf. idem, 1971, pp. 332-38). These arguments, it may be noted, fall within Weber's category of 'rational' because they are factual discussions of the consequences of policies oriented toward particular value ends. None of them fit very easily into the framework of impartial problem solving for which the *Verein* strove, because they involve the issues of class interests and historical development, that is, 'political' issues, which require a rather elaborate 'theoretical' underpinning.

WEBER'S 'POLITICAL' VALUE CHOICE

The doctrine of value-freedom and the theory of values thus functioned for Weber both as a political and a critical tool, and his use of this tool has implications for any understanding of his own political values and any understanding of the meaning he assigned to his own life. Certain political values, at least as these values are conceived by their adherents, can be readily shown to be 'confused' using this tool. Weber clearly cannot be regarded as having adhered to these 'confused' positions. His own values must be selected from those positions that remain. Weber, Aron has suggested:

> had decided once and for all that the supreme value to which he would subordinate everything in politics, the god (or demon) to which he had sworn loyalty, was the greatness of the German nation. I use the term greatness (*Grosse*) although it is not Weber's own: he more often speaks of *Macht* (power), *Machtinteressen* (power-interests), *Machtprestige* (power-prestige), and *Weltpolitik* (international politics) (Aron, 1972, p. 87).

Weber himself came close to this characterization, as when he spoke of 'the "power value" of the nations of the world – which, for many of us is the ultimate value' (Weber, 1956, p. 130).

We have noticed that Weber presented the choice of the fatherland as a value by eliminating some other choices as utopian and by presenting yet others as discreditable, so that it appears that there are no real choices. He constructed similar arguments for subordinate ends. We have mentioned his view that the only genuine alternatives are 'leadership democracy' or 'leaderless democracy.' In another postwar speech we are told that we must choose between having a sham parliament with a bureaucratic authoritarian state which administers the citizens like a cowherd, unfree, without law, and bringing the citizens into the operation of the state. A *Herrenvolk*, however, has no choice (1971, p. 290). In 'Parliament and Government in a newly ordered Germany' he gave suffrage reforms as an example of a 'demand of the hour' which was a 'political necessity' whose obstruction would have the 'terrible consequences' of preventing the nation from ever again having the solidarity of 1914 and of condemning Germany to the status of a 'provincial people without the opportunity of counting in the arena of world politics' (1978a, p. 1462).

These 'political' value choices need not conflict with the value choice of the scientist. We are accustomed to examining the conflict between science and politics from the point of view of the scientist. But it is also necessary to look at the potential problems, especially problems of 'role conflict' between the political and the scientific roles, from the viewpoint of the politician. We might anticipate problems of truthfulness, where the intellectual in politics would be compelled to lie or distort scientific truth to achieve political ends, for real political advantage might be attained by untruthfulness. But by the same token, a true *Realpolitiker* would be realistic enough to know that deception was sometimes demanded in politics, and that one can engage in deception without engaging in self-deception. The person who engaged in self-deception would be acting in an irrational way. But the person engaging in simple deception need not be acting irrationally. The *Realpolitiker* fears scientific truth only if he has been engaged in simple deception. Only the 'romantic' politician, the politician questing after the impossible or believing the impossible to be possible, who is therefore confused or self-deceived, finds himself in genuine conflict with science. So, for Weber, the scientist who is a *Realpolitiker* and the *Realpolitiker* who is a scientist should experience no inherent conflict between the two roles.

Robert Eden has suggested that this solution to the problem of the relation of science to politics is a central element of Weber's philosophy (1983). The theme of inherent conflicts between science of philosophy and politics looms large in scholarly writing, from Plato and the medieval Arabs to Robert Merton (Strauss, 1973, pp. 7-21; Merton, 1968, pp. 604-15). Weber enters the discussion at a particular point. The problem was central to Nietzsche, who urged a form of philosophic leadership. Eden suggests that Weber's resolution of the conflict is his response to Nietzsche. We shall see that the same solution was later turned against 'scientism' by Weber's successors. The solution allowed Weber to concern himself instead with the failings of politics and movements that were unrealistic and the failings of intellectuals who confused fact and value. The idea that if there were neither intellectuals who confused fact and value nor politicians who confused attainable ends with otherworldly, unattainable ones, there would be no conflict between science and politics can serve as a tool for interpreting Weber. Weber was, at least by his own lights, not a political romantic, nor was he confused about the relation of fact and value; so his own conflict between science and politics was not a role conflict but a matter of sparing time to do each task properly. It was only because he was spurned when he attempted to build a political following that he did not himself become a political actor – not because he felt any intellectual conflict between the two spheres.

It is impossible to give a full formulation of the issues over Weber's political values here.[11] However, a few simple misinterpretations can be rejected on the basis of our discussion of Weber's theory of values. We shall limit the discussion to the two main themes in this literature: the questions of whether Weber can be regarded as a 'liberal' and whether he can be exculpated from responsibility for the rise of Nazism. Several difficulties arise in any such discussion of Weber's political views. The understanding of the relationship between Weber's conceptions and Nazism and liberalism depends on one's conception of the essential character of these 'isms.' But their essential character has always been controversial.

The problem of liberalism

In considering the relation between Weber's writing and 'liberalism' one must begin by recognizing that his theory of values excluded as confused most of the central doctrines associated with liberalism, such as the various Enlightenment conceptions of man's natural rights that informed the Declaration of Independence, Utilitarianism, and any other doctrine that interpreted itself as rationally justifiable, such as those of Rawls, Nozick, or

Finnis today. To speak of Weber as a liberal, then, one must exercise great caution, for doctrines that make up what we would regard today as liberalism have their origins among the political philosophies he rejected. This constrains interpretation and qualifies Weber's remarks.

In spite of these constraints, there is a substantial literature that attempts to portray Weber as a Western liberal. Roth says that 'national welfare was Weber's ultimate political yardstick' (Roth, 1971a, p. 68; cf. Nolte, 1963, p. 4; Jaspers, 1962, p. 212; Beetham, 1974, pp. 121, 129), which suggests that 'national welfare' for Weber meant something akin to what writers in the Anglo-American political tradition mean. John Stuart Mill conceived of 'welfare' as equivalent to 'the greatest good for the greatest number,' and it is some version of this notion that informs the modern welfare state. Weber repeatedly rejected such conceptions (e.g., Weber, 1971, p. 12). Bendix describes Weber as a 'defender of the enlightenment against the Russian Threat,' perhaps with Weber's claim in 1918 that Germany could at least boast that she had saved Europe from the Russian knout in mind. This boast makes more sense as a consoling thought in the face of failure of the war than as an expression of Weber's deepest political loyalty to the West. The 'Russian threat' was a large part of liberal imperialist propaganda, but largely for some reasons identified by Ludwig Dehio: 'in the West . . . the idealistic liberal formulas of our imperialists failed us completely. In attacking England, we were attacking the smaller European nations' most obvious historical defender' (Dehio, 1960, p. 93). 'Since in the East their dreams' of guaranteeing the freedom and independence of the smaller nations 'had some foundation in fact, the liberal imperialists were delighted to shift their emphasis from West to East' (ibid., p. 98). A motive for this concern is given in Naumann's cynical remark that 'Small states are promised freedom so that they shall change their masters' (quoted in ibid., p. 88). This is not to suggest that Weber's Russophobia was not genuine, for it was in fact one of the consistent themes of his thought. Nevertheless, for Weber as for the German liberals generally, the thoughts involved a certain amount of self-deception, as when, after the war, he said that 'there was only one power, which under all circumstances willed the war for war's sake and according to its political aims: Russia. . .' (quoted in Mayer, 1956, p. 106).

Bendix neglects to explain that Weber frequently conjoined his denunciations of Russian society and political organization with a denunciation of British and American society and political organization (Weber, 1975, p. 581; cf. Mommsen, 1974a, p. 40), and he avoids explaining how the Enlightenment tradition is to be preserved by fighting the British, or what the 'Enlightenment tradition' can mean apart from such ideas as the affirmation of the rights of man or of the power of reason in deciding questions of the political good and the form of the state.[12] Affection for 'the West' or Europe was never a significant theme for Weber, though it was for some other Germans. On the contrary – as Dehio has pointed out, he and the imperialist academics with whom he was associated

> occasionally let slip some extremely sinister ideas: for example Max Weber's words: 'Let them hate us, as long as they fear us'; or Otto Hintze's threat: 'If the worst comes to the worst, we shall let ourselves be buried beneath the ruins of European civilization' (Dehio, 1960, p. 20).

Nationalism was an Enlightenment ideal, but it was one ideal among others. By speaking of the nation as an 'ultimate' value, Weber raised the problem of the conflict between the nation and other values in his own thought. Interpretations that attempt to reconcile this conflict are usually based on those of Weber's writings that are critical of the German state of his time and on his practical recommendations for reform. These writings are what Roth has in mind when he argues that Weber's support for parliamentary democracy must be distinguished from the nationalistic rhetoric in which it was cloaked. In these writings Weber advocated parliamentary democracy, a 'liberal' form of government. Roth's suggestion is that this was his goal, his nationalist rhetoric merely a means. We mentioned earlier that an immediate difficulty in this imputation of hidden motives for this advocacy is that Weber's letters and private statements give the same nationalistic justifications for this position as do his public statements. England, the great parliamentary democracy of Weber's time, was at the same time the great world power. The possibility that the two facts were connected did not escape Weber; he devoted a good deal of thought to the connection (Weber, 1978a, p. 1420; idem, 1956, p. 130; idem, 1980, p. 446; cf. idem, 1978b, p. 266). The reason that Weber sided with parliamentary democracy, as he made clear, was not that he had determined, as Enlightenment theorists thought they had, that there was a best form of the state. It was because he had determined that this form of the state would be most conducive to the goal of German national power. Accordingly, Weber advocated a particular kind of parliamentary democracy. He did not choose the form that would be most conducive to social justice, or to the preservation of ancient traditions, or to popular self-determination, or to the development of cultural diversity, or to individual freedom in the Western 'negative' sense. He chose the form that would be most conducive to the production of great *Weltmacht-polische* leaders.

Political leadership

In his postwar writings on constitutional problems, Weber called the form he recommended 'plebiscitarian leader democracy.'[13] The notion is best summarized in his famous statement to Ludendorff quoted in Chapter 1. The 'plebiscitarian' version of parliamentary democracy differs from ordinary parliamentary democracy or a party system such as is found in the United States in respect of the function of the leader and of parliament. Parliament was to serve as a nursery for leaders and as a means for getting rid of leaders who had lost the faith of the masses. The leader himself was to rule not by virtue of parliamentary politics, but by virtue of his own charisma. The powers of parliament would be expressly formulated to assure that this was the function it would serve. The leader would be a president, directly elected, and hence would have a political base separate from parliament. The powers of the president would include power to dismiss parliament, to go directly to the people by means of referenda, and to choose his own cabinet members, though these were to be drawn from parliament. Parliament could not remove the president, though the president could be removed by a referendum, if 10 percent of the electorate called for one (Beetham, 1974, pp. 232-3). Weber believed this was in substance how great prime ministers ruled anyway.

> As a matter of fact, the position of the present British Prime Minister [Lloyd George] is based not at all on the confidence of parliament and its parties, but on that of the masses in the country and of the army in the field. Parliament acquiesces (with considerable inner reluctance) (Weber, 1978a, p. 1452).

The significance of the British example was not a matter of the superiority of the system as such but the fact that

> the British parliament became, after all, the proving ground for those political leaders who managed to bring a quarter of mankind under the rule of a minute but politically prudent minority (ibid., p. 1420).

Parliament thus 'became the decisive agent of British world power' (ibid., p. 1419). In short, the true function of parliament was, for Weber, the production of leaders. Its potential for doing so showed itself in the careers of such figures as Gladstone. The feature of Gladstone's career that attracted Weber was his use of parliament as a platform for a direct appeal to the masses, from which he derived his true power (Weber, 1946, p. 106). His true power was, in a word, charismatic: the form of democratic consent and free rational discourse in which this power was exerted merely concealed its true nature (Schmidt, 1964, pp. 289-92; Abramowski, 1966, pp. 156-9).

One can most clearly see that Weber understood parliamentary democracy in an illiberal fashion if one examines his political conception in the light of his value theory. Consider the contrast to, e.g., Mill, who thought there could be rational discourse about ends (or Bryce, who thought of democracy as government by discussion). For Mill, the political leader could rationally persuade the citizenry to revise their values in such matters as the subjection of women or the preservation of liberty; it would be, further, their responsibility to do so in order to achieve social progress. Mill's own efforts against slavery are exemplary of this. This kind of persuasion and relationship between leaders and followers presupposes that the citizens be sufficiently intelligent to make rational, moral responses to those who wished to persuade them. And Mill, accordingly, gave thought to ways in which an appropriate 'political education' for the working classes might be attained. His conclusions strikingly diverge from the whole doctrine of political education we encounter in writers like Weber and Meinecke (Pois, 1972, pp. 18-19). Mill pointed out that

> there is a spontaneous education going on in the minds of the multitude. . . . The institutions for lectures and discussion, the collective deliberations on questions of common interest, the trade unions, the political agitation, all serve to awaken public spirit, to diffuse variety of ideas among the mass, and to excite thought and reflection among the more intelligent (Mill, 1929, pp. 757-8).

For Mill, then, political participation and free discussion is the primary means of political education. The example he gave of political responsibility, the 'good sense and forbearance' of the workers in Lancashire during the cotton crisis, was a result of 'the instruction obtained from newspapers' (ibid., p. 757). The model of democratic political responsibility and rational conduct, for Mill, was cases like these. For Weber, the model was the struggle between irreconcilable viewpoints and the leaders who are their bearers.

The deeper reason for the difference between Mill and Weber is that for Weber there could be no such thing as rational persuasion with respect to ends, save by showing a person the inconsistency in his choices: for Weber, the relation between leader and follower envisioned by Mill, where the people 'judge for themselves of the persons who are and are not entitled to' deference, could only be sham. The leader could only change values by demanding, tricking, or entrancing his followers into a nonrational decision or commitment to him or to his values.[14] Leadership based on reasoned moral persuasion on the part of the leader and rational reflection on the part of the led would be, for Weber, an *epistemological impossibility*. Thus democracy as traditionally understood was for Weber an epistemological impossibility as well. Weber endorsed democracy only in the light of an antidemocratic conception of what democracies actually were (cf. Antoni, 1959, pp. 125-41).

Mill was not the only 'liberal,' of course, and the fact that liberalism has many guises makes problematic any claim about 'liberalism' as a whole. Yet when one ticks off the justifications that liberalism in its various guises might offer for democratic institutions, we find that Weber would have decisively rejected most of them. He called the idea of human rights 'an extreme rationalist fantasy,' and said that 'inviolable rights were no longer appropriate as an idea in modern industrial society' (quoted in Mommsen, 1974b, pp. 418-19). Elsewhere he remarked that 'such concepts as "will of the people . . ." no longer exist for me and are fictions' (quoted in ibid., p. 421).

The 'liberal' justifications he would not have rejected include the value choice of encouraging the development of the autonomous individual, especially the great personality (Fleischmann, 1964, pp. 213, 215, 238; Mommsen, 1965, p. 573; Löwith, 1927, pp. 77, 83, 87; Wegener, 1962, pp. 260-2; Eden, 1983; Strauss, 1953, p. 44). This is a German 'liberal' doctrine whose outstanding feature is that it construes freedom in a 'nonnegative' way. Weber specifically insisted that this value could not be equated with the traditional liberal idea that the power of the state be restricted as much as possible. Such a notion was perhaps suited to a young capitalism. But Weber believed that capitalism would soon begin to stagnate and that this would lead to a complete bureaucratization of all of life as competition gave way to bureaucratic regulation (Mommsen, 1974a, pp. 98-100). 'Everywhere the House of Serfdom is already at hand,' he wrote (1971, p. 63). His solution was to counter the tendency toward bureaucracy. This was precisely the point of plebiscitarian leader democracy. It allowed for and encouraged the rise of leaders who could control the bureaucracy, who could make the unfortunately ineliminable bureaucracy their own tool rather than merely submit to it, as the ordinary man was forced to do. But this is a peculiar sort of freedom, because it consists largely in the freedom either to become a great man by virtue of an inner calling or to become a follower in the great man's cause, to be charismatically enchanted by him (Habermas, 1970, p. 75). It is a type of freedom that transcends the 'negative' freedom of traditional liberalism. Moreover, it potentially destroys negative freedom: Weber supposed that these leaders would engage in international power politics and that 'all internal relationships' should be structured for the purpose of conducting great power politics (quoted in Mommsen, 1974b, p. 85). Presumably this means that 'negative' freedoms would be sacrificed to power considerations, as they are under a state of war or siege.

The issue of similarities to fascism

To call Weber a 'liberal' on the basis of this doctrine involves us in another problem, for this doctrine borders on or is tantamount to Nazism or Fascism. Hitler too affirmed the 'absolute supremacy of the value of personality' and the 'authority of personality in politics' (Domarus, 1965, pp. 73-4). These commonalities are the basis of the frequently made argument that Weber's doctrine stands toward the end in a line of degeneration running from the Enlightenment to Hitler (Hennis, 1959). Karl Löwith, for example, argued that Weber paved the way to the dictatorial state by pleading for irrational, charismatic leadership and for decisionism, which removed the moral unity that could have prevented Nazism. 'It is one step from this doctrine of "decision" and of leadership to the idea of total mental submission to the leader' (Löwith, 1939, pp. 171-2; cf. Lukács, 1962, p. 556). Yet those interpreters who have stated or implied that Weber was a proto-fascist in his political thinking have faced a difficulty similar to those who have characterized him as a liberal, for the essential character of fascism is also controversial. So discussions of Weber's 'proto-fascism' have turned on arguments over the essential character of fascism.[15]

A commonly cited defense of Weber against the charge of fascism is Ernst Nolte's article, 'Max Weber vor dem Fascismus' (1963), which is directed against Mommsen. Nolte's attempt to give a positive characterization of Weber's view illustrates a difficulty shared with other defenses of Weber. In order to defend Weber, Nolte attributes to Weber an implicit natural right conception, which Nolte supposes would have led him to reject Hitler's assignment of Jews and Marxists to the category of 'foe.' Beyond this, Nolte argues that Weber did not believe that a charismatic leader of the magnitude of past prophets could emerge in his epoch, which suggests that Weber merely predicted badly with respect to the possibility of a Hitler rather than shared culpability for creating a framework of law and ideas in which a Hitler could arise.[16]

Although Nolte is perhaps correct in predicting what Weber would have done, this is not precisely to the critics' point. Because Nolte ignores the structure of Weber's ethical conception, he fails to recognize the peculiar meaning of the demands of the leader in a politics like Weber's, which denies the existence of ordinary moral constraints in politics and rejects the idea of criteria of legitimacy that are superior to, and therefore warrant a rejection of, particular demands of the leader. Heidegger's chilling phrase, 'Precepts and ideas are not now the rules of your being: the Führer is your one and only present and future German reality and law,' brings out this problem sharply. For a Weberian, all moral decisions derive from one's ultimate value choice. If the choice is to follow Hitler, either because one identifies Hitler with the sole possibility of national greatness or is enchanted by Hitler's charisma, one has no independent criteria with which to assess Hitler's demands.[17] If Hitler says, 'Kill Jews,' and one is sympathetic to Jews, one can respond either by betraying Hitler – thus showing that one's ultimate value was something other than national greatness or fidelity to the leader – or by obeying. One cannot say, 'This was an illegitimate demand,' because one lacks, and Weber denied the existence of, any supervening criteria of political morality that would warrant an assertion of illegitimacy.[18] This is of course not to say that Weber himself would not have opposed Hitler. But it is to say that Weber's conception excludes the possibility of doing so on grounds of the illegitimacy of the leader's legal demands.

This may seem like an excessively formalistic and unfair point to raise against Weber, for, as we shall see, he did not in any simple sense share Hitlerian values. Yet the point itself is not unfair. For Weber, politics was a matter of choices between extremes, and he was constantly criticizing his opponents for their failure to push the implications of their choices to their logical limits. This is the theme of his *Antrittsrede*, his speech to the *Verein* in 1895, and of his talk on politics as a vocation. This decisionistic style was not compatible with the kind of reasoning about ethics and choice that was retrospectively seen as necessary for resisting Hitler. Even Weber's friend Karl Jaspers, whose philosophy represented a view, if anything, more extreme than Weber's on these matters, found himself, at the end of the Hitler regime, compelled to appeal, in *The Question of German Guilt*, to a whole range of notions of natural law and the rights of man to make retrospective sense of the moral obligations of Germans (1961, pp.

34, 38, 55-6). This incompatibility is a central source of the Weber problem, as it is a significant source for twentieth-century political reflection. Yet it is not the only source that bears on the problems of Weber's values. In the next chapter we shall deal with the broader question of Weber's political values as shown in his design for German politics.

3 Weber's political design

Weber believed that circumstances placed severe constraints on the state, the leader, and the bureaucracy, just as he believed that value choice was severely constrained. David Beetham has argued that Weber supposed that the constraints were, or could be made, sufficiently strong that the practical achievements of liberalism would be preserved, and that this was part of Weber's political intent. As Beetham points out, Weber had expressed a concern for these practical achievements: life, he said, would not be worth living 'without the achievements bequeathed by the age of the "rights of man" ' (quoted in Beetham, 1974, p. 114). On the basis of such remarks Beetham concludes that these practical achievements were 'values' for Weber, and that this moderates his 'ultimate value choice' of 'the nation' and takes some of the edge off his insistent claim that the intellectual basis of natural law had been definitely dissolved.

If we were to approach this argument in the manner of the previous chapter, we could make short work of it. 'Freedom' in the specific sense that concerns Beetham, the sense of civil liberties, was clearly not Weber's ultimate value. Weber would have been, on his own account, compelled to sacrifice this value at the first conflict with a value that was more important to him, as 'the nation' certainly was. Beetham says that there was a conflict in Weber's own values. But he ignores the implications of Weber's ethical conception for such 'conflicts' and that Weber publically construed the existence of such conflicts in the thought of others to be evidence of a lack of intellectual integrity (e.g., Weber, 1980, p. 440).

What are we to make of this? The conflict in values, given Weber's ethical theory, is a more serious matter than Beetham makes it out to be, and Beetham's failure to deal with the issue raises questions about his whole interpretation. But by pointing to conflicts in Weber's own values Beetham opens up the possibility of an alternative strategy of interpretation. In the previous chapter, we approached the problem by seeking the consistency in Weber's explicit claims and in the logical structure of his own justifications and explanations of his views. Beetham's approach differs from this, in ways that may best be shown by an example.

Wolfgang Mommsen, on the basis of a strategy of interpretation of the sort found in the previous chapter, argued that Weber had for various reasons abandoned the ideas of constitutional democracy. One of these reasons was Weber's 'rejection of natural law theory, which had previously provided the philosophical basis for human rights, as being no longer valid or acceptable to modern man. . . . Mommsen,' Beetham says, 'writes almost as if he believed that there could be no constitutional liberalism except on a natural law basis' (1974, p. 113). Beetham rejects this. Once achieved, he suggests, rights could be *protected* by a properly *designed* institutional structure. So Beetham argues that one of the consequences Weber expected from his own plan for German political institutions was a degree of civil rights and liberties, and this aim was part of Weber's motivation in suggesting his plan.

We may call this an 'interpretation from design,' for it argues for an interpretation of Weber's values on the basis of his practical political suggestions and expectations. Such arguments depend on asking what Weber assumed or saw to be the constraints of the political and social situation, how he thought of them, and what he concluded. The difficulty with any interpretation from design is that it must be built up on a great many assumptions and auxiliary interpretations: to understand Weber's view of the constraints, as well as his formulation of his aims, it is necessary to see what he took to be a possible aim, how he would scientifically describe or conceive a political or social situation, and so on. Thus, our discussion of these arguments must of necessity be roundabout and take in a broader range of his writings on politics. The connection to our main theme, the problem of reason and value, is also indirect. One central element of Weber's sense of the political situation was his sense of its cultural possibilities. These expectations must be construed in terms of his sociological remarks on political culture, which in turn reflect his conception of the character of values.

The problem of legitimacy

Weber's discussion of legitimate authority in *Economy and Society* is central to his sociology of politics. The discussion is in many ways peculiar as a piece of sociology. As J. G. Merquior (1980) has pointed out, it is a 'belief' theory of legitimacy, a classification of beliefs about the ultimate basis of authority. Merquior calls the habit of thinking of social phenomena in terms of their ultimate value basis 'culturalism,' and suggests that this way of thinking is nonsociological or antisociological. Yet, curiously, in his 'political' discussions of the Russian situation, written before the war, Weber took the probable fall of the Tsarist regime to be a matter of its ineptness as a regime and discussed the possibilities of a 'constitutional democracy' in terms of the problem of finding a 'social basis,' a set of interests that would work in support of such a regime (Beetham, 1974, p. 115). These 'political' discussions are more 'sociological' than his classification of beliefs.

One reason Weber proposed a belief theory of legitimacy was 'internal': the treatment of legitimacy was part of a broader discussion of association, and Weber's problem in this discussion was to distinguish voluntary associations from the state. The belief in the legitimacy of commands appears to be the only distinguishing mark of political authority. In the essay 'On Some Categories of Interpretive Sociology,' in which Weber first formulated most of these arguments, there is a much clearer aim: Weber was trying to show that a 'sociological' concept of the state may be constructed on a purely individual basis, in terms of the expectations, probabilities of action, and beliefs of individuals. Lukács, in *The Destruction of Reason* (1980), recognized that this argument, despite its forbidding technical character, was a crucial basis for Weber's rejection of nonindividualist social theories. These included Lukács's own doctrine of the proletariat and traditional German theories that made the state into a substantial being. Such theories usually proceeded by trying to show the conceptual necessity of some supraindividual elements in an adequate account of the state. Weber's discussion is designed to show that these elements are not scientifically necessary. The continuing philosophical significance of Weber's definition of the state as a monopoly of legitimate violence derives from the strict ontological individualism of the argument. The style of the argument, which is concerned with the question of the *conceptual* distinction between state authority and other forms of social relation, is also congenial to current discussions of the justification of state power, discussions that focus on the question of the justification of this specific distinctive element (e.g., Nozick, 1974).

Weber called the type of legitimation belief characteristic of modern regimes 'rational-legal,' and, as Poggi recognizes, this category is a sociologized form of the idea of the *Rechtsstaat*. The distinctive feature of the belief is the idea that questions of authority must be settled by reference to written rules. In a curious way this runs together two problems, the philosophical problem of the justification of the law and the question of the sociological character of beliefs about obedience to the state. As Poggi points out, the philosophical problem arises from the idea of the *Rechtsstaat* itself, which forces us to ask for the authority of a rule in a higher rule and thus to ask questions about the ultimate basis of the rules, in the form of the question If the basis of law is a more basic law, what is the basis of the 'most basic' law? This question, put a little differently, has obvious implications for the 'achievements of the age of the rights of man': if the only limit to what can be compelled by law is to be found in the law itself, and laws can be changed, what protection is there against the expansion of the state legal power? (Poggi, 1978, p. 105). If we seek some basis or limitations outside of positive law, such as in a doctrine of the inherent rights of man or just consent, we are back in the doctrinal world of natural law.

Notice that natural law provided both a 'sociological' solution, in the sense of an account of why people accept the validity of law (i.e., because of human nature), as well as a philosophical warrant for the law. Although Weber and other theorists regarded doctrines such as the inherent rights of man or just consent as definitely dead and inappropriate to the modern world, they nevertheless recognized that the question of the ultimate basis of the *Rechtsstaat*, as a matter of logic, needed an answer. Because it could not be answered simply by reference to a more basic law, the answer needed to be in some sense outside of law. The sociological fact that citizens believed that legal enactments should be obeyed was a convenient answer to the question, considered as a question in the philosophy of law. As a sociological account, however, it leaves a great deal to be desired.

The reduction of the problem of legitimacy to a classification of beliefs that are logically at the base of regimes is a deductivist caricature of the sort of reasoning a citizen would go through in considering his loyalties. For the citizen, his interests, the acceptability of alternatives, justice, and so forth would obviously weigh heavily, and he would ordinarily be prepared to obey a regime that conducted itself competently and fairly, regardless of the 'basis' it claimed for itself. The legal base of regimes is an esoteric legal matter, at best, which gets raised only in highly unusual, particularly in revolutionary, situations. Not surprisingly, Weber's account contrasts poorly to earlier writers like Bagehot, who manages, in *The English Constitution*, to give a class analysis of various legitimacy beliefs and to anticipate the idea of the theatre state (Bagehot, 1963, p. 248; Geertz, 1980, pp. 121-36).

Bagehot's interest was different. He was making a kind of comparative analysis; he was not attempting to, and did not, give an answer to the question of what distinguishes a state from a voluntary association. Nor did he regard the decline of natural law ideas as a significant sociological fact, as did Weber. These questions were distractions, and the result of the mixing together of the two kinds of questions, legal and sociological, by converting the *Rechtsstaat* into an ideal-type was that Weber was left with a curiously narrow and formalistic sociological category.

Weber was aware that workaday political legitimation, in the sense of the workaday creation of support for policy, involves much more than 'basic' beliefs, and his practical political analyses reflect this. Yet he attempted to remain within the individualist framework of his sociology. The consequence of this dual commitment for Weber's analytic practice was that, as Mommsen has pointed out, legitimacy was *de facto* equated with success or stability, because a political system without 'legitimacy' in one of Weber's senses is bound to collapse. There is a more complex kind of equation of success and legitimacy as well, which depends on the concept of charisma. Part of Weber's characterization of charismatic authority is a claim about the manner in which charisma persists. The leader, he said, acquires authority 'and retains it only by proving his powers in real life' (1978b, p. 229). His failures are a sign that he lacks the 'mission' he claims for himself. There is another sense of charisma which is also plausibly attributed to Weber. It applies more broadly to institutions and means the prestige and sacredness of a society's institutions, particularly its leading or central institutions (Geertz, 1977, p. 150-1). As Mommsen has pointed out, a similar question holds here. Prestige, he says, 'is always largely dependent on the success of the rulers; hence it will not survive any substantial failure' (Mommsen, 1974a, p. 85). With this we come back around to Beetham's observation that, in Weber's discussion of the fate of the Tsarist regime, simple competence rather than belief was the issue.

So the theory of legitimacy, which appears to be the key to Weber's politics, turns out to be something less. Its importance in understanding Weber's political design is that it supplies two central concepts: bureaucracy, which Weber took to be the embodiment of 'rational-legal' authority, and charisma, which Weber attempted to design in to the political system by a 'plebiscitary' form, in which 'election' has the character of charismatic acclamation (1978b, pp. 239-41).

The balance of interests

Part of the puzzle about Weber's discussion of legitimacy is that interests are not made a part of the theory of legitimacy itself. Elsewhere in the sociological writings, the concept figures prominently, usually in the formula 'material and ideal interests,' a formula that figures in the writings of later Weberians as well. In the sociology proper, the formula represents not so much a theory of interests as a means of turning a phrase like 'interests rule the world' into a definitional truth. Every purpose or aim falls into the category of an interest, so purposive action is by definition oriented to interests. The notion of 'ideal' interests is so broad as to include everything from the rejection of the world to the desire to be good. The highly formalistic, definitional character of this usage supports Merquior's charge of 'culturalism.' Explanation goes back to interests, and an interest, once identified, is not further explained. In the political writings, 'interest' has a slightly more restricted usage and means something like 'any relatively stable purpose that is broadly distributed in some social category.' This usually refers to material interests, such as those of Russian peasants seeking the redistribution of land and German peasants leaving the East Elbian estates. But even in these cases there are 'ideal' elements, such as the Russian peasants' archaic communitarian ideas and the German peasants' desire for 'freedom' (Beetham, 1974, p. 37).

In the political writings, Weber thought of interests as more or less fixed constraints to which the leader must adapt and respond. However much the 'ideal interests' of the Catholic Center Party may have irritated him, for example, he did not envision any scheme to eliminate these interests by another *Kulturkampf*. Indeed, his notion of leadership and his strong-president 'plebiscitarian leader democracy' constitutional scheme were an attempt to preserve, in the face of these interests, a large range for political action by the leader – to insulate the leader from these interests, so to speak, by allowing the parliamentary leadership to represent the interests of groups, and the president to represent the interest of the nation. Weber believed that the national interest was to achieve the world-political power to deal with a world with limited markets for industry, which were already largely divided up between the empires of the time (Mommsen, 1974a, pp. 41-2). The lack of markets would, he feared, strangle Germany as an industrial and, in the longer run, as a military power; so Germany's great need was to secure the economic functional equivalent of Britain's colonies or of Russia's undeveloped outlying regions. Weber was not in any way unique in thinking this: the same thought was the base of the various schemes for an African colonial empire or a German-dominated *Mitteleuropa*, such as Weber's friend Naumann promoted.

Weber's originality in thinking about national interests lay elsewhere, in his discussions of the domestic preconditions for national power, particularly what he called 'social unity.' The task of obtaining social unity – in the short-range sense of obtaining support for decisive political action at the international level – falls to the president, in the strong presidential system Weber promoted late in life; and this task obviously constitutes a large constraint on the ruler.

We can get some sense of how these constraints work by considering the problem that concerns Mommsen and Beetham, the question of the preservation of civil liberties. Weber himself said almost nothing about the subject of preserving civil liberties in Germany, so this particular issue requires a great deal of interpretive reasoning. In speaking of the constraints on the nation, the impossibility of peace and the necessity for struggle, the need for elbow room, and the like, Weber was quite explicit and direct. His scattered remarks on civil liberties, in contrast, are context-dependent and indirect. Mommsen relies on a remark, quoted earlier, to the effect that internal relations must be subordinated to international tasks, for his view that Weber would have had no compunctions about sacrificing civil liberties were there any power advantages to be gained by doing so. As we saw in the last chapter, this willingness is not only consistent with, but – given Weber's notions about ethical reasoning – is demanded by the choice of 'the nation' as an 'ultimate value.'

Beetham's argument is that Weber's constitutional proposals were designed in a way that would preserve civil liberties and that Weber's scattered remarks on the subject show that the preservation of civil liberties was a value for him, as well as a frequent concern of his substantive political analyses of other countries. In his writings on Russia, he was interested in the question of whether a party with a genuinely liberal ideology could find a sufficient social basis on which to succeed. In writings on the United States and Britain, he was concerned to show ways in which the national character had been shaped to favor freedom.

Beetham sees Weber as having had a kind of balance-of-powers conception, in which the balance is produced not by legal but by sociological devices. The aim of the devices is to control bureaucratization, which was Weber's primary concern. He considered bureaucratization to be an evil, a parceling out of the soul, and in this sense destructive to freedom in the decisionistic sense of the capacity to be a personality. One flaw of bureaucracy has to do with the political capacity of the bureaucratic personality. Bureaucrats lack a power sense and a sense of responsibility, the sort of spirit that Weber believed could only be fostered and developed in parliament (Beetham, 1974, p. 77). Nevertheless, he conceded bureaucracy's indispensability and superiority to any other form of organization. So the elimination of bureaucracy is a utopian goal. Checking and controlling it is not. Parliament, if it is sufficiently strong, can counter the state bureaucracy, and capitalist bureaucracies can also serve as a counterbalance (ibid., p. 83). Beetham takes the view, then, that this was the aim of Weber's institutional suggestions.

Because Weber said little about his expectations, Beetham must reconstruct them through interpretation. The first part of this reconstruction takes up Weber's idea that the social and political development of Germany and Russia were similar. Both were places where capitalist development came late and where the liberal tradition, which grew historically out of the practices and individualist ideas of early capitalism, had never developed. In both Germany and Russia the bourgeoisie had not shared power prior to the existence of modern class conflict, when universal suffrage forced them into a subordinate place in an alliance with the establishment. Beetham supposes that this means that in Weber's discussion of the possibilities of liberalism in Russia we get an idea of his expectations for Germany. The second part of Beetham's reconstruction applies Weber's explicit reasoning about Russia to the German case to see what he might have expected for Germany. This in turn lends a new coherence to Weber's diverse observations on Germany. In the writings on Russia, there are two themes. One is what may broadly be called political culture, the other is institutional structure.

Weber suggested that in Russia civil and political freedom depended on tension between various bureaucracies and between bureaucracies and parliament. In these writings, which, it should be noted, date from before the war, Weber 'regarded a strong parliament as a protector of civil rights and liberties . . . . the various freedoms announced in the October manifesto – freedoms of expression, of conscience, of association, of assembly, of the person – remained only token, and could only continue to be so [because of] the absence of an effective parliament' (Beetham, 1974, p. 113). Beetham suggests that one can generalize from this to the lesson that parliaments protect civil liberties. There had been, of course, a significant example of this in recent German history, when parliament rejected the antisocialist laws of 1890 out of fear that the restrictions would be extended to other parties. Moreover, as Beetham points out, even in Weber's wartime essays, which reflect a disenchantment with the idea of a strong parliament and a shift in emphasis to the need for a strong leader, Weber contrived to treat parliament – this time in the case of England under Lloyd George – as a guarantor of civil rights against a plebiscitary leader.

Perhaps this is one interpretive argument too many. By Weber's time the world had experienced enough instances of parliaments that ignored civil liberties that it would have been quite naive for him to suppose that parliaments were, as a general rule, protectors of civil liberties. Weber himself, during the war, expressed a fear that the Philistine bourgeoisie would be so frightened by 'every outbreak of syndicalist putschism' that it would give up its civil liberties (1978a, p. 1461) – in short, that it would respond differently than it had at the time of the antisocialist proposals. The medium for this cowardice presumably would be parliament, and Weber did not imagine that the mere existence of a legally powerful parliament would change the result.

As we have suggested, the more fundamental difficulty with Beetham's argument is that it presupposes a serious inconsistency in Weber's thought about his own values. To validate such a supposition it would be necessary to provide evidence of sufficient weight to overbalance the acknowledged fact of the importance of the consideration of value-consistency for Weber. If Weber had indeed written a great deal on civil liberties – as Beetham concedes he did not (1974, p. 114) – and if the value 'civil liberties' did not so obviously conflict with others, Beetham's interpretation might pass. But the evidence is insufficiently weighty. Moreover, it is unclear why Weber said so little about the conflict, which was a significant theme of liberal political theory of the time. In one place in which Weber did give some idea of how civil liberties ranked as concerns for him, we find that the question 'How can one possibly save *any remnants* of "individualist" freedom in any sense?' and the question 'How will democracy [even in the limited sense of having some check on the power of the bureaucracy] be *at all possible*?' (Weber, 1978a, p. 1403) were not the 'most important.' The most important concern for Weber was the inability of the bureaucratic mentality to act politically, particularly to direct the state in its international dealings (ibid., pp. 1403-4).

The concept of bureaucracy

In Weber's discussion of the political limitations of bureaucracy, as well as in his discussions of the threat of bureaucratization to the soul, the cultural implications of bureaucratization, and the inevitability of bureaucratization, the tone is characteristically hyperbolic. Weber appears to have been arguing two contrary cases. One is that bureaucracy is unquestionably the technically best form of organization, absolutely indispensable to the modern state and to modern capitalism, *because* it is the most rational form of organization – 'as austerely rational as a machine' (Weber, 1978a, p. 1402). Some readers have taken Weber as having presented the view that bureaucracy represents the only possible form of authority in the modern world. Alasdair MacIntyre, for example, argues that once the rational invalidity of all valuative bases of authority is established the sole 'type of authority [that] can appeal to rational criteria to vindicate itself . . . is [that] type of bureaucratic authority which appeals precisely to its own effectiveness. And what that appeal reveals is that bureaucratic authority is nothing other than successful power' (1981, p. 25). At the same time, Weber found a great deal of fault with bureaucracy, so much so that Merquior reverses MacIntyre's view that Weber makes bureaucracy the only justifiable form. In the political writings, Merquior argues, bureaucracy 'was passionately indicted as the main culprit of cultural *illegitimacy* in modern times' (1980, p. 120). Yet the two interpretations are complementary: the doctrine of the indispensability of bureaucracy together with the idea that bureaucracy constituted the greatest of possible threats to freedom, culture, and the nation makes for Weber's fatalism.

Why was Weber so impressed with the threat of bureaucracy? The reason may be found in his deductivist idea of rationality. 'Deduction' from a value choice depends on turning the choice into the rule When means or ends conflict, act in the way that will achieve value *x*. The rule makes all subordinate decisions machine-like in their strictness.

When Weber constructed a sociological ideal-type, it was the same machine-like character of bureaucracy that impressed him. The machine-like character, however, is due to the rationality of bureaucratic procedure, specifically, to the bureaucrat's deductive reasoning from written rules. The ideal-type is strictly dependent on the conception of rationality. If one rejects this conception of rationality, for example by saying that alleged instances of deductive rationality are in fact stylized and partial reconstructions of actual reasoning, one rejects the ideal-type as inadequate, for whenever it is applied, it misdescribes. If one avoids this judgment of inadequacy by appealing to Weber's notion that ideal-types are always misdescriptions that reality never matches, one loses any sense of the inevitability and absolute superiority of bureaucracy. At best, one can claim that the organizations that most closely approximate this ideal are, in practice, more efficient than the available alternatives. And this claim leaves open the possibility of more effective forms of social organization than bureaucracy, a possibility Weber never considered because he *identified* deductive reasoning from rules with substantive perfection, and deviations as substantive imperfections.

In the political writings, the emphasis changes. Recall that for Weber rationality in action, strictly speaking, was an impossibility. Ultimately action must be oriented to ends, and ends are necessarily not rational, simply because, according to this model of reasoning, first premises are by definition not deduced from any prior premises but must be decided (Weber, 1978a, p. 26). In practice, however, decision and deduction are often separate. Indeed, responsible decision and deductive rule following require distinct mentalities, and for Weber, these requirements corresponded to the tasks of the politician and the bureaucrat, respectively: 'the civil servant must sacrifice his convictions to the demands of obedience' (ibid., p. 1438). The politician, in contrast, makes his own value choices, learns to choose in the light of consequences, and develops the character and integrity to stand by these choices.

Political culture, convention, and character

Weber stressed two sets of consequences of the bureaucratic mentality, cultural and political. We have dealt with the political consequences already, because Weber's concern with leadership was formulated in terms of the antithesis between the self-directed leader and the soulless rule-following bureaucrat, and the antithesis between the qualities needed for advancement in a bureaucracy and the qualities needed for advancement in a genuine parliament, such as that of the British. His comments on culture cannot be so readily summarized. They involve a much broader set of issues and occur in a broader set of contexts. In addition, they involve concepts that do not – in contrast to the discussions of bureaucracy – figure prominently in the core doctrine of the sociological writings, and concepts that perhaps are, as in the case of 'tradition', contrary to the concepts used in his sociology.

The difficulty is not Weber's alone, for such subjects as tradition do not fit very well into either liberal political thought or modern social science. Mill, in his methodological writings on social science, which discuss the relations of the various social sciences, recognized that some place had to be given to these subjects. He proposed a science in addition to the sciences of economics, sociology, and psychology, to be called political ethology, which would deal with national character. Weber had his own difficulties with these subjects. The sociological writings on authority reflect the core doctrine: rational-legal authority, as we have seen, is closely dependent on the notion of rationality in the core doctrine. The concept of charisma is similarly dependent on the notion of ultimate choices or decisions: charisma is made intelligible, in Weber's account of it, as a kind of ultimate commitment to a person. *Zweckrationalität* is the deductive articulation of an ultimately nonrational commitment. Tradition is characterized as unthinking, almost reflexive, habitual conduct. At its limits tradition is, Weber argued, not 'action' at all. Thus tradition, being neither deduction nor decision, is reduced to habit, which can in turn be subcategorized in various ways.

'Usage' and 'custom' are defined as habits that persist socially by 'unreflective imitation' (Weber, 1978a, p. 319). One may be conscious of following customs and may follow them for reasons, such as the reason that failure to follow them when others follow them would be inconvenient or contrary to one's self-interest (ibid., pp. 29-30). 'Conventions' are usages that, if violated, lead to a reaction of disapproval (ibid., p. 34). Traditions, conceived in this way, are fixed and unchanging. They may cease to be followed, or may change in character from mere practice to socially sanctioned 'convention' or sanctified 'custom', but their content is, like habit, rigid. This conception led to certain historical expectations, notably the thought that tradition was, in general, doomed. 'Weber obviously thought,' we are told by Edward Shils, 'that traditions had no resistive power. Rationalization was "dynamic," traditions could at best conduct a "holding operation" ' (1981b, p. 300).

The political implications of his general view of tradition will concern us in a later chapter, for Weber's concept and sense of tradition become part of the dispute. As a sociological account of tradition, it contrasts to the view of tradition as ubiquitous, that some shared tradition is necessary for any kind of common action or mutual intelligibility, and that tradition is characteristically in a state of pragmatic adaptation and reconstruction. Shils puts it this way: 'Traditions are indispensible; they are also very seldom entirely adequate. Their sheer existence disposes those who possess them to change them' (1981b, p. 213). If we think of tradition in this way, it is evident that to possess a political tradition of the right kind is a good thing. Weber did not think of tradition in this way, at least in his formal sociological writings. Yet he often mentioned the value of a good political tradition in his political writings.

In the Swiss Cantons, Weber said, 'the population, by virtue of old tradition, thinks in terms of substantive issues and is well schooled in political matters' (1978a, p. 1456). This is clearly meant to contrast to Germany, where the authoritarian state, the *Obrigkeitsstaat*, has precluded any such development. He complained that the greatest manifestation of authoritarian politics, Bismarck, 'did *not* leave behind any political tradition' but rather a nation '*without any political sophistication*' and 'without any political will of its own' (ibid., p. 1392). Similarly, he said,

> Democracy and freedom are only possible where there exists a settled and determined *will* on the part of a nation, not to be ruled like a herd of sheep. It is 'against the stream' of material interests that we are 'individualists' and advocates of 'democratic' institutions (quoted in Beetham, 1974, p. 210; cf. Weber, 1978b, p. 282).

Beetham paraphrases this by saying that 'the only ultimate guarantee of political freedom thus lay in the liveliness of a country's political tradition' (1974, p. 210).

Characteristically, when Weber did give an answer to the question of the source of this 'will,' it was in terms of religion. In *The Protestant Ethic and the Spirit of Capitalism* he commented on

> the relative immunity of formerly Puritan peoples to Caesarism, and, in general, the subjectively free attitude of the English to their great statesmen as compared with many things which we have experienced since 1878 . . . positively and negatively. On the one hand, there is a greater willingness to give the great man his due, but, on the other, a repudiation of all hysterical idolization of him and of the naive idea that political obedience could be due anyone from thankfulness (1958, pp. 224-5).

Two points should be noticed about Weber's remark. First, it fits his core doctrine and his sociology of authority in that it traces the causal chain back to an act of commitment to ultimate values, rather than, say, to the English political tradition that was the source of the *Magna Carta* or the tradition of common law as defended, for example, by Sir Edward Coke. Second, it provides no particular guidance or hope for Germany, for the status of 'formerly Puritan' is not readily acquired, nor is there any form of political education that influences political conduct in a manner analogous to the manner in which the lingering effects of religion influence it.

These remarks on England seem to express an admiration for the English political tradition. Yet there is a puzzle here. When he felt called upon to justify the war, Weber did so in terms of the concepts of tradition, convention, and national character. Germany, he said, had a responsibility to preserve its culture, and to not allow the world to be divided up between the '*règlements* of

Russian bureaucrats on the one hand, and the conventions of Anglo-Saxon society on the other, possibly with an infusion of Latin *raison*' (Weber, 1971, p. 143, translated in Mommsen, 1974a, p. 40). This remark was not a casual aside. Jaspers, as we shall see, repeats it as though it were the core of Weber's political testament, and Jaspers was as personally close to Weber as any scholar. The remark clearly suggests that there was some distinctively German cultural legacy or tradition that needed to be fought for. Indeed, since the struggle is specifically with the Anglo-Saxon and Russian *political* traditions, the suggestion is that there is a distinctively German political tradition or idea to be preserved.

But it is not clear from Weber's writ what this tradition or idea might be. We find him ridiculing the 'nonsensical talk about the contrast between the "West European" and the "German" ideas of the state' (Weber, 1978a, p. 1383), and regretting the acquiescence of the bourgeoisie to the *Obrigkeitsstaat* and the 'feudalization' of bourgeois capital. And though he said such things as, 'If parliament were to fail and the old system were to return . . . . even then one could be grateful to fate for being a German' (ibid.), we do not find him commenting with great favor on any *particular* cultural or political development in the contemporary German scene.

A resolution to this paradox can be found if we supplement Weber's texts on the conventions and character of the Anglo-Saxons with some ambient German ideas to which Weber made some reference, particularly 'individualism' and 'inner freedom,' which had played a role in the German philosophical tradition.

The classic German formulation of 'individualist' ethics was presented in 1821 by Humboldt. It involved the notion that every 'individuality' contains an idea, a purpose, and norms that are unique to it and that it is the individual's responsibility to fulfill. Thus, a person's 'individuality' is a form which it is his responsibility to realize. For Humboldt, the class of 'individualities' included states as well as persons, an application of the concept which was useful as a formulation of the history of the German state. This history could be written as the story of 'the realization of the form' of unification, which could be treated as having existed prior to the reality (Iggers, 1965, pp. 291-4).

Yet the conception had a problem with which German political thought never quite came to terms, that of the relation between the 'individuality' of the person and the 'individuality' of the state. Humboldt assumed that this relation was governed by a 'profound and mysterious harmony' (quoted in Iggers, 1965, p. 291). This same thought was repeated in the writings of others, who constructed a 'German' notion of freedom, unlike the negative 'English' notion of freedom as freedom from the state. According to the German liberal Gneist, whose lectures Weber attended in Berlin (Mayer, 1956, p. 27), 'Society can find the personal freedom, the moral and spiritual development of the individual, only in permanent subordination to a constant higher power' (quoted in Krieger, 1957, p. 460). This kind of freedom came to be called 'inner freedom' and was often contrasted to the negative freedom or merely external freedom of the English.

As a formal philosophical scheme, this individualism had a fatal epistemological flaw, in the form of the question of how one is to know what one's individuality demands; so by Weber's time this was no longer thought of as a serious philosophy but was rather part of the culture, part of a general semiotic structure of oppositions. Weber's personal resolution of these oppositions was to make the demand of one's individuality into the 'decision by which the soul chooses its fate.' On the political level, the puzzle of having freedom yet being subordinated to a higher power was resolved by making a free decision for the nation. Though Weber never formulated the doctrine of individuality, the idea is present in his thought as the doctrine of intellectual integrity, which German defenders of Weber, notably Henrich, have construed as the commandment Become a personality. Jaspers would later formulate it as the commandment Become what thou art. It is in this becoming that one seeks and gains 'inner freedom' and 'individuality.' When Weber spoke of individualism, this is the tradition his hearers would have had in mind; when he spoke of freedom, it is the 'nonnegative freedom' of this tradition that his hearers would have been thinking of.

In many contexts, this tradition supplies the only intelligible interpretation of Weber's words. In his discussion of bureaucracy and the bureaucratic mentality, for example, Weber made an interesting reference to these notions in discussing the Junkers, in a context that is also revealing of his attitude toward those 'Anglo-Saxon conventions.' In this discussion Weber was attacking the celebration of Prussianism. He complained that

> despite the occasional boasting of our literati, it is completely untrue that individualism exists in Germany in the sense of freedom from conventions, in contrast to the conventions of the Anglo-Saxon gentleman or of the Latin salon type of man. Nowhere are there more rigid and compelling conventions than those of the German 'fraternity man.' These conventions directly and indirectly control just as large a part of the progeny of our leading strata as do the conventions of any leading country (1946, p. 390).

The puzzling feature of this discussion is that we are left without any notion of what Weber could have meant in saying that German culture or political tradition is worth fighting for, other than a distinctive potentiality.

Any resolution of the puzzle would be conjectural, but a plausible resolution might be this. Weber agreed, in general, with the widespread German notions that the English and Americans were in some 'inner' sense 'unfree.' The term 'convention,' which Weber defined in his sociological writings as an imitative practice enforced by social pressure, suggests this. Yet we have no clear comparison of the inner life of the Anglo-Saxons and the Germans in Weber's writings. There is some suggestive reasoning in an article on the Protestant sects, where he said that the ascetic inner life of the Puritan was a consequence of sect organization, which, by selecting members on the basis of their inner traits and outward discipline, 'put the most powerful individual interest of social self-esteem in the service of this breeding of traits' (1946, p. 321).

The modern analogue to the sect is the club, which Weber treated as a secularized variant. But the modern club may have had an effect that was the opposite of the effect of sect membership. With secularization the 'individual interest in social self-esteem' could become dominant, leading to conformism and 'inner slavery.' Weber admired the early Puritans for their inner strength but not the contemporary English. Perhaps he believed that Germany was now the country in which inner strength and resistance to conformism was still possible. He never spoke explicitly to this. He did, however, stress the conformist character of American clubs and observed that 'he who despised [joining], as was usual among Germans, had to take the hard road, and especially so in business life' (1946, p. 311). In a footnote to this remark, Weber observed that 'entry into an American club (in school or later) is always the decisive moment for the loss of German nationality' (ibid.). In these remarks there is at least an echo of the idea that the distinctive German cultural legacy is inner freedom. Jaspers later amplified this echo.

The potential of German culture, then, was central to Weber, but also unclear. His complaints about Prussianism, however, are quite clear. The 'form values of the degree-hunter qualifying for duels,' as he characterized them, 'serve as a convenient way of taming men for qualifying as an applicant for officer commissions' (1946, p. 392-3). They

> are simply not suited to serve as a model for the whole nation down to the lowest strata. They are not suited to mold and unify the nation in its gesture as a *Herrenvolk*, self-assured in its overt

> conduct in the way in which Latin and Anglo-Saxon conventions have succeeded (ibid., pp. 390-1).

The Anglo-Saxon conventions stemmed from the social habits of the gentry, who had emerged in the later Middle Ages as the bearers of 'self-government.' The 'Latin-type of personality, down to the lowest strata' is said to be 'determined by imitation of the cavalier as evolved since the sixteenth century' (ibid., p. 391). There is no German analogue to these patterns of the democratization of habits and ideals. Weber suggested that appropriate civil conventions might have developed in the Hanseatic cities, but after unification their incipient development there ceased (ibid., p. 392). So 'the development of a truly cultured "German form" . . . lies in the future' (ibid.).

The democratization of political forms, paradoxically, increases the necessity for a suitable tradition. There are two reasons for this. One is that, in an age of formal democracy, the populace itself must think like a *Herrenvolk*, and this requires a kind of molding of character. The other reason is that a tradition preserves the nation from the bad effects of leadership appeals. Weber, indeed, was impressed by the necessity for a suitable tradition because of a conflict in his own thought. He stressed the necessity for strong leadership, especially in matters of foreign policy. Yet he conceded that the relation between a modern leader and his mass following is inevitably emotional and that the unorganized masses are most susceptible to emotional influence (1946, p. 171). He also believed that emotionality was dangerous, and he was consistently critical of it, both in religious contexts, as in his remark on 'the often definitely pathological character of Methodist emotionalism' (1958, p. 252), and in political contexts (1946, p. 395). When he wrote about the political tradition Germany needed, he stressed the need for 'inner dignity.' But he offered no positive prescription. 'Only this much (in an essentially negative and formal way) can be said, and it holds for all values of this nature: such forms can never be developed on any other basis than upon an attitude of personal distance and reserve' (ibid., p. 393). It is as though he believed that the process of imitating elites would democratize the ideals of reserve, sobriety, and devotion to a calling and that this process would counteract the emotionalizing effects of a public life focused on leadership appeals (Weber, 1971, p. 270). But this seems uncharacteristically optimistic. The more likely effect of the combination of a politics of leadership appeals together with the process of imitation would be a political culture of *Caudillismo*.

Political education

A political tradition in the full sense could not be invented. Yet there was an immediate need for a semblance of a tradition, and Weber repeatedly spoke of a need for 'political education' as a means of achieving the political maturity necessary to face Germany's immediate political challenges (e.g., Weber, 1980, p. 447; cf. idem, 1978b, p. 267). The idea of political education was central for Weber, from the *Antrittsrede* to his pamphlet on 'Parliament and Government in a Newly Ordered Germany.' But it raises several subtle issues of interpretation, one of which is closely connected to questions about the implications of Weber's doctrine of value.

Weber was quite clear about the broadest aims of the program of political education he called for in 1895. 'The aim of our socio-political activity is not,' he informs us, 'world happiness but the *social unification* of the nation, which has been split apart by modern economic development, for the severe struggles of the future' (1980, p. 447; cf. idem, 1978b, p. 267). Social unification was a distant aim, however; political education proper was presented as an immediate task. Speaking to economists, he declared that 'the ultimate goal of our science must remain that of cooperating in the *political* education of our nation' (ibid.). One threat is the wrong kind of economics, the kind that cultivates 'a weak eudaemonism' that 'threatens the natural political instincts with decomposition' (ibid.). The aims of political education as described in the *Antrittsrede*, however, are largely negative. Political education is understood there largely as a matter of ridding the public of misguided notions.

Lawrence Scaff, in a recent article, has argued that the method of education Weber had in mind was 'exposure to the realities of political choice and participation.' 'Weber's support of trade unionism and an activist foreign policy rested ultimately on their educational function for their citizens, on their practical consequence of teaching broad classes of men how to think and act politically' (1973, p. 131). Scaff puts a particular face on this notion. He identifies Weber's concept of political maturity with 'the values of Puritanism – civic commitment, hard work, public responsibility, devotion to a vocation' (ibid., p. 132). Similarly, Robert Eden suggests that this is what Weber thought would be 'the probable consequence of the adoption of [his criterion of the political vocation], as far as its effect on public morality or public opinion' (1974, p. 483).

Doubtless there is a large element of truth in these interpretations. Weber unfailingly praised certain virtues, such as 'reserve,' which he believed to be Puritan in origin (Weber, 1958, p. 235), and he was sensitive to their survival in peoples with a Puritan past. Yet it is not clear how this bears on the German case. Puritanism, Weber believed, was more a part of the English past than its present. Its free institutions may have been based on this past, but the practical relevance of this fact is unclear.

It is doubtful that Weber imagined anything analogous to Puritanism arising to create similar conditions in Germany. If anything, the remarks suggest that Germany would have to be different. That Britain could have free institutions and 'still become a world power' was, for Weber, an anomaly (Weber, 1958, p. 261). When Weber spoke of political maturity and education, he used the terms to cover a wide variety of things. He gave as an instance of immaturity the fact that at the time of Bismarck's dismissal the parties who had supported him did not even demand an account of the reasons for it. 'They did not bestir themselves, they simply turned to the new sun' (Weber, 1978a, p. 1386). This was the domestic political immaturity of a class, and one may find examples of other kinds of domestic political immaturity. But there was always another thrust to Weber's program of political education: education as preparation for citizenship in a world power. And this thrust always dominated.

To see this, it is only necessary to compare the details of Weber's discussion of political education with the use of the term 'political education' by others. The familiarity of the notion of political education is due to the fact that it was a commonplace of English political writing of the nineteenth century that the best means of political education was political participation. We have seen that Mill argued that the way to make the working class worthy of the franchise was to give them experience in democracy at the most immediate levels. By Weber's time, this notion had become the cliché that, as Bryce put it in *The American Commonwealth* (a book Weber greatly admired [Scaff, 1981, p. 1279] and relied upon for his discussions of American Machine politics), 'the town-meeting has been not only the source but the school of democracy' (Bryce, 1893, p. 626). Weber was clearly aware of the idea of participation as 'schooling' as early as the *Antrittsrede*, in the form of Lujo Brentano's idea that the struggles of the English trade unions were a kind of political education for the workers. But Weber deemphasized the 'educational' influence of the unions, with the remark that it is rather a matter of '*the resonance of a position of world power*,' which 'constantly poses for the state great power-political tasks and gives the individual a political training which we might call "chronic" ' (Weber, 1980, p. 446; cf. idem, 1978b, p. 266).

In the *Antrittsrede* he showed no interest in political education for domestic politics. The primacy of foreign policy was understood to imply the primacy of education for foreign policy, and the obstacle here is the 'softening of attitude' that is 'unspeakably narrowing in its effects,' which makes people think they can 'replace political with "ethical" ideals' (Weber, 1980, p. 447; cf. idem, 1978b, p. 267). The later writings, especially 'Politics as a Vocation,' express much the same animus. The technique of education through participation in smaller-scale political units is obviously ill adapted to this aim. Indeed, Weber was explicitly fearful of what might naturally be expected to result from this form of political education, namely 'Swissification' or neutralism and parliament's becoming 'a mere market place for compromises between purely economic interests, without any political orientation to overall interests' (Weber, 1978a, p. 1397).

If Weber had indeed wished to promote democratic tolerance or a willingness to settle for a world political role appropriate to the national circumstances, he would have presumably sought means appropriate to these ends, and we might have heard a good deal more from him about political participation in smaller political units or, as Brentano suggested, in trade unions. The idea that the value of democratic toleration had to be impressed on the population was in the air at the beginning of Weimar. Scheler, as we shall see, took this task as his own, for a while. But Weber contributed nothing to this task, and his own political actions testified to a greater concern with attaining hardness and defeating cowardice. This, then, proved to be the dominant theme in his task of political education: to assure, as Meinecke expressed it in a different connection, that citizens would 'each . . . have a little of Bismarck' (quoted in Pois, 1972, p. 19).

We may be wise in retrospect, and see that this was the wrong emphasis. Although one suspects that Weber would have agreed with Oswald Spengler's caustic observation on Hitler that the 'pathfinder should be a hero, not an heroic tenor,' the remark reveals Weber's neglect of the problem of an ambient German political culture that made the rise of the heroic tenor probable. Others saw this problem more clearly. Jacob Burckhardt foresaw the 'terrible simplificateurs' and 'the great handsome fellow with the talents of a subordinate officer' who would introduce a 'new barbarism' (quoted in Mayer et al., 1970, p. 318). Treitschke himself observed that the Germans find it difficult in times of stress to distinguish the heroic from trumpery (Butler, 1942, p. 290). The Weimar era proved to be such a time of stress.

4 The Weimar era dispute

The postwar context

By the time of Weber's death in 1920, a controversy over his basic conception was underway. The world in which the controversy began was a world irrevocably changed, and a major topic on the agenda of the politics and the scholarship of the era was the matter of dealing with the changes. This included making sense of what had happened in the war, for the censorship imposed by the military rulers was efficient, and the claims of victories in battles frequent, so that the loss of the war was a surprise to the German population. In the aftermath of the war this lack of information was compounded by the attempt to evade the charge of war-guilt and the attempt on the part of various military and political figures to disclaim responsibility for events. For this reason it is difficult to know what to make of the political statements of the war period and after, some of which were based on misinformation.

The 'doubling back' we have noticed between issues of historical interpretation and issues of Weber interpretation occurs with the events of Weimar as well. Schluchter describes the political situation in Munich in early 1919 as an 'unholy alliance of intransigent right wing chauvinism and left wing politics of single-minded conviction (*Gesinnungspolitik*).' Revolutionary leader Kurt Eisner he calls a 'representative of the literary crowd,' who had 'a policy of single-minded conviction, which was unconcerned about its consequences' (1979b, p. 68). This places Weber's own political intransigence in the period in a favorable light, by recapitulating Weber's own opinions as fact: Weber himself, as Schluchter reports, regarded Eisner as 'an example of . . . political romanticism' (ibid.).

The claim that Eisner was unrealistic is oversimple. A frequent historical verdict is that the socialist president of the new republic,

Ebert, was unrealistic enough to trust the forces of the old regime, especially the police and army, in the restoration of order, a policy that discredited his party with its natural constituency and crippled it for the whole Weimar period. Eisner did not make this mistake. In the perspective of the incalculable later effect of German illusions about the war, Eisner's publication of documents indicating German war-guilt, which infuriated Weber, showed a kind of political responsibility and willingness to come to terms with realities. Shortly before the Armistice, when the war was clearly lost, Weber polemicized publicly against those who wanted to act to end the carnage (Grunberger, 1973, p. 44), and in the period after the war we find Weber telling Gustav Stolper, 'I have no political plans except to concentrate all my intellectual strength on the one great problem, how to get once more for Germany a Great General Staff' (Stolper, 1942, p. 318).[1]

Such remarks indicate a streak of political romanticism, which his brother, Alfred, was later to point out. The romanticism was not unmixed, for at times Weber spoke of Germany as finished as a world power. But even at the darkest moments Weber professed to see the possibility of a 'third youth' for Germany (quoted in Mayer, 1956, p. 104).

The period immediately after the war saw a reaction against the intense nationalism of the 'Ideas of 1914' and a rise in pacifism.[2] Weber stood against the tide. He publicly challenged his hearers to prevent the implementation of terms of the treaty, e.g., to 'see to it that the first Polish official who dares to enter Danzig is hit by a bullet.' In her biography, Marianne Weber relates that these views and his national ethic fell flat with the young pacifists and communists, who, as she put it, were hoping for a turning point in world history in accordance with their beliefs (1975, p. 631). Marianne relates that he concluded this particular speech with the appeal, ' "When you have decided to take the course that will then be inevitable, then I am at your disposal, then *come to me*!" These last words, which he spoke with a sweeping motion of his arm . . . were followed by an icy, uncomprehending silence' (ibid., pp. 631-2). Yet he was not entirely without political impact. His advocacy of a strong presidency scheme undoubtedly had an influence on the constitutional commission on which he served, and he influenced a number of academics whose views were later to be important.

Political and cultural developments

For the moment, however, events ruled, not personalities. The immediate postwar period was an economic disaster for Germany.

The food shortages of the war period did not abate for several years. By the time they did, the country was gripped by severe inflation, which had the effect of wiping out the savings of all who had savings, especially the urban middle class, leaving many who were embittered and searching for someone to blame. Continuous difficulties over the payment of war reparations supplied a conspicuous public scapegoat in the form of the Allied governments involved in their negotiation and renegotiation. There was a sort of poetic justice in the reparations problem. The Germans had themselves demanded and received huge indemnities from the 1871 war with France, and had expected to do the same after the World War. Although the reparations were not the root cause of the inflation, it appeared to the public that they were. The parliamentary regime, which made the reparations payments and was forced to make economic decisions to accommodate them, lost prestige for this, as well as for the renegotiations themselves, which were highly public affronts to German pride.

The cultural and moral developments of the period had an animus beyond politics. Their general character can best be seen through their effects in the microcosm of an individual life. Many of the cultural dilemmas have been captured in a revealing human document of the period, Lilo Linke's autobiographical account, *Restless Days* (1935). For the young, the period was a series of painful events and privations, of which the war was just the beginning. Linke, then a young girl in the eastern part of Berlin during the war, recalled that on the piano in her apartment sat a framed photograph of Ludendorff and Hindenburg with the caption: ' "The more enemies, the more honour!" ' (1935, p. 30). She spent long hours in lines with a ration card waiting for meat and bread. When the war ended in failure, the sacrifices went unrewarded, and the ideals were apparently destroyed. The workers seized power in her Berlin district, and their strikes deprived citizens of essential services and created a climate of fear. In the shopping district, 'nearly every window was smashed, either by bullets or stones – the hungry crowds had used the opportunity of the general turmoil to storm the shops and carry away everything that was not clinched or riveted' (ibid., pp. 78-9). The crowds became 'hated and despised enemies, dregs of humanity without any decent feelings. The Fatherland meant nothing to them, they were pacifists and internationalists, and this was the most abusive thing that could be said about anybody' (ibid., p. 82).

The revolution of the workers was soon over. Karl Leibknecht and Rosa Luxemburg were assassinated, and a 'huge procession followed the coffins' through the streets (Linke, 1935, p. 83). But deep social hatreds were formed by the events. The official socialist regime, which had relied on the police and the army to defeat the revolutionary workers, was soon voted out of power, in part a result of the policy of using the army against fellow workers. But stability in private life did not return; the inflation 'destroyed the last vestige of steadiness' (ibid., p. 131).

The quest for 'steadiness' and normal life took novel forms. By 1924, Linke was working as a clerk, and was invited to join the Trade Union for Shop and Office Employees, a group that was nonpolitical but 'verging on democratic ideals' (Linke, 1935, p. 148), which sponsored a youth organization. These 'young Republicans . . . felt neither respect nor love for the pre-war Germany because we did not know anything about it.' (ibid., p. 155). They believed in such ends as international friendship, but their main goal was 'to build up our lives under our own responsibility' (ibid.). The monthly journal of the group published such articles as 'The Creation of a New Community.' Linke's group was a version of the earlier *Wandervogel*, youth organizations that promoted the simpler virtues and provided group solidarity. But youth organizations of all types flourished, 'from the Young Nationals to the Young Socialists, from the Association for German Culture Abroad to the No More War Movement, from the Boy Scouts to the nudists, from the Bible Circle to the vegetarians and the Cyclists Union' (ibid., p. 153). Council Youth houses, set up after the war to provide space for these movements, were peacefully shared. Linke remarked that in those days the youth shared a belief in 'fair play and the existence of a general willingness to achieve the common good.' Later, she pointed out, 'we began to pursue each other with the hatred of deadly enemies' (ibid.).[3]

The youth groups were a means of pursuing personal happiness in a time of uncertainty. 'One joined groups in the hope that they might have a recipe for the best method to achieve it and because one was afraid to be alone' (Linke, 1935, p. 180). The quest for new values and genuine community was an essential part of the youth group movement. This quest raises some delicate questions, especially if one views them exclusively in terms of the political associations of their central ideas, for the Nazis also appealed to this quest for meaningfulness and the true values (cf. Mosse, 1964). Yet the motives were more general, more broadly based than the motives for Nazism and cannot be reduced to it. The culture of prewar Germany did need 'reform.' But the new values that ultimately emerged closely resembled the old values they purported to replace. Several philosophers of the period concerned themselves with providing an intellectual articulation of the quest for community and an explanation for its loss. Far from being the exercises in utopian programmatics these may seem in retrospect, they were a response to a genuine and deeply felt need.

The intellectuals were dramatically affected by the changes of the era as well. The failures of the war constituted an intellectual problem that was more acute than any analogous problem one could imagine today. The war had been, one might say, a philosophical war, in the sense that it was a war that had been consciously imbued, by intellectuals, with the ideas and ideals of the German intellectual tradition. The war was not a result of this tradition, at least not in any simple sense. But the war had been justified, explained, and framed by the great ideas of this tradition. Franz Neumann, describing his student experiences, reported that at the University of Breslau in the spring of 1918 its 'celebrated economist – in his very first lecture – denounced the Peace resolution of 1917. . . . The still more celebrated professor of literature, after having paid homage to Kantian idealism, derived from that philosophy the categorical imperative of a German victory.' In Leipzig 'the economics professor thought it necessary – in October 1918 – to endorse the peace terms of the Pan German Union and of the General Staff, while the historian proved conclusively that democracy was an essentially non-German form of political organization, suitable for the materialistic Anglo-Saxons, but incompatible with the idealism of the Germanic race' (Neumann, 1953, p. 15). After the defeat, the theoretical notions and traditions that figured in these exercises in apologetics were, not surprisingly, subject to reconsideration along with the political notions they had framed.

The peculiar characteristic of the Weimar period, and the one that gives the philosophical struggles of the time such poignancy, was that the political crisis, the cultural crisis, and the ongoing crisis in academic philosophy which resulted from the playing out of neo-Kantianism all were connected together in the intellectual discourse of the time. Personal, intellectual, and social confusion each seemed to be aspects of some deeper historical moment in the history of *Geist*.[4] This came to be called a *Krisis der Wissenschaft*, a term understood to refer not only to academic thought but to the foundations of culture. It was widely believed that some new founding or basing of culture and social life was about to occur out of this crisis – or that the crisis was the beginning of a darkening or debasing of the world. One consequence of this sense of intellectual pregnancy was that there was an unusual amount of dialogue between what ordinarily would have been mutually disregarding schools and movements (cf. e.g., Wurgaft, 1977, pp. 104-6).

Like other ideas of the period, the idea of a 'Crisis' had its origins earlier, in such places as Dilthey's idea of '*die Anarchie der Weltanschauungen*' and Nietzsche's doctrine of the death of God. After the war, Weber's two speeches, 'Wissenschaft als Beruf' (Weber, 1973, pp. 582-613; cf. idem, 1946, pp. 129-56) and 'Politik als Beruf' (Weber, 1971, pp. 505-60; cf. idem, 1946, pp. 77-128), and the violent controversy these speeches engendered focused these issues, and, in the fashion of times, connected them to politics, for these 'nonpolitical' speeches on science and politics as vocations were continuous with Weber's political stance. 'Politics as a Vocation' contains a number of allusions to his political stance and attacks on his political enemies (Weber, 1946).[5] These views are similar to his own prewar views, so in them Weber was clearly taking a stand for the continuation of certain political values of the past and against radical change (cf. Weber, 1973, pp. 1-25; Mommsen, 1974a, pp. 22-46).[6]

Kahler's critique

The intensity of the controversy over 'Science as a Vocation' was indicative of a different climate of opinion. The focus of the disputes had shifted, as did the allegiances of many scholars, particularly younger scholars. In the 'value-freedom' dispute in economics in the prewar period, Weber had attacked the then influential *Kathedersozialisten* for their devotion to bureaucratic solutions to problems of economic policy and for presenting these solutions as scientifically warranted, and had done so by appealing to the conventional philosophy of the time. In the postwar period it was Weber's own conception of knowledge that was subject to attack, and the new dispute was not limited to economics. The speeches were widely distributed and read by intellectuals of all sorts. Edmund Husserl's response to the controversy typified the development of opposition to Weber's views. As Spiegelberg, the historian of the phenomenological movement, points out,

> in the days of his essay on '*Philosophie als strenge Wissenschaft*' Husserl himself took a stand similar to Weber's, though for rather different reasons. . . . But this whole situation changed for Husserl after the First World War. . . . During the war itself Husserl, who lost a brilliant son in action, had refrained deliberately from taking an active part by writing or speaking for the war effort. But in the aftermath he found it impossible to stay aloof from the questions of the day. Now the incapacity and unwillingness of science to face problems of value and meaning because of its confinement to mere positive facts seemed to him to be at the very root of the crisis of science and of mankind itself (Spiegelberg, 1971, p. 80).

Husserl took the view that in 'contrast to the science of the Renaissance, which had been part of a comprehensive philosophical scheme,' the science advocated by Weber in this controversy was a 'truncated science' which 'endangered man, and in fact endangered itself, by a "decapitation" ' (quoted in ibid.; cf. Husserl, 1910, pp. 289-314).

Husserl himself did not engage in direct polemics with Weber and his followers. This was for the most part left to younger scholars, and it is for the most part the younger members of various philosophical camps that figure in the controversy.[7] The most important attack on Weber's position was Erich von Kahler's *Der Beruf der Wissenschaft* (1920). Kahler was a young scholar who had 'devoted himself directly to historical and philosophical writing' and was associated with certain members of the Stefan George circle, especially Gundolf, and was later to carry on a friendly correspondence with Thomas Mann.[8] Kahler's work, the title of which was a play on the title of Weber's speech, was an attack on the conception of the nature of philosophical and scientific knowledge advanced by Weber, as well as an attack on the political conception with which it was linked. The study 'started a lively discussion in Germany and gained Kahler the reputation of being one of the most important thinkers in the German-speaking world' (Winston and Winston, 1975, p. vii).

Kahler's strategy was adopted from the great Hellenizers of the German tradition. He contrasted Weber's conception of disciplined learning to the Platonic conception.[9] This strategy was warranted by Weber's own statements that the idea of science and philosophy as an escape from the cave of ignorance was definitely dead, an 'illusion' which had been dispelled (1946, pp. 140, 143). Plato was used more than once in the Weber controversy, and this should not be surprising, for in Plato preeminently the unity of ideas and community go hand in hand. For Plato, the possibility of the best society is assured through the epistemological possibility of the discovery of a universally true idea of the good and of the cosmos. In contrast, Weber's conception of the possibilities of rational inquiry denied the possibility of any genuine truth about values, apart from the irrefutable principles of 'logic' that comprise his theory of values and entail his methodology. Because these principles also entail his denial of the Platonic idea of a rational good or moral truth, Weber had to deny the possibility of a community or of lives being founded upon such a truth. But the reason for Kahler's appeal to Plato lay deeper than this political or moral point. Kahler pointed out that Weber accepts the present state of *Wissenschaft*, that is, the present attempt to create concepts that order and conquer reality, as the permanent situation of *Wissenschaft* and does not question its presuppositions. Yet the new conception has distinctive aims, which can be shown by comparison to the old: where the earlier conception had emphasized reflection, the new *Wissenschaft* takes endless testing as its task (Kahler, 1920, p. 21). Thus *Wissenschaft* became an attempt to change reality through our reason – its aim, as later sloganeers were to put it, became 'prediction and control.'

The effect of this change in aims, Kahler suggested, is destructive. The generalizations that this new 'science' derives separate man from reality. Life itself is changed by being analyzed in the fashion of the new 'science.' Kahler's thought here is difficult to formulate, but one may get some idea of it by considering that today it is common to say that behaviorism is a mode of description that distorts and diminishes human life. Kahler's point is that the notion that one chooses values subjectively and can directly know only mechanical relations also distorts, and the distortions are not without consequences well beyond scholarship – a point made by critics of behaviorism as well. In particular, he argued, the adherence to a purely technical standard of rational validity, one that legitimates a conceptual relativity in science and in historical inquiry, has a devastating impact on moral life.

The obvious political or cultural effect of Weber's doctrine, Kahler suggested, is that it strengthens the *Fachmann* type (1920, pp. 33-7. The virtue of this type of man is that he masters the 'learnable.' But the price of this mastery is a separation from culture and art, which begin to lose their meaning. The final result is that each man's contact with the organic whole of the community, the *Volk*, is lost. And because of this, proper political leadership and representation become impossible. The present state of politics, marked as it is by strong divisions and disassociations, is in part a consequence of this loss. Kahler pointed out that Weber's conception of politics offers no surcease of this state: all the undisciplined quarrels between parties are legitimated by the Weberian claim that they are 'eternally unresolvable' because they are grounded in the struggle of *Weltanschauungen*.

The community that Weberian men may have among themselves is a new kind of community, a 'unity' only in the sense of its shared basis in unending intellectual advancement. Kahler asked whether this order of ever-changing, progressing life forms is better than the old unity. He denied that it is (1920, pp. 60-3). The fact that man is in constant change itself precludes stable, general values. Furthermore, because Weber's doctrine denies the capacity of our intuition in making value judgments, it foments distrust for others, whose actions and purposes become suspect as to the values they serve. The result of the destruction of objective values, of intuition, and of true community is that human life is pressed into slavery, like the 'leveling' of Kierkegaard. The only solution Weber could see to this was the rise of a prophet. But there were no prophets at hand, as Weber himself observed.

One can scarcely read such writings as Kahler's without seeing in them the oracular image of the future that was to overtake Kahler and Germany. This may be said of several of Weber's writings as well, both 'political' and 'scientific.' Kahler himself drew attention to several of Weber's remarks that had what would much later appear to be of a prescient character, and especially to the suggestion that the solution to the confusion of the time was a new prophet. But Kahler's own emphasis was different. He was more concerned with the men who would hear this call. Weber's remark that the disenchantment of the world creates 'specialists without spirit, sensualists without heart,' a 'nullity' that 'imagines that it has attained a level of civilization never before achieved' (1958, p. 182) is echoed by Kahler's theme that 'the cog-man, the functional man, the success-man,' man as a 'stick of sensations' is everywhere dominant in Germany (1920, p. 65).

Kahler suggested that Weber believed that the creation of men of this new type, whom Weber regarded as 'realistic,' would be politically advantageous for the nation. Kahler thought this was delusive; he claimed that the 'scientific' government leaders have done nothing to help Germany. Men have never been so confused, and this confusion contains a terrible warning from the secret incalculable powers that in the 'rational period' we have become less, not more, capable. Rationalization will bring a new irrationality, for every 'disenchantment of the world' brings a new spell, which exercises its power whether one likes it or not: the 'rational period' can merely be an interregnum (Kahler, 1920, p. 50). The confused men who adhered to the view of reason and life Weber endorsed would face the future with the handicap of the belief that values are merely subjective. They would be unable to make, as Weber could not, an objectively valid moral decision between Napoleon and Jesus Christ (ibid., p. 82).[10] Kahler could not have been surprised at the choice they did make.

Salz and the Weberian response

In reading Kahler, one notes immediately that his analysis treats Weber's work, both his politics and his scholarship, as a whole. In later years Weber's defenders would regard such a critique as an 'ideological' attack, which mixed distinct issues. This was not the contemporary response. The Weber *Kreis* for the most part accepted Kahler's conception of the nature of the conflict between Weber and his antagonists, and they defended Weber's position as a 'philosophy,' i.e., as a unified conception.[11]

The question of the extent to which Weber's views are a 'whole' and a 'philosophy' was the principal subject of an intense dispute between Heinrich Rickert and Karl Jaspers after Weber's death. Rickert made the remark that there was not a fundamental disunity in Weber's thought and personality (1926, p. 237). There was a unity, Rickert suggested, but the political was the dominant thrust – indeed, Weber was too concerned with being a prophet in his scientific work. Weber, as Rickert put it at one point, used science as a weapon (ibid., p. 234). Jaspers agreed with Rickert that Weber's work constituted a unity, but he angrily rejected Rickert's suggestion that this unity was philosophically weak or defective. Instead, Jaspers wished to present Weber as a great moral figure whose life itself as a whole, his words and deeds together, was a 'philosophy' (1926). To this remarkable claim Rickert replied, 'that you construct a philosophy out of Max Weber may be your rightful privilege, but to call him a philosopher is absurd.'[12]

Jaspers's response to Rickert gives one a sense of the attitude of the Weber *Kreis* toward Weber as a man. A whole genre of a sort arose out of this, treating Weber as a 'hero' (e.g., Wilbrandt, 1928; cf. Factor and Turner, 1982, p. 147; Schroeter, 1980, 1982). But the idea of Weber as a hero gives little sense of the way in which those close to Weber understood the practical bearing of his doctrine and stance. The source that is most revealing of this attitude is a work by Arthur Salz, *Für die Wissenschaft* (1921), which was regarded as the Weber circle's response to Kahler's critique.[13] It shows clearly that Weber's view was sharply distinct from such philosophical movements as positivism and phenomenology, on the one side, and such political movements as socialism and conservatism on the other. The impression one gets from Jaspers is that Weber's stance was a kind of establishment existentialism, equally critical of philosophical and political reformers and of those conservatives who wished to return to old ideals, an impression that is confirmed in Salz.

Salz began his critique of Kahler with a cultural diagnosis of his own. The present, he argued, is a time of flux, and therefore people seek the stable and the permanent, which leads to a distrust of modern *Wissenschaft* and a call for a new *Wissenschaft* animated by an entirely different spirit. The call results from a perception of the failure of *Wissenschaft* to lead life rather than merely to serve practical interests. However, Salz said, the perception rests on a misunderstanding of *Wissenschaft*.

Salz began his own account of this misunderstanding of *Wissenschaft* where Weber did, with the problem of the necessity of a division of labor in modern society, a division into *Berufe*, or vocations, and in scholarly life into specialized disciplines. He countered Kahler's lament for the passing of the universal genius with the argument that to have such people we would need to forsake specialization and the fruits of specialization. In doing this we would forsake the great need of the present for educated men who devote themselves to the state as duty rather than 'set themselves up in tension with the state' (Salz, 1921, pp. 16-17).[14]

The *Wissenschaft* Kahler wishes to promote, Salz argued, is personal and egocentric. It creates a 'community' of a peculiar sort, based on the initiation of adepts into a small circle with a leader and with a common intuition. Claims for the validity of such a *Wissenschaft* must depend on the grandiose presupposition of the existence of a unique eternal order.[15] But because there can be no proof of such an order, rational proof is replaced by a kind of faith. Such a *Wissenschaft* is, in a sense, 'teachable,' but here 'teaching' and 'bewitching' are indistinguishable (Salz, 1921, p. 28). The new *Wissenschaft* is, then, something that can appeal only to fanatics, ecstatic visionaries, and holy men; the old *Wissenschaft*, which Weber represents, is for men with the weaknesses of men, but with passionate hearts, love for the truth, and cool understanding (ibid., p. 29). This *Wissenschaft*, Salz suggested, was democratic or demagogic, not esoteric, as is the new *Wissenschaft*; it was valid for all who bound themselves to its purpose, not – as the new *Wissenschaft* is – valid merely to a closed sect. One way of putting this is to say that the universality of the new *Wissenschaft* is universality with respect to scope, or subject matter, but not with respect to validity. The old science was fragmented and specialized but sought universally binding results. The new *Wissenschaft* does not claim to be universally binding. Salz believed that the difference arose from the fact that the foundations of the old science were never finally fixed, but always remained hypothetical and open to change. The new *Wissenschaft*, however, is dogmatic and rigid in its foundations, and is not open to correction by experience (ibid., p. 33).

Salz went on to consider the charge that science 'failed to lead.' Here it becomes apparent that political recriminations were an important source of the conflict over Weber's views. As might be expected, one aspect of Weber's doctrine, his insistence on the inability of *Wissenschaft* to determine rationally the true value scheme, plays a large role in this discussion. Salz defended Weber for 'baring the irrational roots of the act,' thus 'freeing the road for the great heroic action, which stems not from rational, conceptual knowledge, but from the freedom of man' (1921, p. 40). Every great and heroic act, Salz insisted, is irrational. Only 'crass rationalists' and 'Bolshevik reason-worshippers' believe that science guides their action. Salz attacked Kahler for 'adopting the popular reproach' that the 'old' *Wissenschaft*, and specifically *Nationalökonomie*, whose outstanding representative was Weber, failed in the war. Salz remarked that it is not entirely clear whether it is blame for the war itself or for the loss of the war which the critics wish to attach to *Nationalökonomie* (ibid., p. 41). He asks Kahler whether he believes that the war would have been more successful or would have been avoided with his new 'generalizing' *Wissenschaft*, and whether the defeat of the nation would have proved the correctness of the *Wissenschaft* of the victors. It is never said precisely what the 'popular' prejudices Salz mentioned have reference to, but it is evident that this political issue is a significant fuel for the dispute, for the exculpation of *Nationalökonomie* goes on for five pages (ibid., pp. 41-5).

Salz had a clear rhetorical strategy: accusing the critics of Weber of a whole catalogue of political errors and sins, and associating them with popularly disreputable views. The old *Wissenschaft*, he reiterated, was 'statesmanlike,' in contrast to the irresponsibility of the new *Wissenschaft*. In his conclusion, he said that he is sick of hearing 'the shame of the time and our guilt . . . shouted in our face.' At another point he described a French work on the Germans that asserts that they are childish in their morals, incapable of contemplation, and unable to distinguish good and evil, and asked whether this "evil book" is really the last word of French intuition? (1921, p. 87). He associated Kahler with Stefan George, who rejected the war, using the contrast between Weber and George to raise the charge of unpatriotism. A poet, he said, can release himself from the state and be supranational in his orientation, but the scholar cannot: his place is in society and the heart of the time, whose pulse he feels in himself (ibid., p. 58). Kahler and his viewpoint, one is supposed to infer, is un-German, while the adherents of *Nationalökonomie* were true patriots, making their contribution to the state.

Here Weber's references to 'accepting the fate of the times like a man' take on a distinct meaning. Salz urged, as a requirement of 'scholarship,' the acceptance of the state and its needs and avoidance of the temptations of revolutionary change. The fate of the times was understood with a certain idealism, however. For Salz the task of the time was to retain the German cultural treasure, and to show that the Germans alone represented Europe. Kahler's case for a 'new science' contradicts the 'most basic principle of *Wissenschaft*,' that it is always an expression of the life-feeling of the time. A revolution in *Wissenschaft* is made possible, Salz argued, only by virtue of a change in the life-feeling of the time itself. It is romantic self-deception to suppose that one can declare oneself free of this. One might as well, he said, declare one's independence of fate (1921, p. 58). According to Salz, the great revolutionaries of the scientific spirit – Copernicus, Galileo, Kepler, Newton, and Hegel, among others – proclaimed the life-feeling of their time, instead of opposing it.[16]

Ernst Troeltsch, whose views were close but not identical to Weber's, also commented on Kahler and placed his work into a broader context. In 'Die Revolution in der Wissenschaft,' he suggested that the origin of the revolution in *Wissenschaft* precedes World War I and has parallels in the work of Bergson in France and in Croce's attack on positivism in Italy (Troeltsch, 1921, pp. 66-9). He pointed out that it concerns the *Geisteswissenschaften*, philosophy, and history rather than the natural sciences. The target of the revolution is the restrictive conception of rationality. It wishes to resurrect the symbol-creating and intuitive power of the intellect, and to establish a new intellectual order and communal unity on this basis. But what this inevitably amounts to, Troeltsch suggested, is the establishment of a coterie surrounding a personality like Stefan George. Troeltsch found this to be reminiscent of Nietzsche – indeed, at one discussion he heard the phrase 'the *Ubermenschentum* of all' (ibid., p. 67).

Kahler's book, Troeltsch said, is the war manifesto of this new *Wissenschaft* (1921, p. 83). It calls for a new personal *Führertum* and a new *Weltanschauung* under which the young can unify. Troeltsch noted that Weber insisted that this kind of leader and this kind of unified *Weltanschauung* is no longer possible and observed that Kahler does not tell us how this new organic science is possible. Troeltsch said that it is hard to imagine how it could succeed, but remarked that he himself disagrees with Weber on philosophy, and in fact believes that some of Kahler's instincts are closer to the truth (ibid., p. 89). In general, Troeltsch approved of the Salz critique, but found his history of the German *Geist* to be a bit peculiar. Neither book, he thought, provides much that is intellectually essential; they are more important as symptoms. He gave these symptoms a political reading. The movement for the new *Wissenschaft*, he said, is really a 'revolution against the revolution,' that is, against the world-wide revolution of democratic and socialist feeling. It cannot overcome the facts of modern economic and social life: but one cannot simply dismiss it as impotent for this reason – important ideals, he noted, make themselves felt (ibid., pp. 92-4).

Troeltsch's interpretation is not, however, entirely sufficient.

The reduction of the issues to political differences is an oversimplification which is also characteristic of more recent literature, in which each side is labeled as representing a stance like 'liberalism,' 'conservatism' or 'neo-conservatism.'[17] Such a reading mistakes the aims of the participants, who were not partisan in any usual sense, but were concerned first and foremost with establishing a *modus vivendi* for political life and giving this mode an intellectual underpinning. Kahler wished to create a framework of ideas, a *politeia*, in which community and culture would be possible, more than to promote a particular cause. In the context of the time this was an intelligible aim. The 'revolution' of 1919 had not been the sort of revolution that provided a set of common ideals. On the contrary, the SPD, which had power thrust on it, proved to be indifferent about anything beyond the goals that had been part of the party program during the *Kaiserreich*: the eight-hour day, unemployment insurance, and protection of workers' rights (Rosenberg, 1965, p. 38). So there was a need for an undergirding rationale for the common life of the nation. The peculiarity of the situation was that those who sought to provide the rationale were not, as were Lenin and Jefferson, men of affairs as well as men of ideas. The results of this divorce between ideas and the responsibilities of action were predictable, both with respect to practical political discourse and the discourse of intellectuals.

The *modus vivendi* of the Weimar order, in any case, never was underwritten by any widely accepted ideas. The young socialist workers marched with signs reading 'A republic is nothing grand, for Socialism we take our stand' (Eyck, 1963, p. 118). Its academic supporters frequently called themselves 'democrats by necessity' or 'republicans by reason,' making conscious contrast to the kind of loyalty and intellectual commitment people ordinarily have to a political order. The lack of intellectual commitment to the Weimar arrangements, both by scholars and by the citizenry, was one cause of the ultimate failure of the system and its lapse into 'sham constitutionalism' as early as 1923 (cf. Rosenberg, 1965, p. 212). The Weimar regime might be given as refutation of Weber's idea that the form of the state could be considered merely as a technique, specifically a technique for producing leaders. The leaders the 'technique' produced had little loyalty to the arrangements, and they used their followings to wreck and subvert the arrangements. Hitler was merely the last and most dramatic example of this.

A more serious flaw in the reduction of these disputes to political stances is that the philosophical significance of the arguments is obscured. For Troeltsch, who was part of the older generation, the new philosophies appeared as aberrations: they were motivated by what he regarded as intelligible dissatisfactions with the present state of learning, but were entirely inadequate as alternatives. But this was not the sense of the younger generation. The slogan 'Back to Kant,' with which the reaction to Hegelianism had started sixty years earlier, had before the war been replaced in avant-garde philosophical circles with newer slogans. The slogan of phenomenology was 'Back to the things themselves'; another was 'Back to Hegel.' These reflected a widespread sense of the dissolution of neo-Kantianism. They also reflected the diversity of the search for alternatives. The proffered alternatives were often shabby, and it is characteristic of the period that poorly articulated, poorly thought through positions were taken seriously. But this reflected the recognized inadequacies of received philosophy, in the face of which a much wider than usual range of alternatives seemed plausible.

The phrase 'dissolution of neo-Kantianism,' borrowed from Gadamer (1982, p. 40) deserves some explanation. The dominant philosophies of late nineteenth-century Germany were variant forms of the movement 'back to Kant.' Neo-Kantianism proper consisted of the Marburg and the 'Southwest' schools. By an extended usage it included Dilthey and his successors. By an even more extended usage it included Nietzsche and phenomenology. Vienna Circle 'Logical Positivism' itself has been regarded as little more than a late variant of neo-Kantianism. As we shall use it here, neo-Kantianism refers to the body of views broadly including Dilthey, Nietzsche, and the schools. Together these made up a rough consensus, on which Weber relied. The seeds of the dissolution inhered in the project – these were philosophies that inquired into the presuppositional basis of belief or value, and each 'basis' proved to be questionable in one way or another. The dissolution occurred when this project itself was called into question by the insolubility of its central problems, historicism, relativity, and the irrationality of 'bases.' These were not new problems in 1918. But the effect of the crisis of defeat was to sharpen them and bring them to the consciousness of a wider public. Without the defeat, one suspects, the dissolution would have taken more time, for the doctrines in question were diverse in form and style, and therefore not easy to defeat at one blow.

Scheler and the broader dispute

The search for alternatives, and the critique of neo-Kantianism and its variants that accompanied it, was far broader than the Weber dispute, which appears in retrospect to have been little more than an episode in the destruction of the philosophic consensus of the previous century. Yet the dispute played a role in hastening the developments and focusing the issues. At the level of academic philosophy, the issues over Weber merged with issues over historicism and historicist relativism. Weber continued to figure in these disputes, though as time went on he came to be regarded more as a representative of a particular generation.[18]

Max Scheler was the author of a famous *bon mot* about Weber to the effect that Weber was the most perfect representative of the times – and these were the worst of times. In contrast to Troeltsch, he recognized that a major shift in philosophy was in the making and joined wholeheartedly in the search for a new alternative. He also took a different view of the Kahler-Salz dispute: he endorsed Kahler's critique, remarking that he differed with it only on minor points (Scheler, 1963, p. 15).

Like Husserl, Scheler went through a change of views as a result of the war. During the early part of the war, he had been intensely nationalistic. He was loyal to the ideal of the spiritual unity of Europe, but he contrasted what he called the spiritual militarism (*Gesinnungsmilitarismus*) of the Germans to the instrumental militarism of the Western democracies, which he regarded as the cause of the war (Staude, 1967, pp. 80, 82-3). As Scheler changed his view of the war after the breakdown of the German offensive in 1915, he became more involved in the Catholic church, and in time developed a form of non-Thomistic philosophy of religion resembling Augustinianism. He came to realize the inconsistency of this view with the dogma of the church, and became more critical of other aspects of christianity. One might say that once he had acquired the label 'the Catholic Nietzsche,' he showed that the Nietzsche outweighed the Catholic in him. He officially left the church. Soon he was presenting his view more widely as a new *Weltanschauung* which would resolve the spiritual crisis of the time (ibid., p. 243). Scheler's great theme, from his earlier phenomenological studies to his philosophical and theological reflections of the late 1920s, was the nature of values. His argument is complex, but it may be briefly summarized. Because Scheler's later ideas were taken up in part and eclipsed by Heidegger's they had relatively little direct relevance to the later controversy. But in the Weimar period, they constituted a visible alternative. Indeed, in the early 1920s, Scheler appeared as Weber's great opposite.

Scheler's rejection of relativism may be put simply. Consider the value 'good medical practice.' What *counts as* good medical practice varies as our knowledge progresses. But the value remains the same. Relativism, Scheler said, mistakes 'valuations,' the things that count at various times as instances of good medical practice, for the value good medical practice, and concludes from the existence of conflicts in valuations that there are no true values. This was a standard argument in ethics. In the hands of the neo-Kantians it had usually led to an idea of 'formal values' which were 'eternal' but instantiated in radically opposed ways in various historical circumstances. Scheler took a different approach. He admired Nietzsche's command of the range of historical values, and wished to capture the richness of moral life without falling into historicism or nihilism – to capture true values where Nietzsche had found no values.

The notion of 'perspectives' was his primary philosophical device: each 'value stance' amounted to a limited 'perspective' on an eternal order of values. Our situation in apprehending values, in short, is like the situation of the six blind men and the elephant – perspectives disclose genuine values, but each perspective is partial, disclosing only a part of the whole 'eternal order' of values (Schutz, 1957, p. 494). He believed that new values, new parts of the order, can be 'discovered,' especially through the creative force of love. The task of philosophy in the face of the historical richness of alternative values was to make sense of their specific historical manifestations in individuals who were 'moral exemplars' for their period, as well as to account for differences in class 'perspectives' on values. The ultimate aim was to identify the eternal hierarchy of the various values, by exhibiting their relations to one another. How this last task was to be accomplished was the metaphilosophical soft spot in this scheme, a point made by Nikolai Hartmann, another contemporary ethical objectivist (1962, pp. 595-613).

Scheler's attempt to construct an alternative theory of values was not fruitless. It was the source of such insights as his psychological analysis of '*ressentiment*.' Resentment was understood as a reaction to the failure to achieve genuine values and as the basis for the substitution of false but achievable values. Thus resentment figures as an explanation of the historical fact of the pursuit of false values. The Schelerian concept of *Kairos*, the demand of the hour, was to have influence in theology. It also had political implications. As Scheler understood it, a *Kairos* was a moment of opportunity for a particular unique moral insight and action, a moment when one had a special window on to a new facet of the eternal order, so to speak. The postwar period, he believed, was such a time: it demanded common repentance and the rebirth of the idea of Christian solidarity and European community, against individualism and nationalism (Deeken, 1974, p. 119).[19]

In the immediate postwar period, Scheler recognized the need for a new conception of the state and of the university that would meet the needs of democracy (Scheler, 1960a, pp. 398-410). His concern was to recognize the existence and partial legitimacy of the various ideologies of the time, in the belief that the mutual recognition of the validity of different values was essential to a democratic politics. He promoted the idea of adult education centers that would be ideologically neutral but whose instructors would make a point of explaining the various ideologies and discussing them historically and sociologically. In these centers, the instructor would not refrain from stating his own position, but the point of the instruction would be to overcome prejudice and intolerance (Staude, 1967, p. 116). He explicitly attacked proposals for political education designed to foster nationalistic feeling (Scheler, 1960b, pp. 425-6). Yet, like Weber, Scheler did not reject what he saw as the realities of politics. In spite of his concern for the promotion of tolerance, he saw the main problem of politics not as a problem of compromise but as a problem of promoting great leadership, which was also Weber's idea. He also spoke for political realism – perhaps unfashionably, for when he spoke to one of the Catholic youth groups he had admired for creating a new sense of social solidarity, they rejected him as 'Machiavellian' in his politics (Staude, 1967, p. 119). Thus in politics, as in philosophy, he was a transitional figure.

His later philosophical work extended the 'perspectives' device to ontology, by arguing that the 'classical' conception of being and the modern conception of being both 'miss their mark' (Scheler, 1961, pp. 63-7). He said that the ground of being, because it is always 'becoming,' cannot be captured by schemes. Heidegger was to develop and elaborate this hint into a rejection of the ontological bias of Western thought. Scheler did not go so far. Though his later views presupposed the realization of the death of the traditional conception of God, he supposed that acting morally amounted to acting in accordance with the partial but continuing realization of the divine in man. Because he took the divine in man, 'becoming,' to have an objective character, the later views preserved his ethical objectivism.

In accordance with his earlier class analyses of value stances (Deeken, 1974, p. 95; cf. Stark, 1958, pp. 77-8), which suggested that such things as an emphasis on being, spiritualism, idealism, and the search for identities and harmonies were generally associated with higher classes (but not the bourgeoisie!), Scheler did not suppose that this new conception of man could be meaningful to any but an elite. He continued to stress the need for great leaders, and he must have supposed that leadership would come from above. But he could not think of the leaders as *creators* of values, as Weber did. He stressed that the moral exemplars he analyzed (one of which was the 'hero,' another the 'leading light of civilization') were *discoverers* of objective values, not creators. Hartmann also stressed this distinction, which has a crucial political implication: where there is in any sense an objective practical or moral good, there is an objective standard to be 'discovered' by which leaders may be judged (Hartmann, 1962, p. 49).

Scheler remained in the public eye, and continued to the end to present his views to political audiences, such as an assembly of officers in the *Reichswehr* Ministry and the *Deutsche Hochschule für Politik*, with considerable success (Staude, 1967, pp. 225, 228). But his death in 1928 cut off the full development of his ideas, though Heidegger and many others picked up pieces of his position. His most important student, Paul-Ludwig Landsberg, survived to return to a position closer to Catholicism and died in the camps for his anti-Nazi activities (Spiegelberg, 1971, pp. 267-8).

The Nazis found the vocabulary of 'eternal values' sufficiently compelling to try to coopt it and at the same time to reject Scheler's way of thinking about them. Gregor Strasser, writing in 1926, referred to

> a *terrible hopelessness* in the souls of humanity, *a dissolution of all firm values, an instability which looks in vain for stability, stability which it does not find any more in religion and which it has lost in ethics*! '*RELATIVITY*' – that is the keynote of the culture of our times. . . . I do not want to be misunderstood in the word *morality* – morality is always founded only on animate nature, not on supposedly unalterable commands (1978, p. 93).

Similarly for institutions.

> For in *one thing* we must achieve *utter clarity: that FORMS AND INSTITUTIONS ARE CHANGEABLE*, are never right 'as such' and never wrong 'as such': that there is, however, only one 'RIGHT' SPIRIT, only one spirit with a constructive viewpoint, that is the spirit of eternal nature, animated by man, the image of God! (ibid., p. 94).

This vitalist 'spirit,' which he identified with the 'Prussian style' and the 'completion of human existence through both *HONOR* and *DUTY*,' is 'the idea of national Socialism' (ibid., pp. 93-4).

The Schelerian idea of eternal values was clearly as uncongenial to the Nazis as vitalism was congenial. Yet the fact that Strasser chose to attack it shows its significance in the culture at large. If Scheler failed, in the sense that he failed to produce a philosophical consensus to replace the neo-Kantian consensus of the late nineteenth century, he nevertheless succeeded in keeping alive the possibility of a philosophical underwriting of political and ethical practice. His visibility and personal prestige were such that he could represent 'philosophy' as a force legitimating the claims of 'eternal values.' It is evident that this stance was not without effect.

Developments on the Left

The dissolution of neo-Kantianism and the search for alternatives went on throughout academic philosophy and intellectual life. The process was paralleled on the Left, and developments in the intellectual mainstream influenced developments on the Left. But the Left was relatively uninfluential in academic life and offered no general solutions to the philosophical problems of the time. The movements of left-wing thought that arose in the 1920s only became influential later.

The work of Georg Lukács exemplifies the shift in philosophical consciousness. Lukács had been part of Weber's circle and a contributor to the *Archiv* under Weber's editorship. He was in touch with the same philosophical currents as Weber was, prior to his embrace of Communism. The essays of the period 1918-1922, his most influential contribution, show the peculiar sort of continuity of neo-Kantian themes in the rejection of neo-Kantianism that was characteristic of the time. Gadamer speaks of the return to Hegel as 'within and against the dominant neo-Kantian philosophy' and places Lukács in this group (1982, pp. 26-7).

In 'Reification and the Consciousness of the Proletariat,' an essay in the same genre as Kahler's, Lukács attempted to give a history of thought that accounted for contemporary epistemology, particularly the 'dogmatic assumption that the rational and formalistic mode of cognition is the only possible way of apprehending reality' (1971, p. 121). This assumption was a central tenet of neo-Kantianism, which in some forms reduced philosophy to the philosophy of science. Lukács did not think this 'assumption' could be refuted by argument, but regarded it as a condition that was a historical moment in a developing process. The philosophy is merely an articulation of the condition, which amounts to this: we are condemned to a separation between objects and our forms of thought, which are increasingly unable to do justice to the phenomena (ibid., p. 208).

Our knowledge is always 'from a vantage point', and therefore relativized to this vantage point. Hegel made the first steps toward overcoming this, by recognizing that the relation of subject and object, vantage point and thing observed, is a totality. As Lukács understood it, this totality, and the 'objective dialectic' enacted between subject and object which constitutes it (Lukács, 1971, p. 142), could be understood only from the point of view of the total historical process. Rickert's and Weber's arguments that as historians we are conditioned to accept our own viewpoint fail to do this, because they take an uncritical attitude toward our conditioning (ibid., p. 150). But Lukács did not mean to merely deny relativism. He considered that his line of reasoning was more relativistic than that of Spengler or Nietzsche, which was static and dogmatic because it assumed its own historical absoluteness (ibid., p. 187).

Understanding the totality of the subject-object relation from the vantage point of the total historical process is the only means of understanding history. But 'history is the unceasing overthrow of the objective forms that shape the life of man,' and if changes can be understood by their place and function in the totality of history (Lukács, 1971, p. 186), there can be no 'method' in the usual sense: method is part of what is overthrown. 'Only the historical process truly eliminates the – actual – autonomy of the objects and the concepts of objects with their resulting rigidity' (ibid., p. 144). But the historical process is concrete. So to overcome the reification of concepts a genuine historical progression must occur (ibid., p. 198). The indications of imminent change were clear to Lukács. Although historians, blinded by the limitations of bourgeois thought, could not see it, the world proletarian revolution had begun (ibid., p. 157). At the same time, Lukács said, we are recognizing the increasing inadequacy of our forms of thought – a sign that they are historically doomed. The emancipation from these forms and the revolution of the proletariat are but aspects of one process.

The general strategy in the essay is to seek the transcendence of philosophical dilemmas in the deed – 'existentially' rather than through philosophical speculation (Wurgaft, 1977, p. 104). This line of approach was obviously not original with Lukács. The shared ground for neo-Kantianism and its successors of the period was a belief in the impossibility of a philosophical resolution of present-day epistemological antinomies and relativities. Where writers like Weber insisted on a choice within the framework of antinomies, others sought to transcend them – by spiritual revolution, as in Kahler, by authentic being, or by a return to vital forces, as in Strasser. Lukács accepted the rational insurmountability of relativism, as well as its language, particularly such notions as vantage point. He believed that revolutionary action would bring about the resolution of the problems of 'objectification,' which he identified with the Marxian concept of alienation. But he did not offer an argument or proof of this – the universal historical intimations of contemporary proletarian politics sufficed for him, and he believed that there was no firmer ground. There is, in fact, little in the way of argument in the text. He asserted that such things as the 'absolute-relative' antinomy disappear when we become historically conscious, and he asserted the privileged historical (and therefore epistemological) position of the revolutionary proletariat. But this is wholly promissory, just as was Kahler's discussion of a new *Wissenchaft*.

Yet the idea that a left-wing development out of the dissolution of neo-Kantianism was possible was a significant beginning, and a long series of variations on these themes was to follow. These successors are also characteristically marked by a peculiar halfway emancipation from the ideas they purported to reject. A particularly clear example of this is Paul Tillich, whose own disillusionment and dissatisfaction with the ideas of neo-Kantianism, and specifically with historical relativism, represents something of a standard pattern of intellectual development in the period among young left-wing intellectuals. Tillich was exposed to the best philosophers of the time, as well as the major socialists. He was not himself a particularly deep philosopher, however, so the general pattern of development is more easily read in his work.

Tillich took the philosophical situation as it was understood by the Weberians as a point of intellectual departure, conceiving of his time as characterized by the shattering of world views and an understanding of the limits of scientific method (Tillich, 1957, p. 203). But he was careful to distance himself from what he called the older generation of Troeltsch and Weber and refused to accept the historicist standoff (ibid., p. 74). He took the problem of overcoming the situation of the time as a matter of finding an adequate philosophical base, and he rejected the positions that did not solve the problem, such as positivism and the neo-Kantian view of religion as a 'value,' which was also Weber's view. He rejected Troeltsch for his historicism and idealism which, he said, prevented any solution to the problem of action (Tillich, 1966, p. 54). Then, and in later life, he was acutely sensitive to the 'disastrous consequences of Lutheran social ethics' and later spoke of the Lutheran conception 'in its naturalistic versions, namely, in vitalism and fascism' (ibid., pp. 74, 78), a conception exemplified at the time by Emmanuel Hirsch's 'young Lutheran' nationalist theology.

Tillich told us that his personal turning point was the war (1952, p. 7). As with the phenomenologists, he sought a new intellectual foundation for action. He could not accept phenomenology, which he rather curiously described as 'too Catholic' (1966, p. 53).[20] But he found a theological foundation for a resolution to the paradoxes of historicism in the Schelerian concept of *Kairos*, which he understood, as Scheler had, to explain how decisions to act within a historical situation could be, at the moment of a *Kairos*, based on universal truth. In contrast to ordinary moral absolutism, he readily conceded to historicism that one could not force moral or theological absolutes on a historical situation (ibid., p. 78). Universal truth could only, so to speak, reveal itself. Like Scheler, Tillich believed that his own period was a *Kairos*. The 'decision' he envisioned was a political decision for socialism (Tillich, 1977, p. 132). Here the language and intellectual motifs of relativism, especially the notion of decision, merge with its rejection, as they do in a different way in Lukács.

Tillich had numerous connections in socialist circles, including contacts with the important younger socialist intellectuals around the *Neue Blätter*, such as J. P. Mayer (who later wrote important criticisms of Weber and who discovered some of Marx's early manuscripts) (Stumme, 1977, pp. xviii-xix).[21] He had connections to Wolfers (Staude, 1967, p. 228), head of the *Deutsche Hochschule für Politik*,[22] through a socialist study group, the *Kairoskreis* (Stumme, 1977, p. xvi). He also had contact with another movement that was critical of the conception of knowledge associated with Weber's group, the 'Critical Theorists' of the Frankfurt *Institut für Sozialforschuung* (Jay, 1973, pp. 24-5, 31).

Max Horkheimer, the director of the *Institut*, made the crisis of *Wissenschaft* the topic of his inaugural address at Frankfurt in 1931 (Jay, 1973, p. 25). Not surprisingly, Horkheimer connected the crisis of *Wissenschaft* to the crisis of society. He argued that, for a Marxist, science is one of man's productive powers, a 'means of production,' though he was quick to deny that this fact justifies a pragmatist notion of truth or a reduction of the notion of scientific truth to mere accordance with social interests (Horkheimer, 1972, p. 3). The relation between the two crises, said Horkheimer, is that today science, like other means of production, is not fulfilling its function. It is not the rationality of science, as some would say, that is at fault, but the rigidity of the social structure and the rigidity of science. This latter rigidity dates from the struggle against scholastic restrictions: the exigencies of this struggle forced science to limit itself to the task of describing facts without respect to such nonscientific considerations as human betterment. Yet social reality, he said, proved less amenable to this approach, and social inquiry was superficial and was dominated by fetishistically adhered-to concepts. The deficiency, however, according to Horkheimer, was 'not in science itself but in the social conditions which hinder its development and are at loggerheads with the rational elements immanent in science' (ibid., p. 6).

The historical consequence of the devotion to superficialities in the human sciences was that a critique of the foundations of research developed in opposition to these superficialities, thus creating the 'crisis.' Physics, Horkheimer suggested, overcame its own crisis by making revisions in its foundations (1972, p. 6). Something similar but less successful happened in social science. Scheler, he thought, prepared the way for a return to the main issues; but the metaphysical approaches as a group merely rejected science, and thus turned away from the question of the causes of the social crisis (ibid.). Accordingly, Horkheimer pronounced a plague on both houses, that of the old science and of metaphysics, both of which, by virtue of their self-limitation, became 'ideological.' His own solution was to seek a correct theoretical understanding of the social situation that grasped the social and historical processes that were the ultimate causes of the crisis (ibid., p. 9).

Horkheimer did not mention Weber, though he would have identified the general position of the Weberians as a class-interested ideology that was in historical crisis along with the bourgeois class and order. Indeed, there is a clear indifference to Weber in the writings of the main figures in the *Institut*. The reference to Scheler suggests the dependence of the views of the Critical Theorists, at least in these early days, on outside figures. This dependence was not to change, though the outside figures were. Herbert Marcuse, who was a student of Heidegger, was later to develop a curiously Heideggerian Marxist critique of science, which he identified as an ideology opposed to Reason (Marcuse, 1968, pp. 223-4). This argument is close to the spirit of Kahler's.

By the same token, there is considerable continuity between Weber's position in 'Wissenschaft als Beruf' and the position of such persons as Tillich. Critics sometimes regarded Weber's position as the basis of the whole line of development of persons who believed that science or life was ultimately based on nonrational decisions. The sociologist Eduard Spranger, for example, in an article on the idea of presuppositionless *Geisteswissenschaften*, treated Weber and the philosophical anthropologists Rothacker and Litt as representatives of essentially the same view, and he described Tillich and Heidegger, among others, as part of the 'crisis' involving the meaning of science (Spranger, 1929, p. 3).

Spranger's point is telling, for it shows the connection between the new views and the relativism these writers purportedly rejected. He focused on Mommsen's idea of a science without presuppositions. It will be recalled that Weber's view on the matter was subtly stated. He insisted that science as an *activity* has at least one presupposition, the valuative presupposition that the subject matter is worth studying. But Weber carefully avoided saying that science has *metaphysical* presuppositions and appeared to deny it (Weber, 1946, pp. 143-5, 154). Spranger suggested that the situation today is that proletarian 'science,' bourgeois 'science,' Protestant-theological 'science', and the like all exist and are all in a stage of struggle with the others, and that this shows that they do have presuppositions about the world, despite their denials that they do. They are all really alternative metaphysical stances, with their metaphysics concealed (Spranger, 1929, p. 8): in short, they are 'frames' in the older, neo-Kantian sense. Worse, according to Spranger, they lost sight of the true aims of science. The scientist, he reminded, seeks integrative knowledge, the overview of things. Tillich's view, he noted, treats science as instrumental and subordinate to value choice (ibid., pp. 25-6). The correct view, Spranger said, is that science demands the search for objectivity as an ethical law. He agreed that *Wissenschaft* is in crisis (ibid., pp. 25, 29). But the solution to the crisis must be through *Wissenschaft* and its commitment to truth. By pretending to be 'presuppositionless' one only adds to the confusion of scientific language and the anarchy of values (ibid., p. 17) – and the result of this pretense is the inevitable smuggling in of values and presuppositions (ibid., pp. 17-8). This puts into words the gnawing dissatisfaction that Spranger and others felt about contemporary philosophy and thought. But matters were to get worse.

The critics' consensus on Weber

Developments in German academic philosophy during the mid-1920s, sometimes called 'the ontological turn,' transformed the issues and rendered much of the earlier vocabulary of the dispute obsolete. One may notice that Scheler, Tillich, and the others we have discussed are centrally concerned with historicism. The problem of historicism is an *epistemological* problem, a standoff between competing historical standpoints understood in a neo-Kantian fashion as frameworks for seeing the world. For the neo-Kantians, problems of ontology, of what exists, were dependent on epistemology. This reasoning can be reversed, in that one's epistemology could be said to necessarily involve an *a priori* ontology, or a set of ontological commitments. The crucial philosophical problem then becomes 'being,' rather than 'knowing,' and the crucial philosophical question becomes the investigation of 'being' as such. Epistemology, instead of a science, then appears to be little more than special pleading for a particular aspect or view of being, based on a concealed or presupposed notion of what really is. Weber, we shall see, provided a textbook illustration of the point. His 'epistemology' now appeared to be based on an undefended presupposition about the world being a 'meaningless chaos.' Of course, the recognition of the impossibility of deciding ontological claims had implications beyond Weber. It was to prove to be the end of any serious hope for a solution to the epistemological and moral paradoxes of historicism, because these solutions now could be seen to rest on deeper insolubilities about existence.

Heidegger is the great figure of 'the ontological turn,' but it is striking that virtually everyone else writing in this period took a similar step. The history of the phenomenological movement itself is inseparable from this development. Husserl's slogan, 'Back to the things themselves', expresses the frustration with epistemology that underlay the 'turn.'

The first fully developed philosophical critique of Weber's work reflecting the ontological turn was offered in 1927 by Hermann Grab. In this critique, Grab identified himself with Husserl and Scheler, that is, with phenomenology, and accordingly criticized Weber's psychologism, his absolutization of 'spheres of knowledge', and his historicism. Grab's critique of historicism explicitly follows Troeltsch, Mannheim, Scheler, and Hartmann (Grab, 1927, p. 5). The critique of the 'absolutizing' of spheres of knowledge and historical viewpoints is the key to his analysis. He observed that Weber separated rational values, or the value 'rationalization,' from other values and presented it as a nonvaluative concept, 'absolute' in the sense that it is itself not merely another historical value, but an eternally valid form (ibid., pp. 39-46). The 'objective' value order that philosophers have sought to discover, he suggested, would necessarily have a particular, and subordinate, place for this value. So by presenting it as a different type of thing, an 'absolute', in contrast to nonabsolute, merely historical values, Weber made it impossible to discover the proper relations between it and the various other values; and, worse, science becomes, by virtue of its 'absolute' claims for itself, the *enemy* of the other values (ibid., pp. 45 -6). It becomes, as Kahler had suggested, an antireligious, anticultural, antilife power. But the dualism that Weber promoted as 'absolute,' between rational supraindividual truths and values accessible only to the individual through irrational choices, is itself merely a product of its times. So by presenting this dualism as absolute, Weber had himself created a false metaphysicization of the present *Zeitgeist*. Grab would have replied to Weber's defenders who insist that Weber was only 'facing reality,' that the 'reality' he was facing was merely the *Zeitgeist* itself in false metaphysical guise as an absolute (ibid., p. 44). We can put this another way if we recall that for Weber the fact-value distinction was a matter of 'logic.' Grab would have said that this 'logic' is not logic but ontology, an ontology whose world contains only nonvaluative 'facts.'

Similar criticisms were made by Karl Löwith, in an essay on the relations between Marx and Weber (1946, 1932). Weber's thesis in ' "Objectivity" in Social Science and Social Policy' is that what we experience in a historical event is determined by our interest. This means that today, in a world marked by the nonexistence of binding norms, we must create meaning in history by deciding on a value stance. Weber insisted that we keep in mind that this step of choosing a value stance, though it is nonoptional (because no historical fact can be experienced unless this step is taken), is nevertheless nonrational and nonscientific. The effect of this claim is to deny the positivist belief in human objectivity, substituting for it the idea of 'scientific impartiality' toward one's own prejudgments (Löwith, 1932, p. 69). But this substitution does precisely what Weber accused such persons as Roscher and Knies of doing: he inserted the presuppositions of his own world view into the logical structure that he insisted holds for all social science inquiry. This can be seen if we inquire into the ontology built into the structure. The ontology is in fact 'individualistic,' and to choose this ontology is to choose for a particular kind of social philosophy, and against others. His 'eternally valid' structure of social science methodology is in this way 'value laden.' More smuggling in of values occurs in his substantive writings, as when he implicitly affirmed a secular outlook by describing the sociological fact of the removal of religious meaning from the world as an 'unmasking' (ibid., p. 76).

Weber's attitude toward 'rationality' and 'rationalization' is thus philosophically problematic. It is also, Löwith argued, puzzling: Weber portrayed himself as a son of the times in his 'disenchanted' view of the world, but was he really a supporter of the devil of intellectual rationalization, the '*Fleurs du mal*' as Löwith put it? Or did he refuse these flowers? He indicated that some of the products of rationalization are evil. Is the ethical irrationalization of the world another of these evil products, one that defeats the rationalization that produces it? The unity behind this apparent conflict is this, according to Löwith: freedom can today be understood only as freedom within the iron cage of the determinative social constraints arising from rationalization as a social development. One must face the reality of the meaninglessness of God and the world in order to be free (Löwith, 1932, p. 94). This conclusion surpasses mere *historical* value relativism. The Nietzschean and Diltheyan problematic – the claim that there is no longer a foundation for understanding the world – is made into a nonrelative basic moral and epistemological fact, a new foundation. As Löwith put it, Weber created a platform of negation on which the hero could sit (ibid., p. 98).

Löwith suggested a new ordering of the relations between Weber's politics and his science. In the methodological writings, Löwith suggested, Weber made the Nietzschean and Diltheyan problematic into a philosophical truth; in the scientific writings he made it into a sociological fact of the historical present; and the political writings are an exploration of the responses to this problem that are possible in the historical present: in these writings, we discover what the hero in the historical present is and will do (Löwith, 1932, p. 95-6). Thus Weber's view of rationality, his valuative stance toward rationality, becomes fully evident only in these writings. So the logical relation between the methodological, scientific, and political writings is not a matter of each depending on the logically prior writings. The apparent logical priority of the methodological writings is spurious, because the choice of methodological principles is not itself justifiable. It is merely a choice like the choices of Roscher and Knies, one that makes different metaphysical presuppositions. Weber's 'scientific' results are based on this choice, and his political 'solutions' therefore presuppose the 'problem' these results create. So for Löwith, Weber's position was, in the last analysis, merely a politics with an attached metaphysics. But it was also a teaching, a teaching of the true heroic stance in the present. As we shall see, Jaspers was to take this teaching very seriously.

Siegfried Landshut developed a critique that resembles Grab's and Löwith's. Landshut argued that Weber's actual research intention remains concealed, and that the task for the interpreter is to identify the basic position that informs his typologizing and his approach to historical reality. The *explicit* aim of Weber's work is the recognition of the cultural meaning or significance of concrete historical associations and the formation of type concepts and general rules. But these are mutually exclusive tasks. So Weber came to relate reality and concept in an especially peculiar way (Landshut, 1929, p. 39). The concept, according to Weber, does not represent reality: reality is, rather, a meaningless chaos which can never be fixed by a concept. So for Weber his own concepts, his ideal-types, are merely handtools, *ad hoc* instruments determined by the point of the research, and the formation of ideal-types is only a means, not a goal, which serves a purpose with respect to a given research intention (ibid., p. 40). The more common view of concept formation is that concepts capture or mirror reality, and that reality is the *test* of the concept. The discovery of concepts with the right relation to reality *was* the research intention. So with Weber, the research intention must necessarily be located elsewhere.

As Grab and Löwith did, Landshut raised the question of ontology, arguing that Weber's method is comprehensible only when we analyze his underlying view of the nature of reality. He suggested that there are two elements to his view: (1) the infiniteness of real associations and thus their ultimately inexhaustible and incalculable character and (2) the irrationalness of reality, which makes rational explanation the only possible form of understanding. The first element is the doctrine that the endless multiplicity of real associations makes presuppositionless cognition impossible. This doctrine, Landshut suggested, is itself absurd, for it depends on the unproved assumption that reality is chaotic. The actual reason for Weber's view is, instead, the idea that the researcher must make value decisions that orient his work (Landshut, 1929, p. 43).

This suggests that when Weber spoke of a 'rational' understanding of the irrational reality of human action and insisted that this is the only possible understanding, he was simply making one of these value decisions. According to the arguments he has given in support of the first, ontological, claim, direct understanding of human action is not possible. So we are left with understanding particular actions as deviations from what is presented to us as the hypothetical construction 'rational action' (but which is really a particular value choice). The valuative character of this construct can be seen if we consider some of Weber's examples. Weber told us that if one shoots an enemy in following an order, this is rational, but if one shoots him out of revenge, this is irrational (Weber, 1976, p. 4). But to say that acting out of revenge is irrational presupposes a division of *motives* into 'rational' and 'irrational.' It turns out that when Weber applies the concept of 'rationality' in his research, he has merely *selected* certain motives as rational. These motives are those associated with the methodical attitude toward life and conduct characteristic of Western man (Landshut, 1929, p. 59).

Like Marx, Weber was concerned with understanding capitalism, the fact that systematic activity aimed at production has become the destiny of the West, and the fact that the individual feels powerless in the face of these relations. Weber, however, posed a different question than Marx. The intention of Marx was to change the world. Weber accepted the consequences of Marx's position but not its presuppositions. The only presupposition he accepted amounts to a particular division of regions of action into rational and irrational.

Yet this presupposition determines a result. Man becomes 'a

product of his relations,' determined by his systematic activitiy aimed at production. What he can expect is determined by the order of these relations, and therefore what he can hope for is determined by the change in these relations. Landshut suggested that this simply recapitulates the great problem of German Idealism, the cleft between freedom and order. The 'order' of society is the theme of the research: freedom is problematic. But the problem and order is insoluble given this presupposition about the nature of man, for the presupposition denies freedom. Thus a sociology that takes the problem of freedom as its subject in this way saws off the branch on which it sits (Landshut, 1929, p. 155).

The similarities between Grab, Löwith, and Landshut represent with the exception of Henrich, who discussed it after World consensus was not 'ideological,' in any useful sense of this word. Indeed, each of these writers came from different philosophical and political backgrounds. Thus the waning years of Weimar saw the transformation of the Weber dispute from its original form. Spranger, speaking at the beginning of the decade, saw Troeltsch and Scheler as the opposite poles of the debate, with Troeltsch defending an essentially Weberian line (Spranger, 1925, p. 74). By the end of the decade both men were dead. Scheler had been succeeded on the technical philosophical level by Heidegger, with whom he had been associated. But Heidegger's stance toward values was different from Scheler's. Although he was explicitly opposed to 'nihilism,' he denied the possibility of metaphysically grounding or legitimating science or values, and this seemed to many hearers to be an affirmation of the deepest possible nihilism. The denial extended to the attempts at grounding advanced by Weber, as well as to the neo-Kantian tradition generally. But it also seemed to extend to all the other alternatives. So the situation of irrational choice that Weber had proclaimed within the sphere of values now seemed to obtain in the sphere of scholarship and of life as a whole.

The result of the Weimar critique of Weber's methodology was that the basic Weberian conception was abandoned by all sides. After the late 1920s, we find no one of significance who treats the 'meaningless chaos' argument as a serious metaphysical doctrine, with the exception of Henrich, who discussed it after World War II. But even Henrich, Weber's major philosophical defender in this later period, conceded the existence of insurmountable difficulties in Weber's value doctrine (Henrich, 1952, p. 116). We get an early taste of this abandonment in Jaspers, who made Weber into a 'quest' rather than a doctrine, for he knew that the doctrine, taken as a whole, was indefensible. Fate would have it that the place of the rejected metaphysical doctrine was taken by the ‘rejection of metaphysics’ in Vienna Circle positivism. But this anticipates a much later part of the story.

5 Words into action: Jaspers and Heidegger

The puzzles about Weimar and the obscurity of many of its intellectual and political developments are in part the result of a separation between various levels of discourse and thought. Arthur Rosenberg, both a participant in and a historian of the politics of the period, spoke of simple facts being 'concealed beneath a symbolic covering peculiar at all times to German political life. The masses in Germany are in the main incapable of seeing things as they really are, and are prone to attach symbolic meanings to them' (Rosenberg, 1965, p. 281). The most competent and effective politicians of the period, such as Streseman, had the capacity to distinguish the levels and live at both, and thus to act. Few politicians, and few scholars, had this capacity.

The larger political parties represented sectors of society, so each party stood to gain or lose support within one sector against competition from within the same sector – the Independent Socialists, the Social Democrats, and the Communists traded positions as representatives of the working class, for example – but the parties could rarely gain support in other sectors (Abraham, 1979, p. 432; Pinson, 1966, pp. 602-4). The parliamentary deadlock of the *Kaiserreich* was thus recreated in the republic, and the same solution suggested itself: if some 'higher' ideal or a leader who was the bearer of a higher ideal could gain a broader following than the traditional parties, the nation would attain the unity so visibly lacking. The articulation of ideals of *volkisch* unity and the quest for other higher ideals was a pastime of academics of bourgeois and aristocratic origin, although others engaged in it, too. The immediate political relevance of these discussions was slight, however, in the sense that they had little influence in the large parties. So the quest for new ideals as a basis for social unity developed separately from the practical politics of the day. But each influenced the other.

The last years of the Weimar order, from 1930 to 1933, were marked by a constitutional crisis, a politics of personalities, and a high rate of unemployment. Conrad has a phrase that characterizes the era: 'something inherent in the necessities of successful action . . . carried with it the moral degradation of the idea.' Yet, although the political events of the era served to discredit or destroy one party after another, the basic deadlock was not broken. The consequence of this was that the 'symbolic covering' of which Rosenberg spoke began to separate from the political action to which it had previously been connected, however tenuously. Parliamentary politics appeared ignoble *because* it failed to live up to the standards of the political rhetoric of the day. The authors of the rhetoric were not politically liable for events, as were the parliamentary politicians. So the rhetoric, the 'symbolic covering', was not discredited; it remained for politicians and political writers to conjure with. Hitler, of course, drew from the rhetoric of the period. He was to some extent an example of Keynes's remark that 'madmen in authority, who hear voices in the air, are distilling their frenzy from some academic scribbler of a few years back.' A political situation that had grown prosaic and stagnant came to be construed in the most epochal and dramatic terms. The danger in this was that those who demanded the immediate historical realization of the symbols could come to power.

Jaspers's diagnosis of the time

In this period, we find the most dramatic appeal to Weber's *persona*, in two books by Karl Jaspers: *Max Weber: Politiker, Forscher, Philosoph* (1946), and *Die geistige Situation der Zeit* (1931). The two works are superficially about different matters. One is an interpretation of Weber's life; the other is a diagnosis of the spiritual crisis of the time. But the works are closely linked. Weber's analyses of the historical process are the source of most of Jaspers's insights into the spiritual condition of the time. More tellingly, the solution to the spiritual crisis Jaspers arrived at in the one book was to preserve the possibility of heroism, of the emergence of personalities who have the characteristics which, in the other book, he has imputed to Weber.

Jaspers's interpretation of Weber is curiously unlike the image that Weber later acquired. But it has a great deal of plausibility. Jaspers knew Weber, admired him greatly, and derived his understanding of politics from Weber's, apparently learning little about politics or the philosophy of politics from any other source.[1]

Some of the details of Jaspers's version of Weber are perhaps anachronistic, especially at the beginning of the book, where Weber is defended against misinterpretations of his politics. Jaspers pointed out that Weber resigned from the Pan-German League only when he saw that it supported the particular interests of the Junkers, when these were contrary to the national interest. Weber's basic valuative assumption was the life and power of the German *Volk*; his attacks on the monarchy, Jaspers said, reflect this, and not any commitment to natural right (1946, p. 10). Weber himself generally avoided *volkisch* terminology, so the reference to the *Volk* is misleading. But the rest of what Jaspers said is consistent with Weber's statements. Weber's support of parliamentarism was purely expedient, according to Jaspers, and was expressed only to hinder the *Untergang* (ibid., p. 12). His true political aim was to preserve the nobility of man and the world political importance of the nation, so that our progeny will regard us as gratefully as we today regard the Greeks (ibid., p. 26).

Jaspers was as much a party to the ontological turn as the rest of German philosophy, and his defense of Weber was formulated in such a way that it implicitly conceded the major points of Weber's philosophical critics. The thrust of his defense is that Weber did not simply find an ontological stopping point or suppose that the questions of human existence could be answered by *Wissenschaft*, but purposely left these questions open. This argument reiterates what Jaspers said after Weber's death, that Weber's philosophical utterances and positions must be understood in terms of his whole work and that this work must be understood as embodied philosophy, philosophy as quest. The distinctions Weber made, including the distinction between valuative and factual spheres, must be understood as devices for furthering this quest, and not as a definitive metaphysical stance (Jaspers, 1946, p. 44). This does not revive the tradition Troeltsch represented, but it does neatly avoid such criticisms as Grab's, that Weber illegitimately 'absolutized' spheres of knowledge.

In *Die geistige Situation der Zeit*, Jaspers made a historical and cultural diagnosis that was uncannily Weberian. One wonders to what extent it derived from Weber's own talk rather than from the study of Weber's writings that Jaspers had undertaken for the purpose of writing his book on Weber. Yet Weber does not appear in this text as a source. He appears as an example of the sort of person on which the hope of man depends.

The situation of the time as Jaspers described it is grim indeed. The individual today, he said, is being leveled, and life becomes mere function. Youth, because it represents the most efficient functioning, becomes desirable (Jaspers, 1933, pp. 48-9). Bureaucracy is becoming the dominant form, and the participants in it are slaves to function. The winners in the climb up the bureaucratic ladder snub all those who aim at adequate self-expression, because the winners have already given up all selfhood (ibid., p. 54). The consequence of the dominance of bureaucratic forms is a crisis in leadership, for leadership can occur only when the leader is acquainted with others upon whose independent judgment he can rely and who can join with him in following the inner voice. Without true leadership, without a leader who can seize the helm and steer a course of his own choosing, there is no life for the masses (ibid., p. 57). But the very fact that today power ultimately resides in the hands of the masses threatens the possibility of true leadership.

The reasoning here is Weber's. Jaspers's contribution was to put the cultural anxieties underlying the reasoning into words. The list of anxieties is long. Jaspers objected to the dominance of method and the technical order (1933, pp. 58-75), and to the degradation of life. According to Jaspers, the tendency to the break-up of the home is one instance of this degradation (ibid., p. 61); detective novels are manifestations of the savagery of the crowd (ibid., p. 71); and the interbreeding of the races is another expression of this degradation (ibid., p. 87).

At the root of these evils, Jaspers believed, is the tendency to think in a utilitarian fashion. He denounced the Communists *because* they are utilitarians (1933, p. 77). 'Anglo-Saxon positivism' is described as another evil force (ibid., p. 87), and one finds a strong undercurrent of Anglophobia throughout the text. Here and elsewhere, this Anglophobia is connected up to Jaspers's concern for 'freedom.' In a much later text by Jaspers, Weber's remark about the need for Germany to prevent the world from being divided up between Tsarism and 'Anglo-Saxon convention' is understood to indicate that the Anglo-Saxon nations lack 'freedom' *because* in these nations life is pressed into conventional forms.[2] In *Die geistige Situation der Zeit* this interpretation is also placed on unnamed events in the United States that indicate that mass-society is destroying 'freedom' (ibid., pp. 120-1). To what extent Weber shared in these cultural anxieties is open to question. As Lukács later put it, 'since Jaspers harboured a deadly hate of the masses and a quivering fear of them, democracy and socialism, a romantic glorification of earlier ages emerged hand and glove with his polemics against the "shell." ' (1980, p. 520). Weber did not fear the masses, much less quiver about them. But he certainly shared in a deep anxiety about freedom and a fear of the shell, or the iron cage, as this is usually rendered in English translations of Weber.

The concept of freedom played the central role in Jaspers's historical diagnosis. The diagnosis was designed to answer the central question of world politics, which Jaspers took to be Is war justified by the present situation? Jaspers held that participation in war is justified only when true human existence, by which he meant 'freedom' in the German liberal sense of the freely developing personality, is at stake (1933, pp. 111, 207). He concluded that it is justified, that indeed the present situation is the critical period in history with respect to freedom. Perhaps, he said,

> freedom has only existed for a real but passing moment between two immeasurably long periods of sleep, of which the first period was that of the life of nature, and the second that of the life of technique. If so, human existence must die out, must come to an end in a more radical sense than ever before (ibid., p. 241).

These were not the counsels of resignation, for Jaspers believed that the age of titanic bureaucracy which now threatens us could be fought, and freedom preserved. To do so we must first prevent rule by the bureaucrats. This, as Weber insisted as well, requires a particular kind of leadership, unlike the kind found in Weimar politics. Accordingly, Jaspers advised his readers to distrust every politician of the existing order (ibid., pp. 82, 86): these leaders are at best 'gifted functionaries,' who compromise and vacillate in the face of a mass. The mass, however, does not know what it really wants. It is composed of people who are hedonistic, immoral, and devoted to little more than insubordination and getting along with their peers (ibid., p. 119).

Jaspers longed for leaders of the more heroic variety. What the mass really needs, Jaspers asserted, are strong leaders, leaders who are not cowards, leaders who can come to a decision, and who are not willing to use force only when the big battalions are on their side (1933, p. 83). Jaspers was not at all squeamish about the leader's use of authoritarian power for the ends he has 'decided' upon. We must recognize the inadequacy of the rational life order to answer the questions of human existence, he said (ibid., p. 90), and we must recognize the need for decision. According to Jaspers's analysis of power, the power to decide is the power of being, a power that is politically incorporated in the state. Every order exists only through power; the facts of power are the 'obscure foundation of community life' (ibid., p. 98). Our social existence persists in time through the molding influence of power. This and the perpetual struggle of the state against other states are the facts of political life.

Other of Weber's friends took this to be Weber's primary lesson. Michels wrote that in the last years of his life Weber's studies brought him to the conclusion that 'the true motors of the history of peoples could be none other than the factors of power and violence.' Michels understood this insight to be the direct antithesis of Förster's historical-ethical views (Michels, 1934, p. xxv). Jaspers drew a similar conclusion: people who reject the struggle for power out of religious ethical convictions are simply irresponsible (1933, p. 100).

Hitler himself, in speeches soon after Jaspers wrote, embraced the principle of the freely developing personality.[3] Yet Jaspers was critical of the Nazis, though none too explicitly. In a later foreword he explained that he knew little about Nazism in 1930, when the book was written, though he did know something about Fascism.[4] It was not Hitler but Weber who was Jaspers's model of leadership. For Jaspers, the leader must possess charisma; he must make the masses will as he does. He must also have expert knowledge about what is possible in the complex modern world situation and must act on his own strong inner sense (Jaspers, 1933, pp. 102, 113-14). The Nazis did not respect this sort of restraint. Yet some similar ideas were found in Nazi propaganda. As Linke quoted one Nazi, 'the expert will decide, the man who has the confidence of the leader, not the stupidity of the masses or the selfishness of the parties' (1935, pp. 357-8). But there is a further criterion that Jaspers also stressed: a true leader must come from a cultural elite, a criterion which, of course, was fulfilled by Weber. But Jaspers had already told us that it is the fate of people like Weber to be ignored, so he had every reason for the pessimistic belief that things can no longer be saved, even by a new Weber.

Jaspers was anxious about the continuation of elite culture and about the cultural situation in general. Today anything goes: the past is forgotten, and novelty and sensation have taken over – the New Thought, the New Economics, the New Objectivity, and so on, take the place of culture (Jaspers, 1933, pp. 133-4). He heartily endorsed the idea that there was a crisis in science (ibid., pp. 152-8). The cause of this crisis, he believed, is to be found in the mass-life, which has produced a sort of plebeianism in science, where everyone regards himself as able to contribute. But the aims of this degraded science are merely technical, in contrast to true science, which seeks not mere technical adequacy but knowledge. Moreover, he insisted, true science is an aristocratic affair (ibid., p. 155). Plebeianization produces a crisis of purpose in the individual scientist analogous to the crisis in the mass-life. Faith in such a merely technical science can only be a superstition, which not surprisingly then generates an antiscientific superstition (ibid., p. 159).

Weber, Jaspers argued, was not guilty of the error of producing an intellectualist faith. His relativistic sociology purposely leaves man untouched (Jaspers, 1933, p. 176). He realized that sociology, psychology, and anthropology could not answer the decisive questions. By showing the limits of objective knowledge in the task of the apprehension of being, Weber's inquiries showed the falsity of absolute claims, and in this sense he was a liberator of man. Yet devotion to a new Weber cannot solve the crisis of science, for in science the true hero will decline the prophet's mantle. Only in politics, where demogoguery may be essential, would a new Weber seek followers (ibid., p. 202).

The advice Jaspers left his readers with is strongly reminiscent of Weber's advice in 'Politik als Beruf' and 'Wissenschaft als Beruf.' Jaspers advised them to be resolute, like those soldiers in the last war who fought to the bitter end. One's only option today, he said, is to make a fresh start in conjunction with others (1933, p. 144; cf. Weber, 1946, p. 128). One cannot go back to old forms of thought (and especially not to religion) (Jaspers, 1933, p. 230).[5] But there were some new emphases in his advice. The struggle for leadership of the mass now turns, as it turned for Michels, into a struggle against the mass. For Jaspers, the mass and its materialism and demand for equality and majority decision-making is indicative of the destruction of the nobility, and must be fought. The numbers of the truly noble today are small, and this means that the decisive historical moment for human nobility has arrived. Past revolts could succeed without ruining man. But if the great leveling process and the revolt of the masses succeeds, man will be destroyed (ibid., p. 222).

The darkening

Jaspers and Heidegger agreed on one of the most powerful ideas of the era, the idea that an apocalyptic moment had arrived. The consequences of this belief were dramatic enough to need no special comment. But if we focus only on its consequences we are likely to miss the truth it contains. The world into which Jaspers was born, the world of the prewar elite, of private schools in which one's classmates would likely become men of significance, and of an easy and unaffected common high culture – this world was dying. Wittgenstein, in notes for a foreword dating from 1930, has captured the sense of loss.

This book is written for those who are in sympathy with the

> spirit in which it is written. This is not, I believe, the spirit of the main current of European and American civilization. The spirit of this civilization makes itself manifest in the industry, architecture and music of our time, in its fascism and socialism, and it is alien and uncongenial to the author. . . . I realize . . . that the disappearance of a culture does not signify the disappearance of human value, but simply of certain means of expressing this value, yet the fact remains that I have no sympathy for the current of European civilization and do not understand its goals, if it has any (1980, p. 6e).

The loss cannot be simply dismissed as rhetorical excess. But the idea that this loss could be made good through politics, the idea that claimed Heidegger, as we shall see shortly, had fatal consequences.

One must also notice in Jaspers a more subtle kind of substitution of rhetoric and symbol manipulation for substantive political discourse. In reading Jaspers we must remember that in the decade before he wrote Germany went through several crises: a breakdown of constitutional rule; a series of political assassinations – *Vehm* murders – smiled upon by members of the courts, who dispensed 'justice' according to their political sympathy for the enemies of the republic; and wholesale violation of international agreements on disarmament. Indifference to such unheroic, procedural 'values' in the face of 'ultimate values' is a feature of the Weberian way of talking about politics and morals. This had implications for the political style of the Weberians in Weimar. If in retrospect we appreciate the coolness and toughness of the Weberian rhetoric, we must also recognize the irrelevance of this coolness and toughness to the times – as well as its dangerousness. Salz made a curious favorable reference to the 'patriotic' movement then developing in Italy in his anti-Kahler polemic (1921, p. 63). As we have noticed, Jaspers invoked the memory of the 'bitter-enders' and insisted that the great leader acts even when the big battalions are not on his side. In retrospect these must be read as a celebration of the irrational. They prefigure precisely the step that Heidegger was to take. Yet the moral reflection of Weber's critics also failed, in the sense that it did not result in a moral consensus that could resist Hitlerism. This is, of course, an unfair standard, for it was not the object of these thinkers to 'produce' a moral consensus to defeat an unforeseen evil. But their cultural reforms failed by their own standards. Their ideas failed in their aim of underwriting a new unity. In some of the cases where Weber's opponents were influential – as was the fate of Stefan George and Gundolf – their usable ideas were appropriated by the Nazis.

Again, one's assessment of these failures involves 'doubling back.' For the Weberian, the failure of the new *Wissenschaft* and its variants to attain a moral consensus was rooted not merely in the circumstances of the time but in the philosophically mistaken belief in the existence of an 'eternal' or final order of values of some sort. If the Weberian position on the nature cf values and the situation of the time is true, the critics must be judged as well-meaning but confused ideologues who contributed nothing to events other than confusion itself. If a philosophical position similar to that of the critics is true, the Weberians must be judged as celebrants of irrationalism in morals and politics and heralds of the irrationalism that was to come.

Of the intellectuals implicated in the events, center stage was held by Heidegger, who was acknowledged in Germany as the greatest philosopher of the time. He had secured this distinction in a famous debate with Ernst Cassirer, in which Cassirer was decisively defeated (Lipton, 1978, pp. 156-8).[6] Thus, any action on his part in support of the new order would serve to legitimate it, and, indeed, his conduct was at first unambiguously designed to serve the particular tasks of legitimation the regime faced. As Löwith pointed out, this occurred at a crucial time for the regime, and Heidegger's decision to support the regime 'resounded everywhere' (1946, p. 350). While Heidegger was rector at Freiburg, his students marched in closed ranks to vote in Hitler's plebiscite, after having heard a rousing speech by Heidegger. After his first year as rector, his conduct became more ambiguous: he resigned the rectorate, and some students profess to having found implicit criticism of the regime in his lectures. Yet Heidegger himself did little to aid attempts at his exculpation, and in later statements and editions of his work he failed to completely recant his earlier views. Moreover, his later writings reflect many of the same political impulses as his earlier pro-Nazi pronouncements.

Heidegger was the most significant thinker to deal with the sort of metaphysical problems that the Weimar debate over Weber had rested on. Thus, a positive assessment of the validity of Weber's views implies some assessment of Heidegger's philosophy: where Heidegger and Weber shared conclusions, there is a question of the connection between these conclusions and the events. But this may amount to a rather negligible connection, and, as we shall see, there is considerable dispute as to whether there was any great relevance of Heidegger's philosophy for his political actions. At one extreme is Leo Strauss's remark that Heidegger was 'intellectually the counterpart to what Hitler was politically' (1978, p. 2).

At the other is the view that Heidegger's philosophy has no particular relation to his politics, and that his political errors were understandable as the folly of a politically uneducated person.

Heidegger's political ideas were far from unique among German intellectuals, and in a sense Heidegger's experience and conduct is representative of this class and of the effect of these ideas. So Heidegger is relevant as an example of the development of political attitudes that were one condition for Hitler's success. These attitudes had earlier origins, in the long decline of German liberalism, and are essential to an understanding of the view of the world situation that was shared both by many of those who stayed in Germany and many of those who left after 1933. Weber too shared some of these views.

The political remarks found in Heidegger's 1935 lectures, published as *An Introduction to Metaphysics* (1959), are not much more than allusions to these widely held ideas. The same fears we encountered in Weimar, of leveling, the destruction of human freedom, technology, and of the intellectual consequences of academic specialization, are Heidegger's fears. The image of Germany as the little but spiritually great nation between the huge but culturally void colossi of Britain and Russia is also Heidegger's image, though Heidegger updated this notion to identify America and Russia as the barbarian mass-societies. The term 'technology,' which is Heidegger's summary concept of the present intellectually dominating force, and which corresponds roughly to Weber's 'disenchantment of the world,'[7] is closely connected to Heidegger's political and historical conception of America and Russia. They are, he said, 'metaphysically the same, namely in regard to their world character and their relation to the spirit,' and this sameness consists in the fact that the demonic influence of technology, meaning broadly a whole way of relating to the world and ordering society, is at its farthest advance in these societies (ibid., p. 45).

For Heidegger, the state of science, its specialization and concern with solving well-packaged problems, is, as it was for Weber, a historical necessity. But for Heidegger, it is an expression of the 'darkening of the world,' which in turn is an expression of our concern with 'beings' rather than with our true calling to be shepherds and watchers of 'Being'. In contrast to Weber, Heidegger supposed, as had others in Weimar, that a university reform that served to combat the effects of specialization, the primary academic manifestation of a concern with 'beings,' was both practically possible and desirable. His motivations for accepting the rectorate at Freiburg were connected with this. He sought to bring the intellectual life of the university into closer relation to the spiritual life of the nation, and, within the university, to reorder the relations between the disciplines in accordance with their true nature, a task in which, as it turned out, the Nazis had no interest (cf. Moehling, 1977, 1972; Heidegger, 1959, pp. 48-9).

Heidegger's works after World War II were extremely pessimistic. In these works liberalism was held to be a last foolish gasp before the total negativity of Marxism engulfs us. But Heidegger once considered National Socialism to be a protest against this darkening, and he wrote of the world situation in a way that suggested that it was Germany's destiny (and responsibility, as the only truly philosophic modern nation) to make this protest (Moehling, 1972).[8] In the metaphysics lectures of 1935, he described 'the inner truth and greatness of' National Socialism in the framework of these ideas about the darkening. In a parenthetical comment that was perhaps inserted later, he added that the inner greatness of National Socialism is bound up with 'the encounter between global technology and modern man' (Heidegger, 1959, p. 199).

'Fate' and the end of philosophy

The relation between these notions and the Weberian world view is complex. Weber did not see any point to a protest against the fate of the times, although he and Jaspers did see the realm of the great leader as a realm in which freedom could perhaps be preserved. 'Freedom' understood in this way is not very different from the 'freedom of the personality' one can seek through Nazism – understood as the pursuit of the absolute value of personality, which we have already encountered in Hitler's thought. Heidegger traveled along the path of intellectual development marked by Weber and Jaspers, and beyond. Jaspers, it may be noted, did not draw any sharp line between his ideas and Heidegger's, though he thought Heidegger's embrace of Nazism was politically naive. However, Heidegger drew a sharp line between himself and the Heidelberg Liberals associated with Weber. In a letter in 1934, Heidegger denounced another academic to his Nazi sponsors for belonging to 'the liberal-democratic circle of Heidelberg intellectuals around Max Weber' (quoted in Jaspers, 1978, pp. 14-15).

At a more fundamental philosophical level, there is another kinship between Weber and Heidegger. Heidegger publically attacked 'intellectualism,' which Weber said he 'hated as the worst devil,' and which Jaspers also denounced. Heidegger identified intellectualism as an 'outgrowth of an already prepared tradition which is bound to traditional western metaphysics' (quoted and translated in Bronner, 1977, p. 170; cf. Heidegger, 1959, p. 122), and his attack on this kind of metaphysics was philosophically more successful than Weber's. Stated briefly, Heidegger took it to be his task to, as present terminology would have it, 'deconstruct' the 'metaphysical' tradition: to show the metaphysical quest for an absolute ground to be a false quest, or at least a falsely absolutized quest. '*Physis*, *Logos*, *Hen*, *Idea*, *Energia*, Substantiality, Objectivity, the Will, the Will to Power, the Will to Will,' as Heidegger pointed out, all have been taken as the 'ground of Being,' with the idea that an ontological grasp of this ground legitimizes science or philosophy (Heidegger, 1957, p. 64). Considering this series of 'grounds' shows us that there is something wrong with the quest for the ground of being itself, for it is a quest that always fails. Yet we can think of the quest in another way. Construed phenomenologically, each new 'ground' is nothing more than a revelation of 'Being' out of concealment. We need not think that there is any end-point to this process. But when we cease treating the quest as a quest for the one ground of being, we move from the form of thought characteristic of the Western philosophical tradition, which always seeks an absolute ground, to what Heidegger called the 'other thinking.' Scheler's last work prefigured, albeit obscurely, this development of Heidegger's thought.

Heidegger himself directly applied his antimetaphysical critique to the framework that his immediate predecessors worked within, especially to the philosophies concerned with the contrast between the Is and the Ought and the idea of 'value,' and with the establishment of new values. He traced the origin of this usage of 'value' to Kant. In the nineteenth century, the empirical world of the sciences came to take in the historical and economic sciences, which directly endangered the role the Ought had for Kant. As a result, he suggested, the subsequent history of philosophy has been dominated by this task: Ought must establish some self-subsistent foundation of its own. Nietzsche's philosophic failure, Heidegger argued, is a result of 'his entanglement in the thicket of the idea of values, his failure to understand its questionable origin.' The problems Heidegger saw are not mere philosophic problems, but problems with our whole manner of talking about 'value.' The distinctions that inhere in this philosophical framework 'permeate all knowledge, action, and discourse even when they are not specifically mentioned or not in these words' (Heidegger, 1959, pp. 199, 200). Yet Heidegger did not offer a way through this thicket to 'the true center of philosophy.' He said only that

> Even if a future philosopher should reach this center – we of the present day can only work toward it – he will not escape entanglement, but it will be a different entanglement. No one can jump over his own shadow (ibid., p. 199).

In dealing with Heidegger's views on moral matters, we are faced with a problem we were faced with in understanding Weber. The structure of his philosophic conception precludes any derivation of obligations or values, though there are some substantive – and negative – implications. With Heidegger, as with Weber, a distinctive conception of the historical situation underlay his understanding of the nature of present choices. Fate and destiny became the crucial rhetorical categories in place of the ordinary moral categories. In both cases, it was believed that these ordinary moral categories had reached the moment when their philosophical insubstantiality had been made historically manifest. But in both cases no course of action was directly ordained by this realization. Weber attempted to define the range of possible choices for his hearers. Similarly, Heidegger's own actions provided the practical model his hearers wanted. He did not, at least at the early part of his association with the Nazis, disabuse his hearers of the lessons they drew from the example of his conduct. The ambiguities in his speeches were perhaps studied. As Löwith observed of Heidegger's rectoral speech, 'the listener hesitates whether he ought to dig into the Presocratics or join the ranks of the S.A.' (1946, p. 351).[9]

If one conceives of morality as something that demands an extramoral or supramoral foundation, i.e., in the fashion of traditional Western metaphysics, one will naturally suspect that the views of a Heidegger or a Weber also have a foundation beyond morality, a metaphysical foundation, but one that is concealed by the design of the philosophy. Thus construed, Weber's and Heidegger's rejection of metaphysics conceals an acceptance of a historical metaphysic of fate (cf. Strauss, 1953, pp. 26-8, 1972a). The substitution of one metaphysic for another is not without effect. As a historical matter, it is likely that views like Heidegger's and Weber's acted as a solvent of moral conceptions that involved the idea of a 'ground' of morality and were, to use Heidegger's phrase, 'outgrowths of traditional western metaphysics.' The new 'historical' metaphysic provides a 'ground' for a new 'morality' – specifically, the morality that appears to meet the demands of destiny. In this sense, Heidegger's was a Nazi philosophy. The difficulty faced by any such interpretation is that Heidegger's own arguments apply to, and refute, any historical metaphysic of this kind. So to accept the interpretation one must accept a radical inconsistency in Heidegger.

Much of Heidegger's later writing is strongly reminiscent of the themes of 'Wissenschaft als Beruf.' In *The Question Concerning Technology* (1977), he denounced science as a way to happiness. In his letter on Humanism, he denounced the naive intellectualist faith in humanity. This suggests a parallel interpretation to Weber. Both believed themselves to be speaking to the community of the disillusioned. But Heidegger's community contained those who were disillusioned with Weber's philosophy as well.

Heidegger had enormous contempt for 'Nazi philosophy,' and this raises a question about the place and character of Nazi philosophy. Because there were indeed people who were generally regarded as 'Nazi philosophers,' and because they did formulate rejections of large portions of the received philosophical tradition, one might suppose that many of the questions about 'responsibility' for the events of 1933 that inevitably lurk behind this dispute could be directly settled by going to Nazi philosophy and seeing how it accorded with previous philosophy. But the positive positions of the 'Nazi philosophers' were eclectic combinations of elements drawn from the Weimar scene, and not exclusively, or even largely, from any particular camp. Nor did the group known as Nazi philosophers represent the consensus of the philosophers and intellectuals associated with Nazism.[10] Heidegger's views were far from the views of the Nazi circle and his eminence was such that he felt no compunctions about publicly attacking them. Spann and Klages, who were regarded by some as sympathizers of the regime, also held views that were clearly distinct from 'Nazi philosophy' (Grégoire, 1955, p. 684). So 'Nazi philosophy' was not the sort of thing that could be displayed as the unitary successor of unitary preceding views. All one can appropriately ask, in drawing connections, is for indications of how the atmosphere in which Nazism became possible – the atmosphere of popular nihilism of which many writers speak – was formed (Butler, 1942, p. 198; Löwith, 1964; Lukács, 1962, p. 536). Kuhn put this point nicely when he stated that while one cannot blame the existentialists and historicists for the Nazis, they did prepare people to accept this new secular revelation (1943, pp. 21-2). For Heidegger this is especially apt. As Peter Gay has observed, Heidegger gave no one reasons not to be a Nazi, but good reasons for being one (1968, p. 83).

6 Nazism, fascism, and the later dispute

However transient the specific philosophical disputes of the time may come to seem in the broader sweep of the history of philosophy – and indeed today it is difficult to see them as much besides late or postneo-Kantian factionalism – at that time they were insurmountable. Because the ethics and philosophy of the time sought to speak directly to the problems of life, the Babel they created had unusually broad effects. Talk about the relativism of the age was a commonplace among literate persons, sufficiently so that Nazi propaganda could refer to it with the expectation that the reference would be understood. Not a few of the intellectuals who experienced the Weimar period, as we shall see, drew the conclusion that the philosophical confusion in general, and relativist and nihilist arguments in particular, were part of the cause of the moral and political confusion. Indeed, it is difficult to read the philosophy of the era without sensing a certain ineluctability in the succession of the 'revolution of nihilism' to the '*Krise der Wissenschaft*.'

We have seen that Weber's views were very early blamed for such consequences. This had been a theme of Kahler's. When the Nazis came to power, the point was made again, by persons opposed to Weber's views and the views of persons associated with him. Aurel Kolnai, in *The War against the West*, wrote, perhaps unfairly, that

> Michels, like many other exponents of 'value-free' sociological research, stout believers in the inevitable necessity of inequality and domination 'under whatever guise,' is as partial to fascism as he is fond of assuming an air of statistical and scholarly impartiality (1938, p. 386).

Other writers had much earlier spoken of Weber as a nihilist. Emil

Lederer, an editor of the *Archiv*, described him this way in 1925 (noted by Speier in Lederer, 1979, p. 289). So when books like Hermann Rauschning's *Revolution of Nihilism* (1939) came out, the making of connections between Nazi ideas and earlier 'nihilists' was inevitable.

The problem of the intellectual origins and associations of Nazism and Fascism stemmed largely from claims and features of the movements themselves. Both were self-described revolutions of the spirit – social movements with philosophical claims. These claims were not always clear, though it is clear that Weber and the value-free social scientists were not their intellectual sources, in any direct sense. But the problem of the intellectual origins of Nazism and Fascism needs to be included in the story of the development of the dispute over Weber's doctrine of values, not because of any direct line of development or any similar historical thesis, but simply because the problem affected the development of the dispute. There were general and diffuse 'connections' between both Weberian and anti-Weberian ideas and various ideas in the camps of the dictators. This created a problem that later thinkers had to face in using and evaluating the earlier ideas. The association with Nazism and Fascism proved to be a historical sieve through which several important ideas did not pass. It is to be expected, then, that the character of the ideas resurrected after the war would be different from the full constellation of ideas in Weimar, and this is what occurred. When the dispute reemerged after the war, each side had dropped certain distinctive ideas but had acquired others that were not implicated in the political events.

Michels and the Fascists

The only figure whose work had developed in close relation to Weber's who had a prominent role in the political events was Robert Michels. In the early part of his career, Michels had striven to attain in his own work the kind of separation between values and scientific inquiry that Weber had recommended. Weber himself had a hand in this, having written to his younger friend letters that were both critical and encouraging (Röhrich, 1972, p. 52). The personal relationship between the two did not survive World War I. Michels, who settled in Italy when his career was blocked in Germany, found himself and Weber on opposed sides in the war. When Michels applied the doctrine of national honor on the Italian side and sought, in the Swiss press, to give an account of the Italian position in terms of Weber's notions of 'the honor of power' and power politics, Weber was irritated. He wrote to Michels, advised him that it was better to be silent in some circumstances, and then attacked the 'barbaric tastelessness' of Italian art. With this their friendship ended, at least, as Michels said in his memorial address on Weber, 'in its most valuable personal form' (quoted in ibid., p. 119).

Michels's views were never far from the lessons of Weber's political thought. Moreover, Michels was an admirer of Weber as a 'great personality,' much as Jaspers was. There is a curious text in which Michels presents short biographies of a series of personalities including Weber, Sorel, and others, in a way that is intended to show how these personalities are to be admired (Michels, 1927). The decisive contribution of Weber to Michels's thought, however, was the concept of the charismatic leader – the *capo carismatico*, as Michels called him. Michels's path to this concept was tortuous, however. At the beginning of his career he was a Socialist. But his disenchantment with the party leadership and the party bureaucracy led him first to a critique of this leadership and then to a general critique of party organization. This was the famous Iron Law of Oligarchy, the doctrine of the inevitability of inequality and domination to which Kolnai's comment, quoted earlier, refers. In Italy, these doctrines were an explicit part of political practice. The liberal Mosca argued that since rule by an elite was inevitable, the important political question was the *quality* of the elite. Pareto, 'the Marx of Fascism,' extended this argument against the liberal bourgeois elite to which Mosca himself belonged by claiming that this elite was in decline, especially in France and Italy. The positive implications of this argument were clear – a new elite must rise, or the nation will decline.

The Fascists claimed to be this new elite, and Pareto and Michels went along with the claim: Pareto called the rise of Fascism 'a splendid confirmation of the predictions of my sociology' (quoted in Beetham, 1977, p. 165). Weber agreed with the view that rule by the few was inevitable, and his idea of leadership involved the notion of a pool of potential leaders, a pool which he thought of as having common social characteristics. Jaspers, one may recall, emphasized precisely this point in his *Die geistige Situation der Zeit*, where he wrote of the need for a cultured class of potential leaders and used this notion in his implied criticism of the Nazis. Weber was less clear than this about the social characteristics of the pool of potential leaders. His remarks on the subject are largely negative: the German bourgeoisie, the workers, and the bureaucrats all, he believed, had failings that made them incapable of political leadership. In his final writings, Weber emphasized the need for sufficient leisure and means for politics, and this suggests, as Struve has more recently argued, that Weber never emancipated himself from the idea that the leaders should come from 'the bourgeoisie and from *grand seigneurs* among the nobility' (Struve, 1973, p. 136). This was very far from the Fascist idea of a self-proclaimed elite.

The distinctive feature of Michels's later writings is the combination of the Paretian idea of the circulation of elites with the idea of the charismatic leader who rises from the masses. The 'Duce,' Mussolini, according to Michels, was '*il capo carismatico*' (Röhrich, 1972, p. 157). But Weber's idea of the leader as a kind of prophet who chooses his own values was not Michels's idea. Michels observed 'that when Mussolini speaks, he translates in a naked and brilliant form the aims of the multitude. The multitude itself frantically acclaims, answering from the profundity of its own moral beliefs, or, even more profound, of its own subconscious' (Michels, 1949, p. 126). Elsewhere he stressed the group psychology of these emotions. 'The *Führer* is assisted by a *Gefolgschaft* of young enthusiastic men who contribute to decisions by the atmosphere of their very existence rather than by explicit manifestations of their will – by *Stimmung* (mood) rather than by *Stimme* (vote)' (quoted in Kolnai, 1938, p. 150). The emphasis here is different from Weber's; it does not portray the relation between leader and follower purely decisionistically. The leader, for Michels, articulates a preexisting moral foundation, mood, or psychological need.

The difference may be interpreted in various ways. Certainly Michels's way of describing Mussolini's appeal is truer to the psychology of the follower's side of the leader-follower relationship in general. But one also suspects that the Italian moral tradition circumscribed the realm of politics and therefore the possibilities of political leadership in a way the German tradition did not (cf. Mitzman, 1973, p. 337). When Michels praised the Italian moral sense, he was making an implied contrast to the German moral tradition. The resistance of Italian officialdom to the wartime demands to round up Italian Jewry perhaps reflects this difference: in the Italian tradition the sphere of politics was not morally autonomous, but was subordinate to everyday notions of civility and decency. One might say that the 'abstractions' of the Catholic natural law tradition, such as the idea of common humanity, took on tangible form in this bureaucratic resistance.

Michels was not a philosopher, however, and nowhere did he give a philosophical articulation of these matters. What is missing most conspicuously in Michels's writings is an articulation of the basis of his value-free sociology. The idea of the irreconcilable clash of *Weltanschauungen* and of the present as an intellectual crisis, so prominent both in Weber's work and in the work of his Weimar followers, did not figure in Michels, though one might have expected it to, in view of Mussolini's own self-professed relativism and admiration for German philosophical relativism. Weber's discussion of the Fatherland as an ultimate value was couched in terms of commitment; when Michels chose Italy as a new *patria*, he did not describe this choice in the terminology of 'ultimate value decisions,' and indeed did not speak of it in a philosophically self-conscious way at all (Mitzman, 1973, p. 337). Similarly, Weber attempted to impress Michels with the necessity for separating fact and value in Michels's own scholarly work, which he described as a 'vivisection' (Röhrich, 1972, p. 52). The doctrinal basis of Weber's position, which was apparently not shared with or of interest to Michels, did not figure in the discussion. Roth, in describing the later history of the doctrine, spoke of 'Science as a Vocation' serving as 'the vade mecum of many a sociologist' (Roth, 1971b, p. 36), a phrase that suggests a separation between the philosophical argument on values and scientific value-neutrality as a personal scholarly ideal or morality. Weber's discussions with Michels suggest that this separation was there from the start.

Another reason for Michels's neglect of the problem of value choice is to be found in the structure of elite theory itself. If one emphasizes the 'inevitability of elite rule' and regards any elite as the bearer of a political tradition, the only significant 'this-worldly' political question comes down to the question of supporting or supplanting this elite. The room for 'decision' is correspondingly reduced. The *capo carismatico* must not only have a following but must have a whole new elite behind him, ready to rule. His decisions are not the absolute ones envisioned by the Nazi *Führerprinzip*, because the elite constitutes the true basis of his rule, as for all rule. To violate his bond with the elite is simply to invite being overthrown. Indeed, this was precisely the historical lesson of elite theory – political leadership by itself is nothing, for history is the rise and fall of elites as a whole. The kind of doctrine of the nature of morality needed to underpin such theories need not be especially elaborate. Since elite theory deals in 'inevitabilities,' it obviates moral questions, for 'ought' implies 'can.'

'Inevitability' or 'impossibility' arguments are a path from science to action when they are construed positively, as Michels, following Pareto and Mosca, construed elite theory. Weber would not have done this, for he would have regarded the determination of a 'good elite' as a valuative decision. But Weber used a similar argument, the idea of the rule of the few, negatively, against 'true socialism' and 'true democracy,' as did Michels. Inevitability arguments of one sort or another figure more heavily in the work of Weber's later followers, who emphasize his 'realism' and deemphasize his doctrine of what Salz called 'the irrational roots of the act.'

Weber and Michels differed revealingly in their attitude toward parliament. Michels rejected parliamentarism, which he saw as a weak form, but saw with clarity that a charismatic leader would not allow himself to be fettered by mere parliaments.

> It is useless, anti-historical and anti-scientific to hope that dictators, having happily initiated their political work, will abdicate at the height of their power, since abdication is an act of weakness. . . . The charismatic leader does not abdicate, not even when the water reaches to his throat. Precisely in his readiness to die lies one element of his force and his triumph (quoted in Beetham, 1977, p. 176).

Weber did not discuss possible conflicts between the principle of charisma and the idea of parliamentary constitutional forms. He professed no loyalty to constitutionalism *per se*, and his view of parliament as a means of producing leaders fits well with Weimar cynicism about the parliamentary and presidential structure. Delbrück and Meinecke, whose views on politics were not far removed from Weber's, spoke of the system that used a strong president to control parliament as '*Ersatzkaisertums*' (Töpner, 1970, p. 135). Michels saw that an *Ersatzkaiser* would not feel, as Hindenburg felt in the 1930s, any loyalty to the arrangements that prevented him from becoming a real Caesar or acting like the Kaiser had in the old system. It may be said that popular loyalty to a *politeia* (a 'constitution,' in the broader sense) as a value may be regarded as a *de facto* precondition for the preservation of the sort of arrangement Weber envisioned as 'plebiscitarian leader democracy' against the charismatic power of the leader. Weber's way of thinking about values as ultimate choices fit this kind of loyalty poorly.

Steding and the Nazis

Michels was not the only follower of the dictators who was an expert on Weber. In Hitler's camp there was a young historian who had written a dissertation on Weber, Christoph Steding. Steding was a peculiar figure in many respects, so his writings support few conclusions about the problem of continuity. He was always spoken of as the 'alone' or the 'individual' and was never well assimilated into the Nazi intellectual effort (Heiber, 1966, p. 505). He was a student of the liberal historian Wilhelm Mommsen, and had been supported by a Rockefeller foundation grant before becoming a protegé of the Nazi historian Walter Frank and a member of his *Reichsinstitut für Geschichte* (ibid., pp. 501-6).[1]

Steding's work on Weber, published in 1932, contains a number of suggestive ideas. He begins with a discussion of liberalism, in which he makes the point that 'we are all the sons and heirs of liberalism.' As an antiliberal himself, Steding nevertheless polemicized against the widespread 'blind hate against everything that is liberalism' (quoted in Heiber, 1966, p. 503). As part of a reconciliation with the liberal past, he argued, we must reflect on men like Weber. So Steding saw Weber as a champion of liberalism and saw recent German history, including the *Kaiserreich*, as liberal.

Weber's whole existence, Steding suggested, was devoted to self-emancipation (Steding, 1932, p. 16), and his underlying scientific concern was to bring about the consciousness of the modern rational *Fachmann*. Weber's scientific tasks and his own task of self-emancipation were not, according to Steding, actually distinct, and as a consequence his work did what science allegedly could not do – gave an interpretation of the meaning of the contemporary world. Weber's sociology, he argued, amounted to seeing the historical world through a temperament, or a kind of historical poetry or fiction – a remark perhaps meant to recall Gundolf, who explicitly used historical writing as a means of capturing the heroic in the past (ibid., pp. 29-30). In the English revolution, the revolutionaries referred to the Book of Samuel and the prophets – and not the New Testament or the Book of Kings. Weber, similarly, found in the prophets a model for contemporary political leadership. Indeed, as Steding pointed out, some of the sentences in the *Sociology of Religion* appear virtually unchanged in the political writings (ibid., p. 32). Here politics, science, and self-emancipation come together, for Weber himself identified with this type of leader. When he wrote of the prophets 'scientifically' he projected his own perspectives into the minds of the prophets. And this, as Steding noted, is warranted by Weber's methodological writings, which insisted that a *subjective* starting point is the inescapable condition of *objective* historical science (ibid., p. 32).

The methodological critique of Weber is familiar to Steding, who cited some of it; but it is not his main concern. The main thrust of the book is to distinguish the tradition that Weber embodied in his politics, his science, and his personality from another German tradition. The contrast here is crucial to understanding one strand of divergence between Weber and the viewpoint represented by the movement of reaction against modernity that broadly included Spann, Heidegger, and Steding, as well as many other corporatist thinkers. If one keeps Jaspers in mind, the character of the divergences between the two strains of thought can be kept clear. Where Jaspers feared mass-society and supposed that the only hope for the preservation of human dignity or nobility lay in the possibility of preserving a class of persons with the moral capacity for great political action and leadership, the tradition critical of the city and the bourgeoisie saw the difficulties as the consequence of the bourgeois, urban, impersonal character of society. There is a deep theoretical basis to the divergence between these traditions, which may best be seen in terms of Michael Oakeshott's argument that modern European political thought is based on two distinct medieval ideas, *societas* and *universitas*. They represent two modes of human association, each of which came to represent an exclusive conception of the character of the state (Oakeshott, 1974, pp. 199-200). The unsettled dispute between these interpretations, Oakeshott has suggested, reflects the equivocal character of the state itself. The idea of *societas*, or 'partnership,' fits more closely to Weber's individualistic view of the state and its basis. The idea of *universitas*, or 'corporation,' fits the German alternative more closely.

The philosophical articulation of a distinct political theory of the state was the concern neither of the Weberians nor of this other strand of thought. Such a theory would inevitably demand a basis outside of itself, as for example in a theory of human nature; and neither side, in the historicist aftermath of Hegelianism, could see its way clear to an explicit appeal to such a basis. Besides, they did not construe the issues as simply 'political.' To appeal to an intellectual basis outside of political thought supposes that an untroubled basis for agreement exists outside of political thought. And this no one supposed: everything about the culture, they thought, was in dispute. So when Steding wrote, he dealt with the questions in the broadest *historical* sense, distinguishing the cultural, regional, and ethnic traditions of which Weber was bearer and embodiment from its contraries.

In this perspective, Weber was a Puritan bourgeois. He opposed the rural and traditional. 'Rationalization' was specifically contrasted to the traditionalism of the farmer. Modern science, technology, and capitalism, according to Weber, are ultimately rooted in the demystification of the world advanced by the prophets. Weber's own struggle against bureaucracy, Steding suggested, was akin to Amos's struggle against kingly bureaucracy. And this provides us with the crucial clue to understanding Weber's own struggle as a person: he saw himself as part of this historical movement, indeed as one of its prophets. For him, as Steding put it, rationalism was an existential position (1932, pp. 42-3).

Bureaucracy and prophecy as well as prophecy and tradition have historically been opposed. When the bureaucracy is strong, as was the Egyptian bureaucratic priesthood, prophecy is stifled. Not coincidentally, the Egyptian state represented the epitome of unfreedom for Weber. In a broader sense, all social forms with the character of *universitas* – bureaucratic or 'traditional' forms – repelled Weber. Weber had, Steding pointed out, a great interest in the social types that were modern parallels to the prophets. His proposed study of newspapers reflected this impulse. Journalists live a hazardous, 'outsider' existence, for which Weber had great sympathy. He thought that this 'emancipated' life was a precondition for developing a certain kind of character (Steding, 1932, pp. 50-1).

Weber's own conduct, Steding suggested, reflected Puritanism. Even Calvin, Steding pointed out, recognized the 'cry of the people.' When Weber finally acted politically, he sought acclamation and sought a structure of leader selection that demanded acclamation. Steding noticed that this political form presupposes a particular conception of the political community – or more precisely, a conception opposed to the idea of community. The bases of community – the belonging group, the family, the caring church – were not part of Weber's political conception, which excluded these supraindividual and irrational powers (Steding, 1932, pp. 87-9). As Steding put it, it was accepted by Weber as self-evident that the only mode of association suited to the modern world is *Gesellschaft*, and not *Gemeinschaft*; Weber's effort was directed against the kind of supraindividual value hierarchies characteristic of the *Gemeinschaft*, or *universitas*, mode of association. The Weberian conception of politics, and especially of the politics of parliamentary party-struggles, was reinforced by the value-relativism that informed Weber's sociological writings. Steding found a Puritan element here, as well. The structure of bourgeois political parties, according to Weber, parallels that of the Puritan sects – they are autonomous associations of free individuals, where members are chosen after rational deliberation. The underlying contrast is to rural life, which, as Weber himself emphasized, was never, except for the Donatists, congenial to Puritan thought (ibid., p. 93).[2]

Nazism as a sieve

The selective effect of Nazism on subsequent thought was both great and complex. 'Liberalism', and things called 'liberal,' went through a revival after Hitler's defeat, as much because the Nazis had attacked 'liberalism' as because Germany had a usable liberal tradition. More often, terms and ideas had become tainted by their adoption by the Nazi philosophers, ideologists, and sympathizers. Some of these terms simply dropped out of subsequent discourse; some survived, but were used with much greater care by later writers. Both the term 'relativism' and the term 'intuition,' which figured on opposite sides in the Salz-Kahler exchange, were put to use by 'Nazi philosophy.' The term *Schau*, connoting intuition, largely dropped out of later discourse, and 'relativism' came to be used with great care. Because many writers, such as Radbruch and Alfred Weber, specifically abandoned both the term and the substance of relativism and other writers merely sought to change the emphasis of the doctrine, the history of the term relativism is particularly complex.

The relativism of the early 1920s appealed to Mussolini, as Mussolini appealed to the relativists of that time. In 1921, Mussolini spoke of relativism as 'Germany's philosophical revenge which may herald the military revenge,' and, combining both terms, stated that 'everything I have said and done these last few years has been relativism by intuition' (quoted in Kuhn, 1943, pp. 21-2). But it was in connection with racialist thinking that relativism acquired its most odious associations. The notion of an appropriately German and National Socialist *Weltanschauung* was underpinned by the idea that *Weltanschauungen* were relativistically true but that the relativism corresponded to racial types: hence 'racial relativism,' which takes a place formerly held by historicist relativism, and which produces analogous difficulties.

The key difficulty this doctrine creates is that it is unclear precisely how one is to know whether one's *Weltanschauung* or science corresponds to one's own racial type. The solution to this is intuition, which provides a kind of test of racial appropriateness. Another difficulty is that merely admitting racial relativism, and being committed to a particular view because of its racial appropriateness – which has the effect of avoiding the creation of an individual relativist dilemma – does not solve the question one really wishes answered, the question of the superiority of one view over another. Put differently, the 'racial' qualification of relativism changes the problem of relativism, because the question of superiority no longer dictates that one must make a choice between alternatives – one is, so to speak, fated to one's racial *Weltanschauung* – but it does call for some sort of reassurance of the special and unique value of the German view. One could scarcely fail to feel the need for such reassurance, in light of the fact that this *Weltanschauung*, and the race it corresponds to, was being held up by the leaders as a value that is threatened with extinction by the Western nations and Russia, which must be defended by war. The need is not philosophical, but it is a need nevertheless, which can be satisfied only by some sort of 'absolute' affirmation, either of the *Weltanschauung* or the race. The solution to this quandary was to affirm the absolute and special value of the race, a notion that much of German propaganda from the earliest days of the movement for unification lent credence to.

For the many nonracialist Germans, such devices as Heidegger's notion of the special philosophical greatness of the German language must have taken the place of racial ideas in securing their acquiescence to or support of the Nazi regime. The ubiquity of the idea that there was something uniquely German that was threatened and needed to be preserved by force is remarkable. Conjoined with historical relativism, it led to the same conclusions as did racial relativism. As Kolnai quoted Mowrer: 'For most cultured Germans are so proud with historical relativity that they deny the existence of any "absolutely" higher forms. Each people, they believe, has a right to its own peculiar culture, and no one can be ranked "above" another; they are merely different.' As Kolnai has glossed this, ' "We" are at liberty to consider ourselves as unconditionally superior, indeed the Salt of the Earth; not on the ground of a Standard we have managed to answer, but because there is no such Standard by the test of which Our pretension could be rebutted' (Kolnai, 1938, p. 236). Some prewar remarks by Haiser show the practical implications of this conclusion. 'The values of the group are pitted against the values of the foreign group as it were incommensurably. . . . Hatred of foreign things and love of one's own tribe (*Stamm*) are alike a duty and a pleasure.' And again, 'Thy fatherland bids thee hate the stranger's estranging custom; by loving thy nation's foe thou soilest the Creator's name' (quoted in ibid., p. 46).

Ideas like these form the symbols and oppositions in terms of which philosophical ideas of 'scientific' claims can become intelligible in the context of demagogy. The audiences of the demagogue, whether composed of scholars or ordinary people, do not need such things spelled out, nor are these audiences interested in minor variations in the form of the utterances (as they would interest an audience of competent scholars as scholars). Frequently, political speech-making consists in the creating of impressions by the appeal to and selection from familiar symbols and oppositions. Describing this general set of symbols and oppositions involving Germany's place in the world and the nature of its struggle with other nations as bearers of values and customs serves simply to show the framework in terms of which Weber's variations on these images were heard by his audience. Needless to say, although Morgenthau's world image (which we shall discuss in the next chapter) may be regarded as a later variation, this semiotic structure became a casualty of the war.

The substantive political thinking of Nazism presents difficulties that resemble the difficulties with Nazi philosophy, and that, in the same way, taint certain ideas. The 'continuity thesis' rests in part on the point that Hitler's foreign policy ambitions took the same form as certain earlier imperialist strategies, and that Naumann's advice in his widely read book, *Mitteleuropa*, resembles Hitler's approach (Vermeil, 1955, pp. 46, 51, 54). Such power-political rationales for regional hegemony, needless to say, were not spoken of after World War II. Similarly, the Nazi and Fascist appropriations of both the notion of an elite and of the leader and the mass tainted these terms as well. The term *Führer* has permanently acquired connotations that make it a red flag.

The ethical ideas that were most tainted by the Nazis' use included a number of concepts associated with what Löwith, in writing of Heidegger, called the mode of catastrophic thought of the German generation of the time after World War I. 'Basically,' Löwith suggested, 'these notions and terms are the expression of the bitter and hard resolution of a will which affirms itself in the face of nothingness, fiercely disdaining happiness and compassion' (Löwith, 1946, p. 354). Associated with this attitude were the Nazi doctrines of personal sacrifice, commitment as against compromise, and especially the belief, raised to the level of doctrine, in 'unsentimentality,' or ruthlessness in politics. 'Great history is not made by suave people; it is made by strong men – who are strong because they are absolutely hard men.' The author of this remark is the Nazi theoretician Rosenberg (quoted in Kolnai, 1938, p. 201). Weber's postwar speeches on politics and science reflected the same mood, and it is no surprise that later Weberians were not to stress these aspects of his conception of the demands of the day. Earlier, Weber was regarded as a paragon of a particular attitude, a 'dry and often cruel approach to reality' (quoted in Masur, 1961, p. 191). It should be recognized that these modes and attitudes were an explicit part of a public scholarly tradition. Jaspers, in his *Psychologie der Weltanschauungen*, claimed to be following Hegel, Kant, Kierkegaard, Nietzsche, and Weber. The latter three were praised for their vehemence (Jaspers, 1922, pp. 12, 14). Certainly vehemence was part of Weber's personal style as well. Radbruch, who knew Weber well, described him as being, in his practical behavior, an ethical absolutist and rigorist (Radbruch, 1951, p. 88). Some writers have regarded this style as an essential part of Weber's message, of his 'philosophical anthropology,' in which the resolution and devotion demanded by one's ultimate choices is a large theme. Because phrases like 'decisionlessness' were used by persons like Carl Schmitt during the Nazi era to describe the kind of political attitude they opposed, later interpreters, insofar as they wished to defend Weber, had to present this style *cum* philosophical anthropology with considerable care, if at all (Schmitt, 1940, p. 272).[3]

The concept of 'decision' in general became tainted. The concept was, however, ubiquitous. The Nazis had a 'Year of Decision,' Spengler had a book he entitled *The Hour of Decision* (1934), Tillich had one he called *The Socialist Decision* (1977), and so on. Yet the term had more specific associations. The term 'decisionism' was associated with the legal thought of Carl Schmitt, who, like Heidegger, was a public supporter of the Nazi regime and wrote in support of it. Unfortunately, the term proved, much later in the Weber dispute, to be a red herring. It attracted a number of authors in the 1960s, who sought to claim that Weber was not a 'decisionist,' thinking that this 'disproved the Nazi connection.' The matter was further confused by Habermas's use of the term to characterize a mode of relation between experts and political decision makers.

The term 'decision' had a distinctive role in Schmitt's account. Schmitt was impressed with the power to declare a state of exception (or state of siege), i.e., to suspend the law. The interesting peculiarity of such declarations is that, although the power to declare a state of siege may be granted in law, it is not itself subject to rules that define the conditions justifying a state of siege. The decision to declare a state of exception is thus not 'bound by rule' as are the ordinary operations of courts and bureaucracies. But at the same time, the power to declare an 'exception' can only be intelligible as a suspension of an ordinary state of affairs, where the law operates normally. Thus the power of the 'exception' is by its nature 'occasional,' dictated by the extreme circumstance, but not by rule.

At the occasion where decision is demanded by the situation, we are, according to Schmitt, governed by no rule but the demands of the occasion. Moral, theological, metaphysical, and economic considerations, as well as law, are never authoritative in this, the purely political moment. Yet political moments are given by fate. After a political decision, a new order, based on this decision, can arise out of disorder. Schmitt took the Nazi regime to be a new emerging concrete order. So the moment of decision was, in Schmitt's view, ended, and the individual, far from being free to choose, was ethically bound to the law of ordered community life.

At times, Schmitt wrote as though he wanted to reduce the state to decision – to the decision to define the categories 'friend and foe,' and to the 'highest instance' of this, the readiness to die and kill for the state, which defines the political realm. Weber spoke in ways that are congenial to this, as when he said that

> war does something to the warrior which, in its concrete meaning, is unique: it makes him experience a consecrated meaning of death which is characteristic only of death in war. . . . This location of death within a series of meaningful and consecrated events ultimately lies at the base of all endeavors to support the autonomous dignity of the polity resting on force (1946, p. 335).

Schmitt saw this as a way out of the relativism of the liberal bourgeois. The fact that in war the readiness for death and killing is the 'ultimate' gives the facts of war and the threat of war a superiority over other political aims.

One may raise a good many questions about Schmitt's doctrine as a philosophical scheme. Schmitt used Cromwell and his implacable hatred toward Spain as the model of great politics. Cromwell saw Spain as a 'natural' enemy; he did not think he had merely 'decided' to place it in the category of 'foe.' Schmitt rejected Cromwell's self-understanding, but he nevertheless accepted a category of natural enemy; the wars between Greeks and barbarians he took to be an example of this. This suggests that there is a natural order of the world and of human things which is not a matter of 'decision,' and that this is Schmitt's hidden metaphysic. But the existence of this order means that there is no moment of pure decision – for even in the political moment, when normal political order no longer suffices, the natural order remains. But Schmitt did not deal with problems at this level, as Löwith repeatedly pointed out in his critique, so it is obscure as to whether he was a decisionist in Weber's sense or not (Löwith, 1934-5). Schmitt's criticisms of Weber, in *Legalität und Legitimität*, do not reflect credit on Weber. Schmitt suggested that in Weber the parliamentary legislative state reverts to the earlier situation of absolutism in that it creates 'the great right of unconditional obedience' (Schmitt, 1932, p. 15). Schmitt was no democrat, but he believed that legitimacy, in the normal situation, should derive from more basic values. The Weberian doctrine that the bureaucracy is merely a technical means, he pointed out, following Smend, does not allow the civil servant to reject unjust commands (ibid., p. 16). In the 1950s, consistent with this earlier statement, he observed that the ultimate implication of Weber's view of legitimacy as formal legality is the practice of the Nazis' quasi-legal seizure of power.

Schmitt's legal doctrine of 'decisionism,' and Schmitt as a personality, were tainted by the association with Nazism. But his specific legal doctrine had little to do with the later debate or uses of the term 'decisionism,' which fit Radbruch's usage more closely. Much else was tainted as well. The social ideas of the Nazis stressed the organic unity of the *Volk* and the idea of an all-encompassing party that corresponded to the whole – all supra-individual concepts of the sort Weber had no taste for. These particular organic or corporativist ideas were the most strongly tainted of all, for there was no direct revival of them in later German scholarship.

7 The emergence of the dispute in England and America

With the rise of Hitler many Weimar as well as Austrian intellectuals were dispersed over the world, and in their attempts to come to terms with their new situations we can find the beginnings of the recasting of the Weimar dispute. Part of this recasting took the form of coping with the political traditions and forms of the Western regimes: J.P. Mayer, Leo Strauss, and Karl Mannheim all made contributions to the question of the foundations – moral and intellectual – of the Western democracies. Another part of the recasting took the form of coming to grips with the American situation: Hans J. Morgenthau reformulated Weberian ideas to apply to the new place of the United States in world politics, Joseph Schumpeter to the problem of socialism and the future of democracy. Another part of the transformation of the dispute involved the coming to grips with the philosophical traditions outside Germany by displaced Weimar scholars encountering the displaced Vienna Circle, as well as American Pragmatism, British ethical theory, and various intellectual attitudes characteristic of American and British intellectual life, such as the optimistic scientism of the American social sciences.

The rise of Hitler raised another problem. It put the German tradition, in the broadest sense, in a new light. Accordingly, of the traditions the emigrés had to cope with, it was perhaps their own that produced the greatest amount of reflection, and to some extent the Weber literature was to become an appendage to these reflections, for Weber was read as a part of the problematic tradition that produced Hitler. After World War II, the reconsideration of the German tradition also became a central concern of the intellectuals who stayed in Germany, as we shall notice later.

To a remarkable extent those German scholars who emigrated

preserved the Weimar issues in their scholarship. There were many reasons for this: one was that the philosophy of the English-speaking world seemed extraordinarily backward – persons like Bertrand Russell and John Dewey seemed to have retained a faith in science long after neo-Kantianism had shown the insubstantiality of such a faith. The culture, particularly of the United States, seemed degraded, fulfilling the conventional German wisdom about mass-societies. Consequently, mass culture became something of an obsession for émigrés at both ends of the political spectrum. In light of this, the continuation of Weimar perspectives should perhaps be no surprise: the frame of reference the emigrés could best use to make sense of the events was the one they brought with them, and events could be construed to conform to it. Sometimes their perspectives proved to fit with native concerns, and this produced subtle distortions.

THE ENGLISH CRISIS OF CULTURE

In England, there had been a discussion of culture that paralleled the Weimar discussion, but it proceeded in the framework of a different style and in the face of a metaphilosophic tradition in which a philosophy that failed to accord with truth and reasonableness as ordinarily understood was *prima facie* suspect. Locke called the philosopher an 'underlaborer', and later English philosophers, empiricists and Platonists alike, generally agreed with this in practice. So the discussion of culture was not to take the form of a philosophic dispute, but primarily of discourse on literature and religion.

Karl Mannheim and the extension of the Weimar perspective

Karl Mannheim, who had been an active participant in German sociological circles, emerged as a significant figure in English intellectual life. He brought a socialism oriented to 'planning' which found a sympathetic audience in England. Although Mannheim was one of the emigrés most open to new ideas – his work reflects a close reading of American social psychology, for example – the Weimar themes are there as well. Mannheim's early work, in the 1920s, dealt with conservatism as an ideology and led him to an understanding that there was more to the modern conservative impulse than traditionalism or reaction. But during this period Mannheim was still trapped in the epistemological paradoxes of historicist relativism. His final resolution of these paradoxes in *Ideology and Utopia* (1936), his 'relationism' and concept of the 'free-floating intellectual,' was not well received, but it enabled him to ignore the neo-Kantian dilemmas. The example of Lukács, whose concept of 'totalities' resembled Mannheim's, must have weighed heavily. As a 'free-floating intellectual,' he was freed from the fear that his own reflections on morality and culture were 'ideology.'

In his wartime essay 'The Crisis in Valuation' (1943), Mannheim proceeded from the standard observation that the moral unity of medieval society had been broken down by liberalism. Modern societies lack a common moral framework: such basic moral categories as crime, freedom, and discipline, and such basic policy categories as education and leisure have no common definition. Yet it was widely agreed that it was bad to live in a society where norms are unsettled, and Mannheim agreed with this as well. He quotes with ironic approval the remark of a Fascist political scientist that 'a bad decision is better than no decision' (1943, p. 15). This general crisis, Mannheim said, has been analyzed in two ways. The 'Idealists' said that the spiritual crisis was the cause of the crisis in civilization: 'To them all the struggles of history were due to the clash between different forms of allegiance to authority or to changing valuations' (ibid.). The Marxists put it the other way around. Mannheim agreed with the Marxist recognition of the fact that culture depends on social situations, but he rejected the use of 'class' as the sole means of conceiving these situations. Thus his own causal formulation retains elements of both views.

The underlying problem of valuation, Mannheim argued, is that the values of small-scale societies, the Christian values, must be 'translated' into large-scale terms. As he put it, the intention of the original values, rather than the form, must be preserved. It is exemplary of Mannheim's openness to the American tradition in social science, as well as of a common practice among the emigrés to seek Anglo-American sources, that Charles Horton Cooley is given as the author of this notion. The institutional reasons why this 'translation' has not occurred include the fact that the educational system is still oriented to the parochial world of the past, one result of which is that today we have a variety of political and religious philosophies that neutralize each other. Authority, in Mannheim's version, went from a basis in tradition, to one in natural right, to a utilitarian basis, to, finally, 'the endless arbitrary claims of charisma' (1943, p. 21).

Mannheim never simply transposed Weimar notions and remedies onto the Western democracies in a purely procrustean way, and he recognized that the style of British politics was quite different from that of Weimar.

> If you come over from the continent one of the things that strikes you most is that over here it seems to be a part of the accepted ways of life to leave unsaid many things which elsewhere would be plainly stated. . . . differences in opinion are rarely fought out in full, and hardly ever traced back to their final source (1943, p. 66).

This style of life, he admitted, has 'intrinsic value' (ibid.), but he believed it cannot be expected to survive; it has survived this long only because of England's security and wealth. During the war and in the postwar period, he said, it will be vital for its leaders to understand that these are passing customs which will, in the future, require reasonable alternatives (ibid., p. 64).

Here and elsewhere it is unclear what Mannheim had in mind as 'reasonable alternatives'. 'Planning' is the word he used to describe the family of techniques he had in mind, and he was concerned to make the term as harmless sounding as possible, because he was aware that it smacked of totalitarianism. He candidly admitted that the methods he was suggesting did not differ essentially from those of the totalitarian regimes, save with respect to their ends. But this he took to be a significant difference, enough difference to think of democratic planning as a 'third way' between liberalism and dictatorship. Liberalism itself he took to be simply doomed: the defenders of capitalism and the antiplanners had a 'suppressed awareness' of what was going on in the world – they simply did not acknowledge the changes that had taken place and would have to take place (1943, p. 67). One may note that here the Jasperian notion that the present is a passing moment of freedom between two long eras of unfreedom is turned into the claim that liberalism was no more than a transitional period between two forms of closed society (Mannheim, 1950, p. xi).

The 'planning' of values is at once the most touchy area of 'planning' for a liberal audience and the area in which the echo of Weimar thinking in Mannheim's thought is loudest. What planning in the realm of values is to achieve resembles, superficially, the cultural reform envisioned by Weber's opponents in Weimar, such as Kahler, which also involved the notion that the development of the human personality required a new moral and philosophical order. Just as some of the cultural reformers of the 1920s looked back to the medieval hierarchy of human values as exemplary of the type of intellectual system that man needed, Mannheim looked back to medieval Catholicism as possessing social techniques suited to the present time and social circumstances. Like the church, Mannheim taught the need for a coherent system of values 'without which modern society cannot survive' (1943, p. 111).

> The more the age of planning proceeds, the more it will become likely that these recommendations will take the shape of a consistent system similar to the Summa of St. Thomas. . . . Religious and moral recommendations, as we have called them, will therefore tend not only to lay down some principles, but also a set of concrete patterns of behavior, the image of satisfactory social institutions and a whole world view as a connecting link between them (ibid., pp. 110-11).

Mannheim of course did not suppose that this order could be simply concocted. He thought that it would require inventiveness and experimentation, under democratic control. But he believed there was no alternative: noninterference with values and silence on the subject of the common good leads to débâcles like the Weimar Republic, and ultimately prepares the ground for total submission (ibid., p. 25). For Mannheim, the crucial difficulty, the one that stood in the way of a recognition of the need for a new political and social form based on planning, was the persistence of parochial viewpoints. What is needed, he argued, is 'total awareness' (1950, p. 64), which is distinguished from class consciousness and other 'partial group experiences' because it is the synthesis of these group experiences. This resembles Scheler's impulse of the immediate postwar period to use the sociology of knowledge as an educational means of reconciling the conflicts between *Weltanschauungen.* The spirit of Mannheim's sociology of knowledge, as of Scheler's during the postwar period, was not to treat inquiry as the 'road to suspicion', but rather as the '*tout comprendre*' that becomes '*tout pardonner*.' Academic over-specialization, he went on to point out, also stands in the way of total awareness. Thus, like the reformers in Weimar, educational reform became his central preoccupation (Remmling, 1975, pp. 108-21).

The problem of tradition

For Mannheim, the lesson of Weimar was that the 'liberal' approach to values leads to disaster. Germany, by virtue of its special trials, was the first nation to go through this disaster. But the lessons apply equally to England. In this ready application of the lessons of Weimar to other 'liberal' regimes we may see this most striking and characteristic feature of the development of the controversy over Weber's thought and of midcentury development of German perspectives on the political and social situation of the world. For Mannheim, and as we shall see for such diverse figures as Morgenthau, Schumpeter, and Habermas, there was no essential difference between the German liberal regime and the 'liberal' regimes of England and the United States.

In England, this reasoning came up against a body of thought that dealt with the problem of culture in its own ways. There were several main variants in this body of thought, which were distinguished in several respects. One line was represented by defenders of political versions of economic liberalism, and this group included such students of von Mises as Hayek, whose *Road to Serfdom* (1944) made him into a public figure. Another variant was the conservatism of Michael Oakeshott, who criticized Hayek for turning the English tradition into an ideology, and who developed an account of rationalism and tradition that represents a fundamental alternative to Weber's account of Western rationality. The *Dublin Review*, edited by Christopher Dawson, was the locus of a Catholic discourse on culture that included non-Catholics as well. T.S. Eliot, in his writings on the possibility of a Christian society and on the nature of a 'culture,' took up these same issues. These various authors were aware of one another, and they recognized the differences between each other, which consisted of the degrees to which they regarded liberal economics as central, religious sympathies, which ranged from secular to Catholic, and politics, which ranged from Tory to liberal to socialist.[1]

The contrast between these thinkers and Weber was not 'political', in the sense of a difference in their location on a spectrum from left to right, for the center of gravity of this tradition was conservative-liberal, which describes Weber as well. But there were fundamental differences with respect to the core Weberian ideas on reason and values. In these writings we find, in addition to Oakeshott's rejection of the separation between reason and tradition, an alternative to Weber's broader historical notion of the destruction of past values by the rationalization of life that depends on a sense of the continuity of Western culture, and a view of politics that reflects these differences.

Although Mannheim was not, in any simple sense, a Weberian, his discussions of England continued Weber's thoughts, and Mannheim was a target for several of these writers. We have seen that Mannheim believed that civility or the rules of the game were ultimately a doomed feature of British political life, and that the unwillingness to fight differences out in full, he thought, could not survive. He connected the British political style to Chamberlain's unwillingness to face the unpleasant facts of Hitler's regime (1943, p. 65), and to the 'suppressed awareness' of the defenders of capitalism, the antiplanners, who could not grasp the changes that were now overwhelming the old economic political forms (ibid., p. 67). Elsewhere, in a particularly Weberian phrasing, he spoke of the functional rationalization of society, which neutralized substantial morality or sidetracked it into the private sphere, and of the tendency to 'do away with substantial irrationality, retaining merely those customs which facilitate the smooth working of social relations (1950, p. 67). Custom and substantial morality, in this picture, live on borrowed time – when 'functional rationality' demands, they are done away with. This picture is precisely what Oakeshott, Dawson, Hayek, and Eliot rejected.

One aspect of the rejection may be seen through a consideration of Polanyi's concept of the 'tacit dimension,' which corresponds to what Oakeshott calls 'practical knowledge' as distinct from 'technique' (Oakeshott, 1962, p. 8; Polanyi, 1966). To say that there is a 'tacit dimension' to scientific knowledge, or that a tradition has no essence and cannot be reduced to rules, but is rather a matter of 'habits of behavior, adaptable and never quite fixed or finished' (Oakeshott, 1962, p. 21), is to point out that there is a nonrational or irrational dimension to science or to tradition. The sense of 'irrational' in these contexts is the literal (and, philologically, the root) sense: there are no 'reasons' given for that which is contained in the 'tacit dimension'; it rather is to be acquired, as skills, sensibilities, and tastes are. Rationalists ignore that, as Oakeshott says, 'an activity consists in knowing how to behave' (ibid., p. 96). A body of practice is inseparable from scientific reasoning or rational political conduct. The tacit dimension is, one may say, this inseparable thing one must master in order to reason and to understand reasons.

Whatever one may think of this view of the matter (or of whether the irrational-rational distinction is appropriately applied to it), it has a very different emphasis from what might be called 'decisionistic' irrationalism. The 'tacit dimension' is, after all, something that is more or less stable, though it is not fixed and unchanging. One cannot 'choose' to 'assume' it. Education into a tradition is an education of one's affections, one's sense of fitness, and of one's capacity to reason, weigh, and distinguish. To be educated into the tradition of modern physics, to take one of Oakeshott's examples (1962, p. 128), is to acquire such things. To 'decide' for a tradition can only be to decide to try to enter into it and master it; the act of decision itself – in contrast, for example, to an act to 'decide for the nation as one's highest value' – stands in relation to mastering the tradition as decision to seek a physics degree stands in relation to becoming a master physicist. The decision itself is nothing – the acquisition everything.

Oakeshott speaks to the question of the implications of this for the problem of the nature of 'rationality' in his essay 'Rational Conduct,' which is a classic in the tradition, discussed in Chapter 2, of nondeductivist accounts of 'rationality.' For Oakeshott,

> the only significant way of using the word 'rational' in relation to conduct is when we mean to indicate a quality or characteristic (and perhaps a desirable quality or characteristic) of the activity itself, . . . the quality concerned is not mere 'intelligence', but *faithfulness to the knowledge we have of how to conduct the specific activity we are engaged in.* 'Rational' conduct is acting in such a way that the coherence of the idiom of the activity to which the conduct belongs is preserved and possibly enhanced (1962, pp. 101-2).

More generally, to reason is to reason within an open-textured tradition of giving and acting on reasons, in terms of a body of practices of reasoning which is itself open to revision.[2] For Oakeshott, education in a political tradition, or in any other great tradition, is not the learning of doctrines or technical means. 'Since a tradition of behavior is not susceptible of the distinction between essence and accident, knowledge of it is unavoidably knowledge of its detail: to know only the gist is to know nothing. What has to be learned is not an abstract idea, or a set of tricks, not even a ritual, but a concrete, coherent manner of living in all its intricateness' (1962, pp. 128-9). T.S. Eliot, in his discussion of the Christian society, makes a similar point about Christianity. Where Weber saw Christian ethics as resting directly on specific beliefs about salvation and consisting in a technique of salvation, Eliot thought of Christianity as an ethos or way of life (1968).

This difference has significant historiographic implications. The *Protestant Ethic* dealt with a change in values that was peculiarly congenial to the idea of value choice as 'decision.' The theology of the reformers, which emphasized the need for a personal act of faith or submission, seemed to justify regarding the actions of the believers in these terms. But one cannot find a comparable decision at the basis of the rest of the Western moral tradition, and certainly not at the basis of the 'democratic virtues' or the civilizing conventions that made the liberal form of rule possible in Britain. What one finds instead is 'continuity.' Writers like Christopher Dawson, for example, stressed the degree to which modern morals, law, and political thought rested on the achievements of the medievals (1956).[3] In Weber's sociology, there is no place for this sort of development, save under the headings of 'rationalization' and 'the disenchantment of the world': if tradition strictly speaking is unreflected upon by those who follow it, it therefore cannot readily be conceived to change, 'on its own,' so to say, even over a few hundred years. So the positive development of a moral framework seems possible, in Weber's sociological scheme, only through the action of the charismatic prophet, through revelations, secular or religious, or through decision.[4]

These historiographic differences made for different perceptions of the present cultural situation. Writers like Eliot and Dawson felt that the tradition was 'imperilled, but not doomed utterly' (Kirk, 1971, p. 110.) Eliot sought a solution in a Toryism that had 'a religious foundation for the whole of its political philosophy' (quoted in Kirk, 1971, p. 198). In the 1930s and during the war, the continued political importance of the religious tradition was especially evident. As Dawson, writing in Eliot's *Criterion*, quoted Karl Barth, 'Theology and the Church are the natural frontiers of everything – even of the Totalitarian State' (quoted in ibid., p. 232).

Many writers whose views were far from Dawson's and Eliot's Christian stance shared in seeing the continued political importance of tradition. Tawney spoke of making the culture more widely available within English society. Huxley, writing to a friend in 1938, drew this lesson from Bertrand Russell's recently published book *Power: a new social analysis* (1938):

> any society which indulges in searching criticism of hallowed beliefs and institutions breaks through that crust of decency and prepares the way for the use of naked and entirely cynical power. . . . political decency has always been bound up with the acceptance of traditions and the end of one has always meant the end of the other (Mitchison, 1982, p. 635).

These were ideas with a long English tradition. They reflect Burke and Johnson as much as they do any contemporary disputes.

Mayer and Weber's political legacy

J.P. Mayer, who had been Archivist for the Social Democratic party and the primary book reviewer for the *Vorwärts*, the SPD party paper, escaped to England and became involved with the Labour party. During the last part of the war he was on the faculty at the London School of Economics. While remaining in the ambit of Laski and Tawney, he became friendly with Dawson and Eliot, published in the *Dublin Review*, and had his work edited by Eliot at Faber. His Weber book, *Max Weber and German Politics*, dates from the period during which Eliot was writing 'Notes toward the Definition of Culture' (1968, pp. 83-202), which was addressed to the same themes.

The Weber book reflects this ambience, as well as, in a broader sense, the French tradition of Tocqueville and Taine, which Mayer wrote on in the same period. Mayer did not see the British and German political infrastructure as being essentially alike, and he saw Weber's misinterpretations of British political life as being at the core of his political conception as a whole, and as revealing its fundamental weakness.

Mayer noted that although Weber visited the British Isles and was a sensitive traveler he misunderstood what he saw in England. Mayer was not surprised by this.

> Countries with old traditions like England and France can only be understood if one shares the common life of their peoples. Only then will you see more than 'conventions,' you begin to ask and to understand how these strange manners came about. Perhaps after years, if you are lucky and have patience, you will penetrate behind the facade and suddenly you may discover the secret norms which guide the Englishmen (Mayer, 1956, p. 43).

As a student of Tocqueville, Mayer knew the difficulties in attaining this sort of knowledge. But his criticism goes deeper than the point of social anthropological methodology. Behind it is a tradition of thinking about the moral basis of political life that figures in Tocqueville and in Taine, who is quoted at length by Mayer in his *Political Thought in France: from revolution to the Fifth Republic.*

> For eighty years our publicists have reasoned themselves blind concerning constitutions; I know one among the most eminent who would transport that of England or the United States to France, and asks two years only for rendering the nation accustomed to it. . . . In fact, nearly all Europe has attempted or adopted the English system. . . . Consider how grotesque the result has been. . . . The constitution of a state is an organic thing . . . another cannot assimilate it, the outside merely can be copied. Underneath institutions, charters, written laws, the official almanac, there are the ideas, the customs, the character, the condition of classes, their respective position, their reciprocal sentiments; in short, a ramified network of deep-seated, invisible roots beneath the visible trunk and foliage. It is they which feed and sustain the tree. Plant the tree without roots, it will languish, and will fall at the first gust (quoted in Mayer, 1961, p. 78).

Mayer made a similar point in his study of Weber, which was first published about the same time, during the war. The 'secret norms which guide the Englishmen,' he said, their 'unconscious tradition,' includes moral strength, 'tolerance, fairness, love of freedom,' and 'not the *raison d'état* of the power State' (1956, p. 43). Without an understanding of these traditions, speculation about forms of state is sure to lead to misjudgments, and Weber, Mayer suggested, made them.

Mayer suggested several reasons for these misjudgments in comparison, beyond the sheer difficulty of understanding, as Oakeshott would say, 'a way of life in all its particularity.' The common law was, for most of the English writers we have been considering, a paradigm instance of a tradition. Weber, whose perspective was formed by legal training in a nation without a strong, living tradition of state law, did not, Mayer suggested, grasp its significance in England (1956, p. 102), and he believed too readily that it would be swept away by the processes of rationalization and bureaucratization (ibid., p. 147). At the same time, Weber failed to understand the continuity of values.

> Weber had only a glimpse of the underlying values of the West – in spite of the *Protestant Ethic*. He failed to understand that these values inherent in and interwoven with the Western world were not yet destroyed by the impact of rationalization and the steel age (ibid., p. 105).

In part, this was a result of Weber's German chauvinism, for, as Mayer pointed out, he 'never reflected on the wealth of value-patterns which underlie the American-Anglo and French civilizations' (ibid., pp. 120-1).

Weber's misunderstanding of the Western moral tradition, Mayer argued, vitiates his analysis of British politics. Weber, he said, separated 'political technique from traditions and moral valuations which are in fact interwoven with the power-element' and is therefore too ready to see forms of the state merely as techniques (1956, p. 82). This, Mayer argued, is a mistake. Although 'Weber has clearly seen the basic religious and moral element' in the *origins* of Anglo-Saxon politics, 'what he failed to realize is the phenomenon that the basic religious and moral element does not disappear in the modern British and American state structure, though it is covered by ever more secularized layers' (ibid., p. 57). Mayer also pointed to the continuities that exist in France and England: the change from

> the old party system based on notabilities, to the modern one, based on bureaucratic organization, does not proceed by a sudden break. The old structures, particularly in countries with long-standing political traditions like France and England, are

mixed up with the modern organizational forms; and this sometimes to the advantage of the latter (ibid.).

Weber's failure to see this led to an error in his prescriptions for Germany: he placed too much blame on Bismarck for the failures of German politics, and not enough on the native tradition of authoritarianism, which derived from German Protestantism, the practice of using crippled NCOs for village teachers, and compulsory military service. These traditions, Mayer said, 'permeated the whole of German society' (ibid., pp. 78-9).

Weber's apparent blindness to the consequences of this German tradition for democracy led him to overlook the conflict between the principle of charisma and the parliamentary principle. 'Weber's conception that the highest office of the *Reich*, once it was open to the political struggle, might provide an aim for young and untried "charismatic leadership" was romanticism *pur sang*,' Mayer said. Mayer, like Michels, saw that the dictator would not yield even when the water had risen to his throat. But Mayer drew the conclusion that only a political tradition – custom or "convention" and morals together – could limit charisma in its destructive forms. Weber, having failed to understand 'convention,' failed to see this.

Mayer's book was published at the point during the war when it was evident to insiders that Hitler would fail, and reconstruction was on many minds. Mayer suggested that 'Christian collectivism' should be an element of the solution. He echoed Dawson and Karl Barth in saying that the 'Christian Churches have become the refuge for many Germans who were unable to accept the National Socialist policy of a totalitarian Nihilism' (1956, p. 122), and pointed to the 'strong and persevering' 'confessional' element in Germany. 'In our view,' Mayer said, 'a Christian, mainly Catholic, element in this new political structure of Germany will be very likely' (ibid.). But the 'Utopia of German power-politics,' Mayer said, 'is for ever finished' (ibid., p. 123).

THE AMERICAN CONTEXT

Mayer and Mannheim were exceptional for finding a place in English academic life; few other Germans did. The United States proved more hospitable. American culture and American political and academic traditions proved to be more diverse and less absorptive than English traditions. German ideas, and German quarrels, tended to survive in a less diluted form. The emigré community had buried its quarrels for the period of the war, however, so no book analogous to Mayer's was written in the

United States, and the Weimar dispute did not immediately revive. When Weber's ideas were presented, in a piecemeal fashion, they were inserted into disputes and traditions that had developed largely independently of the German disputes.

Academic values

Discussions of the American academic tradition traditionally focused on the protection of a weak professoriate and emphasized arguments for toleration.[5] The 1915 'Declaration of Principles' of the American Association of University Professors might have been taken from Mill or Bagehot. 'In the interpretation of the general meaning and ends of human existence and its relation to the universe, we are still far from a comprehension of the final truths' (AAUP, 1922, p. 496). This is not value-relativism but scepticism and antidogmatism. When American authors of the 1920s wrote on German developments they rejected them.[6] Roscoe Pound, in a commencement address at Oberlin in 1927, observed that 'reasoned search for what ought to be in politics and in law has been under attack. . . . The neo-individualist followers of Nietzsche told us it was wrong. The superman was not to be held down by fetters of reason forged in the interest of weak humanity' (1927, p. 573). Pound rejected this, and the rejection is mutual: Radbruch, in his *Law Quarterly Review* article of 1936, rejected American 'substantive' philosophy of law, specifically mentioning Pound (1936, p. 542).

In the social sciences a new set of distinctions was developing, but one that was not fundamentally at variance with the Mill-Bagehot notion of the basis of toleration or with Pound's notion of the reasoned pursuit of the Ought in politics. A good benchmark here is William F. Ogburn's 1929 presidential address to the American Sociological Society. Ogburn, a 'scientifically' oriented sociologist, turned to the question of the 'betterment of men' in connection with the contrast between sociology and social work. He made the contrast not on the Weberian ground that one activity is goal oriented and value laden and that the other is value laden only to the extent of its choice of vocabulary, but on the grounds of the scientist's need for patiently waiting until all the evidence is in and the social worker's need for immediate action. In the future, he said, 'social problems will be so urgent that one cannot wait on the "suspended judgement" of the scientist. . . . Hence action will often be based on approximate knowledge' (Ogburn, 1930, p. 9). He did not believe that this meant that sociology would abandon the concern for the betterment of man. Indeed, he said, in

> the future the subject matter of the social worker and of the sociologist will be the same, in large part, except that the field of the sociologist will be larger and will encompass that of the social worker. The interests of the social worker and of the sociologist will also have more in common. For a large group of sociologists will deal with the practical problem of human betterment. And to a certain extent the motivation of the social worker and of the sociologist as a human being will tend to be the same (ibid., p. 8).

Ogburn's concern was to distinguish the scientific in sociology from 'various non-scientific procedures that are now so intertwined in the so-called scientific pursuits of the social scientists' (ibid., p. 2). The nonscientific elements he had in mind include the writing of eloquent and colorful articles. More generally, he wished to affirm a contrast between 'scientific' activities and 'intellectual' activities. 'Intellectual processes,' he said 'are combined usually with feelings. . . . But in the scientific work of proof, of establishing real enduring knowledge, thinking must be freed from the bias of emotion' (ibid., p. 4).

There is a parallel here to Weber's demand for coolness. But for Weber, it is in politics as well as science that this attitude is demanded. For Ogburn, it is demanded in science and only at a specific point, in the 'long, careful, painstaking work' of 'proof or verification' (1930, p. 5). Ogburn's only argument for what was later to be called value-free sociology turns out to be a prudential one, relating to the 'temptation to distort conclusions in the interest of emotional values' (ibid., p. 9). He said that 'it will be desirable to taboo our ethics and values (except in choosing problems)' (ibid., p. 10). But this prudential 'tabooing' is not based on the idea that the values of the policy-makers are fundamentally problematic.

Only in the 1930s did the issues begin to take on a different shape, in part because the advocacy of socialism became a concern to critics of the university. The 'head of the department of economics in one of our large universities,' forced to defend his instructors, did so by defending their 'non-partisanship and objectivity.'[7] He remarked that he had

> come through to a sort of faith, if not conviction, that while fundamental values are matters of sentiment more than of reason, conflicts of interest can usually be adjusted by negotiation – discussion and due process of law – that is, through tolerance and peaceful persuasion. It may be, however, that there are certain conflicts of economic interest so deep that no amount of 'reasonableness' will suffice. When we are confronted

> with such a situation, the only thing to do is to stand firm for our constitutional rights.[8]

One notices here a distinct shift from Pound's defense of the reasoned pursuit of the Ought. But the writer's expectation that due process and the constitution will suffice as a framework for dealing with value disputes is still far from Weber, as is the vocabulary. Terms like 'sentiment' are an inheritance from Scottish moral philosophy. They are designed to mark and explicate the contrast between the Is and the Ought, but they do not necessarily imply relativism – indeed, in the hands of the most distinguished members of the tradition, the concepts were used to account for the moral unity of man *beneath* surface differences. So in this tradition a form of the fact-value distinction was important, but *not* to mark out a realm of fundamental and irresolvable conflicts over values. This 'head of the economics department' was a sceptic, after the fashion of the 1915 AAUP Declaration. Scepticism was very common, particularly in the form of the view that there was no known technique for knowing or proving values. But this view was not the same as decisionism and did not lead to the same results, any more than Sidgwick's conclusion that utilitarianism was unprovable led, in England, to a rejection of utilitarianism in practice. The problem of justification was not taken to amount to failure of the valuative, moral, or political ideas themselves, nor to open up the possibility of a new range of choices, nor to create a new situation of choice. The concepts of 'decision' and 'responsible decision,' which were widely used to characterize the situation in Germany, were simply not part of the discussion in the United States, either on the technical, philosophical level or on the public, political level. Indeed, the discussion remained broadly within the liberal tradition. The task of ethical theory or political philosophy was taken to be the *salva veritate*, specifically the *veritate* of liberal civility. Both sides to the philosophical dispute claimed liberalism, or some substantial part of it, as their own, and in the later stages of the dispute, during the war, the conflict hinged on the question of whether an acceptable defense of democracy was possible apart from the affirmation of immutable values.

The Dewey-Hutchins dispute

John Dewey had distinctive views on ethical theory and the fact-value distinction, and this made him a target for such figures as Mortimer Adler, who made disputes over philosophical doctrine into a visible, public matter, and connected them to disputes over educational reform, democracy, and America's world role. Robert Hutchins, president of the University of Chicago, put these issues into the pages of *Life* magazine and other such highly public forums.[9]

The dispute over the defense of democratic values reached the highest peak of public visibility in an exchange in which Hutchins and Dewey squared off in the pages of *Fortune*. Part of the significance of the dispute in connection with the Weberian doctrine of values was that the position Hutchins took foreshadowed the influential critique of Weber later articulated by Leo Strauss. Dewey's response to Hutchins was quite as far from Weber as from Hutchins. But the connection to Hutchins shows one of the ways in which European traditions hostile to Weberianism were reborn in the United States.

In the *Fortune* article, Hutchins took a 'natural right' view of the basis of the American creed and of the issue in the war.

> We know that there is a natural moral law, and we can understand what it is because man has a nature, and we can understand it. The nature of man, which is the same everywhere, is obscured but not obliterated by the different conventions of different cultures. The specific quality of human nature . . . is that man is a rational and spiritual being (Hutchins, 1945, p. 180).

Nor was Hutchins alone in holding this view. At Chicago there was a core of persons with similar views, including Adler and John Nef. Nef, who was one of the forces behind the establishment of the Committee on Social Thought, held a kind of salon at his home, at which Catholic natural law thinkers, such as Frank O'Malley and Waldemar Gurian, were frequent guests (Stritch, 1978, p. 442). Gurian, the founder of the *Review of Politics* in the late 1930s, was a German-educated Catholic who was part of the emigration. In the 1920s, he had been a student of Scheler's and did his doctoral dissertation under him. Jacques Maritain was then approaching the summit of his influence among American Catholics, and this lent great prestige to the revival of natural law views (ibid., p. 443).

Dewey, speaking as the most prominent living American philosopher, took both natural law and natural right to task in his reply to Hutchins. The conflict, as he saw it, was over the intrusion of scientific ways of thinking into the domain of moral and political questions. Dewey's views were widely known, and he was as hostile to the classics as Hutchins was in favor of them. Both agreed that the function of traditional metaphysics was in underwriting practice. As Dewey said,

> Metaphysics is a substitute for custom as the source and guarantor of higher moral and social values – that is the leading theme of the classic philosophy of Europe, as evolved by Plato and Aristotle (1948, p. 17).

But where Hutchins accepted this tradition, Dewey rejected it:

> These eternal objects abstracted from the course of events, although labeled Reality, in opposition to Appearance, are in truth but the idlest and most evanescent of appearances born of personal craving and shaped by private fantasy (1929, p. 436).

For Dewey, science and morals were essentially similar as intellectual endeavors. He was an instrumentalist in his philosophy of science and in his ethics.

> Is there an impassible gulf between science and morals? Or are principles and general truth in morals of the same kind as in science – namely working hypotheses that on one hand condense the results of continued prior experience and on the other hand direct further fruitful inquiry whose conclusions in turn test and develop for further use the working principles used? (1944, p. 186).

Dewey's answer to the latter question is that they are, and that this explains the ultimate mutability of moral ideals, an answer which placed Dewey in opposition to natural right doctrines as well as, in its notion that there is no radical methodological distinction between science and morals, to Weberianism.

Dewey's response to neo-Kantianism was to object to the philosophical distinctions in terms of which philosophical views like Weber's (and for that matter those of past philosophy generally) were framed. The aim of pragmatism as a philosophical movement, as Dewey conceived it, was to dissolve the standard philosophical distinctions. Thus, in writing on education, Dewey attacked distinctions between theory and practice (1944, p. 155). In writing on ethical theory, he attacked the means-end distinction and the fact-value distinction, and this is where his relevance to the Weber controversy is the greatest, for Weber relied heavily on both. Considering Dewey also serves to show how closely the Weberian dilemmas are connected with the particular philosophical tradition in which these distinctions are central.

In his technical philosophical writings, Dewey attacked the means-ends distinction on the philosophical level by arguing that it stems from the 'failure to make an empirical investigation of the actual conditions under which desires and interests arise and function' (1970, p. 413). Desires, he suggested, arise when there is something lacking in the existing situation, 'an absence which produces conflict in the elements that do exist' (ibid.). An 'end-in-view' is formed and projected which is designed to resolve the conflict: whether it will or will not is a matter for empirical inquiry. Value-relativism is an example of the doctrines that arise from this failure; as Dewey put it, the doctrine that 'any desire is as "good" as any other in respect to the value it institutes' (ibid., p. 436) is an extreme response to the kind of theory that 'isolates desires as sources of valuation from any existential context' (ibid., p. 435). The two theories play on each other, for one is tempted 'to escape from the frying pan of disordered valuations,' by jumping 'into the fire of absolutism' (ibid., p. 436).

Valuations, Dewey argued, are capable of being empirically observed, in the historical and cultural-anthropological sense. This sort of knowledge does not warrant 'valuation-propositions,' i.e., purely normative statements. But when we consider the way in which valuations change we notice that knowledge of the conditions of achieving valuations and knowledge of the consequences of their achievement is also empirical; it becomes evident that this knowledge sooner or later 'would surely lead to revaluation of desires and ends that had been assumed to be authoritative sources of valuations' (1970, p. 439). Similarly, when

> investigation shows that a given set of existing valuations, including the rules for their enforcement, be such as to release individual potentialities . . . in a way that contributes to mutual reinforcement of the desires and interests of all members of the group, it is impossible for this knowledge not to serve as a bulwark of the particular set of valuations in question (ibid., p. 440).

Because our knowledge of consequences and conditions changes, our valuations are not fixed but develop, and no abstract theory can suffice to judge these valuations. Development of this sort, based on the idea that values that have good results are supported by the fact that they have good results and the idea that new ones come out of existing ones by showing defects in existing ones, seems like lifting oneself by one's own bootstraps. But this is an impression that, Dewey said, results from a failure to consider how valuations may be brought into relation with one another, which always involves looking at conditions and consequences.

Dewey drew from this some implications for sociology and cultural anthropology that clearly distinguish him from the Weberian conception of the social sciences. We need, he said, systematic empirical investigation of traditions, customs, and institutions with respect to their conditions and consequences

(1970, p. 441), and especially to see the role of cultural conditions in the formation of desires and valuations (ibid., p.443). The result to be expected of this goes right to the core of the fact-value separation.

> The separation alleged to exist between the 'world of facts' and the 'realm of values' will disappear from human beliefs only as valuation-phenomena are seen to have their immediate source in biological modes of behavior and to owe their concrete content to the influence of cultural conditions (ibid., p. 444).

This sociology, far from being predicated on the fact-value separation, was, for Dewey, a means of breaking it down. Breaking it down, as Dewey made clear, is really a matter of cultural reform. Moreover, and here Dewey made a wartime sociological observation of his own, it is a reform demanded by the present, where 'the split between the affectional and the cognitive is probably one of the chief sources of the maladjustments and unendurable strains from which the world is suffering' and is probably a fact that is essential to an adequate explanation of the rise of dictatorship (ibid., p. 445). As he pointed out, today's

> emotional loyalties and attachments are centered on objects that no longer command that intellectual loyalty which has the sanction of the methods which attain valid conclusions in scientific inquiry, while ideas that have their origin in the rationale of inquiry have not as yet succeeded in acquiring the force that only emotional ardor provides (ibid.).

What we need now, he said, is for 'the head and the heart [to] work together' (ibid.).

Morgenthau as a Weberian

There was no 'Weberian critique' of Dewey's ideas labeled as such. Reinhard Bendix, who was an undergraduate in the United States, had been exposed to Dewey's *Human Nature and Conduct* before reading Weber, and he took Weber to have roughly similar views. Perhaps this was a common impression; Weber's interpreters in the United States did little to correct such impressions. The general reason for this was the muting of public dispute between emigrés during the 1930s and the war. 'Solidarity' against Hitler, together with the precarious hold many émigrés had on academic positions, enforced the muting. In these circumstances, the confrontation between Weberian ideas and the ruling American ideas on politics and science was to take different forms, one of the most revealing of which was Hans J. Morgenthau's wartime polemic, *Scientific Man vs. Power Politics* (1946).

In a recent autobiographical statement, Morgenthau acknowledged the Weberian origins of his thought. He tells us that while he was preparing for his legal examinations in the 1920s, he attended a 'seminar on Max Weber's politics and social philosophy, based on the latter's political writings,' in Munich in the faculty of law. 'Weber's political thought,' Morgenthau recalls, 'possessed all the intellectual and moral qualities I had looked for in vain in the contemporary literature inside and outside the universities' (1977, pp. 6-7). The director of this seminar, Professor Karl Rothenbucher, had suitable credentials for such a seminar. Marianne Weber has told us that in 1919, Rothenbucher and Weber had met and talked at length, and Weber reported that he had taken great pleasure in their discussion, for he had found Rothenbucher's political views to be very close to his own (Weber, 1975, p. 664).

Weber's ideas were to form the backbone of Morgenthau's work; yet Morgenthau acknowledged the importance of Weber as a source only late in life. At the time he wrote *Scientific Man vs. Power Politics*, there was no such acknowledgment. This is easily understood. As one may well imagine, it would have been self-defeating for Morgenthau to have presented his views as 'a German theory of politics,' or to have stressed the German origins of his views, especially in the early 1940s.[10] So Morgenthau adopted a procedure that permitted him to present Weberian views with their full polemical force, without the disability of their origins. The procedure was to reconstruct Weber's position in Anglo-American terms, such that when he criticized Anglo-American thinkers, he appealed to the authority of other Anglo-American thinkers. This was a procedure that sometimes led to odd results. In one passage, A.S. Eddington, James Jeans, and Alfred North Whitehead are used to support the notion that the world is ultimately unknowable (1946, p. 135). In another passage, Abraham Lincoln is quoted against the ethic of 'good intentions' and for 'the ethics of responsibility' (ibid., p. 186). In both cases the underlying thought is Weber's. Yet Weber is not mentioned in the book. In spite of this, it is evident that the basic structure of Morgenthau's argument in this book has simply been taken over from Weber: Morgenthau argued that a person may potentially choose various moral positions or make various ultimate value choices, and that reason and rational dialogue cannot settle the questions between these choices.[11]

For Weber, the role of reason with respect to value-oriented action is limited to considerations of consistency of means to ends and between ends. There is a large class of persons who Weber said do not really devote themselves to any cause or end, but who let their lives 'run on as an event in nature,' that is, governed by impulses (1949, p. 18). Morgenthau extended the role of reason to include the 'harmonization' of impulses as well as bringing into harmony means to ends and ends to ends (1946, pp. 157-8). This is an accommodation to Hume, but a minor one, for the core of Morgenthau's position is his recapitulation of the distinctive Weberian argument showing the existence of rationally irresolvable conflicts. The core of the argument is that irresolvable conflicts can arise even with the most modest of political questions.

> the question, 'Who shall produce aluminum?' is itself capable of different interpretations according to the interest or emotion which seeks satisfaction. One may . . . qualify the question under the point of view of private vs. public enterprise, capitalism vs. socialism, corporate vs. individual ownership, monopoly vs. competition, private vs. public interest, and so forth; and in each particular instance the use of the same reasoning powers will produce a different answer. Reason has not one answer to the question, 'Who shall produce aluminum?' It has as many answers to offer as there are conflicting interests and emotions striving for different ends (ibid., pp. 159-60).

Morgenthau called this the 'irrational determination of reason,' and the irreducible irrationality of choice.[12]

The critique of liberalism and legalism

The tradition Morgenthau opposed, because it 'misunderstands the nature of man, the nature of the world, and the nature of reason itself,' he called 'rationalism' (1946, p. 204). In philosophy and social science, we are told, this tradition appears as scientism, in political thought as liberalism, and in foreign policy thinking as legalism. Morgenthau had some obvious reasons for dealing thoroughly with liberalism that Weber did not have. Unlike Weber, Morgenthau was writing in a political environment dominated by liberalism. His targets make up a revealing list. Bentham, Marx, Herbert Spencer, Dewey, Lester Ward, Robert Lynd and Karl Mannheim were all criticized for their scientism and optimism (ibid., pp. 4, 33), and Gladstone, Wilson, and Briand make the 'politicians' section of his list. The thinkers with the right view, at least of foreign policy, are Thucydides, Machiavelli, Richelieu, Hamilton, and Disraeli. What makes them right is that they 'conceive the nature of international politics as an unending struggle for survival and power' (ibid., p. 42).

Dewey had been prominently involved in the 'outlawry of war' movement, and Wilson envisioned an international legal order to settle international disputes. They represent the 'legalism' Morgenthau rejected. Events showed that Morgenthau was right in holding that legalistic formulae would not prevent war, and he was right in identifying legalism as a characteristically American way of thinking about political matters. But he was perhaps wrong in his account of its origins. It derives not so much from 'rationalism' as from a tradition in which the law is regarded in a particular way. The common law tradition, especially in the hands of such persons as Sir Edward Coke, holds the law to be above and to constrain the ruler. The American concept of constitutionality involves the same sense of the law as a substantive constraint apart from and opposed to any authority.

One interpretation of the failure of legalism might be this: legalism in international affairs mistakenly presumed the generality of a sense of the law which was in fact not general but part of the particular substantive political traditions of Britain and the United States. The 'legalists' in international affairs mistook the use and wont of British and American political culture, and the ways in which men of good character and disinterested motives act within this culture, for the way in which decent and properly aware men everywhere act. Further, they assumed that the law could be understood as they themselves understood it, as something separable from and prior to ideological differences and conflicts, and believed that it could be relied on, at least ordinarily, to regulate those differences and conflicts.

Morgenthau's account of the failure of legalism is quite different. For Morgenthau, the mistake of the legalists is a mistake about the nature of politics, a blindness to the character of political life as a struggle of interests; 'legality' can only be a cover for this struggle, a cover that obscures from us and deceives us about the facts of interest. 'What is obvious in . . . claims to justice – be it "just" wage, "justice" for an ethnic minority, or the "justice" of a war – is the coincidence of the claim to justice with the self interest of the claimant' (Morgenthau, 1974, p. 164). For Morgenthau, 'justice' is illusion; struggle is real.

The same argument applies more generally to liberalism. Liberalism, as Morgenthau understood it, is the belief that matters of policy are open to rational reconciliation both domestically and between nations. Weber, of course, denounced these 'rationalistic' notions of politics and insisted that both domestic and international politics are ruled by a struggle based on valuative and material interest. Against the 'liberal' point of view, Weber and Morgenthau took the reductive view that politics is not 'public reason' or about 'just government,' as it appears to be, but is struggle. Thus, for Morgenthau, 'politics among nations is not about the just governance of the nations of the world, but about the struggle of interests. For the liberal, the Weber-Morgenthau view is essentially antipolitical, in the same sense that Marx and Saint-Simon are antipolitical; for both, politics is an illusion whose essential meaning is a struggle whose basis is outside of politics or outside of political discourse.

Morgenthau's positive theory

'Realism,' in contrast to liberal internationalism and other utopianisms, sees politics as it really is, a struggle between interests, and Morgenthau's position has been a development of this viewpoint. 'Realism' and 'utopianism' became technical terms in his metatheoretical account of the 'theory of international politics.' 'Utopians' correspond to Weber's category of persons who have chosen ends that cannot be achieved in this world by any known means but who do not recognize that these ends cannot be achieved. 'Realists,' for Morgenthau, are persons like himself whose choices reflect an acceptance of the fact that to act in international politics entails the doing of evil.

One can see why Morgenthau regarded Weber as possessing special moral qualities and why Morgenthau regarded conduct that is ordinarily considered immoral to be truly moral. Morality in foreign policy, as Morgenthau understood it, is equivalent to the intellectual integrity of the person who subjects himself to the discipline of consequentialist moral discourse and therefore limits himself to choices of attainable ends. Thus, in *Scientific Man vs. Power Politics*, the case against scientism and liberalism is a moral one. 'The moral blindness of scientific man' consists in his failure to appreciate the Weberian fact of the essentially tragic character of human life – a fact that follows from the ultimately inescapable risk of doing evil in the course of political action, the irrationality of the valuative choice, and the rational irresolvability of conflicts arising from these choices (1946, pp. 168-209).

'Realism' in this sense is consistent with Weber's own views. But Morgenthau's development of these ideas took an apparently un-Weberian twist, for it eventuated in a theory that purports to be practice-informing, something that Weber presumably would have held to be impossible. The nature of this departure can be seen through a consideration of the way the two handled the problem of the concept of interests. Weber's concept of interest is summarized in this famous passage:

> Interests (material and ideal), not ideas, dominate directly the actions of men. Yet the 'images of the world' created by these ideas have very often served as switches determining the tracks on which the dynamism of interests kept actions moving (see 1946, p. 280).

Morgenthau quoted this passage with approval in *Politics among Nations: the struggle for power and peace* (1978, p. 9). The passage is peculiarly written. As we have noticed, the parenthetical qualification of the use of the term 'interest' is crucial, for the notion of 'ideal interests' rather takes the force from the claim that it is not ideas that dominate the actions of men. The term 'directly' used in qualification of 'dominate' is also important. The very subtle chain of influence from Calvinist religious ideology to the 'spirit of capitalism' was surely 'indirect,' yet Weber ascribed to this historical influence very substantial effects, such as the economic dominance of Protestant Europe and the disproportionately Protestant character of modern business, which he observed in his own time (1958, pp. 35-7). The Calvinists' interest in their own salvation, which Weber claimed to be the ultimate source of these great effects, is an ideal interest; so one should also be mindful that the phrase 'material and ideal' broadens the notion far beyond the usual meaning of 'interests.' Specifically, it treats ultimate value choices, which are ordinarily regarded as values in contradistinction to interests, as merely another category or type of interest.

Some commentators, ignoring the parenthetical qualification, have interpreted Weber as having been an heir of Marxism who believed in some sense that material interests were determinative of action in history. According to these commentators, Weber's importance lies in his emphasis on the role of ideas as 'switchmen' (e.g. Warner, 1970).[13] These commentators fail to notice that one consequence of this interpretation is that it puts Weber in the position to offer an evaluative account of social life; for he can evaluate various moral stances in respect to their power to enable adherents to achieve their true, material interests or, to put it another way, evaluate valuative choices in terms of their correspondence to their adherents' true interests. This would amount to a method of evaluating the rationality of value choice, by considering value choice as an instrumental act. Morgenthau did not interpret Weber in this way. He treated values and interests as Weber did, by considering interests to be dictated by value choices, material and ideal. But the institution of the nation-state creates an anomalous situation: in international politics, according to Morgenthau, interests can be rather precisely defined.

Morgenthau argued that the nation-state is going to be a fixture in world politics for the foreseeable future. The structure of world politics in a world of nation-states is such that no nation, whatever its goals (whatever its 'value choices,' so to speak), can escape from the necessity to guide its actions by technical considerations of power. Any nation wishing to survive and pursue worldly goals has a 'national interest' that is relatively fixed by the fact that any serious deviation from the pursuit of this interest, in the context of world politics, will lead to defeat. Therefore, the idea that any nation can pursue policy contrary to its interests for such purposes as the satisfaction of 'moral principles' is utopian.[14] In short, the boundaries of realism or worldly goal attainment in international politics are very tight. So for Morgenthau, an objective, practice-informing theory of international politics is possible without departing from the Weberian strictures against normative theory.

An interesting difference between Weber and Morgenthau appears at the point of the consideration of what ends are attainable in this world. Morgenthau, in his discussion of the old and the new nationalism, described the old nationalism as the view that 'the nation is the ultimate goal of political action, the end point of the political development beyond which there are other nationalisms with similar and equally justifiable goals' (1962, vol. 1, p. 187). This was Weber's value choice. Morgenthau rejected this choice, on grounds that would have appealed to Weber. He argued that nationalism contained a paradox (which became apparent only, as it happens, after Weber's death). Instead of creating a just world order of free nations, nationalism, (especially of small nations and peoples) became 'the great disruptive and anarchical force of the interwar period' as a consequence of the breakup of the Turkish and Austro-Hungarian empires (ibid.). The goal that nationalism sought, namely national freedom, turned out to be unattainable as a consequence of this anarchy and disruption. It became, in other words, an illusion, and therefore could not be the proper goal of politics understood as 'the art of the possible,' that is, understood as an enterprise based on an ethic of responsibility. If nationalism can no longer be realistically regarded as an attainable end, it becomes 'utopian,' and the responsible politician is compelled to seek other goals.

Offical responsibility and leadership

This style of argument is not contrary to Weber's; indeed, it resembles Weber's discussion of the present inevitability of democratic forms of state, which was similarly designed to place 'empirical' limits around the discussion of political alternatives

(Weber, 1978a, p. 1461). The striking departure occurred when Morgenthau gave an account of the nature of the moral responsibility of the officials of the national state, using the example of Lincoln. Lincoln justified his own war policies on the ground that he had a responsibility to save the union. For Morgenthau, this justification amounted to saying that the official has an inherent official responsibility for the maintenance and survival of the state of which he is an official.[15]

> The individual may say for himself: *Fiat justitia, pereat mundus*; but the state has no right to say so in the name of those who are in its care. . . . Yet while the individual has a moral right to sacrifice himself in defense of . . . a moral principle, the state has no right to let its moral disapprobation . . . get in the way of successful political action, itself inspired by the moral principle of national survival (Morgenthau, 1962, vol. 1, p. 10).

One notes immediately that Morgenthau used certain terms in these arguments that Weber would have hesitated to use. For Weber, the state is not a moral object except by virtue of an individual's decision. One can, as an individual, choose to devote oneself to a particular state or ruler, or accept the legitimacy of a state or ruler. But the state has no reality apart from such decisions or beliefs of the subjects of the state. Weber's type of nationalism combined, in one individual value decision, a personal value choice and an acceptance of the legitimacy of the demands of the state.

If one rejects this value decision, as Morgenthau did, it is unclear precisely what is the source and character of one's obligation to the state. Indeed, the theory of obligation, deontology, is a notorious weak spot in philosophies that hold that the ultimate seat of values is in individual value decisions, for according to such theories one could have no obligations other than those one freely assumes. Given this, it is paradoxical for Morgenthau to tell officials what their responsibilities or moral obligations are, since these are not defined by any general principles of obligation or political conduct, but ultimately rest only on their own value choices. Since Morgenthau went to considerable trouble to deny that value positions can be rationally founded, it is obscure how he could claim to offer rational grounds for assertions of the obligations of officials.

Weber faced this problem squarely by denying that the leader has any obligations to his followers or, in fact, to anything but his own value commitments. This does not mean that the statesman is unconstrained in his actions; of course he is constrained by the situation. Weber meant merely that he is under no *moral* obligation to serve the best interests of his followers or, for that matter, to preserve the state itself, as Morgenthau claimed.

But this raises some questions. If one considers the kind of politics Weber wished to maximize, the politics of leaders who command irrational devotion, as distinguishing a type of political community in contrast to the type of political community based on reasoned valuative persuasion, one suspects that it is this latter type of political community that would have the greater unity and ability to deal with true foreign enemies and the former type that would be subject to the most divisive conflicts. In the plebiscitary regime, the enemies of the leader would not merely be foreign enemies but would be domestic opponents as well. Indeed, the distinction between foreign and domestic enemies would dissolve, for it would lack any principled basis. Further, there is no assurance that the value positions of the leader who would command the greatest following would conduce to national greatness. Morgenthau's account appears to avoid this difficulty. But his conception of the moral obligation of officials to preserve the state serves to reduplicate these difficulties in Weber's conception, in different guise.

For Morgenthau, the duty of the official to preserve the state may well set him against the desires of the subjects, or many of the subjects, of the state. Far from being a hypothetical possibility, this is in fact the permanent condition of foreign policy-making in the United States. In order for the maker of foreign policy in the United States to succeed in his task for preserving the state (in the extended sense of serving its permanent interests), his policies must meet the requirements of sound foreign policy dictated by this task and also meet the requirement of keeping popular support. It is revealing that in Morgenthau's discussion of this problem, the matter is stated entirely in terms of the effectiveness of policy. The policy-maker is warned that effective policy requires popular support. Yet Morgenthau did not mention any moral responsibility of the policy-maker in a democratic regime to obtain the consent of the governed for these policies. He said merely that the statesman must 'impress upon the people the requirements of a sound foreign policy by telling them the facts of political life . . . and then to strike a compromise which leaves the essence of a sound foreign policy intact' (1962, vol. 1, p. 387). In short, the statesman must deal with the people in precisely the way in which one deals with a foreign power.

When one recalls Weber's phrase 'the domestic political form must be structured for the purpose of fulfilling foreign policy tasks,' one wonders about Morgenthau's conception of the location of the moral limits on the statesman's conduct toward his own countrymen (Weber, 1971, p. 443). When, for example, is deception allowable? Is a permanent policy of public deception allowable? It is evident that deception that fails may cause a loss of popular support, and responsible policy may then become extremely difficult to obtain. But this is the case with deception in international dealings as well. Is there any special obligation of the statesman to tell the truth to his own political community apart from such considerations of expedience? To pose these questions is merely to bring out the peculiarity of the relation between the official and the political community that is implicit in Morgenthau's conception; no limits on official conduct or obligations of the official to the political community follow from Morgenthau's account. On the contrary, the epistemological premises of this conception preclude the possibility of rational justifications for claims about limits or obligations, so they could only flow from an individual's personal moral code.

Morgenthau's place in American discourse

Morgenthau illustrates one of the ways in which Weber's views were inserted into the American debate, and how they were transformed and obscured in the course of this insertion. Weber's views grafted nicely on to a literature that had developed in the 1930s on 'the crisis in liberalism,' as Dewey had entitled a chapter in his 1935 book (1963). The 'crisis' had to do with the conflict of welfare and state power with various liberal rights. The upshot of the dispute was that there were issues of principle in liberalism concerning the welfare activities of the state and the extent to which these activities could appropriately override property rights, and that these issues were not easily resolved on the level of principle or at the level of interests. The issues themselves were not new, but they were newly raised by the actions of the Roosevelt administration and the widespread bitterness and distrust that accompanied them.

Pragmatism and scientism were commonly associated with interventionism. Dewey's view, for example, was that 'natural rights and natural liberties exist only in the kingdom of mythological social zoology' (1935, p. 17). Liberals and particularly economists committed to these doctrines often attacked the philosophy underlying these claims. Hayek's *The Counter-Revolution of Science: studies on the abuse of reason* (1952) is representative of this genre. Frank Knight had similar criticisms. His own essay 'The Sickness of Liberal Society' (1947) was a commentary on the Dewey-Hutchins debate. He rejected pragmatism and scientism but at the same time rejected what he saw as the 'preaching' of Hutchins and Adler, as well as Maritain.

Morgenthau had many of the same targets. He pursued them in a different way, by adapting the German idea of the *Krisis der Wissenschaft*, which served him as a frame for the 'Crisis of Liberalism'. In the first chapter of *Scientific Man vs. Power Politics*, the 'Crisis' of our civilization is identified in a section called 'The Crisis of Philosophy' (1946, p. 2). Since there actually was no crisis of philosophy in American scholarship, Morgenthau redefined 'philosophy' as 'the largely unconscious intellectual assumptions by which the age lives' (ibid., pp. 2-3). The 'crisis', he said, was induced by the failure of Wilsonian liberal internationalism and the rise of Hitler (ibid., pp. 4-7). Thus liberalism, like pacifism, showed itself to be utopian and self-defeating.

Antiutopianism was also a large part of Knight's and Hayek's arguments, but there were some significant differences between their antiutopianism and antiscientism and Morgenthau's. Knight evaluated *Scientific Man vs. Power Politics* when it was submitted to the University of Chicago Press; he took it for a good critique of 'scientism.' In his prepublication evaluation, he made a remark that shows the gap between his views and Morgenthau's. 'As in the work as a whole,' Knight said, 'the title speaks of science, [but] the discussion immediately turns to reason.'[16] Knight wished to reject the claims of scientism, and he did so in a way that reflected scepticism. He saw both Dewey and Hutchins as claiming that they had a technique for resolving disputes or solving ethical problems, and he denied that they do. But nothing about power-politics and the ethical irrationality of this world follows from the nonexistence of a technique. So Knight treated the disputes over economic rights as a practical threat to the liberal tradition. But he remained firmly within this tradition himself. If he believed that there was no rational solution to these particular problems, he did not take this to imply the fundamental irrationality of ethical and political questions. Morgenthau, like Weber, took this step.

Morgenthau's influence was primarily in the academic area of international relations. He was a decisive influence on Henry Kissinger. Yet Morgenthau's metatheoretical ideas were never particularly influential or, for that matter, understood, save as an explication of 'Realism.' He opposed the 'behavioralism' that developed in political science in the United States and opposed the war in Vietnam on grounds of *Realpolitik* – oppositions that earned him the support of radical political scientists in his successful bid for the presidency of the American Political Science Association. The invisibility of his philosophical roots must be accounted for in part by the rise of a philosophic movement that was superficially similar, at least with respect to the problem of values. The story of the later dispute over Weber is in large part the story of the entanglement and confusion with Logical Positivism and other movements during the postwar period in the United States and Germany.

8 The issue reframed: positivism and value-free social science

The 1940s brought a new set of circumstances: the end of World War II and the beginning of the cold war, the rapid expansion of the universities and the social sciences, the rise to influence of the philosophy of Logical Positivism, and the changed significance of science in the wake of the atomic bomb. Weber's doctrine of the place of values in the social sciences and his view of the vocation of science took on meaning as an explication of a solution to some of the new problems of the university, and it was in connection with these issues that the doctrine of values proper became widely recognized in the United States.

Morgenthau's critique dealt with a constellation of interrelated ideas. He took pragmatism, scientism, liberalism, and legalism together to correspond to the Weberian ideas, which he used as a more or less unified conception of science, politics, and an account of values. In America, however, this use of Weber was anomalous. The typical pattern was the piecemeal appropriation of Weber's ideas, and the deemphasis of the uses of the value theory as a technique of criticism. Parsons's discussion of Weber in *The Structure of Social Action* (1968), which first appeared in 1936, said nothing about Weber's politics, and discussed Weber's doctrine of values only in connection with methodology and the Parsonian project of the construction of a 'voluntaristic theory of action.' Reinhard Bendix's *Max Weber: an intellectual portrait* (1962), which introduced Weber to a generation of students, is emblematic of the fragmentation: far from being an 'intellectual portrait,' it did not deal with Weber's political or methodological writings, and it gave no hint of the existence of the Weimar critique.[1]

The insertion of Weberian language

The reasons for the fragmentation of Weber's views were closely connected to the reason for their ready adoption. We can understand this through a consideration of one of the earliest uses of the language of the Weberian doctrine of values in the United States, in a polemic against James Bryant Conant's 1947 American Association for the Advancement of Science presidential address, 'The Role of Science in Our Unique Society.' Conant's topic is the place of science in the preservation of American democracy; he argued that 'our solidarity as a nation depends on our acceptance of [certain] ideals and a concerted effort to move continuously toward the social goals implied' (1948, p. 80). The ideals provide a purpose for the social sciences – the 'study of the many problems arising as a consequence of our endeavours to keep our society prosperous, strong and democratic' (ibid.). Conant was perfectly aware that this line of reasoning goes against the idea 'that science is neutral as far as value judgments are concerned.' This view he characterized as 'one of those three-quarter truths fully as dangerous as half truths' (ibid., p. 81). Social science he considered to be analogous to medical science, whose practitioners also had to clarify their standards of value. He considered there to be a broad range of common social goals in the United States which 'might form the basis of agreement' among social scientists. These included 'the goals of equality of opportunity, a maximum degree of individual freedom, and a wide distribution of centers of initiative' (ibid., p. 82).

Conant's statement is striking as an articulation of a view of the social role of social science that was characteristic of the American university tradition. Twenty years earlier, and perhaps ten, it would have excited little hostility. In the postwar period things had obviously changed. Robert Bierstedt, son-in-law of the chair of the Columbia sociology department, attacked Conant, using arguments that were soon to become commonplace in sociology. Bierstedt's argument is distinctly Weberian; yet Bierstedt did not, as Morgenthau did, attack the American political tradition. He applied the argument solely to the question, as the title of his paper reads, of 'Social Science and Social Policy.'

The paper is reminiscent of Weber's dispute with the Social Policy Association. Sociology, Bierstedt says,

> is a science or it is nothing. And in order to be a science it must diligently avoid all pronouncements of an ethical character. As a science it cannot answer questions of value. It can have no traffic with normative statements because there is no logic of the normative. It can deal, as can the other sciences, only with

> questions of fact, with propositions, with statements capable of being true or false. . . . This non-ethical or non-normative character of science is . . . one of its primary characteristics, along with objectivity, communicability, verifiability, and relativity. The scientific method as such provides no technique for answering questions of value [or] for determining ultimate ends (1948, p. 312).

Neither Conant in 1947 nor the *Katherderalsozialisten* in Weber's time, of course, had claimed that the scientific method provided a technique for determining ultimate ends. Conant, indeed, had gone out of his way to deny that science did any such thing.

The real issue between Bierstedt and Conant lies elsewhere. Bierstedt was anxious that sociology appear to be a science. So he wished for sociologists to imitate what he took to be the characteristics of science.[2] His specific idea for doing this is an institutional one, formulated in terms of roles: the role of the scientist and the role of the citizen, we are told, must be distinguished. 'To adopt another course is to prostitute the prestige of science and of a scientific reputation,' and to risk confusion with 'social prophecy' (Bierstedt, 1948, p. 314).

The means of separating these roles is to consider 'ethical neutrality . . . normative silence, and . . . objectivity' as 'virtues' for the scientist in performing his role (Bierstedt, 1948, p. 317). This does not preclude some participation in public life. But this participation, as Bierstedt envisioned it, should be 'decisionist,' in Habermas's sense. 'Once the values of a society are determined and once the goals are set, the sociologist should be able, when he does not know the answers, to initiate researches which will supply them' (ibid.).

The argument for this conception of the role of the sociologist is no more than a straw-man argument conjoined with the imposition of a false dichotomy, which makes the one side of the dichotomy, Bierstedt's conception of the role of the sociologist, appear to be the only acceptable possibility.[3] Conant's actual suggestion was never addressed. But the anxiety to appear scientific must have been overwhelming at the time, as it has been for many social scientists since. And this must have supplied enormous power to the semiotic structure that Bierstedt's dichotomy presupposes, which makes science the opposite of 'normative.' This particular insertion of Weberian language into a non-Weberian issue – the anxiety of sociologists to appear scientific – led to a peculiar result. We find Alvin Gouldner, writing in 1964, attributing to Weber the view that university teachers have no right to believe in and be committed to values. Gouldner takes the 'opposite view,' 'that professors are like all others, entitled and perhaps obligated to express their values' (quoted in Bruun, 1972, pp. 36-7). This opinion, as Bruun points out, is 'in fact identical with Weber's own position' (ibid, p. 36). Other distortions arose from construing Weber's views in terms of the Anglo-American tradition. Schumpeter, in his *History of Economic Analysis*, explained Weber's dispute with the *Verein* in this way. 'The epistemological problem in itself,' he said, 'is neither very difficult nor very interesting and can be disposed of in a few words . . . with reference to the English environment: and specifically Senior, Cairnes, and Sidgwick' (1954, p. 805).

In the course of this assimilation, the Weberian doctrine and phrases such as 'the relativism of values' came to serve as a new reading of the skepticism of the Anglo-American tradition as 'relativism'. This was in part justified by the historical development of the Anglo-American thought itself, a point made by Schumpeter in mentioning Sidgwick, whose *Methods of Ethics* showed the futility of the established approach to the proof of the utilitarian principle (1954, pp. 806-7; Sidgwick, 1874). But Sidgwick was nevertheless not a value relativist, and neither were the skeptics in this tradition, so this new reading was a distortion.

The translation of the term *Wissenschaft* also, and fortuitously, helped the acceptance of Weberian language. Weber's doctrine was presented by his American admirers as a plea for disinterested scholarship and value-free *science*. Frank Knight had noticed a related shift in Morgenthau's argument between 'science' and 'reason' (1947). The shift in terminology from 'Wissenschaft' to 'science' made the argument for value-free *science* extremely plausible (Brecht, 1970, p. 141) – no one wishes to claim that valuative preferences, however well warranted, can refute or disprove the results of empirical inquiry, or that 'ideology' should replace empirical study. But this was not what Weber's critics in the Weimar period wished to claim either. '*Wissenschaft*' is a far more inclusive term than 'science' (ibid., p. 142). Strauss's translation, 'philosophy or science,' correctly brings out the point that Weber's negative thesis – the denial of ultimate rationality to all moral or political choices – is far more sweeping than the slogan 'value-free science' indicates. It says that one cannot intelligibly ask questions about, e.g., the meaning of science, its value, or the value and rational adequacy of political and cultural positions – an extremely implausible claim. And to exclude the task of answering such questions from the university, on the grounds that all such questioning is merely the struggle of one equally baseless value position against another, is even less plausible (ibid., p. 143). Put differently, in its original form, Weber's position is a philosophical thesis in need of an elaborate explication, not a self-evident truth contested only by 'ideologists.' So in the course of accommodating Weber's views to the American environment, these Weberian arguments were deemphasized or treated as platitudes about science. At the same time, the positive aspects of Weber's view of values, especially the doctrine of the necessity of irrational decision and of value-struggle, were ignored or soft-pedaled.

The absorption of substantive analyses

The anxiety to appear scientific, and the code of 'normative silence' which followed from it, had another effect. Weberian ideas about politics and Weberian sociological concepts, which were self-consciously constructed to appear value-free, became more attractive to the new generation of social scientists trained after the war. So Weberian concepts and arguments were imported piece by piece to fill particular needs. Sometimes they were identified with Weber. Sometimes they were not – other authors simply presented the Weberian ideas as their own, as Morgenthau had, without identifying their source. This had the peculiar result that standard Weberian arguments were widely known before Weber's own formulations were translated. When they were translated, the arguments seemed familiar and not particularly distinctive.

A good example of this process was Schumpeter, Weber's close friend and, with Morgenthau, the Weberian with the greatest impact on American intellectual life. Though Schumpeter's economics was not much influenced by Weber, his political and sociological writing was. His *Capitalism, Socialism, and Democracy* has a great deal to do with Weber. Schumpeter's historical view of the inevitability of socialism has more than a passing similarity to Weber's discussion of future bureaucratization. The inevitable sharpening of struggle in the political and economic spheres provided the motive force for this development in Weber's writings. Schumpeter argued the point somewhat differently. In his famous presidential address to the American Economic Association in 1950, he argued that inflation would ultimately create circumstances that will make socialism a political inevitability. This was a notion gleaned from the Weimar experience.

The parallel to Weber's views to be found in the discussion of the theory of democracy in *Capitalism, Socialism, and Democracy* is even closer. In this section he argued against what he called 'the classical theory of democracy,' which he understood to be based on the notion that government is an expression of the will of the people. Weber, it will be recalled, also denounced the notion of the 'will of the people' as a fiction. Schumpeter argued similarly, following (but not citing) Weber's 'Socialism' speech, that the will of the people may be said to be expressed through democratic institutions only in such circumstances as Swiss democracy. The Swiss were mostly small-scale agriculturalists, and there were few large businesses. The political issues that arise for such a society can be understood by all, and do not require professional expertise (Schumpeter, 1950, p. 267). In short, these communities have a 'public.' This is not Schumpeter's terminology, however. Schumpeter put the issue the other way around, by saying that modern societies ordinarily are dominated by the 'crowd' and crowd psychology.

From this Schumpeter concluded that the classical theory is no longer applicable; accordingly he offered an alternative 'theory of democracy' which he suggested should replace the classical theory in the minds of politically sophisticated persons. The theory says that 'the democratic method is that institutional arrangement for arriving at political decisions in which individuals acquire the power to decide by means of a competitive struggle for the people's vote' (Schumpeter, 1950, p. 269). This theory, Schumpeter said, 'is of course no more definite than is the concept of competition for leadership' (ibid., p. 271). The classical theory, he observed, did not leave room for 'a proper recognition of the vital fact of leadership' (ibid., p. 270). When Schumpeter applied this theory, he chose Weber's example of Gladstone as a 'Plebiscitarian Dictator.'

> Gladstone had resigned the leadership years before and tackled the country single-handed. But when the liberal party under this impetus had won a smashing victory, it was obvious to everyone that he had to be again accepted as the party leader – nay that he had become the party leader by virtue of his national leadership and that there simply was no room for any other (ibid., pp. 275-6).

'Now,' Schumpeter went on, 'this instance teaches us a lot about the working of the democratic method. . . . It is the oversized specimen of a normal genus' (ibid., p. 276). Parliamentary authority, as Schumpeter echoed Weber, becomes something of a fiction. The leader always becomes to some extent independent, a personal leader with a foothold outside parliament and party. This 'puts a whip into the hand of the leader the crack of which may bring unwilling and conspiring followers to heel' (ibid., p. 277).

Putting aside the question of the truth of this account of the example, we can recognize the similarities to Weber. But there are differences that are notable as well. Schumpeter ignored the normative 'just consent' elements of the classical theory and did not consider that the preservation of a 'public' is a normative requirement of democracy. He presented his own view entirely as a historical thesis. Clearly, he would not have believed that the creation of a democracy living up to the 'classical theory' was a future historical possibility. But he did not treat the classical theory as a delusion based on a false conviction that rational 'just consent' is, in value-tainted spheres, an epistemological possibility as Weber did by his insistence on the present historical realization of the philosophically based problem of 'rationally irreconcilable value conflict.' The whole issue of value conflict simply did not figure in Schumpeter's account.

Stripped of its associations with the Weberian idea that a 'classical' democratic order based on rational value agreement is now a philosophical impossibility as well as a practical impossibility, this account of democracy appears to be straightforwardly historical, and neither 'valuative' nor 'philosophical.' Similar transformations were made with other Weberian ideas. The thesis of the rationalization and ethical irrationality of the world was, for example, transformed into a 'value-free' historical observation about 'the end of ideology.' Weber could then be interpreted, retrospectively, as someone who had understood this historical 'fact.'

Postwar Germany

The destruction of the Hitler regime, the end of the war, the occupation, and the emergence of the cold war made for a German context quite unlike the earlier context of the dispute. The political situation of Weimar was not allowed to recur. The occupation authorities imposed a political order. The legitimacy of this order, in theory, rested not on the consent of the governed but on the Occupation Statute, which was succeeded only in 1955 by the ratification of the Paris agreement (Grosser, 1971, p. 79). In practice, under the statute, the occupation authorities in the West gradually granted autonomy in various areas, as the situation warranted. So the new regime was not subject to the same constitutional disputes as the Weimar regime. At the same time, the Germans, divided by the Iron Curtain, felt the cold war as did no other nation.

The immediate result of the end of the war was a great outpouring of reflections on the German experience itself, and there was an extraordinary demand for explanations of the meaning of the German catastrophe. Helmut Thielicke, a prominent Protestant theologian, recalls that

> when the universities were reopened after the German capitulation in 1945 they were filled with ragged figures . . . former officers . . . refugees from the Eastern territories . . . and also many who came from prison camps. All of them . . . were hungry, for the blessed stream of American CARE packets had not yet reached us. . . . Intellectually, however, it was a glorious time. Before us sat a generation which had been shrewdly and cruelly misled by the holders of power. And now they faced a world of rubble and ruins; not only their homes, but also their idealism, their faith, their concepts of value were shattered. But the vacuum in their hearts cried out to be filled. At the same time these young people were profoundly skeptical (1969, p. vii).

Thielicke lectured on Nihilism, to which he tried to give a Christian response. Nihilism was a common theme. For the German intellectuals who lived through the war, the war seemed to be the fulfillment of the sense of catastrophe to which Nietzsche referred in the second aphorism in *The Will to Power: an attempted transvaluation of all values* (1924). By the end of the war, it seemed instead that not civilization as a whole, as Nietzsche had said, but Germany in particular had been destined for catastrophe and that Germany in particular had to draw its lessons. Nihilism became regarded as a curse which must be forced to lift rather than as a fate which had to be faced. Not surprisingly, natural law and natural right ideas found new respectability, and on the philosophical level a good deal of what was written was motivated by the question of how much could be appropriately conceded to these ideas.

Weberians as well as anti-Weberians were prominent in the reconsideration of the German experience. Both Jaspers and Spranger wrote important books.[4] Radbruch, who also played a 'prominent part in the attempt to help Germany find her bearings and to build a new scheme of values from the ruins of the Nazi debacle' (Friedmann, 1960, p. 192), came to regard the Weberian legal relativism he had previously taught as in part responsible for the easy acceptance of Nazism (ibid., p. 205). Just before his death, Radbruch was moving to a legal conception that incorporated more natural law elements, as in such remarks as 'where the contradiction between the positive law and justice reaches so intolerable a degree that the law of unright law must cede to justice, the force of positive law must yield to the higher demand of justice' (quoted in ibid.).[5] Yet these developments were paralleled by a development that put Weber in a more favorable light: the attempt to find liberal democratic roots in Germany, in the course of which Weber was presented as a distinguished German forefather of the then forming German republic. This set up the controversy over Weber's liberalism that followed in the late 1950s and the 1960s (Aron, 1970, pp. 297-8; cf. Roth, 1971b, p. 46).[6]

The writings of the immediate postwar period cannot always be taken at face value. Some of the reconsideration of the German political past and German philosophy took the manifest literary form of rewriting the past in ways that excused or minimized the responsibility of particular persons or ideas. In several cases, notably books by Jaspers and Meinecke, their explicit admission or acceptance of collective German guilt and the admission of the intellectual responsibility of the German tradition is constructed in such a way that the intellectual responsibility of Meinecke and Jaspers as individuals is minimized. In Meinecke's case, for example, there is a curious blindness about Naumann, with whom Meinecke had been politically associated. Where others stressed the continuities between Naumann's ideas and Hitlerism, Meinecke managed to find nothing but virtue in Naumann (Meinecke, 1963, pp. 22-4).

Jaspers's writings presented an even more peculiar picture. Lukács described Jasper's transformation bluntly. 'Since Jaspers was an existentialist, irrationalist, Kierkegaardian and Nietzschean, nobody in Hitler's time could raise a concrete objection to him [i.e. Hitler]. Now, after Hitler's downfall, Jaspers discovers . . . reason' (1980, p. 829). Indeed, Jaspers's new argument, presented in *The Question of German Guilt*, differs from his earlier views. He continued to speak of the importance of power in community life, and claimed that it inevitably produces guilt. 'Every human being is fated to be enmeshed in the power relations he lives by. This is the inevitable guilt of all, the guilt of human existence' (1961, p. 34). Where Weber had drawn the conclusion that the inevitability of guilt rendered Christian morality irrelevant to politics, Jaspers now drew a different conclusion. This inevitable guilt, he said, 'is counteracted by supporting the power that achieves what is right, the rights of man,' and this creates a new standard: 'failure to collaborate in organizing power relations, in the struggle for power for the sake of serving the right, creates basic political guilt and moral guilt at the same time' (ibid.). Failure to meet this standard was the basis of German guilt. We mentioned in Chapter 2 that this was an appeal to natural law, and Jaspers himself stressed this when he said that the Nuremberg trials were justified by 'human rights and natural law' (ibid., p. 55). Jaspers also used the book to attack another philosopher (apparently Heidegger), and suggested that this philosopher was culpable for encouraging Nazism (ibid., p. 111). Although Jaspers had said similar things to those said by this philosopher, he did not deal with the obvious question of his own culpability.[7]

Another conspicuous figure in the reconsideration of the German past was Weber's younger brother, Alfred. His book, *Farewell to European History*, shows the distance the experiences of the war had put between his views and his brother's. Though the two had never held identical views, it will be recalled that they were closely identified during the struggle with the Social Policy Association. But Alfred's later ideas on these issues were very different.

The 'cardinal sin' of German political thinking, in the post-1870 period, Alfred Weber argued, was the placing of the state beyond the moral sphere.

> It was a sin that cost it dear, since in this way the whole body-politic which, all through the Middle Ages, had been under the sanction of the Church – the individual ordering his life, his happiness, his fortune, his spiritual being by this and this alone – became something quite arbitrary (A. Weber, 1977, p. xviii).

Once the humanitarian ideals of the eighteenth century gave way to the rise of appeals to 'National Interest,' 'all respect whatsoever for decency and honor' was thrown aside. The present war, he said, has finally collapsed 'the whole *raison d'être* of a-moral state-action with its plausible justifications' (ibid.). The lesson of the war is 'that all forms of power politics, since these, as Clausewitz might say, carry war in themselves as the continuation of statecraft by other means, must be exterminated at the root' (ibid., p. xv).

The doctrine Alfred Weber identified as the 'cardinal sin' had passed through Treitschke, his brother Max, in 'Politics as a Vocation,' Simmel, who made an important contribution to it by formulating the idea of 'autonomous spheres,' and in the 1920s Carl Schmitt, whose *The Concept of the Political* (1976) said that the sphere of politics was defined by war and the threat of war. Thus, to say, as Alfred Weber did, that in accounting for the catastrophe it is cowardice to blame everything on Hitler (A. Weber, 1977, p. 152), and to then designate this doctrine as the 'cardinal sin,' apportions blame to these persons. But Alfred Weber was concerned to regard the development of this idea in the broadest perspective. Thus Nietzsche bears the brunt of his attack, though he too is seen as part and parcel of the spiritual disintegration in Europe in the nineteenth century. 'We can say with confidence,' Alfred Weber told us, 'that the spiritual outcome of secularism with its historicisms and relativisms was bound to be Nihilism, as Nietzsche was quite right in thinking' (ibid., p. 137). And Nietzsche himself, precisely because of his 'time-conditioning,' the historical circumstance of the collapse of the old abstractions, could not escape from Nihilism. 'Only when we can see this world again and are ready and able to experience it in ourselves and take our bearings by it, shall we be on the road to the conquest of Nihilism' (ibid., p. 139). But, as Alfred Weber reemphasizes often, the 'experience' includes values. 'The official morality of Christianity . . . is nothing less than a formalized accentuation of value deriving wholly from the preconceptual and fundamental experience on which Christianity rests; from the experience of the transcendental oneness of mankind' (ibid., p. 138).

The path back, he suggested, is through the improvement of the 'average *character quality* of the masses.' By character quality, he said, 'we mean the inflexible will to come to one's own judgment and the resoluteness to act accordingly even to one's own disadvantage' (1977, p. 164). The qualities he had in mind, as he made quite clear, have more to do with 'the psychology of the English workers – or . . . the outlook and basic assumptions of the average North American' (ibid., p. 165).

> 'Self-control' and 'self-government,' whoever does not know that these are not mere catchwords but fundamental *facts* born of the Anglo-Saxon character, obviously has no conception of what this war is about. . . . Government of the masses in freedom is principally a question of character formation . . . it is facilitated by old traditions (ibid.).

The first order of business for Germany, accordingly, is to revive the urge to freedom and independence of character that prevailed in Germany during the sixteenth century (ibid., pp. 164, 169-70). This view of the problem of character resembled Max Weber's, but differed in the decisive respect of the intent behind the reforms. For Max Weber, the aim had been to create a people who could count in world politics. For Alfred Weber, this aim was part of the problematic past.

However unoriginal Alfred Weber's views might seem, they represented a decisive turning away from Weberianism. The older form of Weberianism, defined by Weber's own views taken as a whole, was clearly no longer a tenable position. The inevitable consequence of this for the Weber dispute was that the tainted doctrines were deemphasized by Weber's admirers and explicators, and this in turn had the effect of making Weber appear more like a positivist, an appearance which, in Germany, was compounded by the usage of the term 'positivist.'

Although the term shows up with some frequency, it is used with astonishing looseness. In Thielicke's book on Nihilism, based on his 1945 lectures, we are told that 'this basic scientific attitude and method which regard the fragmentary, discontinuous data of the world as the only facts available to scientific knowledge we call positivism. It is therefore always combined with a nihilistic view of the world' (1969, p. 63), and that 'in the last analysis all dictatorship is coupled with nihilism; or more precisely, it is coupled with the *positivistic* form of nihilism' (ibid., p. 74). Thielicke substantiates this connection by reference to a 'positivist student of the law' of Bismarck's time who 'jeered at' jurists who inquired 'after the total context in which the law itself was incorporated and within which it served a useful function' (ibid., p. 65). This jurist said this was 'really searching for something that transcends and that those who do this are nothing more than metaphysicians disguised as lawyers' (ibid., p. 66).

Thielicke's use of the term captures the basic semiotic – the conceptual grid – in which it is embedded: positivism means the 'separated' and the 'immediately given', and this means historicist relativism or nihilism as opposed to the 'connected', the transcendent, and the realm of orderliness beyond immediate experience. In this semiotic structure, Weber is a 'positivist.' But the semiotic itself confuses the historical issue of Weber's place in relation to the philosophical movement of Logical Positivism as distinct from such movements as pragmatism and ordinary language philosophy, which are also frequently labeled as 'positivist.' The history of the dispute over values and methods after the war is in large part a history of this confusion and of the attempt, by some of the heirs to the Weimar dispute, to read these other movements through this semiotic structure. Weber differs substantially from the other movements that have carried the label 'positivist.' We have already seen Morgenthau's Weberian criticisms of scientism and pragmatism. Yet similarly large differences hold between Weber and the philosophical views of Logical Positivism *proper*. To understand these differences, some technical and historical background is necessary.

LOGICAL POSITIVISM AND THE DISPUTE

Logical Positivism was well received in the United States, for it fitted with the admiration for science which Morgenthau noticed and criticized. It had some similarities to Weberianism. But the intellectual and historical background of the movement was very different, and the attitude of the positivists toward values was also significantly different. The main line of Logical Positivism developed from the work of the Vienna Circle, a small group of individuals who agreed on the rejection of metaphysics and on certain issues relating to the problem of logical analysis of scientific propositions. Their views on ethical issues, and on ethical theory, were much more diverse, although some similarities of approach remained.

The linguistic turn

The key element of the Logical Positivist program was the task of constructing a criterion of meaningfulness and a particular conception of the significance of this task. Weber's conception superficially resembles the Positivist's conception in that he appealed to the notion of meaning and frequently used the expressions 'meaningful' and 'meaningless.' In an account of the function of value discussions, after identifying four kinds of deductions and determinations possible in value discussions, he described them as 'far from being meaningless' (1949, p. 21). This seems to imply some kind of criterion based on a distinction between 'meaningful' and 'meaningless'. But his use of these terms is not the same as the Positivists', for he also spoke of 'meaningful value judgements' as though the criterion of meaningfulness also demarcated categories of value judgment (ibid., p. 60, cf. pp. 52-3). The doctrine of meaning behind these remarks has more to do with the Diltheyan notion of the 'meaning' of the world, and with the idea that we must create this 'meaning' ourselves, an idea to which Weber subscribed (ibid., p. 57).

The Logical Positivists' innovation was to define the problem of meaningfulness in terms of sentences. The formulation of the problem in these terms presupposes an important shift in perspective. In discussing the development of the Weber dispute in Weimar, it was pointed out that the 'ontological turn' had led to a reformulation of issues which earlier, in the period of neo-Kantian dominance, had been formulated in epistemological terms. The development of the problem of meaning involved a similar shift in terms from epistemology to the theory of meaning, broadly understood to include, in C.W. Morris's terms, syntactics, semantics, and pragmatics. The ontological turn occurred after Weber's death. The linguistic turn was contemporary with Weber, but the implications became recognized slowly, whereas the ontological turn completely transformed German philosophical discourse in the space of a few years.

The starting point for this linguistic shift is the philosophy of Gottlob Frege, the founder of modern symbolic logic and, on some accounts, the founder of modern philosophy of language.[8] One of Frege's views was presupposed by the task the Positivists had set for themselves. Frege held that names had meaning only in the context of sentences, and he took sentences to be the subject of a theory of meaning. Thus, when the famous 'Verificationist Criterion of Meaning' was formulated, it referred to sentences. According to the standard formulation of this criterion, 'A sentence has empirical meaning if and only if it is not analytic and follows logically from some finite and logically consistent class of observation sentences' (Hempel, 1959, p. 111).

The style of formulation here is crucial: only when the issue is stated in terms of meaningfulness of *sentences* does the task of the Vienna Circle become distinguished from the rest of post-Cartesian epistemology and metaphysics. To put this differently, when Weber spoke of 'meaningful' and 'meaningless' value judgments, he could distinguish them only by reference to a general epistemological or metaphysical stance. The terms as he used them thus recapitulated his epistemology and metaphysics.

Defined in terms of sentences, the problem takes on a quite different character. It becomes autonomous, in this sense: once one sets out to frame a criterion distinguishing between 'meaningful' and 'meaningless' sentences, the Positivists supposed, one would be forced to recognize that one could not draw the line to include particular favored statements in the category of 'meaningful' without at the same time including statements one clearly wished to regard as meaningless.[9] Their expectation was that anyone wishing to design the criterion to let in sentences about such things as essences would find that the criterion also let in sentences about the intelligences that rule the orbs, or other occult entities, which no one would want to regard as the subject of empirically meaningful sentences, or at least which the adherents of the doctrines seeking admittance would not be willing to consider. In short, the epistemological disputes of nineteenth century philosophy could apparently be obviated by the structure of the problem itself.

But Frege's work was almost certainly unknown to Weber, and when Weber spoke of the 'Logicians' of the time, he mentioned Windelband, Simmel, and Rickert, none of whom ever wrote a sentence on 'logic' in the sense of Frege's *Begriffsschrift* (1970). The fact that Weber's work is innocent of the Fregean thesis that 'meaning' is something that is definable for sentences places it in the post-Cartesian, 'epistemological' tradition rather than in the tradition that takes the philosophy of language to be central. So with Weber, the issues took the 'epistemological' form and the problem of meaningfulness did not arise as a distinct 'linguistic' problem. The epistemological and metaphysical claims that would have warranted Weber's usages of the term 'meaningful' would have been rejected, as it happens, by the Logical Positivists as 'meaningless.'

Historically, this should not be surprising. Often Weber discussed the presuppositions necessary for an inquiry or claim, a typically neo-Kantian move. The whole strategy of the Positivists was opposed to this. Schlick remarked that the

> misleading view (introduced by the 'Neo-Kantians') according to which objects of a science are not simply 'given' to it but are themselves 'given as problems' will not lead anyone to deny that whoever wishes to understand anything must first know *what* it is he wishes to understand (1962, p. 3).

The possibility of any such knowledge is, of course, precisely what Weber denied, on grounds of the claim that 'reality' consists of an 'infinitely manifold stream of events' such that all

> analyses of infinite reality which the finite human mind can conduct rests on the tacit assumption that only a finite portion of this reality constitutes the object of scientific investigation (Weber, 1949, p. 72).

To give some idea of how far removed this is from Positivism, consider that Carnap in 1932 considered the question of the existence of a real external world to be a metaphysical and therefore meaningless question (see Carnap, 1959, p. 77). *Any* assertion taking the form 'Reality is . . .' would be beyond the pale of meaningfulness for the Positivists.

A crucial methodological difference arises from these differences. The Positivists held that the language of physics constituted a basic language for all the sciences, and that this fact enabled the 'unification of science' into a single (albeit elaborate) theory with a *single* object and object-language. In contrast, Weber supposed that each science departed from certain presuppositions. For Weber, one may have a science of jurisprudence, just as one has a science of physics, by making certain presuppositions (the existence of which, of course, limits one's conclusions) about an object, 'the law,' and then inquiring into the facts about this object. One might think that this conception would also let in theology, in some sense, as a 'science'. Weber implicitly conceded that it would, but went on to say:

> As a rule, theologies, however, do not content themselves with this . . . presupposition. They regularly proceed from the further presupposition that certain 'revelations' are facts relevant for salvation and as such make possible a meaningful conduct of life (1946, p. 154).

For the Positivist, who rejects this conception of the constitution of an object and insists that a science must be based on sentences describing, so to speak, 'raw feels,' neither theology nor jurisprudence can be a science. Otto Neurath was particularly harsh on the scientific claims of Kelsen's 'Legal Positivism,' precisely because he made such presuppositions as Weber described, in such statements as 'the state . . . is a distinctive reality' which 'resides not in the realm of *nature* . . . but in the realm of spirit' (Neurath, 1959, p. 307). Weber, of course, considered the cultural and historical sciences to require language distinguished from the physical sciences.

The similarities between Weber and the Positivists thus turn out to rest largely on the common endorsement of the fact-value distinction and agreement, although limited, on the relevance of causal explanation to human action. However, significant differences occur with respect to the form of the fact-value distinction and the uses to which it is put.

Positivist ethics

The primary difference in the conceptions themselves is that Weber assumed that ethics is teleological in character, and that 'ultimately' the difference in value stances amounts to different *choices* of ends, ends which he claimed were 'rationally irreconcilable.' The Vienna Circle Positivists did not conceive of the problem in this way. Their views on ethics ranged from Carnap, who generally agreed with C.L. Stevenson's 'emotivist' analysis of ethical utterance (Stevenson, 1937), to Schlick, who presented an ethical theory resembling utilitarianism. It is not necessary to go into the fine points of these doctrines in order to show their similarities and dissimilarities to Weber's own view, since the fine points are largely devoted to questions of the analysis of sentences, a matter Weber said nothing about. Suffice to say that the Positivists based their conception of the distinction between facts and values on the consideration of the logical form of statements of facts and the sentences that express valuative or moral things. One version of the distinction maintains that facts are expressed by statements, while moral and valuative things are expressed by imperatives. An apparently descriptive sentence like 'George is good,' according to this view, has a misleading surface form – its true meaning is the imperative, 'Be like George.' Relations of implication do not hold between imperatives and statements, any more than they do between questions and statements, and this is why facts do not imply values, nor values facts.

The thesis that Carnap formulated at the end of his life, which he called the 'Thesis of non-cognitivism,' expresses the common opinion of the Circle.

> *If* a statement on values or valuations is interpreted neither as factual nor as analytic (or contradictory), then it is noncognitive; that is to say, it is devoid of cognitive meaning, and therefore the distinction between truth and falsity is not applicable to it (1963, p. 999).

There is a significant sense in which Weber agrees with this. But Weber went on to claim that rational reconciliation of alternative value choices is impossible (1949, p. 19). Carnap's 'Thesis' entails that 'rational reconciliation' is unintelligible in the first place, because value statements lack truth-values; thus both the claim that 'rational reconciliation' is possible and its denial are meaningless.

This has direct and differing implications for the world-historical and social attitudes of Weber and the Positivists. For the Positivists, it was not unreasonable to expect that the advance of science – at least through its negative effect on superstition – would lead to social progress, and one member of the Circle, Otto Neurath, was adamant that it would. These attitudes were common among politically unsophisticated intellectuals, then as now. The sheer naivete of the attitude provided the basis for the genre of antiscientistic writings mentioned in the previous chapter. The Positivists were not 'scientistic' in the sense that they had elaborate schemes for the reconstruction of society, but they certainly shared in the belief that a society in which scientific rationality had a larger place would be a better society.

One basis for this optimism is evident in Schlick's remark that

> there are wide regions in which the unanimity and security of moral judgments is substantiated. The modes of behavior which we group together under the names reliability, helpfulness, sociability are everywhere judged to be 'good' while, for example, thievery, murder, quarrelsomeness pass for 'evil' so unanimously that here the question of the common property can be answered with practically universal validity (1962, pp. 13-14).

The elimination of superstition and error, together with basic moral commonalities, makes, on this view, for more rather than less moral commonality. Emotivism is also consistent with the idea that basic commonalities in human makeup lead to basically common moral attitudes. Weber's world-historical conception derives in large part from the contrary view, that value conflict is inevitable. Indeed, Weber supposed that 'the disenchantment of the world,' of which the Positivists certainly were agents in their rejection of superstition and metaphysics, would lead not to more moral unanimity, but less. As Weber put it:

> Our civilization destines us to realize more clearly these struggles again, after our eyes have been blinded for a thousand years – blinded by the allegedly or presumably exclusive orientation toward the grandiose moral fervor of Christian ethics (1946, p. 149).

For Weber, the source of past moral unanimity in Europe was Christianity, not commonalities in human makeup.

The closest parallels to Weber's reflections on the historical problem of value conflict as a social phenomenon in the Positivist literature are discussions by Viktor Kraft, a member of the Circle, and Hans Reichenbach, who was not a member of the Vienna Circle but of the small 'Berlin group' of Logical Positivists. Reichenbach pointed out that such extreme individualistic moral alternatives as the ethics of Nietzsche's superman or Machiavelli's prince 'have never been carried through except on paper' (1951, p. 286). His explanation of this is almost Durkheimian: moral volitions, he suggested, are 'originally group volitions' (ibid., p. 285). The 'value conflicts' that do occur in society are not Weberian 'endless struggles' but are learning experiences which lead one to 'adjust oneself to group will' (ibid., p. 297). He showed that he did not intend by this phrasing to lend support to authoritarian regimes, however, by remarking that 'only a distorted morality can argue that our will is bad if it is not the response to a command from another source' (ibid., p. 292). Thus, for Reichenbach, as for Schlick, desires deriving from one's human makeup do not inevitably lead to irreconcilable value conflicts.

Kraft's *Foundations for a Scientific Analysis of Value*, first published in 1937, presented a similar argument, which goes much farther on the matter of meaningfulness and in the criticism of prior theories of value. In this text one can discern the outlines of what might be considered as the pragmatist-positivist critique of Weber. Like Dewey, Kraft rejected the form of the problem as given by the neo-Kantians and Scheler as a false dilemma: the alternatives are not 'absolute values' and sheer 'choice.' Kraft quotes Rickert's remark that a value is something 'that has neither real nor ideal existence, but nonetheless is something,' and his claim that 'Irreal values exist as a separate realm apart from all real objects, which likewise constitute a realm of their own' (quoted in Kraft, 1981, p. 3). Kraft suggests that it is a short step from this abstracted notion of values to the view, presented by Scheler and others, that values can be known only through intuition. Indeed, Kraft argued, Scheler merely changed the Kantian terminology of the *a priori*, which fits Rickert's concept of value, to a terminology that distinguishes two kinds of 'experience.' Scheler considered experience of values to be 'pure, immediate experience' as distinct from ordinary experience of natural objects, which he treated as mediated by 'the positing of a natural structure' (Kraft, 1981, p. 4).

Kraft's alternative to this dilemma resembles Dewey's. He pointed out that we always start with values already given by tradition, which he understood as life experience conditioned by place and circumstance. Such values are caused, and therefore are nonarbitrary. As the causal conditions of collective life change, the values change, by various social processes, such as the adoption of values from other members of a group by learning, suggestion, and imitation (1981, p. 156). We do not face the question of the validity of particular values in abstraction from these conditions and processes. The artificiality of writings like Nietzsche's derives from this. 'Despite all the divergence' between Nietzsche and his enemies, Kraft pointed out, 'a large cluster of traditional valuations are agreed upon, because each person is compelled to acknowledge them by the conditions of his culture circle' (ibid., p. 164). Even philosophies that renounce the world, such as Buddhism, tacitly presuppose as self-evident some valuations in common with the culture they 'reject' (ibid., p. 185). But this is a limited claim. Kraft did not claim that science can dictate valuations, much less absolute values in the sense of Rickert or Scheler. At most, he believed, science can serve in the assessment and revision of 'posited' values (ibid., pp. 184-5).

Because there are no strong implicative relations between the philosophical views of the Logical Positivists and their politics and cultural stance, these may appear to be entirely accidental connections. This would be a misleading appearance, for Logical Positivism does exclude some views. When the Positivists rejected metaphysics on grounds of empirical meaninglessness, they obviated the type of cultural despair that derives from the philosophical discovery of the nonexistence or unknowability of values. Weber was in the grip of this discovery. For him, if something was not to be found in the 'meaningless chaos' of the world, it had to be irrationally or nonrationally chosen. The Logical Positivists' approach to the problem allowed them to say that although ethical sentences are not empirically meaningful, they have some other meaning – prescriptive or emotive, perhaps. Indeed, the Positivists were in a sense compelled to come up with such analyses. These analyses were not very good answers to the problems of ethical theory, i.e. the problems of giving a philosophical characterization of morals or sentences about what persons ought morally to do, but their approach does not in any straightforward way leave morality entirely up to 'decision.' Nevertheless, the approach does not exclude a decisionistic analysis of values, and, as a historical matter, probably served to make such an analysis more plausible.

For German audiences, the most important 'positivist' was Karl Popper. Popper claimed he was not a positivist, and he was in fact not a member of the Vienna Circle. But his views and concerns were close to those of the Logical Positivists in many respects, including the question of the 'demarcation' line between science and nonscience. Popper was a decisionist, and this lends plausibility to the later argument that decisionism is the 'obverse' of positivism. His views on the subject are perhaps best expressed in *The Open Society and Its Enemies*. He told us that the

> dualism of facts and decisions is, I believe, fundamental. Facts as such have no meaning; they can gain it only through our decisions. Historicism is only one of many attempts to get over this dualism; it is born of fear, for it shrinks from realizing that we bear the ultimate responsibility even for the standards we choose (1966, pp. 278-9).

His own decision was different from Weber's.

> We can interpret this history of power politics from the point of view of our fight for the open society, for a rule of reason, for justice, freedom, equality, and for the control of international crime. Although history has no ends, we can impose these ends of ours upon it; and *although history has no meaning, we can give it a meaning* (ibid., p. 278).

For Weber, it would be a 'factual' question as to whether one could impose such an order on the future without falling into utopianism. He believed that one could not – that the question of whether *any* remnants could be saved in the coming age of bureaucracy had to be laid aside in favor of a question he took to be more fundamental: the question Can leadership be preserved against the bureaucrats? The priority of this question depends on Weber's analysis of the problem of controlling bureaucracy, whose triumph would mean bondage (Weber, 1978a, p. 1402) and the parceling out of the human soul (Weber, 1956, p. 128). So the difference from Popper rests on Weber's belief in the limited range of genuine possibilities for the future, as well as in the choice he made in the face of these possibilities. Popper's decision was for 'negative utilitarianism,' i.e., to prevent as much suffering as possible. The practical implications of this choice are not clear, however, since it is unclear how, for example, the sufferings of the Gulag are to be weighed against the suffering caused by war, or whether the temporary sacrifices of war will prevent the Gulag. Weber would have unambiguously preferred the sufferings of war, simply for its release of the potential for human greatness and meaningful sacrifice – in contrast to the soullessness of the bureaucratic machine.

Positivism and value-free social science

The rise of positivism alone, one suspects, could not have led to a self-consciously 'value-free' sociology and political science, such as emerged in the United States in the 1950s. A position like Conant's on the proper role of the social sciences would have been more congenial to the Positivists. Indeed, in the early years of American Positivism one finds attacks on the developments in the social sciences in a Positivist vein. In 1949, Felix Kaufmann, part of the Austrian emigration and a positivist fellow-traveler, presented a rather Deweyan critique, in the framework of a linguistic analysis, of the doctrines of value-freedom and value-neutrality in political science. He suggested that 'the extent of disagreement on fundamental ethical standards is usually overrated' (Kaufmann, 1949, p. 347) and that the differences between the standards underlying the usage of ethical statements and the standards underlying such scientific usages as 'problem' and 'confirmation' are also overrated (ibid., p. 349). Both types of standards, he argued, involve less than perfect agreement, but both involve substantial consensus. 'What really separates the different ethical doctrines is primarily disagreement about the *relative rank* of universally accepted moral standards. . . . And this disagreement results in opposite suggestions for the resolutions of moral conflicts' (ibid., p. 351). In cases where scientific conclusions are disputed on grounds of disagreement over such usages as 'confirmation,' we do not embrace irrationalism, and, Kaufmann argued, specifically against Weber, neither should we do so in the case of analogous disputes in ethics or political philosophy.

These arguments were of no avail against the deep need to be 'scientific' which one finds in articles like Bierstedt's. At a different level, in the postwar period there was a gradual shift toward relativism of a sort in the culture of the educated, especially in the United States. This new conventional wisdom, which is perhaps too close to us in time to gain a suitable comparative perspective on, was a peculiar mix of tolerance, belief in 'rights,' faith in the virtues of the oppressed, together with antinomianism and antiauthoritarianism. Each of these ideas has visible roots in the liberal tradition, but the philosophical arguments of the Positivists, existentialists, and of Weberianism doubtless played some part in the amalgam. Some 'Weberians' later came to speak as though Weber's views were largely consistent with this conventional wisdom, particularly in the sense that both Weber's thought and the conventional wisdom were uncongenial to 'ideology.' This was perhaps the most durable of all the adaptations and insertions of Weberian ideas into Anglo-American thought.

9 The later form of the critique

Eric Voegelin has complained that in the 1960s in the social sciences he had 'to observe a boring repetition of the very situation in which [he] grew up . . . inasmuch as the contemporary methodological debate in America lives to a large extent on the revival of the earlier German ideologies, methodologies, value theories, Marxisms, Freudianisms, psychologies, phenomenologies, hermeneutic profundities, and so on' (1978, p. 7). Habermas makes a similar point in looking at the history of German philosophy over the past fifty years. 'What strikes one to begin with is the astonishing continuity of schools and of principles of inquiry. The theoretical rudiments which dominated philosophical discussion in the 1950s and 1960s originated in the German language area as early as the 1920s' (1971b, p. 634).

Some of the elements of the later disputes, especially in the Anglo-American intellectual world, were new. The Logical Positivism that became 'the standard interpretation' in American philosophy of science was unknown to the Weimar disputants; the war discredited some competing ideas, as we have seen; and the critique of Weber in Weimar had largely discredited Weber's metaphysics. Because it was possible to hold Weber's ethical views independently of his metaphysics, later Weberians who wrote on the philosophy of science ordinarily discarded the metaphysics and combined a largely Weberian ethical theory with some form of positivism or another linguistic-turn philosophy of science – often Popperianism, in Germany – that preserved the fact-value distinction.[1] As we shall see, this gave the critics of Weberianism a more difficult job, for they were compelled to argue for implicit connections between these substitute doctrines and Weber's ethical theory, whereas Weber had made these connections explicitly.

In the earlier dispute, both critics and defenders had read Weber in roughly the same ways. What Weber had said had been discussed primarily in terms of validity and only secondarily as an interpretive problem. The later dispute was to a much greater extent historical, a dispute over what Weber had meant and what his political life had meant. Immediately after the war, the textual dispute over the meaning of Weber's writ, especially his philosophical writings, emerged. The historical literature on Weber developed largely in the wake of Wolfgang Mommsen's great study, *Max Weber und die deutsche Politik, 1890-1920*, the first edition of which was published in 1959. And hovering over the later dispute, present even when unmentioned, was the historical fact of Nazism.

Another feature of the later dispute, which derived from these other developments, was a high degree of confusion about what the issues were. The term *Krisis der Wissenschaft* had been used in Weimar in much the same way by all sides. The defenders of Weber's position in the 1960s, in contrast, set themselves up as defenders of science or rationality itself against those who wished to junk science and substitute ideology in its place (Bendix, 1971; Roth, 1971b). This was *not* the way the issues had been formulated in Weimar. There, both critics and defenders saw it as a clash between alternate conceptions: there had been nothing quite comparable to the attempt to delegitimate the opposition that was the hallmark of the 1960s. One may recall, for example, Troeltsch's favorable remarks on Kahler, and the participation of both sides in a dialogue, which, however heated it became, remained a dialogue. One can only be impressed by the extent to which personal relations between scholars on very different sides of the issues had remained warm and stable during Weimar. This has not been at all characteristic of the later dispute, which has often involved deep personal bitterness and antagonism.

In Germany, the issues were crystallized by the '*Positivismusstreit*' in Germany sociology in the 1960s, between the Frankfurt School and its opponents. The Critical Theorists relied upon the binary opposition, discussed in Chapter 8 in connection with Thielicke, between nihilistic positivism and, as they put it, Critical Reason. This was an oversimplification that produced its own difficulties. It lumped Weberians together with Positivists and positivists of quite different types together with one another. For example, Karl Popper found himself the figurehead of the 'positivism' the Critical Theorists wished to attack.

The left-wing critique of Weber

The synthesis of Marxism, Hegelianism, and Freudianism achieved under the title 'Critical Theory' had not been a part of the original dispute, although the synthesis contained elements from many of the philosophical traditions that had differentiated in the 1920s. The philosophically inclined members of the Frankfurt *Institut* in the 1930s had said little about Weber until after the war. The members of the early *Institut* who had the most to say about Weber were Karl Wittfogel and Franz Neumann, and Neumann was something of a Weber admirer (Wittfogel, 1924, 1931; Neumann, 1942, 1953). After the war this changed. In *Eclipse of Reason*, first published in 1947, Horkheimer characterized Weber as an opponent of objective reason. Weber, he said, 'adhered so definitely to the subjectivistic trend that he did not conceive of any rationality – not even a 'substantial' one by which man can discriminate one end from another.' This, Horkheimer observed, 'is itself a stepping-stone in the renunciation of philosophy and science as regards their aspiration of defining man's goal' (1974, p. 6). On the Left, this was a characteristic way of thinking of Weber – as one of a long series of subjectivist thinkers, distinguished only by the strength and unqualified character of his commitment to a particular view of rationality and rejection of the ambitions of philosophy, particularly philosophy embodying dialectical reason.

Horkheimer's opinion resembles Lukács's discussions of neo-Kantianism, and this suggests that Critical Theory, at least in its critique of Weber and neo-Kantianism, is largely derivative from Lukács. But matters are not so simple. As we have seen, Lukács's critique itself resembles other critiques of Weber and neo-Kantianism of the 1918-1922 era. Horkheimer's critique also resembles these critiques, and in particular shares the core ideas of the 'return to Hegel.' These were, as we have also seen, common ideas of the Weimar period, and were shared and developed by mainstream philosophers as well as the Left.

So the extent to which Lukács's views were originally shared by the Frankfurt School is open to dispute. However, there is little question that they diverged very early.[2] The primary reasons for the divergence have to do with different interpretations of historical events. *History and Class Consciousness* was a document of the 1918-1922 period in another sense. It was based on the expectation that the 'world revolution' then in progress would succeed. It did not, so the Critical Theorists, in contrast, were theorists of the failure of the proletariat.

Lukács pinned his hopes for change in philosophy on philosophic change's being an 'aspect' of the proletarian revolutionary process, and he suggested that philosophic change would not be the leading edge of the process. For the Critical Theorists, these were dead hopes, precisely *because* of the failure of the proletariat to achieve proper revolutionary consciousness, a failure later to be explained by these theorists in terms of psychoanalytic accounts of 'authoritarianism,' or, more broadly, 'alienation.' Alienation thus took on, for the Critical Theorists, a more fully autonomous historical role than it had played for Lukács or Marx. This new role was a response to an explanatory necessity, the failure of the proletariat, that Marx and Stalinism did not face. These differences, together with the facts of Lukács's political career, led to two parallel but quite different developments.

The primary formulation of Lukács's views on Weber is to be found in *The Destruction of Reason*, completed in 1952. The date of the work is perhaps misleading. Lukács had faced the problem of the German associations of his own thought much earlier, in 1934, when he recanted his past views for his patrons in the Soviet Union. As Morris Watnick points out, *The Destruction of Reason* is 'largely an elaborate gloss' on this recantation (1962, p. 150). If anything, however, it gave Lukács a better opportunity to distort the positions he rejected in order to conceal the similarities between his own position and the positions he rejected.

The book itself was an extraordinary feat. It required broad familiarity with the German philosophical sources. The characterizations of the various figures paraded before us are frequently telling and clever. In the case of each philosopher or thinker discussed, Lukács showed the place of the 'irrational' or of 'the limits of reason' in his thought, and considered the attitude each author took toward these limits. He then ascribed political motives for these positions. The motives are invariably antiproletarian and antirevolutionary, or at least historically reactionary. Jaspers's rediscovery of reason, for example, is attributed to the fact that 'today "reason" is dedicated to refuting Marxism as irrationalism was previously' (Lukács, 1980, p. 829).

Lukács's task of labelling thinkers as irrationalists was made easy by the fact that the philosophers he criticized were post-Kantians, most of whom formulated their views in a foundationalist manner, by seeking a basis for particular *a priori* premises or structures of thought. These bases are, by definition, not 'rational' in the sense in which reasoning *from* the premises is rational. They can only be matters for intuition, the will to will, decision, history, culture and the like, all of which Lukács classified as 'irrational.' Such philosophies as Pragmatism, which reject this entire framework of basis-seeking, can be treated as irrationalist simply for rejecting the problem of a rational basis (Lukács, 1980, pp. 20–2).

Consequently every philosophical alternative could be described as irrationalist.

The net result of these arguments, as Kolakowski observed, was that, for Lukács, 'all philosophers who do not profess Communism in its current orthodox form, i.e. Stalinism, are irrationalists and therefore Nazis 'objectively' if not by actual conviction' (1978, p. 286). Kolakowski goes on to say that

> It would be hard indeed to find a more striking example of anti-rationalism than that afforded by Lukács's own philosophy of blind faith, in which nothing is proved but everything asserted *ex cathedra*, and whatever does not fit the Marxian schemata is dismissed as reactionary rubbish (ibid.).

This raises the question of the rational adequacy of Lukács's own views, a question which cannot be taken up here. It must suffice to say that Lukács believed himself to have a rational basis for his own philosophy. But this basis was largely identical in structure to those he rejected. Consider 'vitalism,' a philosophy he singled out for particularly harsh treatment. He stressed the idea that the core of vitalism was the antinomy between 'rigidity' and 'life,' an antinomy to be resolved by the irrationalist choice of 'life.' He had no trouble in showing the fascist associations of these ideas, which, incidentally, were common in circles of which Lukács had been a member. In describing Jaspers's views, Lukács wrote that 'For everything objective about knowledge he used the scornfully ironic term "shell" (*Gehäuse*), thereby restating the old vitalistic antithesis of the alive and the moribund' (1980, p. 517). This is a Weberian term as well, the term Parsons translated as 'cage' (cf. Turner, 1982). Lukács said nothing about the use of such ideas in his own thought of the same period – such as his insistence that bourgeois thought was rigid and 'reified,' and that the validity of a decision for the proletarian cause was warranted by evidence of its revolutionary vitality. These usages suggest a close symmetry between the early Lukács's argument and the Nazi use of vitalism. Both used vital forces to bring about an extraphilosophical resolution to the paradoxes of relativism: for Lukács, the resolution was through the vital forces of history; for the Nazis, it was through the vital force of race.

The Critical Theorists did not suppose that matters were so simple, and indeed Adorno went so far as to call *The Destruction of Reason* 'The Destruction of Lukács's Reason' (quoted in Kolakowski, 1978, p. 284). This perhaps reflected their quite different circumstances. The Critical Theorists needed an account of these matters that stood on its own, apart from the authority of the party. We have noted that the account they developed was constructed from available philosophical materials, and these included materials drawn from sources Lukács denounced as irrationalist. Weber's ideas were among these materials, as were Marxist, Freudian, and Hegelian ideas. Thus much of the common ground between the Critical Theorists and Weber was also shared with the young Lukács of *History and Class Consciousness*. As Bryan Turner suggests, the relation between the Critical Theorists and Weber is a matter of overt criticism and covert reliance, particularly in the case of Habermas (1981, p. 65). The reliance is on Weber's ideas of rationality. Weber and the Critical Theorists agreed that ideas of natural law are archaisms and that the present stage of historical development is characterized by the dominance of instrumental rationality, a dominance enforced by capitalism and the facts of international competition. They assessed bureaucratic life in similar ways, as 'alienated' or as a kind of spiritual bondage. They accepted similar views of Protestantism as the source of the cold rationality of the modern era (ibid., pp. 61-105). But they differed in their hopes for the future: Weber saw no alternative to this dominance by instrumental rationality; the Critical Theorists believed that there was, in the form of dialectical reason.

From the point of view of the earlier dispute, the quest for an alternative made for some strange bedfellows. Herbert Marcuse, a member of the Frankfurt School in the 1930s and a defender of a Hegelian species of Marxism, stands as an example of what might be described as Heideggerian anti-Weberianism. Though Marcuse disavowed Heideggerian political thought, his Heideggerian philosophical roots are evident. His critique of Weber, 'Industrialization and Capitalism in the Works of Max Weber,' nicely captures the Heideggerian sense of the nature of thinking, though with a decidedly un-Heideggerian Marxist twist. According to Marcuse, Weber's 'spiteful fight against the socialist efforts of 1918' was motivated by his belief that 'socialism contradicts the idea of occidental reason,' as well as by his nationalism (1968, p. 201). 'Whatever capitalism may do to man, it must, according to Weber, first and before all evaluation, be understood as necessary reason' (ibid., p. 202). Furthermore, 'to understand the world-historical situation is, for Weber, to understand that one must capitulate to it.' 'The Ought shows itself in the Is,' Marcuse said (ibid., p. 203), specifically the Is which is concretized in the formal theories of rationality and domination in *Wirtschaft und Gesellschaft*: technical rationality and the inner rationalization of life are presented, as Marcuse quoted Weber, as the 'absolutely *inescapable* condition of our entire existence' (quoted in ibid., p. 204).

Thus for Weber, Marcuse claimed, 'formal rationality turns into capitalist rationality' (1968, p. 204). And at this point Weber's 'critique stops, accepts the allegedly inexorable, and turns into apologetics – worse, into the denunciation of the only possible alternative, that is, of a qualitatively different historical rationality' (ibid., p. 208). Heidegger's 'other thinking' and 'shepherding of Being' may perhaps be understood as such a rationality, though 'rationality' suggests a misemphasis, because Heidegger presented his alternative not as another step in the series of 'rationalities' or groundings since the Greeks, but as an ending and repudiation of the series.

The claim that Weber was the representative of a kind of rationality, one that is connected to capitalism, which it is our historical task to overcome, was the common view of the later Frankfurt School, though one that was ordinarily formulated in a more Hegelian and less Heideggerian way. The date of this critique is significant. Marcuse's paper was published in 1964, and was inspired by Wolfgang Mommsen's book of 1959, particularly by the suggestion, moderated in the second edition, of a link between Weber and Nazism. It was such uses of his argument as Marcuse's that led Mommsen to revise his book. Yet the need for this stimulus is revealing. Weber was simply not the central villain for the older generation of the Frankfurt School, but always and only an instance of a much larger errant group. The identity of this larger group of errant thinkers, and the question of the character and historical roots of their errors, was to be a large theme of these writings. It was Habermas's contribution to give a broad historical answer to these questions which dealt more successfully with later forms of positivism.

In the United States, Marcuse and the Frankfurt School had many followers among radical students in the 1960s and early 1970s. But the critic with the most serious and ultimately perhaps the most significant following was another emigrant, Leo Strauss. Strauss and Habermas both have a similar relation to the Weimar critique: they incorporated the technical arguments against Weber made in the context of the *Krisis der Wissenschaft* and tried to interpret the same general issues more broadly, by applying the arguments to other movements, by placing the issues into the framework of a much broader and more systematic historical and philosophical analysis, and by formulating a broader concept of the crisis. Neither argument can be fully explicated here, but the distinctive uses of the basic arguments can be shown.

The Straussian critique

Strauss traced the origins of the modern crisis, which he

understood as a crisis in valuations, to the rejection of classical political philosophy. He pictured Machiavelli, Hobbes, Rousseau, and Locke as the authors of a new 'natural right'; Weber and Heidegger appear as late, nihilistic versions of the rejection. Social science positivism and behavioralist political science he considered to be subject to most of the same criticisms he made of Weber; indeed, he described Weber as 'the leading social science positivist.'[3]

Strauss began his treatment of Weber by a consideration of historicism, which Weber's conception of the social sciences had attempted to correct. He pointed out that

> Historicism asserts that all human thoughts or beliefs are historical, and hence deservedly destined to perish; but historicism itself is a human thought; hence historicism can be of only temporary validity, or it cannot be simply true (1953, p. 25).

The historicist does not say that historicism is only of temporary validity – it 'thrives on the fact that it inconsistently exempts itself from its own verdict about all human thought' (ibid.).[4]

Weber had attempted to avoid this inconsistency by employing the fact-value distinction: he argued that value ideas are historically relative, but that the validity of the propositions of social science is objective and universal, or transhistorical. Thus the historicist-relativizing consequences of the thesis are restricted to a limited aspect of social science, the value aspect. The 'validity of the propositions' is accounted for 'positivistically,' and therefore nonrelativistically (Strauss, 1957, p. 351).

To say that the only thing that is transhistorical is the validity of the propositions of social science is to say that everything but validity is historically relative. The picture this suggests looks something like this: reality is like a quiz show, where the contestants can only be asked questions with 'yes' or 'no' answers. Each of us approaches reality with historically bound conceptions. So the only knowledge we can have of reality is limited to the kinds of questions we can, within our *Weltanschauung*, ask. This means that the knowledge of social reality that we as coparticipants in a certain *Weltanschauung* have is not really competitive or commensurable with the knowledge of the participants in other *Weltanschauungen*, because they are operating within a different set of possible questions. In effect, then, there is no one knowable reality for social science, but as many knowable realities as there are self-consistent valuative starting points for approaching reality. Reality becomes knowable for us by virtue of an essentially arbitrary decision to act in a certain way toward it. The significance that things have is not in the things themselves; it is breathed into them, as it were, by this decision.

Strauss invited us to notice how Weber's conception would contrast with a social science that claimed that there could be genuine knowledge of the true ends of man. In such a social science, the arbitrary character of the first step, deciding on a point of view from which to approach reality, would be eliminated; the science could proceed from a valid frame of reference as opposed to various partially valid or invalid frames of reference. This would have obvious bearing on questions of theory and practice.

> Based on genuine knowledge of true ends, social science would search for the proper means to those ends; it would lead up to objective and specific value judgments regarding policies. Social science would be a truly policy-making, not to say architectonic, science rather than a mere supplier of data for the real policy makers (Strauss, 1953, p. 41).

The central thesis of Strauss's life work is that this sort of social science, which the classical political philosophers had sought, should still be sought. It is the possibility of such a science, Strauss said, that is the real target of the fact-value distinction. The rejection of the possibility makes sense only if one denies that there can be any genuine knowledge of the Ought. Weber, of course, denied that man can have any knowledge of the true value system, on the grounds that there are various value systems whose conflict cannot be solved by human reason.

Strauss pointed out that this doctrine, which he described as the real major premise of Weber's conception of social science,

> necessarily leads to nihilism or to the view that every preference, however evil, base, or insane, has to be judged before the tribunal of reason to be as legitimate as any other preference (1953, p. 42).

Yet, Weber's case for his position is peculiarly slight. His attempt to demonstrate the insolubility of value conflicts involves only three or four examples. Strauss disposed of these as badly conceived, except for one example: the conflict between a this-worldly orientation and an other-worldly orientation (ibid., p. 70). Strauss pointed out that if we grant that social science, as a this-worldly orientation, is legitimate, this conflict raised by Weber appears to be irrelevant to the project of classical political philosophy. But Weber refused to grant this premise.

At the root of Weber's rejection, Strauss suggested, seems to be the fact that, in the long struggle between theology and philosophy, or science in the full sense of the term (i.e., in the sense of the integrative and overarching pursuit discussed in Weimar), neither side has managed to refute the other. Philosophy must grant that revelation is at least possible. Yet to grant this means granting that the philosophic life may not be the right life, since revelation might demand another kind of life, for instance, a life of obedient love. So, for Weber, the commitment to science is, at root, unfounded or based on an act of faith, which is contrary to its nature; it requires the 'sacrifice of the intellect,' which is abhorred by science or philosophy (Strauss, 1953, pp. 71-2). Thus Weber reduced his own position to a level equal to any other position, for he can make no claim that his act of faith is better than any other act of faith. In short, he reduced it to the level of decision. This line of argument should be familiar, for it is the Weimar critique.

Strauss pointed out that the classics took a view of knowledge that was opposed to this. Socrates had conceived of philosophy as an ascent from opinions to knowledge or truth that is made possible and necessary by the fact that opinions about what things are contradict one another. A recognition of these contradictions forces one to go beyond opinion toward a consistent view of the nature of the thing involved. This consistent view makes visible the relative truth of the opinions. As Strauss stated it, the 'opinions are thus seen to be fragments of the truth, soiled fragments of the pure truth' (1953, p. 124). This conception is implicit, he said, in the practice of both Plato and Aristotle, who proceeded from the various commonsense or prescientific views on the topics they had considered. Philosophy is thus concerned with a reality that common sense, by virtue of its perceived contradictions, points to. In short, the possibility of philosophy or science is established through a consideration of the prescientific understanding of reality. When Strauss called for the restoration of the classical political philosophy, he was not simply calling for the revival of Platonic or Aristotelean political conceptions. He was calling for the restoration of the idea of proceeding *from* and perfecting the prescientific understanding of things.

What this strategy does *not* do is what Weber quite explicitly did do – claim that scientific understanding involves a *break* with the prescientific understanding of social life. Weber had proceeded from a rejection of the prescientific understanding of reality. As he saw it, science is based on a specific view of reality, and scientific understanding consists in a specific transformation of reality. As Strauss formulated it, Weber's reality is

> an infinite and meaningless sequence, or a chaos, of unique and

> infinitely divisible events which in themselves are meaningless: all meaning, all articulation, originates in the activity of the knowing or evaluating subject (1953, p. 77).

The scientific view of social life, the 'value-free' view, is by its defining premise a denial of the validity of prescientific knowledge. The citizen, the political man, does not make the fact-value distinction. He is as sure that he can judge good and bad as he is that he can judge 'factual' statements, and when he speaks about political things he speaks about the two things together. Weber's whole conception supported the legitimacy of a break with this prescientific view by the sociologist.

But Weber, Strauss argued, was unable to carry through this break consistently. Nor have current sociologists. A simple example is given to illustrate this. When a sociologist conducts a survey, he gives his interviewers all sorts of instructions; but he does not tell them: address your questions to human beings, and not to dogs, trees, and so on. Nor does he tell them how to identify human beings. This knowledge is presupposed. It is a part of the prescientific understanding that is not 'replaced' by science (Strauss, 1972b, p. 225). But social science is dependent through and through on this knowledge; the 'scientific view' rejects the prescientific understanding only to let it in through the back door. If we consider Weber's conception in the light of this dependent relation, the scientific view changes from forming an *alternative* to prescientific understanding to forming a *modification*. As a modification, Strauss said, the scientific view can only make sense on the basis of a coherent and comprehensive understanding of that which it attempts to modify.

The new political science, he argued, does not proceed in this way. It adopts the positivist conception of science as a programmatic presupposition. Yet it is forced, in the course of attempting to carry out its program, to examine this presupposition in a way that Weber refused to examine it. Strauss reasoned as follows. In the study of political institutions, the new political scientist must at some point consider the ideologies that have had a part in shaping these institutions. The various teachings of political philosophers are one kind of 'ideology.' These teachings may have had only a minor political role – but to determine this one must know these teachings as they were meant by the teachers. In such study, the political scientist will encounter his own presuppositions, the scientistic presuppositions, for these too are a part of the history of ideology. Because these presuppositions are a modification of the principles of modern political philosophy, which are in turn a modification of those of classical political philosophy, which in its turn is a self-conscious modification of the prescientific understanding of the world, they must be examined as modifications. And in doing this, the new political scientist cannot avoid consideration of 'the possibility that the older political science was sounder and truer than that which is regarded as political science today' (Strauss, 1972b, p. 229). He must do so because it is impossible to see how a coherent account can be given of such developments without formulating precisely this possibility. The new political scientist is thus forced to account for the possibility and character of his own enterprise in a way that is consistent with his enterprise. And in formulating this account, the new political scientist must transcend the self-limitations of social science. Thus the history of political philosophy, far from being merely an exotic branch of the history of ideology, is the direct route to the examination of the presuppositions on which any understanding of politics rests.

Habermas and the self-critique of sociology

Jürgen Habermas began his inquiry in *Theory and Practice* with the central Straussian observations. The classical political tradition is dead; it has given way to 'the establishment of political science on the model of the modern experimental sciences' (1973, p. 41). Classical political philosophy now seems alien to us because it was a doctrine of *praxis* as opposed to *techne*, that is to say, it was concerned with prudent understanding as opposed to instrumental or technical mastery, 'prediction and control.' Machiavelli was the first to deal with political questions as a matter of technique, divorced from the ethical considerations of classical political science; but Machiavelli did not give an account of his writings as 'science.' Hobbes was the first to do that, and it was Hobbes who first became entangled in the ambiguities of the idea of a causal, mechanistic science of man.

Habermas goes beyond Strauss in his account of these ambiguities. He notes that Hobbes assumed that 'as soon as insight into the mechanics of the societal state has been gained, the technically required arrangements can be fashioned to produce the correct social and political order' (1973, p. 72). Theory was to inform practice as technical knowledge informs instrumental action. But this relation creates a paradox:

> The same human beings whose behavior was initially conceived as an object of nature, in the necessary causal interconnections of institutional compulsions and modes of reaction given with human nature, must at the same time assume the role of subjects

> who, with the knowledge of these interrelationships, are to fashion the better arrangements. They are as much objects of the conditions to be investigated as subjects of the conditions to be changed (ibid.).

The claim of theory to inform practice thus becomes problematic. The ideal order or even just the better order cannot be conceived in theory structured in this way without 'changing the structure of the theory itself' (ibid., p. 78). The goal – the ideal or better order – is by definition inconsistent with the laws of nature, because the laws of nature causally produced the existing order.

The difficulty thus took on two aspects. First, the relation between the theory and political practice had to be accounted for in such a way that politics could still be 'guided' by knowledge of the laws governing the 'natural order' of society. Hobbes papered this problem over. The Physiocrats tried to solve it by turning politics into a kind of epistemological tribunal: they wished to install the monarch as 'the guardian of the "Natural Order" of society which they have analysed theoretically; the monarch, however, does not gain insight into the laws of the *ordre naturel* directly – he must allow this insight to be mediated for him by the *public éclairé*' (Habermas, 1973, p. 77). This is what, in a later period, John Stuart Mill ridiculed as the idea that one *ought* to 'obey' the laws of nature. In the Physiocrat's conception, public opinion has the task of determining what the laws of nature are, in order to obey them. The second aspect of the difficulty was the critique of ideology. Any conception of the political good that is inconsistent with the political order produced by the causal laws of nature must therefore be fantastic and illegitimate, as would an invention that presupposed the suspension of gravitational forces. If it is said that something about the actual order is evil, the speaker need only be shown that this thing arose through causal, law-governed forces.

Habermas claimed that this 'bourgeois critique of ideology' can only be negative. Once the notions of the natural order and law become positivistically understood, they can only be used for 'dissolving the empty formulas of Natural Law' (1973, p. 120). 'Moral questions, and questions of practice, are thus deprived of any rational basis or foundation' (ibid., p. 115). Yet Marx, no less than Hobbes, the Physiocrats, and Locke, is entangled in these ambiguities. The problem of resolving them, Habermas points out, is the axis upon which subsequent controversy within Marxism was forced to turn. Marxism came to occupy an ambiguous position, 'between philosophy and science.' The work of Marx is conceived of as a critique of ideology, especially a 'critique of political economy,' as the subtitle of *Das Kapital* reads. Engels understood the critique positivistically, such that

> the correct ideology was distinguished from the false solely according to the criteria of a realistic theory of knowledge. The socialist *Weltanschauung* was the only correct one, because it correctly 'depicts' (*abbildet*) the cosmic law in nature and in history (Habermas, 1973, p. 228).

This self-understanding was to become the foundation of the official Marxism of the Soviet Union. The development of the positivistic self-understanding of Marxism was paralleled and in some respects surpassed by the development of the positivistic self-understanding of academic sociology. The difficulties of official Marxism and the difficulties of academic sociology are thus of a piece, and the critique of official Marxism applies, *mutatis mutandis*, to academic sociology.

Sociology cannot escape the problems of its positivistic self-understanding. Sociology is itself a social phenomenon and is therefore a subject of sociological inquiry. Indeed, as Habermas remarks, 'Only when role theory is referred back to the activity of the sociologist itself do the fundamental problematics begin to emerge' (1973, p. 208). Thus, according to Habermas, the sociology of sociology plays for positivist sociology a role analogous to the role that Strauss said the history of political thought plays for behavioralist political science. It forces the foundational issue of self-understanding.

The problem of self-understanding forms the point of departure in Habermas's major middle work, *Knowledge and Human Interests* (1971a). The strategy Habermas adopted was to take the Marxism critique of knowledge as a point of departure for a new epistemological conception or self-understanding of social science. The Marxian critical tool was the demonstration of connections between ideas and class interests. Habermas gave an account of the dominant self-understanding of the social sciences, positivism, with an eye toward seeing positivism as an embodiment of certain interests. He went back to the historical origins of positivism to bring out these connections. He also examined the work of Dilthey and Peirce, because both these philosophers *reflected* on the purposes of reasoning. Dilthey reflected on hermeneutic reasoning, and conceived of its point as instrumental; Peirce reflected on science and came to the same instrumentalist conclusions. Positivism in its developed form, i.e., Logical Positivism, denies the possibility of speaking meaningfully about the value or interest significance of science and thus puts such self-reflection out to the pasture of meaninglessness.

Instrumentalism has some peculiar features as an interpretation of science that it does not share with Logical Positivism. If a scientific theory is an instrument, it must be an instrument with a purpose – the concept of instrument is inseparable from the concept of purpose or end. Thus, an instrumentalist interpretation of scientific theory presupposes the meaningfulness of questions about ends. But, although scientific theory may be distinguished from other kinds of theory by reference to the distinct purposes of theories, an instrumentalist philosophy of science does not *recommend* the characteristic ends of scientific theory over the ends of other kinds of theory. Nor does it deny the possibility of other ends and other kinds of theory. The instrumentalist interpretation thus invites self-reflection on the purpose of science. In contrast, Habermas argues that the Logical Positivist denial of the meaningfulness of reflection on interests is a form of false consciousness (1971a, p. 315).

This is a difficult point. To judge a philosophical position 'false consciousness' one must examine it against the standard of 'true consciousness.' The step of adopting the standard is fraught with well-known risks of relativism and circularity. Habermas developed a solution to the problem of relativism by accepting the notion that 'interest' governs cognition, and by identifying a particular interest, which he calls the 'emancipatory interest,' as the source of a nonrelative purpose which is a basis for the evaluation of consciousness. His point in *Knowledge and Human Interests* ultimately rests on this account, but its import can be shown more directly. The Positivists interdict a class of possible claims when they deny meaningfulness to questions about purposes. In effect, they also suppress the interest represented by the interdicted claims about ends. But they do not suppress all interests: they do not suppress the one that is built into the scientific enterprise, the interest summarized in the expression 'prediction and control,' which Habermas calls the interest in 'technological control.'

This hidden relation between positivism and interest has profound social implications in a social setting where political matters are transformed into scientific or 'technical' questions, as they are in the modern welfare state. The implications arise in this way. The 'object domain of the cultural sciences,' Habermas points out, is not constituted only by considerations of method but is 'confronted as something already constituted' (1971a, p. 193). In Straussian terms, there is a relevant prescientific understanding of the things studied by the cultural sciences. The scientific understanding that the technocrat uses is different from this prescientific understanding. But this difference is concealed or obscured by the refusal of positivism to reflect on the difference. So the technical control of society exercised by the state is based on an unexamined transformation *from* practical needs understood prescientifically *to* goals that can be formulated in terms open to technical control. An example may clarify Habermas's idea. Suppose that there is a desire to wipe out poverty. 'Poverty' must be defined in a way such that 'the poor' can be identified and action can be taken. This transformation becomes a *distortion* of the meaning of the term 'poverty,' unless there is some informed consensus on the part of the public to the effect that it is an acceptable substitution. In a technocratic society, power becomes the power to make these transformations of meaning without this informed consent. The power to distort communication in this way becomes the basis for domination. The only check on the power would be the loss of the loyalty of the masses to the state. This problem can be made technically manageable in the short term, but the use of the techniques ultimately generates a 'legitimation crisis.' Put simply, the child who becomes cynical by watching quasi-fraudulent television commercials also applies this cynicism to the state's claim to legitimate authority and to all the sorts of activities that, in liberal theory, are assigned to 'the public.' A new relation between the dominant class and the rest of society emerges. The loyalty of the masses is assured by assuring their affluence. But the public realm must be 'confined to spectacles and acclamation' (Habermas, 1970, p. 75), and this confinement requires that the distortions of communication can be kept from examination. Thus the positivism that prevents reflection and the fact-value separation (which Strauss takes as central) become key obscuring ideologies, preventing practice from being brought under rational valuative scrutiny.

Habermas has fitted this argument into a critique that best applies to Weber. Like Strauss, Habermas argues that Weber's positivistic account of method contradicts his hermeneutic intention of understanding the cultural significance of the present; his positivism limits 'the social sciences to a cognitive interest, valid for the production of knowledge which can be utilized technically' (Habermas, 1972, p. 63). Moreover, Weber was 'positivistic enough not to allow himself to reflect upon the connection between his methodological perspectives and rules, and the results of his social analysis' (ibid., p. 65). The other side of the coin of the positivistic account of scientific knowledge as technical knowledge is a particular ethical conception, 'decisionism,' the doctrine that evaluative and prescriptive assertions are distinguished from scientific claims because the basis for these assertions can be nothing other than a 'decision' that cannot be further justified. Decisionism is the obverse of positivism in this sense: if all knowledge worthy of the name is technical or instrumental, the *ends* or *purposes* of the techniques or instruments when put into practice must be fixed in a way that ultimately is arbitrary or irrational, in short, an unfounded 'decision.'[5] So for Habermas, the positivistic self-understanding of science implies a particular ethical theory, decisionism. This pair of doctrines is the basis of the fact-value distinction and therefore is the basis of the problem of theory and practice. And Weber was the principal architect of this pair of doctrines in the recent social sciences. We shall return to the difficulties in this account of the relations between the two doctrines.

One of Habermas's important contributions is the development of the concept of 'the ideal speech situation,' which is the end sought by the emancipatory interest. The notion of 'communicative distortion' is specified through the concept of the ideal speech situation. This concept is based on a particular theory of discourse. Habermas holds that a language game 'rests' on a background consensus about the truth of certain beliefs and the correctness of certain norms (McCarthy, 1973, pp. 139, 142). The ideal speech situation is a hypothetical state of discourse in which there are no constraints on raising questions about elements of the background consensus and coming to a revised consensus. Where there are such constraints, deviant or distorted communication occurs. One of the paradigmatic kinds of distortion is the case of domination, where one of the parties to interaction cannot be forced to justify his statements. The essence of domination, in this view, is that the dominator can avoid accounting for his acts or statements. Distortion may also arise from neurotic incapacities of the speech participants which prevent them from participating in discourse about particular elements of the background consensus. A consensus that arises through distorted communication is a false consensus.

The doctrine has practical implications: in a society in which the ideal speech situation does not obtain, philosophy must take sides against distortion, in favor of nondistorted communication. The interest in nondistorted communication amounts to an interest in emancipation, which is a political interest. So the drive for genuine knowledge and the drive for the political goal of a nondistorting political order coincide. Further, there is a unity of theory and practice, demanded by considerations of consistency: epistemology must formulate a political ideal and end; when it does not, it cannot aim at its own fulfillment, because it does not aim at establishing the conditions for its fulfillment.

Habermas rejects the classical solution on grounds that are

revealing of the character of this alternative standard. The attempt to treat the political order as a portion of the cosmological order, he argues, is itself a mystification that conceals the interest of classical philosophy.

> Theory in the sense of the classical tradition only had an impact on life because it was thought to have discovered in the cosmic order an ideal world structure, including the prototype for the order of the human world. Only as cosmology was *theoria* capable of orienting action. . . . Theory had educational and cultural implications not because it had freed knowledge from interest. To the contrary, it did because it derived *pseudonormative power from the concealment of its actual interest* (1971a, p. 306).

The actual interest of classical philosophy was to purge the world of demons or archaic super-human powers so that the individual ego could develop. The individual emancipated himself by identifying his ego with abstract laws of the cosmic order. The basic ontological assumption of a structured self-subsistent world order thus served an emancipatory psychological function in the communication system of the polis.

From the point of view of the ideal speech situation, the consensus the classics achieved was in part a result of the constraint that the members of the speech community, the philosophers, had a common psychological need. This need was not a matter that entered into the discourse, because it was common to all members of the community. Because it was not the subject of disagreement between members of the philosophic speech community, it did not become problematic in the discourse of the community. Discourse was thus constrained, just as discourse is restricted by the positivist's refusal to enter into dialogue on certain claims on grounds of their alleged meaninglessness.

There is a troubling feature of this analysis of the classics. The person who claims to be in the ideal speech situation and to have arrived at his conclusions through discourse in the ideal speech situation is analogous to the radical historicist described by Strauss, who claims to be living in the absolute moment in history, the moment at which the historicity or historical boundedness of all previous thought stands revealed. One may ask the radical historicist whether this 'knowledge' that he lives in the absolute moment is not also historically conditioned and therefore suspect. The claim to be in the ideal speech situation is also conditioned by the speech situation. If the speech situation is one in which the distortions are self-concealing or inaccessible to discourse, such as were the conditions of classical philosophy, the speaker may mistakenly suppose himself to be free of the distortions, and he will have no way of checking this out within the language games of his speech community. Habermas characterized the process of emancipatory discourse in psychoanalytic terms as a self-formative process. The psychoanalytic patient, like the participant in self-reflexive emancipatory discourse, marks his success, he suggests, by his recognition of the successful continuation of a self-formative process. But how does one distinguish success? Do not paranoids and schizophrenics go through a self-formative process? Is this not successful? If not, how precisely does one distinguish success here? It may be suggested that groups of persons who believe in auras and astral projection satisfy neurotic narcissistic impulses through their participation in the discourse, and agreement with the consensus, of these groups. Is not the development of the ideology and practice of such groups an example of theory-guided action developed through discourse, of the self-formative development of a speech community? The Positivists have answers for such questions: according to the verification criteria of meaning, the assertions about auras and astral projections would be meaningless. Habermas rejects such criteria but fails to provide a satisfactory substitute for them. His own explanations, as with the radical historicist's claim to be speaking in the absolute moment, are subject to the same suspicion as all other claims – that they are based on the consensus of a speech community acting under conditions of communicative distortion.[6]

The limits of the critiques

Both Strauss's critique and Habermas's critique work effectively against Weber, for Weber has an undefended metaphysics, as the Weimar critiques established. Yet the extension of these critiques to Positivism is fraught with difficulties. Habermas and Strauss have both approached the difficulties in terms of a thesis suggested by Weber himself, the thesis that science has a significance which must somehow be accounted for. Weber said that it cannot be accounted for scientifically, but that the value of science is presupposed. The fact-value distinction is the source of this paradox, which has figured in positivist as well as in Weberian writings (Rudner, 1969). Habermas dealt with the problem by considering the positivist interdiction on questions of this sort as an ideology that props up an order, i.e., in terms of the sociology of knowledge.

Strauss's approach to criticism proceeded from an idea stated in the last line of *Thoughts on Machiavelli*: while 'philosophy must beware of wishing to be edifying, it is of necessity edifying' (Strauss, 1969, p. 299). Strauss convicted his opponents on the basis of the erroneous or self-negating implications of their explicit teaching that the person living the political life or the life of the mind must draw. He regarded several kinds of consequences, such a nihilism, as self-negating. The remainder are alternative doctrines of natural right and can be defeated on grounds of their own inadequacies or their inferiority to the classics as a doctrine of natural right. Weber he charged with nihilism. Other positivists he charged with teaching a manifestly inferior, but concealed, natural right.

This strategy in itself raises a difficult point of hermeneutics. Peter Winch, in a discussion of Evans-Pritchard's imputation of 'contradiction' to Zande thought, remarked that 'it is the European, obsessed with pressing Zande thought where it would not naturally go – to a contradiction – who is guilty of the misunderstanding, not the Zande' (1970, p. 93). In one sense this same point can apply to individual thinkers. In saying that a thinker has 'hidden the nihilistic consequences of his own thought from himself,' as Strauss has said of Weber, one must be very careful that these consequences show up only by pushing the thinker's thought where it would not go for reasons inherent in the thinker's own doctrine.

Strauss got into precisely this difficulty in his critique of 'social science positivism.' In the epilogue to Storing's collection of critiques of behavioral political scientists, Strauss recognized that his opponents hold their scientific claims to be without normative implications. He denied that they are: the theories of the new political scientists have, he said, 'grave political consequences. . . . The Is necessarily leads to an Ought, all sincere protestations to the contrary' (1962, p. 319). Strauss held such consequences to be evident to common sense. 'Everyone knows what follows from the demonstration . . . that there is only a difference of degree between liberal democracy and communism in regard to coercion and freedom' (ibid.). The difference between Strauss and Habermas rests on the question of *how* these consequences flow from positivist social science.

For Habermas, positivist social theory can only resolve into a critique. To this extent, then, and only to this extent, does positivist political science or the bourgeois critique of ideology have normative implications. The relation between this critique and decisionism is, however, never spelled out by Habermas in the form of a logical analysis of the implicative relations between the doctrines. The critique does not, in any clear sense, *entail* decisionism. Strauss agreed that positivist political science serves as a critique and has negative implications for the central concepts of classical political theory, such as the idea of wholes and the idea of the common good. But Strauss also wished to insist that there are positive normative implications of the new political science – that it *warrants* a specific conception, namely the rational society or the nonideological regime. Strauss made the connection in this way: the new political scientists make an assumption that value choices are irrational.

> One thus arrives at the notion of the rational society or of the non-ideological regime: a society that is based on the understanding of the character of values. Since this understanding implies that before the tribunal of reason all values are equal, the rational society will be egalitarian or democratic and permissive or liberal: the rational doctrine regarding the difference between facts and values rationally justifies the preference for liberal democracy – contrary to what is intended by that distinction itself. In other words, whereas the new political science ought to deny the proposition that there can be no society without an ideology, it asserts that proposition (1962, p. 324).

But how precisely does one 'arrive' at this notion of the rational society? If Weber is the 'greatest representative of social science positivism' (Strauss, 1957, p. 351), it is not clear that the notion applies to him, for, as Löwith pointed out, Weber did not simply embrace rationalization. Further, whatever the personal preferences of the positivists might be regarding the 'rational society' or permissive egalitarianism, neither idea derives very directly from the positivist canon. If one can be a positivist without being committed to such preferences, there is no necessary connection between the preferences and positivism.

The argument that the fact-value separation promotes 'permissive egalitarianism' is perhaps not central to the Straussian critique. The question is whether the difficulty that is encountered here – that in order to make these criticisms of the positivist position it often proved necessary to reformulate it and supplement it by some nonpositivist (and perhaps counterpositivist) premises – is a difficulty that arises in the central arguments as well, such as the argument on the significance or meaning of science. The central Straussian criticism is that Weber's conception of facts and values has nihilistic consequences, and that these nihilistic consequences necessarily extend to and deny the justification of his own position. This does not readily extend to Logical Positivism. For the Logical Positivists, the question of the value of science or the justification of science is not a scientific question; it is not needful of a scientific answer, for there could be no scientific answer. The point of the fact-value separation, the claim that facts and values are absolutely heterogeneous, is that factual claims properly understood and value claims properly understood cannot conflict. But claims that are falsely understood or that are misrepresentations, such as political advice that claims to be based on nature, may indeed conflict with factual scientific claims. They may also conflict in the sense that when the standards of evidence used to evaluate scientific claims are applied to political advice, these standards prove inapplicable and therefore do not serve to warrant the claim that the advice is based on nature. For the Positivist, the conflict is not a scientific conflict. It is rather a conflict between scientific claims and pseudoscientific claims, those that cannot be warranted by these standards. A 'scientific claim' for or against the value of science would, in turn, be a misrepresentation or falsely understood claim as well. If one makes no such claims, no such conflict arises. So Strauss's extension of the argument founders on the self-understanding of positivism. To convict positivism of inconsistency, one must supply premises that this self-understanding precludes. Minimally, one must supply the premise that science must be rationally justified. This premise is not part of the positivist canon, at least not the modern positivist canon. Indeed, it may be said to be the chief claim of the Logical Positivists that science does not have what E. A. Burtt called 'metaphysical presuppositions' (Burtt, 1927), that indeed it has no presuppositions at all but is distinguished from metaphysical 'argument' by the criterion of meaningfulness.

The criterion of meaningfulness, as we suggested in the previous chapter, is now a dead letter. But one may notice that it was a source of difficulty both for the adherents of Positivism as well as for its critics, as Hempel's discussion in 'The Empiricist Criterion of Meaning' makes clear (Hempel, 1959). For the critics, the temptation to supply additional foundational premises and to reconstrue Positivism as a form of the philosophical approach that is the source of these supplied premises – such as historicism, relativism, or (as we have seen in Habermas's case) instrumentalism – has sometimes been overwhelming. Two conspicuous instances of this arise in connection with figures involved in the Weber controversy. Strauss, in a course at Chicago in 1962, 'used Ernest Nagel's *The Structure of Science* [1961] to illustrate what he meant by affirming that if positivism understood itself, it would necessarily transform itself into historicism' (Gildin, 1975, p. xiii). The argument he offered hinges on a passage in Nagel's book that suggests that it is 'only a contingent historical fact' that science aims at achieving explanations prescribed by the principle of causality: 'it is logically possible that in their efforts at mastering their environments men might have aimed at something quite different' (Nagel, 1961, p. 324). For Strauss, who thought of the principle of causality as a foundation of modern science, this amounts to an admission that modern science is 'only one of a number of ways of pursuing knowledge and . . . no more defensible rationally than any of the other ways' (Gildin, 1975, p. xv).[7] Nagel, however, did not think of the principle of causality as a foundation or premise of science, but rather as one form among several logically possible forms of explanation. The possible forms of scientific explanation, further, are all within the empiricist criterion of meaningfulness, which he did *not* describe as logically arbitrary or 'historical.'

An earlier example of an attempt to collapse Positivism into the same category as historicism is to be found in Max Horkheimer's 1930s article, 'The Latest Attack on Metaphysics,' in which Otto Neurath is accused of 'Super-relativism' on the strength of a remark to the effect that, as Horkheimer quoted him, 'We recognize the demands of relativism.' Horkheimer compared Neurath's relativism to Mussolini's and concluded that 'relativism, which is without philosophical justification, is an element of a social dynamic which moves toward authoritarian forms' (Horkheimer, 1972, p. 165). What Neurath actually said is less dramatic. The remark, which was misquoted by Horkheimer, occurs in a passage in which Neurath considered the question of the status of the 'logical and mathematical instruments' used by the sciences. He suggested that these too are corrigible, e.g., by the proof of contradictions, and that their apparent certitude is only a matter of degree. He noted one implication of this rather narrow point, which is that, to the extent that the mathematical aspects of a scientific theory are not absolute, the terminology of 'correspondence with the world,' which is absolutistic, is inappropriate (Neurath, 1936, p. 189). The mathematical aspects of the theory, which are corrigible, are not directly tested by comparison with the world. Thus the sentences that are compared to the world are, in this sense, 'relative' to the logical or mathematical framework of the theory, and therefore their truth cannot be a simple matter of correspondence to the world. So what Neurath actually said about relativism is quite different from what Horkheimer would have preferred him to say. He said that he 'recognizes in principle' what he described as the 'unreasonable claims [*l'exigence*] of relativism,' but this 'recognition' is applied solely to 'the traditional absolutistic terminology' of correspondence (ibid.). This is not 'super-relativism.' But the fact that Horkheimer has been tempted to distort Neurath's remarks in this way is suggestive of the strength of the wish to see the issues of Positivism and historicist relativism as identical.

The difference between the issue with Weber and the issue with the Positivists is in the problem of meaningfulness. As we have seen, Weber lacks a 'criterion of meaningfulness' that can plausibly be said to be 'nonmetaphysical' in character. This criterion figures heavily in the formulation of positions like Nagel's. So Weber was clearly vulnerable to the criticisms of the Weimar ontologists, who were able to make the point that Weber's metaphysics was no more firmly based than the metaphysical stances he so bitterly opposed.

The extension of the critique to Anglo-American philosophy

An analogous structure of interdictions gets in the way of extensions of the Weimar critiques to other philosophical movements.[8] Habermas has devoted the most effort to this problem. We have said that Habermas argues that a language game rests on a background consensus about the truth of certain beliefs and the correctness of certain norms, and that these should always be open to challenge. This claim, it should be pointed out, contrasts to the notion of the nature of the consensus in a language game in Wittgenstein, from whom the notion of language game was taken. Rush Rhees has described the 'consensus' in Wittgenstein's conception of language game in this way:

> We see that we understand one another, without noticing whether our reactions tally or not. *Because* we agree in our reactions, it is possible for me to tell you something, and it is possible for you to teach me something (quoted in Winch, 1958, p. 85).

For Wittgenstein, the consensus would be no more than the common use of the rules that make up the language game: it does not rest on anything 'outside' the language game. Habermas wishes to say it does. His view seems to be this: we can always talk *about* the rules of the language game, and sometimes what is said about these rules or usages leads us to change what we are doing and adopt new rules or usages. In some contexts this may be a plausible picture. Particular legal usages may be discursively justified by arguments involving the rule of precedent, on which there is a consensus in Wittgenstein's sense. But discourse in the law is almost unique in this respect.

In other contexts, it is implausible to speak of 'justification' of the rules. One can certainly talk about arithmetic. But what can one say to *justify* it? What can one say about the classical French cuisine and its standards that would justify them? One can perhaps explain arithmetic or the French cuisine, but such explanations consist not in justification but rather in showing or explicating. Someone can show you how to do sums, until sooner or later you catch on, and it may help for you to hear explications like, 'Think of it this way – pretend you have three apples in this pocket, and . . .' Similarly, you can come to learn the fine points of the French cuisine, to 'develop a palate.' But in doing this, you would never hear a 'justification,' nor would you learn what a justification of the rules or criteria would look like.

Habermas is compelled to deny that showing or explicating can suffice as justification. This is a point of some importance. If he were to say that it does suffice, he would be forced to give up his case against the Logical Positivists, who hold that science does not stand in need of justification, but only of explication or analysis. So to protect his metascientific theory, Habermas must demand that discourse on science involve something stronger than mere explication or analysis. This is a demand of doubtful coherence. 'Justification' is an especially strong term. From Wittgenstein's point of view, if there are no criteria for calling something a justification, no criteria for distinguishing 'mistakes in the argument,' then it is conceptually misleading to call it a justification at all. In analyzing the self-reflective significance of the claims of psychoanalysis, Habermas argued that they cannot be 'subjected to externally imposed standards, whether of a functioning language game or of controlled observation' (Habermas, 1971a, p. 269). A Wittgensteinian philosopher would suggest that by leaving the control of an established language game the claims would go beyond the bounds of intelligibility.

The difficulty Habermas encounters here in giving an account of the connection between talk about a language game and the truth or validity of the language game has a parallel in Strauss's critique as well. In demanding a metaphysical justification of science, Strauss demanded something both Weber and the Positivists denied could be given. Habermas, in arguing that all discourse rests on a 'background consensus' which must be open to discursive justification if it is to be a true consensus, demands that science, among other activities, be 'justifiable.' Wittgensteinians would reject this demand, for they would reject the view that the 'justifications' actually serve as, or constitute, justifications at all. As we have seen, Weber's rejection of the problem of justification collapsed in Weimar under the attacks of such critics as Grab, Landshut, and Löwith, who all showed that Weber's rejection of these questions was ultimately based on just another metaphysical stance. Analogous attacks have been made on the Wittgensteinian rejection. Roger Trigg, in his recent *Reason and Commitment* (1973), has suggested that this rejection makes Wittgenstein into a believer in 'commitment' not unlike Tillich. Stanley Cavell, who is not a critic of Wittgenstein, has shown similarities between Heidegger and Wittgenstein on the Kierkegaardian questions (Cavell, 1964).

The questions that produce these similarities have the form, 'Should I choose to believe what is true?' 'Should I be moral?' and 'Should I be a part of a community at all?' (and are taken to mean, e.g., 'Should I be moral?' not in a specific instance but 'in general'). Such questions are radically different from ordinary questions of morals and politics, which are questions of applying moral criteria to particular cases, of weighing considerations, or of making choices between concrete alternatives. The ordinary questions direct us to the particular facts of the situation at hand. These other questions direct us to 'ground' or foundational answers. To say, as Wittgenstein might, that there is no ground or foundational answer to such questions, that here there can be no more than commitment, is not to say that therefore there is no knowledge, no morality, but only commitment. It is merely to say that there is no 'foundation' of knowledge and morality, i.e., no basis apart from the language games one plays. It is noteworthy that Trigg, who regards the Wittgensteinian view as objectionable, does not argue that it leads to moral confusion or political disaster, for he does not confuse the two types of questions.

Perhaps it was Heidegger's mistake to think that at the moment of Hitler's ascension the two questions had fused, so that the absolute historical moment had arrived. But it was not Heidegger's mistake alone. The whole point of Tillich's concept of *Kairos* was that the fundamental moment of decision had arrived as an immediate historical fact, demanding commitment. Weber's whole approach depended on regarding the two types of questions as differing only in degree. If one follows Weber in this respect, combining the immediate historical question and the Kierkegaardian question demanding commitment, then one may say, as Steven Lukes has, that Weber's view of the nonrationality of morality is a matter of common consent in contemporary philosophy (Lukes, 1974, pp. 167-8). But if one does not follow Weber and Heidegger here, as contemporary Anglo-American philosophy generally does not, the lack of a foundational justification that gives reasons, e.g., for being rational, or for being a part of a community, or for being 'moral in general,' does not produce nihilism in the face of *particular* questions of belief, moral action, or membership in a community. There is no special difficulty about these particular questions, because the means of answering them is at hand, in the particular facts of particular cases.

The reason the German and recent English traditions in ethical philosophy stand so starkly opposed on this point is that one reason behind the development of these English traditions and their guiding idea of learning 'how ethical language actually works' is that this task was conceived as a corrective to the kind of doctrines that flourished in nineteenth-century Continental idealist philosophy. Thus where Heidegger worried that we are not great enough to live up to the philosophy of the idealists, this English tradition denied that the terms the idealists were enthralled with, such as 'freedom,' meant what the idealists had taken them to mean. The philosophical doctrines that arose in the German tradition in response to such things as the problem of the conflict between freedom and necessity were thought to be pseudo-problems, to be correctly resolved by attending to actual usage. Indeed, if one wishes to take the 'analysis of ethical language' contained in ordinary language philosophy as a 'teaching,' it is largely the teaching that the two types of questions are different, and that particular facts settle particular ethical questions and settle them in intelligible ways.

'Foundational' questions, or the historical 'choices' with which the German tradition was so concerned, are clearly questions of another type: those in this English tradition would say that the problems solved by attending to the particular facts in a particular case just cannot be solved by the means for solving the other kind of questions, and vice versa. They would further question whether the foundational questions are intelligible at all. In any case, from the confusion of these two types of questions, moral trouble is likely to follow, because the confusion necessarily distracts us from the facts that settle particular questions of right and wrong.

Nothing could be more alien to this teaching than the idea that one must substitute the foundational kind of question for the mundane questions in order to be truly sublime or noble, or that the truly sublime and noble is inevitably something that goes beyond mundane morality. Yet this is implicitly Weber's teaching, especially to those aspiring to leadership: the identification of 'freedom' with going beyond mundane morality and acting on one's 'decision.'

Strauss regarded contemporary Anglo-American philosophy as of a piece with Weber because his own conception, and, he believed, the classical conception are based on the notion that it is possible and necessary to seek answers to both the 'ground' or foundational and particular questions by one more or less unified account. So this philosophy, which denies the possibility of a philosophical or rational answer to the 'ground' or foundational question, necessarily appeared to him as 'nihilism.' One of his followers, Stanley Rosen, has pursued this line of argument in detail in his book *Nihilism: a philosophical essay*, (1969; see also idem, 1980). An analogous contrast obtains between certain forms of contemporary Anglo-American philosophy and neo-Thomism, which also stresses the necessity of grounding.

In recent years there has been something of a return to the problems of substantive moral philosophy within Anglo-American philosophy. In particular, there has been a reopening of meta-philosophical questions about the nature of moral rationality and deliberation. This reopening has brought about more critical assessments of Weber's views, within the context of a broadening of the common ground with traditional ethics. It should be pointed out that some Catholic writers, notably Kenny, Geach, and Anscombe, have always regarded the teachings of the church and 'ordinary language philosophy' as reconcilable.

The rehabilitation of deliberation

The primary common ground between the Weber critics is over the question of the character of moral deliberation, which they do not believe can be reduced to 'decision.' Some of the critics treat Weberianism as an incident in a general foundationalist attack on deliberation. For example, Richard Rorty has developed an antifoundationalism that construes Heidegger, Wittgenstein, and Dewey as attacking the Platonic and Kantian enterprise of 'grounding' belief and action. Rorty's views are the same as those he attributes to the Pragmatists – he rejects the idea of a theoretical basis for practice, and holds that a theory is no better than the practices it underwrites. He characterizes the Platonic-Kantian conception of philosophy as an attempt to provide a spurious substitute for deliberation:

> All the Platonic or Kantian philosopher does is to take the finished first-level product, jack it up a few levels of abstraction, invent a metaphysical or epistemological or semantical vocabulary into which to translate it, and announce that he has *grounded* it (1980, p. 729).

This deconstruction is perhaps itself a 'strong misreading.' He contrasts standard philosophical practice to his own, pragmatist, view that

> the pattern of all inquiry – scientific as well as moral – is deliberation concerning the relative attractions of various

> concrete alternatives. The idea that in science or philosophy we can substitute 'method' for deliberating between alternative results of speculation is just wishful thinking (ibid., p. 724).

He regards the relativists' despair over the lack of such methods, and their drawing of dramatic practical conclusions about moral life from this lack, as similarly faulty (ibid., p. 728). Both relativists and Kantians are distracted from the concrete by a spurious ideal of 'method' or 'technique.'

> The relativist who says that we can break ties among serious and incompatible candidates for belief only by 'non-rational' or 'non-cognitive' considerations is just one of the Platonist or Kantian philosopher's imaginary playmates, inhabiting the same realm of fantasy as the solipsist, the sceptic, and the moral nihilist (ibid.).

John Finnis, in his recent *Natural Law and Natural Rights*, makes a similar point about the drawing of these conclusions. Weber, he says,

> slides from saying that *empirical science* cannot adjudicate between values to saying that such adjudication is beyond reason and objectivity altogether, and is a matter of faith, demonic decision, radical subjectivity. (But this is just a slide.) Like Sartre after him, Weber relies mainly upon certain ethical dilemmas, in which it is, he thinks, impossible to show that one of two competing ideals or morally motivated courses of action is superior to the other. . . . But all these dilemmas arise from the *complexity* of ethical considerations; they do not show that all value-judgments, or even all ethical value-judgments, are likewise perplexed and beyond rational discrimination (1980, p. 51).

Finnis goes on to make some points about foundationalist construals of natural law. Aquinas, he points out, held that the grasp of natural law is 'simply one application of man's ordinary power of understanding' (ibid., p. 400), and is thus distinct from the 'foundational' question of the cause of natural law. Grasp of the natural law does not, in other words, depend on any sort of theology or metaphysics. However, Finnis does not, as Rorty does, reject foundational questions: the problem of the cause of the natural law is not, for him, a pseudoproblem.

Rorty and Finnis, of course, do not represent the mainstream of Anglo-American philosophy. In the 'mainstream,' as well, however, there has been a falling away from Weber-like views. This is especially evident in recent ethics. John Rawls's *A Theory of Justice* (1971) introduced a term for the aim of ethical reasoning, 'reflective equilibrium,' and Norman Daniels, in a series of important papers, extended and clarified this conception of ethical reasoning by the concept of 'wide reflective equilibrium.' These writings fall squarely in the tradition of thinking of morals as a matter of principles, in contrast to writers like Oakeshott, who regard this tradition as a primary source of the modern Babel (1962, pp. 59-79). Yet they do, *contra* Weber, legitimate the selection and revision of these principles as 'rational.'

The process consists in seeking consensus by seeing whether our considered judgments match our principles, and correcting failures to match by revising our principles, which in turn generates new considered judgments on specific cases, which in turn bears on the principles – a mutually correcting procedure, but one that is fallibilistic, i.e., does not pretend to produce final truths. The kind of rationality involved in narrow reflective equilibrium, as Daniels puts it, has a strong similarity to the rationality of choosing a syntactic theory, while 'choosing between competing moral conceptions in wide equilibrium has a close analogy to the problem of choosing between alternative deductive logics' (1980, p. 21). The novelty of these accounts of the methods of ethics rests on their rejection of the idea that ethics could be founded on some Archimedean point outside of ethics. These methods do not seek a nonmoral foundation for morals – they begin with our moral judgments and show the rationality of the process of revision of moral judgments, and identify an aim for the process.

Hilary Putnam, who is also close to the American mainstream, takes a related line of attack on Weber.[9] 'Let us recall,' Putnam says,

> that when Max Weber introduced the modern fact-value distinction, his argument against the objectivity of value judgments was precisely that it is not possible to establish the truth of a value judgment to the satisfaction of *all possible rational persons* (1981, p. 174).

Putnam goes on to suggest that

> In a disguised form Weber's argument is a Majoritarian argument; he is appealing to the fact that we can get the agreement of educated people on 'positive science' whereas we cannot get such an agreement on ethical values. It is interesting to contrast this stance with Aristotle's: Aristotle said that of course in ethics we should always try to get the agreement of the Many, but very often we know that realistically we cannot.

> Sometimes, elitist as it sounds to present day ears to say it, we are only able to convince the wise; and of course we have to rely on our own judgment to tell who are and who are not the wise (ibid., p. 177).

This suggests a rehabilitation of rational deliberation. As Putnam puts it:

> It is plausible that one of the highest manifestations of rationality should be the ability to judge correctly in precisely those cases where one cannot hope to 'prove' things to the satisfaction of the majority. It seems strange indeed that the fact that some things should be impossible to prove to everyone's satisfaction should become an argument for the irrationality of beliefs about those things (ibid., p. 179).

The rehabilitation of deliberation suggests a quite different, and less heroic, picture of Weber.

Weber believed he had discovered the limits of reason. Perhaps it would be better to say that he had discovered the limits of a particular philosophical tradition. Weber's foundationalism, his conception of rationality as quasi-deductive reasoning, his devotion to the standard philosophical distinctions, notably the distinction between means and end, all mark him as a child of nineteenth-century philosophy. These three features of his philosophical vocabulary also generate his doctrine of value – if a good reason for action can only be an 'end,' and choices between ends must be justified in a quasi-deductive way if they are to be justified at all, one is naturally faced with a difficulty over the justification of the 'ultimate' end – indeed, it is a contradiction in terms.

Vocabularies can be shells, too, and Weber construed the happenings of his moral world through this shell. The pathos of Weber's career is, in part, the pathos of his intellectual bondage by this set of philosophical ideas. Weber's successors today often show themselves to suffer from the same bondage – the relentlessness of their insistence on this philosophical vocabulary is unrelieved by the philosophical detachment necessary to examine these concepts. Weber's critics used this very relentlessness against him, for they noticed that the argument for the impossibility of a quasi-deductively 'justified' ethics could not be limited to ethics, but applied as readily to the 'justification' of science, of ontology, and to the distinction between science and ethics itself – for one can ask for the 'ultimate presuppositions' behind these things as well.

Weber took the nineteenth-century vocabulary that produced these paradoxes as a kind of fate to be submitted to. Yet the idea that ethics is a matter of deductive or quasi-deductive reasoning from value choices or principles is not a given. One might better take the Weberian problem of the impossibility of justifying an 'ultimate' end-choice as a *reductio ad absurdum* of the idea that ethical deliberation, or, more broadly, *phronesis*, consists in the use of 'more ultimate' values to deductively decide conflicts between 'less ultimate' values. Substantive moral conflicts occur, and one may be unable to settle them very satisfactorily – but when this happens, morality does not collapse, or become irrational, as an inconsistency makes a theory collapse. Far from it. When one acts in a morally competent fashion, one acts in recognition of the *validity* of the various claims on one. By turning the fact of the moral difficulty of politics into the 'tragic character of politics,' or by describing issues as matters of, e.g., 'theology vs. survival,' limited practical issues are obscured and overdramatized. Turning an everyday issue into a Kierkegaardian Either/Or courts turning politics into tragedy in fact, as well as rhetoric.

The pathos of Weber's career does not extend to the careers of his successors. In this respect, Jaspers was right: Weber was a seeker. To be seekers today we must go beyond the cage of Weber's own philosophy. Weber, who taught detachment with respect to 'ideal-types,' did not teach detachment with respect to the doctrine at the base of this teaching. Today we must cultivate this detachment or openness anew. Part of the Weberian heritage is that a number of crucial substantive themes – the problem of the aims of social science, the theme of the continuing relevance and significance of the various substantive political traditions, and parts of the substantive problems of legitimacy, constitutions, democracy, leadership, and international relations – were reductively redefined or defined away in accordance with Weberian premises about the nature of 'values' as 'choices' and the fact-value distinction, as when Morgenthau treated the concept of justice as no more than an expression of particular material or ideal interests. These reductions now appear to have been no more than an episode. Such is the cunning of historicism. But the episode is not yet complete.

Notes

Chapter 1 Problems of context and interpretation

1 These movements are described at length by Anderson in the chapter 'Propaganda Organizations in the German Empire' (1939).

2 Ralf Dahrendorf lists Roth among those who made 'relentless attacks' on the SPD in *Society and Democracy in Germany* (1969, p. 175).

3 Indeed, the doctrine that a developed and nurtured sense of community and common ideals is impossible in the modern world has been suggested to be false in precisely the context of work organizations, where Weber believed that rationalization, specialization, and routinization would, under the pressure of competition and struggle, go farthest. The experience of recent years is that the organizations Weber believed to be the ultimate in efficiency have proved unable to compete with Japanese organizations and Japanese-model Western organizations which emphasize nonspecialization, communitarian forms, common articulated philosophies of worklife, and so forth, and are also more productive. (Cf. Ouchi, 1981.)

Chapter 2 Reason and decision: Weber's core doctrine and value choices

1 Even the 'weathermen' of the Students for a Democratic Society (SDS), it will be recalled, believed the weather was blowing their way.

2 'Non' is simply a variant of the latinate prefix for negation, 'in', which is the root for the 'ir' in 'irrational.' The term 'nonrational', used by some Weber commentators (though not by Weber), is designed to avoid certain connotations of the established use of 'irrational,' particularly the hint of fanaticism, which stems from a traditional contrast between rational and animal.

A variant of this contrast is the distinction between systematic or methodical and erratic or disciplined and undisciplined. Weber placed a great deal of emphasis, in his historical accounts, on this distinction. He did not attempt to find a single definition covering all these distinctions, though he claimed that 'ultimately they belong inseparately together' (1946, p. 293). In his discussions of values and their relation to rationality (e.g., 1978a, p. 26) he generally used it in a much more narrow, quasi-deductive sense.

3 Some writers have regarded this style of using science to reason about practical decisions by eliminating illusory choices to be among Weber's greatest contributions (Albert, 1971, pp. 98-101). Schluchter emphasizes certain weaknesses of this style of reasoning (Schluchter, 1979b, pp. 106-12; cf. Kocka, 1976, pp. 289-90).

4 Weber argued this way with respect to the idea of admitting value discourse to the university, when he said, 'If, however, one wishes to turn the university into a forum for the discussion of values, then it obviously becomes a duty to permit the most unrestrained freedom of discussion of fundamental questions from all value positions.' However, he considered this a *reductio* of his opponents' position (Weber, 1949, p. 8).

5 Walter Bagehot, whose 'Metaphysical Basis of Toleration' is perhaps the source of Weber's language, supposed that there are 'ultimate truths of morals and religion' (Bagehot, 1889, p. 356).

6 The relation between the broad category of 'dispelled illusions' and the apparently broader category of the historically inappropriate is not clear. Consider a remark by Schluchter. 'Weber wants to prove that there are historically adequate and inadequate valuations, depending on their intellectual rationale. He considers it demonstrable that the positively religious person cannot be a "contemporary"' (Schluchter, 1979b, p. 81). Weber did not say that a 'return to the churches' involves a lack of intellectual integrity, nor did he include religion among the 'illusions' he spoke of. He said only that it requires an 'intellectual sacrifice' (1946, p. 155). Schluchter seems to presume that a choice that requires an intellectual sacrifice is *eo ipso* defective. Weber, who perhaps had in mind that all religion involves faith, did not say this, though he may have believed it. He said only that the arms of the church are open to the person who 'cannot bear the fate of the times like a man.'

> An intellectual sacrifice in favor of an unconditional religious devotion is ethically quite a different matter than the evasion of the plain duty of intellectual integrity, which sets in if one lacks the courage to clarify one's own ultimate standpoint and rather facilitates this duty by feeble relative judgments (ibid.).

In his eyes, he said, the religious return ranks higher than the sort of academic prophecy that does not clearly recognize that, in the classroom, 'no other virtue holds but plain intellectual integrity' (ibid., pp. 155-6). This suggests that the religious man can sacrifice the intellect and retain his integrity – as long as he recognizes that he has made the sacrifice. The intellectual integrity of the religious person thus flows from the fact that he decides, and faces the consequences of his decision; the person who seeks to avoid 'decision,' e.g., by 'relative judgments,' lacks integrity.

It should be noticed that the persons falling into this second category often simply disagreed with Weber's philosophical doctrines of the relation of reason and value, and rejected the idea of decision. The existence of the disagreement does not stop Weber from denouncing them for lacking intellectual integrity. Thus in practice Weber's category of intellectual integrity derived from his philosophy of values, and was not simply an independent standard.

7 *Gesinnungsethik* has been translated as: 'ethic of sheer commitment to ultimate values' by Guenther Roth (1976, p. 266); as 'ethic of sentiment' by Kurt Wilk in translating Radbruch (1950, p. 92); as 'ethics of intention' by Strauss (1953, p. 69); as the '*morale de la conviction*' in Raymond Aron's 'Introduction' (1954, p. 44. Cf. also Maurice Weyembergh, 1972, p. 14); as the 'ethic of ultimate ends' by Gerth and Mills (Weber, 1946, p. 120); and as '*l'ethique de l'intention ou* (*fausse*) *conviction*,' by Fleischmann (1964, p. 231).

8 Roth, for example, fails to make this distinction and reads Schluchter as arguing that Weber was a pragmatist in some broader sense than the narrow sense Habermas uses in the context of discussing the relation of experts to political discourse. The misunderstanding here is a misunderstanding of philosophical pragmatism.

9 It is misleading to dismiss this non-Weberian conception of the tasks of the university, as does one of Weber's defenders, as the view of 'extreme right-wingers' (Roth, 1971b, p. 51). In Weimar, when pedagogy became an important concern, forms of this conception were widely defended, by figures as far apart on the political spectrum as Spranger (1925) and Tillich.

10 One must take care in interpreting these affirmations of the tragic character of power. Peter Gay criticizes Meinecke by saying that this 'very vision of power as a tragic phenomenon is an unfortunate philosophical habit inherited from German Idealism; it gives a practical question metaphysical dignity, which must lead not to analysis but resignation' (Gay, 1968, p. 95). The point applies equally to Weber's vision.

11 Weber's statements of his position (e.g., 1971, pp. 13-14) have been qualified by some writers to emphasize that Weber was more fundamentally, or at least significantly, concerned with the country (Weyembergh, 1972, p. 16) or the preservation of German culture (Beetham, 1974, pp. 119-47; Aron, 1972, p. 87) or even 'human freedom' (Beetham, 1974, p. 210) in a certain sense of this term (Jaspers, 1962, p. 212; Mommsen, 1974a, pp. 95-115). Jaspers said that in 1920 Weber came to the conclusion that the individual nation was no longer the highest value, but that what was most important now was the solidarity of the free Western nations, and that now Germany must affirm a Western type of political freedom (Jaspers, 1962, p. 205; cf. Beetham, 1974, pp. 141-2). Walter Struve, however, has denied that there was any significant change in Weber's dedication to the power of the national state and has suggested that this goal took precedence over 'national culture' and even over the needs of the people as a whole (Struve, 1973, pp. 117-18). Ernst Nolte has pointed out that in January 1920 Weber was still saying that every power must be

employed to reestablish Germany's greatness (Nolte, 1963, p. 13).

12 The claim that Weber went through a change of heart after the war, seeing Germany's new role as part of the Western bloc, has a long history. There is some basis for the claim. Weber had long taken the view that an understanding with England that would have prevented the war was possible, and believed that there were cultural reasons that made this possible. But Weber nevertheless always presented the West as the lesser of two evils. When he discussed the 'unavoidable' fact of American world domination or 'Anglo-Saxon world domination,' he described it as 'very unpleasant.' It is instructive to notice that Jaspers, who after the Second World War made the claim that Weber saw Germany's future role as a matter of taking the side of the West (1962), had read Weber differently in the Weimar era, as seeing the Anglo-Saxons and the Russians as threats on a more nearly equal footing, as we shall see in a later chapter. Some writers have seen Weber's attitude toward the Anglo-Saxon world as a more important determinant than his attitude toward Russia. Weyembergh goes so far as to claim that Weber's devotion to imperialism was instrumental, an imperialism designed essentially to break British world hegemony (Weyembergh, 1972, pp. 131-2).

13 The concept of plebiscitarian leader democracy has been the subject of a large controversy, and indeed, as Struve remarks, much of the debate over Mommsen's work has 'narrowed down to the question of the relation between National Socialism and Weber's conception of plebiscitarian leadership' (Struve, 1973, p. 115). The significant texts include those of Mommsen (1974b, pp. 418-53; 1963; 1965), Nolte (1963), Karl Loewenstein (1966, pp. 63-90), Beetham, (1974, pp. 215-44), Johannes F. Winckelmann (1952), Christian von Ferber (1970), and Gustav Schmidt (1964).

14 It is revealing that when Weber spoke of the values of the syndicalist and the persons he persuaded to syndicalism, he did not use the term 'persuade', a term suggesting moral reasoning, but used the causal term 'induce' (Weber, 1949, p. 24).

15 The whole genre of literature on Weber designed to distinguish his ideas from those of the Nazis tends to convey a misleading impression, because the arguments for a connection between the ideas of Weber and the Nazis are generally held to tougher standards than are similar arguments in the history of ideas. Nolte certainly does this. Beetham goes out of his way to give Weber the benefit of the doubt as a liberal and an enlightened nationalist. He would doubtless reject, as intolerably vague, an argument that said, for example, that there was a natural connection between Weber's doctrine of leadership and support for Nazism. But he himself argues 'that there was a natural connection between elite theory and support for fascism,' and applies this to Mosca, whose differences with the Fascists – both theoretically (he would never have called Mussolini's following an elite) and practically – were very conspicuous (Beetham, 1977, p. 163).

16 Along these same lines, various writers have emphasized that Weber foresaw *de facto* restrictions on the leader that would have limited his

power. Weyembergh has emphasized that the leader would be limited by his own practical calculations of the chance of success of a venture and by the fact that each person must choose for himself between following the leader and not following the leader (1972, pp. xxix-xxx). Situational constraints like the multiplicity of parties and the federalist structure also would limit the leader (ibid., p. 439). Nolte (1963, pp. 11, 23). Beetham (1974, p. 114), Giddens, (1972, pp. 22-3). Kocka (1976, pp. 295-6), and Loewenstein (1966, p. 41) emphasize that parliament and party structures serve as restrictions (cf. Kocka, 1976, pp. 289-90, 295; Beetham, 1974, pp. 133-4, 138-9, 239, 243; Abramowski, 1966, pp. 58-9). However, when Weber himself spoke about the role of parties in a plebiscitarian democracy he claimed that it was 'decisive' that 'those who direct the party machine . . . keep the members of parliament in check' and are 'in a position to impose their will to a rather far reaching extent. . . . The man whom the machine follows now becomes the leader, even over the head of the parliamentary party' (Weber, 1946, p. 103). 'The broad mass of deputies function only as followers of the leader and the leaders in the cabinet, and follow them blindly, as long as they are successful. And this is as it should be' (Weber, 1971, p. 348).

17 One reader has asked whether a choice 'to follow Hitler' can, in Weber's theory, count as a value choice. Weber's critic in the immediate postwar period, Julius Jacob Schaaf, spoke to this general issue by pointing out that Weber confused the thing valued and a 'value' (1946, p. 61). Scheler emphasized a similar point in developing his alternative to Weber's views. There is nothing apparent in Weber that precludes counting Hitler himself as a value. The 'fatherland,' which Weber himself described as a value, is, like Hitler, a particular historical entity, not a general concept.

18 The Vietnam protestor had access to such principles in the form of the doctrine of war crimes and the claim that the war itself was criminal or illegitimate. The Weberian would deny there were any such universally obligating or action-justifying principles as the idea of war crimes. Thus a Weberian in the situation of Vietnam objector would be faced with a choice between support and betrayal of the country on the basis of irrational commitment to values such as the 'values' of natural law. The 'natural law' adherent would not be faced with 'betrayal' as an alternative. He would simply be faced with a moral dictate.

Chapter 4 The Weimar era dispute

1 Godfrey Scheele is another who was critical of Weber. He pointed out that, far from desiring a dialogue with the Marxists, Weber resigned from the postwar party he was first allied with because it was too ready to compromise with Marxism (1946, p. 50). Scheele was critical of Weber's constitutional ideas, especially involving leadership, which he characterized as 'all rather prophetic of Nazi doctrine' (ibid., p. 51), and noted both the apprehensiveness of the Democrats about presidential power and Weber's embrace of it, as when he told the

socialists that they too accepted the notion of a dictator, because dictatorship of the masses required a dictator (ibid., p. 50; Weber, 1971, p. 499). Scheele also pointed out the differences between American, or French, notions of 'rights' and those of the Weimar constitution, written under the influence of a different 'liberalism.'

2 The bitter-enders who wished to continue the war, for example, figure in the mythology that later developed about the postwar and late-war period. Nevertheless, such dramatic events as the disintegration of the navy through a general mutiny obviously involved a widespread repudiation of the militaristic outlook of the prewar and war years. In some social settings this change in attitude was very shortlived; in others it never happened at all.

3 Certainly this is an exaggeration.

4 An account of the sides taken by academics in these political-intellectual disputes is available in Kurt Töpner, *Gelehrte Politiker und politisierende Gelehrte* (1970).

5 One finds that Kurt Eisner is the target on pp. 118, 120, F.W. Förster on pp. 122-4. It would of course be wrong to say that these speeches *entail* his political stance, but the 'choices' the listener is left with by these speeches are few indeed; so the links between the 'value-free analysis' and the 'values' are close (cf. Mommsen, 1974a, pp. 29, 32-3).

6 Michels, for example, specifically said that the imperialist thought of the past and the concerns of the *Antrittsrede* were retained by Weber in the last years of his life (1927, p. 111).

7 One should not suppose that people like Stefan George had followers and Weber did not. Gadamer, a student in the early Weimar period, recalls a meeting where followers of George, Tagore, von Gierke, and Weber spoke (Gadamer, 1977, p. 25).

8 This correspondence has recently been published by Winston and Winston, under the title *An Exceptional Friendship: the Correspondence of Thomas Mann and Erich Kahler* (1975). Not too much should be made of these personal ties, however. Gundolf was also a friend of Arthur Salz, of whom we shall hear more, and an admirer of Weber.

9 Another example of comparison to the Greek conception of science, which is to be an underlying theme of this literature, from Jaspers and Bultmann through Strauss, is the critique of Weber's speech by Ernst Robert Curtius in 'Max Weber über Wissenschaft als Beruf' (1919).

10 The desolated men Kahler described are especially reminiscent of the central figure in Alberto Moravia's novel *La Conformista*.

11 'Already a series of philosophers have tried to "construct" him,' reported Kantorowicz, who specifically mentioned Honigsheim and Jaspers (1922, p. 256). In this period, in contrast to the more recent literature, the tendency was for Weber's followers to claim to find unity, and for critics to emphasize his incoherence or inconsistencies.

12 Jaspers's bitterness toward Rickert long outlived Rickert himself. In his 'Philosophical Autobiography,' Jaspers recounts this and other unpleasant incidents with Rickert (1957).

13 Weber's association with Salz is described by Marianne Weber (1975, pp. 369, 452; cf. Käsler, 1979). When Scheler spoke of 'Weber and his

friends,' he mentioned Salz, Jaspers, and Radbruch (1963, p. 19).

14 Stefan George, who was well known to both Salz and Kahler (though neither was properly part of his circle), is the referent of these remarks.

15 Salz did not go so far as to use such phrases as 'natural law' or 'natural right' to describe the presupposition of a 'unique eternal order.' At the time in Germany there was no significant doctrinal stance self-identified as 'natural right,' and natural law philosophy was a Catholic concern. However, it was clearly understood that the contemporary understanding of society, including sociology as a discipline, derived from the rejection of *Naturrecht*, a point made by Sombart in a discussion of the history of sociology in 1936. It is of interest to note that here Sombart gives Stammler, the subject of a methodological attack by Weber, as an example of a contemporary *Naturrecht* thinker (1936, pp. 4-6).

16 Karl Jaspers described Weber as a 'substantial manifestation of our time' (1921, p. 27).

17 Fritz Ringer discusses this dispute in terms of his concept of 'mandarism.' As John Torrance observes, Weber 'is the historical hero of the story' as Ringer tells it (Torrance, 1974, p. 159). Others have seen the matter differently. R.H. Samuel and R. Hinton Thomas, for example, said that 'Weber's lecture may be described as a defence of the orthodox tradition of German scholarship, and in it are reflected the virtues of that tradition and also its weaknesses, especially considered in connection with the democratic movement' (1949, p. 122).

Ringer's account of the speech is idiosyncratic. He claims that all that Weber's 'Science as a Vocation' speech 'excluded was the search for ultimate values in the cultural philosophy of the German Idealists' (1969, p. 356). Weber's text itself lists more dismissed doctrines. Ringer then tries to claim that Salz was 'somewhere near the center of the mandarin spectrum in his views,' on the grounds that he 'denounced the utilitarianism and rationalism, the "leveling" and despiritualizing tendencies' (ibid., p. 361). As we shall see in the next chapter, Jaspers, who was close to Weber, also denounced these things. The idea that academic specialization had gone too far, which Ringer takes as a right-wing or 'mandarin' idea, was also the view of such nonmandarin socialists as Paul Tillich (1966, p. 35). One might also point out that the Lauenstein Cultural Congress of 1917 and 1918, where Weber had made his famous challenge to the Kaiser to prosecute him for *lèse-majesté*, and which had such themes as 'The Meaning and Tasks of our Times' and 'The Leadership Problem in Cultural and State Affairs,' were sponsored by the neo-Conservative publisher Diedrichs (Stark, 1981, p. 136). The point is that these various labels were inadequate to their task throughout this period: the themes the 'neo-Conservatives' appropriated, including those Ringer mentions, were also found in the writings of Jaspers, Scheler, various socialists, and others. They were neither the property of an academic aristocracy nor of any political camp.

18 By, e.g., Paul Tillich in *The Protestant Era* (1957, p. 74; see also Scheler, 1963, pp. 13-26).
19 It should be noted that Scheler backed away from the 'communal' aspects of this view (Collins, 1944, p. 676).
20 Like Scheler, Tillich was an advocate of university reform, and in 1931 he proposed a return to the old antiprofessional idea of the university (Tillich, 1966, p. 35).
21 The manuscripts were published as: Siegfried Landshut and J.P. Mayer (eds) *Der historische Materialismus: die Frühschriften von Karl Marx* (1932).
22 Participants in the *Deutsche Hochschule für Politik* included: Max Scheler, Arnold Wolfers, Arnold Brecht, Sigmund Neumann, Hajo Holborn, and Theodor Heuss.

Chapter 5 Words into action: Jaspers and Heidegger

1 'Max Weber's political thought coined my own,' Jaspers testifies in his 'Philosophical Autobiography' (1957, p. 57; cf. Manasse, 1957).
2 'Posterity will hold [us] responsible, . . . if the world be divided between the Russian whip and Anglo-Saxon convention. It is our task and opportunity to salvage between these two a third: The spirit of radical liberalism, the freedom and manifoldness of personal life, the magnitude of the occidental tradition. This was Max Weber's attitude which I now shared' (Jaspers, 1957, pp. 55-6).
3 E.g., Hilter's speech at Düsseldorf on January 27, 1932. The text of the speech is included in Max Domarus's *Hitler: reden und proklamationen, 1932-1945* (1965, pp. 73-4). 'The basic principle of life (he tells them) is war, which, translated into social terms, means "absolute supremacy of the value of personality."'
4 This foreword appears only in the Anchor edition of *Man in the Modern Age* (1957; see p. v). All subsequent citations will refer to the Holt edition.
5 Cf. Max Weber, 'Science as a Vocation' (1946, p. 155), where the old forms are reserved for those who cannot bear the fate of the times.
6 Lipton's sympathies are with Cassirer.
7 Jaspers's phrase 'the life of technique' is intermediate between the two.
8 Moehling's defense of Heidegger's political conduct passes by this issue. He makes much of Heidegger's notion of *Heimat* and his self-characterization as a Swabian peasant, without noticing the highly specific ideological implications of this. Diedrichs, the 'neoconservative' publisher, had a whole set of 'Hearth and Homeland' authors (Stark, 1981, pp. 97-8). Moehling also never considers that Heidegger's opinion that German was the only modern language in which it was possible to philosophize had political implications. Put together with his view that philosophy was the key to life, and that Germany was threatened on both sides by barbarism, this had a clear meaning for his listeners. Moehling takes Heidegger's attacks on 'nihilism' literally, without considering the common argument that his own position

reduces to nihilism (see Bronner, 1977, pp. 173-4).

9 Another discussion of Heidegger's relation to his audience is found in Henry Pachter, 'Heidegger and Hitler: the incompatability of *Geist* and politics,' (1976).

10 The figures in the grouping are discussed and identified by F. Grégoire (1955, p. 683-4).

Chapter 6 Nazism, fascism and the later dispute

1 The subsequent career of the book Steding wrote at Frank's *Reichsinstitut* (which had to be completed by his wife and Frank after his death in 1938) indicates the degree of looseness in official thought in this period. Frank changed the work in minor details to make it appear more anti-Semitic and therefore acceptable. But even this was not enough to make it entirely acceptable, for it was critical of Nietzsche, who had been made into a Nazi luminary. Though he was enamored of Hitler (as Steding said, the third time he saw Hitler he thought of Hegel's words about the *Weltgeist* on horseback, when he saw Napoleon ride past (Heiber, 1966, p. 505)), he was less enamored of the Nazis, who are criticized in the book (ibid., p. 519). The book was also used by Schmitt to criticize the Nazis (ibid., p. 513). The official verdict on it was mixed: Heydrich approved it and wrote a report on it (ibid., p. 525), and Himmler blocked its use as school material because of Steding's rather negative view of racial ideology (ibid., p. 526). It then became the subject of a wide controversy: Rosenberg vilified it from a racialist perspective (ibid., pp. 526, 528), while the *Frankfurter Zeitung* attacked it from a liberal perspective (ibid., p. 522). Frank continued to defend it, however, and in spite of severe opposition, five editions were published by 1944 (ibid., p. 532).

2 The theme of the Catholic-integrated-rural versus the Puritan-dualist-urban was a source for many writers. Schmitt, in his pre-Nazi period, discussed it, and it was probably a source for Heidegger. Schmitt made the interesting point that the technology-nature dualism is a Protestant conflict, and that the Catholic view not only cannot be reduced to the 'nature' side of the dualism, the dualism would not even arise in the Catholic conception of nature. 'Mastering Nature . . . will remain eternally alien to the Catholic conception' (Schmitt, 1931, p. 42).

3 Interpretations of Weber as a philosophical anthropologist include those of Dieter Henrich (1952, pp. 105-31, esp. pp. 118-23) and Walther Wegener (1962, pp. 258-63).

Chapter 7 The emergence of the dispute in England and America

1 This is not to obscure the differences between these writers, which are sometimes strong. For example, Oakeshott makes the crucial point that writers like Hayek, in attempting to turn the 'English tradition' into something like self-conscious ideology, capitulate to the reductive, doctrinal *style* (1962, p. 21). Oakeshott takes this kind of capitulation to be central to the modern European moral predicament

(ibid., p. 79).

2 J.C. Nyíri has recently argued that there is considerable continuity between Oakeshott's views and Wittgenstein's. He goes so far as to suggest that Wittgenstein provides Oakeshott with the logical starting points or premises to his 'large-scale conclusions about society and history' (1982, p. 64).

3 For Dawson, as well as for J.P. Mayer, the idea of 'Europe' was central. They considered certain German thinkers to be Europeanists, successors to and oriented to the European tradition as a whole, and in this sense opposed to the Germans who believed in German uniqueness. Uniqueness was, of course, a Nazi notion, though by no means confined to the Nazis.

4 The work of Edward Shils is in some respects an attempt to develop the insights of this Eliotine tradition in sociological contexts. His key phrase 'center and periphery,' for example, comes from Eliot (Eliot, 1968, p. 148). Yet Shils also wishes to combine these insights with Weber's sociology. He does this by appealing to the broader sense of charisma found in the writings of Rudolph Sohm, Weber's source for the concept (Weber, 1946, p. 246). Sohm described the development of the charisma of the institution of the church over the early centuries of Christianity. Shils generalizes the idea to suggest that the central institutions of a society, such as the central state, have a charismatic endowment. The sticking point for any reconciliation of Weberianism with the English writers on tradition discussed here is the concept of tradition itself. Shils sides with these writers. He rejects Weber on tradition and takes the view that traditions are indispensable, even for scientific 'rationality' (1981b, pp. 107-20).

5 A main theme of 'The 1915 Declaration of Principles' is that the proper discharge of the function of the professoriate requires 'that the university teacher shall be exempt from any pecuniary motive or inducement to hold, or to express, any conclusion which is not the genuine and uncolored product of his own study' (AAUP, 1922, p. 494).

6 Edward Purcell discusses the atmosphere of the 1930s and 1940s in the United States in great detail and provides an exceptional collection of examples of positions on value questions, from social science to law. His discussion is aimed at supporting a certain historical thesis. According to Purcell, a 'relativist democratic theory . . . had been clearly formulated and widely accepted in the late thirties and forties' (1973, p. 236). He connects this development to what he calls 'scientific naturalism.' The difficulty with this thesis is that the term 'relativism' is made to cover such a wide range of viewpoints that the claims become trivially true. The range of application of the terms 'relativist' and 'absolutist,' as Purcell adopts them, comes from their epithetical use. Thus he describes anyone who is not an 'absolutist' as a 'relativist,' in spite of the fact that virtually none of the people thus categorized labeled themselves relativists and in most cases took care to deny or reject the "relativistic" implications of their substantive morality.

Pragmatism is an instance of this. As Rorty says,

> The association of pragmatism with relativism is a result of a confusion between the pragmatists' attitude toward *philosophical* theories with his attitude towards *real* theories. James and Dewey are, to be sure, metaphilosophical relativists, in a certain limited sense. Namely: they think there is no way to choose between incompatible philosophical theories of the typical Platonic or Kantian type. Such theories are attempts to ground some element of our practises on something external to these practices. Pragmatists think that any such philosophical grounding is, apart from elegance of execution, pretty much as good or as bad as the practise it purports to ground. They regard the project of grounding as a wheel that plays no part in the mechanism (1980, pp. 728-9).

Whatever the ultimate merit of such reasoning, it is not, as Purcell seems to think, simple relativism.

If Purcell's category of 'relativist' is oversimple, his category of 'absolutist' is so narrow that virtually no one in fact fitted in it. It is well to remember that Catholic natural law (which he takes to be paradigmatic of 'absolutism') always retained a large place for prudential considerations and that the prudent application of natural law in different situations could underwrite quite diverse political practices. The eminent contemporary spokesman for natural law, Jacques Maritain, emphasized that it was a misunderstanding of natural law to think of natural law as a list of fixed, universally applicable, substantive, and highly specific moral and political rules: only the command to do good and avoid evil remains fixed (1951, p. 98). Maritain is an 'absolutist' in a philosophical sense, without being an absolutist in the sense that he affirms such a list, or holds that there is no range of legitimate disagreement in politics among rational persons. Similarly for Leo Strauss and John Hallowell, who are also given as examples of absolutism by Purcell. Indeed, it is questionable whether anyone of significance was an absolutist in Purcell's sense.

7 'Economics and Sociology in the University,' correspondence in May, 1935, between the president and the head of the department of economics in one of our large universities, (*School and Society* (1935), vol. 42, pp. 893-97). A major element of the demand for nonpartisanship and objectivity was a reaction to the excesses of the universities during World War I. Julien Benda's *Trahison des Clercs* is the most famous text of this reaction, but Americans contributed as well. Datus Smith complained about the making of moral judgments by the university during the war (1937, p. 413). His point was that tolerance of value discussion is essential and that the university disrupts this by taking sides in what should be a matter of free dispute between scholars. In short, for Smith, the university has an obligation to be impartial, scholars to present their case.

8 'Economics and Sociology in the University,' (*School and Society* (1935), vol. 42, p. 897). Carl Friedrich, writing in *Harper's* in 1936, made similar points. With the intimidation of school teachers 'we are

confronted by an attack upon the Constitution.' He went on to say that 'a teacher who is convinced that Karl Marx was right and tries to explain why he thinks so is better than a teacher who talks contrary to his convictions. If Karl Marx was wrong – and I have no doubt he was – the good sense of his pupils will by and by discern the limitations of their teacher's analysis, they will compare it with other teachers' different ideas and interpretations and will come to a reasoned conclusion' (1936, p. 176).

9 Adler's activities and his relation to Hutchins are dealt with in Adler's autobiography (1977, pp. 149-71).

10 *Scientific Man vs. Power Politics* originated as a lecture entitled 'Liberalism and Foreign Policy' at the New School in 1940 and was expanded into a book with the support of the Social Science Research Committee of the University of Chicago. The economist Frank Knight, a great admirer of Weber and the translator of his course notes on economic history, is acknowledged in the preface.

11 Morgenthau's connections to Weber are almost entirely neglected in the literature. The significant exception is Gottfried-Karl Kindermann (1977, pp. 29-40).

12 There are many other correspondences between Weber and Morgenthau. Morgenthau repeated Weber's conclusion in 'Politik als Beruf', that one cannot act politically without violating Christian principles (Morgenthau, 1962, vol. 3, p. 15; Weber, 1978b, pp. 216-17). No compromise is possible between the great commandment of Christian ethics, 'Love thy neighbor as thyself,' and the great commandment of politics, 'Use thy neighbor as a means to the ends of thy power.' It is *a priori* impossible for political man to be at the same time a good politician – complying with the rules of political conduct – and a good Christian – complying with the demands of Christian ethics. In the measure that he tries to be the one he must cease to be the other (Morgenthau, 1962, vol. 3, p. 15; Weber, 1978b, pp. 217-18). Morgenthau's example of the error of mixing up ordinary ethics and politics is Weber's own example of the pacifist whose refusal to participate in war encourages more war (Morgenthau, 1946, pp. 173-4). In these passages Weber is not cited, though on rare occasions he does appear in Morgenthau's texts.

13 An analogous issue arises in the writings of Pierre Bourdieu, who uses such notions as symbolic power and symbolic capital (1977, p. 47). The difficulty, in both the case of Weber and Bourdieu, is that the force of the notions derives from the thought that ideas, rationalizations, and motives can be reduced to or explained by 'interests'. As we noticed in Chapter 3, the extension of the concepts of interest or capital to include the ideal or symbolic makes this reduction definitional rather than explanatory, robbing it of its force. Thus the terms retain their explanatory force in appearance only. On Bourdieu, cf. Jenkins (1982).

14 As Morgenthau put it, the nation-state is a product of history, a fact which cannot be overcome. Hence its permanence for the calculable future and the relative permanence of the policy dictates of inter-

national politics (1962, vol. 1, p. 108).

15 Morgenthau's distinction follows from a long line of German thinking on the problem of the relation of public and private morality which starts, as Weber pointed out, with Luther, who 'relieved the individual of the ethical responsibility for war and transferred it to the authorities' (1946, p. 124). Discussions of the intellectual history of this problem may be found in: Franz-Martin Schmölz, 'Das Dilemma der politischen Ethik bei Max Weber,' (1962); Eric Voegelin, 'Max Weber' (1930); Friedrich Wilhelm Förster, *Weltpolitik und Weltgewissen* (1919); idem, *Politische Ethik und politische Pädagogik* (1918); Otto Baumgarten, *Politik und Moral* (1916); Heinrich Scholz, *Politik und Moral* (1915); Heinrich von Treitschke, *Politik*, (1897). Characteristically, Morgenthau makes Lincoln his American 'antecedent,' and ignores the German sources of the tradition (1962, vol. 1, p. 110).

16 Frank H. Knight papers, Regenstein Library, University of Chicago, Chicago, Ill.

Chapter 8 The issue reframed: positivism and value-free social science

1 Cf. Edward Shils, 'Some academics, mainly in Chicago' (1981a), for his account of his education in Weber's work.

2 How 'relativity' makes it onto this list of characteristics of science, or what Bierstedt meant by it, is never made clear. One imagines he meant value-relativity, but nowhere is this stated, nor are any specific arguments for value-relativism ever given.

3 The language of 'purity and danger' here brings to mind David Bloor's application of Mary Douglas's concept to Frege's logical writings.

4 Jaspers's work was used by the American occupation authorities in Japan in the political reeducation of the Japanese.

5 In this text Friedmann discusses at length the controversy over the precise nature of Radbruch's revision of his earlier views (1960, pp. 195, 202-9).

6 Roth's claim that the liberal opponents of Weber in the 1960s 'had been influenced by natural law doctrines in the wake of the American reeducation efforts after 1945' is doubtful. Alfred Grosser points out that the American sector was not large; the effects of educational efforts were short-lived and slight (1971, pp. 48-50).

7 The Jaspers story takes more twists. Hannah Arendt portrayed him as a heroic 'inner' resister to Nazism, though, as Walter Laquer points out, 'there is no known evidence that Professor Jaspers . . . ever "resisted" in the Arendt-heroical sense.' Here and elsewhere, Laquer suggests, her 'filial piety' for Jaspers 'prevailed over intellectual integrity' (1979, p. 75).

8 This is a controversial claim. The most extreme defense of it is found in Michael Dummett, *Frege: Philosophy of Language* (1973, p. 667).

9 This same autonomy contained the seeds of destruction for Logical Positivism, since, as it turned out, the lines could not be successfully drawn. The issues are examined at length in Dudley Shapere, 'Notes toward a post-positivist interpretation of science' (1969).

Chapter 9 The later form of the critique

1 The leading 'positivist' *cum* Weberian of this sort is Hans Albert, who simply dispenses with what he calls Weber's 'questionable ontological justification' and absolutization of his cognitive interests (1972, p. 47).
2 The parting of the ways came early in the area of aesthetic theory, the area that was the intellectual center of gravity for both Lukács and the Frankfurt School. Slater discusses harsh criticisms of Lukács in the early 1930s. These criticisms contain *in nuce* all the issues over the autonomy of reason from the proletariat which later separated Lukács from the School (Slater, 1977, pp. 127-30).
3 Strauss's critique of Weber is the source of the central Straussian arguments against recent social science; indeed, passages in the important Straussian statements, 'What is political philosophy?' (1957) and 'Political philosophy and the crisis of our time' (1972b) are taken almost word for word from the chapter on Weber in *Natural Right and History* (1953).
4 Usually radical historicism has been the prelude to renewed attempts to find a way out of the paradox. Hegel supposed that there was an 'absolute moment' in which the fundamental riddles would be fully solved. But, as Strauss has pointed out, 'one cannot simply assume that one lives or thinks in the absolute moment; one must show, somehow, how the absolute moment can be recognized as such' (1953, p. 29). This demonstration must be claimed to be exempt from the historicist judgment on thought, so the paradox merely arises in a new form over this claim.
5 Notice the shift to 'knowledge.' Whether ethical notions are knowledge is an issue with many ramifications, many of which revolve around whether ethics is a matter of propositions, or principles, as distinct from, say, the possession of virtue, or the mastery of an idiom.
6 According to McCarthy, Habermas conceded this difficulty (McCarthy, 1973, p. 146).
7 Notice, again, the substitution of 'knowledge,' which is not a positivist term.
8 Eric Voegelin, in an interesting paper, attempts to show that interdiction is built into modern empirical science from the time of Newton, and cites Newton's reply to Leibniz to the effect that he could not understand a particular Leibnizian formulation. This 'I do not understand' is the Logical Positivist response to 'metaphysical' questioning (Voegelin, 1948).
9 Putnam and Rorty (1979, p. 363) both refer to German critics of Weber: Putnam to K.-O. Apel, Rorty to Gadamer.

Bibliography

AAUP American Association of University Professors (1922), 'The 1915 declaration of principles,' *American Association of University Professors Bulletin*, vol. 8, pp. 490-507.

Abraham, David (1979), 'Constituting hegemony: the bourgeois crisis of Weimar Germany,' *Journal of Modern History*, vol. 51, pp. 417-33.

Abramowski, Günter (1966), *Das Geschichtsbild Max Webers: Universalgeschichte am Leitfaden des okzidentalen Rationalisierungsprozesses*, Stuttgart, Klett.

Achinstein, P. and Barker, S.F. (eds) (1969), *The Legacy of Logical Positivism*, Baltimore, Johns Hopkins University Press.

Adler, Mortimer J. (1977), *Philosopher At Large: an intellectual autobiography*, New York, Macmillan.

Albert, Hans (1971), *Plädoyer für kritschen Rationalismus*, Munich, R. Piper.

Albert, Hans (1972), *Konstruktion und Kritik: Aufsätze zur Philosophie des kritischen Rationalismus*, Hamburg, Hoffman & Campe.

Anderson, Pauline R. (1939), *The Background of Anti-English Feeling in Germany, 1890-1902*, Washington, DC, American University Press.

Antoni, Carlo (1959), *From History to Sociology: the transition in German historical thinking*, Detroit, Wayne State University Press.

Aron, Raymond (1954), 'Introduction,' in Weber (1954), pp. 34-57.

Aron, Raymond (1970), *Main Currents in Sociological Thought*, vol. 2, Garden City, NY, Doubleday (Anchor Books).

Aron, Raymond (1972), 'Max Weber and power-politics,' in Stammer (1972), pp. 83-100.

Ayer, A.J. (ed.) (1959), *Logical Positivism*, Chicago, The Free Press.

Bagehot, Walter (1889), *The Works of Walter Bagehot*, ed. Forrest Morgan, vol. 2, Hartford, Travelers Insurance Co.

Bagehot, Walter (1963), *The English Constitution*, London, Fontana.

Barkin, Kenneth D. (1970), *The Controversy over German Industrialization, 1890-1902*, Chicago, University of Chicago Press.

Baumgarten, Otto (1916), *Politik und Moral*, Tübingen, Mohr.

Baumont, M.; Freid, J.H.E.; and Vermeil, E. (eds) (1955), *The Third*

Reich, New York, Praeger.

Beckerath, Erwin von; Popitz, Heinrich; Siebeck, Hans Georg; and Zimmermann, Harry W. (eds) (1962), *Antidoron: Edgar Salin zum 70. Geburtstag*, Tübingen, Mohr.

Beetham, David (1974), *Max Weber and the Theory of Modern Politics*, London, Allen & Unwin.

Beetham, David (1977), 'From Socialism to Fascism: the relation between theory and practice in the work of Robert Michels, Pt II. The Fascist ideologue,' *Political Studies*, vol. 25, pp. 161-81.

Beetham, David (1981), 'Michels and his critics,' *Archives Européennes de Sociologie*, vol. 22, pp. 81-99.

Ben-David, Joseph and Clark, Terry Nichols (eds) (1977), *Culture and Its Creators: essays in honor of Edward Shils*, Chicago, University of Chicago Press.

Bendix, Reinhard (1962), *Max Weber: an intellectual portrait*, Garden City, NY, Doubleday (Anchor Books).

Bendix, Reinhard (1970), 'Sociology and the distrust of reason,' *American Sociological Review*, vol. 35, pp. 831-43.

Bendix, Reinhard (1971), 'Sociology and the distrust of reason,' in Bendix and Roth (1971), pp. 84-105.

Bendix, Reinhard and Roth, Guenther (1971), *Scholarship and Partisanship: essays on Max Weber*, Berkeley and Los Angeles, University of California Press.

Bierstedt, Robert (1948), 'Social science and social policy,' *American Association of University Professors Bulletin*, vol. 34, pp. 310-19.

Böhme, Helmut (1967), 'Big-business pressure groups and Bismarck's turn to protectionism, 1873-79,' *The Historical Journal*, vol. 10, pp. 218-36.

Bourdieu, Pierre (1977), *Outline of a Theory of Practice*, Cambridge, Cambridge University Press.

Brecht, Arnold (1970), *The Political Education of Arnold Brecht: an autobiography, 1884-1970*, Princeton, Princeton University Press.

Bronner, Stephen Eric (1977), 'Martin Heidegger: the consequences of political mystification,' *Salmagundi*, no. 38-9, pp. 153-74.

Bruun, H.H. (1972), *Science, Values, and Politics in Max Weber's Methodology*, Copenhagen Munksgaard.

Bryce, James (1893), *The American Commonwealth*, vol. 1, New York, Macmillan.

Burtt, E.A. (1927), *The Metaphysical Foundations of Modern Physical Science: a historical and critical essay*, New York, Harcourt, Brace & Co.

Butler, Joseph (1896-97), *The Works of Joseph Butler*, ed. W. E. Gladstone, vol. 2, London, Oxford University Press.

Butler, Rohan d'O. (1942), *The Roots of Rational Socialism, 1783-1933*, New York, E.P. Dutton.

Carnap, Rudolf (1959), 'The elimination of metaphysics through logical analysis of language,' in Ayer (1959), pp. 60-81.

Carnap, Rudolf (1963), 'Replies and systematic expositions,' in Schilpp (1963), pp. 859-999.

Cavell, Stanley (1964), 'Existentialism and analytical philosophy,' *Daedelus*, vol. 93, pp. 946-74.

Collins, James (1944), 'Catholic estimates of Scheler's Catholic period,' *Thought*, vol. 19, pp. 671-704.

Conant, James B. (1948), 'The role of science in our unique society,' *Science*, vol. 107, pp. 77-83.

Curtius, Ernst Robert (1919), 'Max Weber über Wissenschaft als Beruf,' *Die Arbeitsgemeinschaft. Monatsschrift für das gesamte Volkshochschulwesen*, vol. 1, pp. 197-203.

Dahrendorf, Ralf (1969), *Society and Democracy in Germany*, Garden City, NY, Doubleday (Anchor Books).

Daniels, Norman (1980), 'On some methods of ethics and linguistics,' *Philosophical Studies*, vol. 37, pp. 21-36.

Dawson, Christopher H. (1956), *The Making of Europe: an introduction to the history of European unity*, New York, Meridian Books.

Deeken, Alfons (1974), *Process and Permanence in Ethics: Max Scheler's moral philosophy*, New York, Paulist Press.

Dehio, Ludwig, (1960), *Germany and World Politics in the Twentieth Century*, New York, Alfred A. Knopf.

Dempf, Alois; Arendt, Hannah; and Engel-Janosi, Friedrich (eds) (1962), *Politische Ordnung und menschliche Existenz: Festgabe für Eric Voegelin zum 60. Geburtstag*, Munich, C.H. Beck.

Dewey, John (1929), *Experience and Nature*, New York, W.W. Norton & Co.

Dewey, John (1935), *Liberalism and Social Action*, New York, G.P. Putnam's Sons.

Dewey, John (1944), 'Challenge to liberal thought,' *Fortune*, vol. 30, pp. 155-7, 180-90.

Dewey, John (1948), *Reconstruction in Philosophy* (enl. ed.), Boston, Beacon Press.

Dewey, John (1963), *Liberalism and Social Action*, New York, Capricorn Books.

Dewey, John (1970), 'Theory of valuation,' in Neurath et al. (1970), vol. II, pt 4, pp. 379-447.

Domarus, Max (1965), *Hitler: Reden und Proklamationen, 1932-1945*, vol. 1, Munich, Süddeutscher Verlag.

Dorpalen, Andreas (1957), *Heinrich von Treitschke*, New Haven, Yale University Press.

Dummett, Michael (1973), *Frege: philosophy of language*, New York, Harper & Row.

Eden, Robert (1974), 'Political leadership and philosophic praxis: a study of Weber and Nietzsche,' Ph D diss., Cambridge, Mass., Harvard University.

Eden, Robert (1983), *Political Leadership and Nihilism: a study of Weber and Nietzsche*, Tampa, University Presses of Florida.

Eliot, T.S. (1968), *Christianity and Culture: the idea of a Christian society* and *notes toward the definition of culture*, New York, Harcourt Brace Jovanovich (Harvest).

Eyck, Erich (1963), *A History of the Weimar Republic*, Cambridge,

Mass., Harvard University Press.
Factor, Regis A. and Turner, Stephen P. (1982), 'Weber's influence in Weimar Germany,' *Journal of the History of the Behavioral Sciences*, vol. 18, pp. 147-56.
Ferber, Christian von (1970), *Die Gewalt in der Politik: Auseinandersetzung mit Max Weber*, Stuttgart, Kohlhammer.
Finnis, John (1980), *Natural Law and Natural Rights*, New York, Oxford University Press.
Fischer, Fritz (1967), *Germany's Aims in the First World War*, London, Chatto & Windus.
Fischer, Fritz (1975), *War of Illusions: German policies from 1911-1914*, New York, Norton.
Fleischmann, Eugène (1964), 'De Weber à Nietzsche,' *Archives Européennes de Sociologie*, vol. 5, pp. 190-238.
Förster, Friedrich Wilhelm (1918), *Politische Ethik und politische Pädagogik*, Munich, E. Reinhardt.
Förster, Friedrich Wilhelm (1919), *Weltpolitik and Weltgewissen*, Munich, Verlag für Kulturpolitik.
Frege, Gottlob (1970), 'Begriffsschrift,' in Van Heijenoort (1970), pp. 1-82.
Friedmann, Wolfgang (1960), 'Gustav Radbruch,' *Vanderbilt Law Review*, vol. 14, pp. 191-209.
Friedrich, Carl (1936), 'Teacher's oaths,' *Harper's Magazine*, vol. 172, pp. 171-6.
Gadamer, Hans-Georg (1977), *Philosophische Lehrjahre: eine Rückschau*, Frankfurt am Main, Klostermann.
Gadamer, Hans-Georg (1982), *Reason in the Age of Science*, Cambridge, Mass., MIT Press.
Gay, Peter (1968), *Weimar Culture*, New York, Harper & Row.
Geertz, Clifford (1977), 'Centers, kings, and charisma: reflections on the symbolics of power,' in Ben-David and Clark (1977), pp. 150-71.
Geertz, Clifford (1980), *Negara: the theatre state in nineteenth-century Bali*, Princeton, Princeton University Press.
Giddens, Anthony (1972), *Politics and Sociology in the Thought of Max Weber*, London, Macmillan.
Gildin, Hilail (1975), 'Introduction,' in Strauss (1975), pp. vi-xxi.
Gordon, Frank J. (1981), 'Liberal German churchmen and the First World War,' *German Studies Review*, vol. 4, pp. 39-62.
Gordon, Michael R. (1974), 'Domestic conflict and the origins of the First World War: the British and the German cases,' *Journal of Modern History*, vol. 46, pp. 191-226.
Grab, Hermann (1927), *Der Begriff des Rationalen in der Soziologie Max Webers: ein Beitrag zu den Problemen der philosophischen Grundlagen der Sozialwissenschaft*, Karlsruhe, G. Braun.
Graham, George J. and Carey, George W. (eds) (1972), *The Post-Behavioral Era: perspectives on political science*, New York, McKay.
Grégoire, F. (1955), 'The use and misuse of philosophy and philosophers,' in Baumont et al. (1955), pp. 678-709.
Grosser, Alfred (1971), *Germany in Our Time: a political history of the*

postwar years, New York, Praeger.
Grunberger, Richard (1973), *Red Rising in Bavaria*, New York, St Martin's Press.
Habermas, Jürgen (1970), *Toward a Rational Society: student protest, science and politics*, Boston, Beacon Press.
Habermas, Jürgen (1971a, *Knowledge and Human Interests*, Boston, Beacon Press.
Habermas, Jürgen (1971b), 'Why more philosophy?' *Social Research*, vol. 38, pp. 633-54.
Habermas, Jürgen (1972), 'Discussion on value-freedom and objectivity,' in Stammer (1972), pp. 59-66.
Habermas, Jürgen (1973), *Theory and Practice*, Boston, Beacon Press.
Hartmann, Nicolai (1962), *Ethik* (4th ed.), Berlin, de Gruyter.
Hayek, Friedrich A. (1944), *The Road to Serfdom*, Chicago, University of Chicago Press.
Hayek, Friedrich A. (1952), *The Counter-Revolution of Science: studies on the abuse of reason*, Chicago, The Free Press.
Hayek, Friedrich A. (1960), *The Constitution of Liberty*, Chicago, University of Chicago Press.
Heiber, Helmut (1966), *Walter Frank und sein Reichsinstitut für Geschichte des neuen Deutschlands*, Stuttgart, Deutsche Verlag-Anstalt.
Heidegger, Martin (1957), *Der Satz vom Grund*, Pfüllingen, G. Neske.
Heidegger, Martin (1959), *An Introduction to Metaphysics*, New Haven, Yale University Press.
Heidegger, Martin (1977), *The Question Concerning Technology and Other Essays*, New York, Garland.
Hempel, Carl G. (1959), 'The Empiricist Criterion of Meaning,' in Ayer (1959), pp. 108-29.
Hennis, Wilhelm (1959), 'Zum Problem der deutschen Staatsanschauung,' *Vierteljahrshefte für Zeitgeschichte*, vol. 7, pp. 1-23.
Henrich, Dieter (1952), *Die Einheit der Wissenschaftslehre Max Webers*, Tübingen, Mohr.
Herr, Richard and Parker, Harold T. (eds) (1965), *Ideas in History: essays presented to Louis Gottschalk by his former students*, Durham, Duke University Press.
Honigsheim, Paul (1968), *On Max Weber*, New York, The Free Press.
Horkheimer, Max (1972), *Critical Theory: selected essays*, New York, Herder & Herder.
Horkheimer, Max (1974), *Eclipse of Reason*, New York, The Seabury Press.
Husserl, Edmund (1910), 'Philosophie als strenge Wissenschaft,' *Logos*, vol. 1, pp. 289-314.
Hutchins, Robert Maynard (1945), 'Toward a durable society,' *Fortune*, vol. 27, pp. 159-60, 194-207.
Iggers, Georg G. (1965), 'The dissolution of German historism,' in Herr and Parker (1965), pp. 288-329.
Jaspers, Karl (1921), *Max Weber: Rede*, Tübingen, Mohr.
Jaspers, Karl (1922), *Psychologie der Weltanschauungen* (2nd ed.),

Berlin, Springer.

Jaspers, Karl (1926), *Max Weber* (2d ed.), Tübingen, Mohr.

Jaspers, Karl (1933), *Man in the Modern Age*, New York, Holt; translation of (1931), *Die geistige Situation der Zeit*, (2nd ed.), Berlin, Walter de Gruyter.

Jaspers, Karl (1946), *Max Weber: Politiker, Forscher, Philosoph*, Bremen, Storm (unchanged from 1931 ed.).

Jaspers, Karl (1957), 'Philosophical Autobiography', in Schilpp (1957), pp. 5-94.

Jaspers, Karl (1961), *The Question of German Guilt*, New York, Capricorn Books.

Jaspers, Karl (1962), 'Bemerkungen zu Max Webers politischen Denken,' in Beckerath et al. (1962), pp. 200-14.

Jaspers, Karl (1978), *Notizen zu Martin Heidegger*, Munich, Piper.

Jay, Martin (1973), *The Dialectical Imagination: a history of the Frankfurt School and the Institute of Social Research, 1923-1950*, Boston, Little, Brown.

Jenkins, Richard (1982), 'Pierre Bourdieu and the reproduction of determinism,' *Sociology*, vol. 16, pp. 270-81.

Kahler, Erich von (1920), *Der Beruf der Wissenschaft*, Berlin, Bondi.

Kantorowicz, Hermann (1922), 'Notizen,' *Logos*, vol. 11, pp. 256-9.

Käsler, Dirk (1979), *Einführung in das Studium Max Webers*, Munich, C.H. Beck.

Käsler, Dirk (1983), 'In search of respectability: the unreality of "*Wirklichkeitswissenschaft*". The controversy over the destination of sociology during the conventions of the German Sociological Society 1910-1930,' *Knowledge and Science*, vol. 4, pp. 227-72.

Kaufmann, Felix (1949), 'The issue of ethical neutrality in political science,' *Social Research*, vol. 16, pp. 344-52.

Kegley, Charles W. and Bretall, Robert W. (eds) (1952), *The Theology of Paul Tillich*, New York, Macmillan.

Kehr, Eckart (1930), *Schlachtflottenbau und Parteipolitik, 1894-1901*, Berlin, E. Ebering.

Kennedy, Paul M. (1980), *The Rise of the Anglo-German Antagonism, 1860-1914*, London, Allen & Unwin.

Kindermann, Gottfried-Karl (1977), *Grundelemente der Weltpolitik*, Munich, Piper.

Kirk, Russell (1971), *Eliot and His Age: T.S. Eliot's moral imagination in the twentieth century*, New York, Random House.

Knight, Frank H. (1947), *Freedom and Reform: essays in economics and social philosophy*, New York, Harper & Brothers.

Kocka, Jürgen (1976), 'Kontroversen über Max Weber,' *Neue Politische Literatur*, vol. 21, pp. 281-301.

Kolakowski, Leszek (1978), *Main Currents of Marxism: its origin, growth, and dissolution*, 3 vols, London, Oxford University Press, vol. 3, *The Breakdown.*

Kolnai, Aurel (1938), *The War against the West*, New York, Viking Press.

Kraft, Victor (1981), *Foundations for a Scientific Analysis of Value*, ed. Henk L. Mulder, Dordrecht, D. Reidel.

Krieger, Leonard (1957), *The German Idea of Freedom*, Boston, Beacon Press.

Krimerman, Leonard I. (ed.) (1969), *The Nature and Scope of Social Science: a critical anthology*, New York, Appleton-Century-Crofts.

Kuhn, Helmut (1943), *Freedom Forgotten and Remembered*, Chapel Hill, University of North Carolina Press.

Labedz, Leopold (1962), *Revisionism: essays on the history of Marxist ideas*, London, Allen & Unwin.

Landshut, Siegfried (1929), *Kritik der Soziologie: Freiheit und Gleichheit als Ursprungsproblem der Soziologie*, Munich, Duncker & Humblot.

Landshut, Siegfried and Mayer, J.P. (eds) (1932), *Der historische Materialismus: die Frühschriften von Karl Marx*, 2 vols, Leipzig, A. Kröner.

Lane, Barbara M. and Rupp, Leila J. (trans. and with an introduction by) (1978), *Nazi Ideology before 1933: a documentation*, Austin and London, University of Texas Press.

Laquer, Walter (1979), 'Re-reading Hannah Arendt,' *Encounter*, vol. 52 (March), pp. 73-9.

Lederer, E. (1979), *Kapitalismus, Klassenstrukter und Probleme der Demokratie in Deutschland 1910-1940: ausgewählte Aufsätze mit einem Beitrag von Hans Speier und einer Bibliographie von Bernd Uhlmannsiek*, ed. Jürgen Kocka, Göttingen, Vandenhoeck & Ruprecht.

Lilge, Frederic (1948), *The Abuse of Learning: the failure of the German University*, New York, Macmillan.

Linke, Lilo (1935), *Restless Days: a German girl's autobiography*, New York, Alfred A. Knopf.

Lipton, David R. (1978), *Ernst Cassirer: the dilemma of a liberal intellectual in Germany, 1914-1933*, Toronto, University of Toronto Press.

Loewenstein, Karl (1966), *Max Weber's Political Ideas in the Perspectives of Our Time*, Boston, University of Massachusetts Press.

Löwith, Karl (1932), 'Max Weber und Karl Marx,' *Archiv für Sozialwissenschaft und Sozialpolitik*, vol. 67, pp. 53-99; portions trans. as 'Weber's interpretation of the bourgeois-capitalistic world in terms of the guiding principle of "rationalization"', in Wrong (1970), pp. 101-22.

Löwith, Karl [Hugo Fiala] (1934-5), 'Politischer Dezisionismus,' *Revue internationale de la théorie du droit*, vol. 9, pp. 101-23.

Löwith, Karl (1939), 'Max Weber und seine Nachfolger,' *Mass und Wert*, vol. 3, pp. 166-76.

Löwith, Karl (1946), 'Les implications politiques de la philosophie de l'existence chez Heidegger,' *Les Temps modernes*, vol. 14, pp. 343-60.

Löwith, Karl (1964), 'Max Weber und Carl Schmitt,' *Frankfurter Allgemeine Zeitung*, 27 June.

Lukás, Georg (1962), *Die Zerstörung der Vernunft*, Neuwied am Rhein, Luchterhand.

Lukács, Georg (1971), *History and Class Consciousness*, Cambridge, Mass., MIT Press.

Lukács, Georg (1980), *The Destruction of Reason*, London, Merlin Press. Originally published as *Die Zerstörung der Vernunft*.

Lukes, Steven (1974), 'Relativism: cognitive and moral,' pt 1, *Proceedings of the Aristotelian Society*, suppl. vol. 48, pp. 165-89.
McCarthy, T.A. (1973), 'A theory of communicative competence,' *Philosophy of the Social Sciences*, vol. 3, pp. 135-56.
McGuinness, Brian (ed.) (1982), *Wittgenstein and His Times*, Chicago, University of Chicago Press.
MacIntyre, Alasdair (1981), *After Virtue: a study in moral theory*, Notre Dame, Ind., University of Notre Dame Press.
Manasse, Ernst Moritz (1957), 'Max Weber's influence on Jaspers,' in Schilpp (1957), pp. 369-91.
Mann, Thomas (1956), *Betrachtungen eines Unpolitischen* ('Letters from an Unpolitical Man'), Frankfurt a/M., S. Fischer Verlag.
Mannheim, Karl (1936), *Ideology and Utopia*, London, Kegan Paul, Trench, Trubner.
Mannheim, Karl (1943), *Diagnosis of Our Time: wartime essays of a sociologist*, London, Routledge & Kegan Paul.
Mannheim, Karl (1950), *Man and Society in an Age of Reconstruction*, New York, Harcourt, Brace.
Marcuse, Herbert (1968), *Negations: essays in critical theory*, Boston, Beacon Press.
Maritain, Jacques (1951), *Man and the State*, Chicago, University of Chicago Press.
Masur, Gerhard (1961), *Prophets of Yesterday: studies in European culture, 1890-1914*, New York, Macmillan.
Mayer, J.P. (1956), *Max Weber and German Politics* (2nd ed., rev. and enl.), London, Faber & Faber.
Mayer, J.P. (1961), *Political Thought in France: from revolution to the Fifth Republic* (3d ed., enl.), London, Routledge & Kegan Paul.
Mayer, J. P.; Crossman, R.H.S.; Kecskemeti, P.; Kohn-Bramstedt, E.; and Sprigge, C.J.S. (1970), *Political Thought: the European tradition*, Freeport, NY, Books for Libraries Press.
Meinecke, Friedrich (1963), *The German Catastrophe: reflections and recollections*, Boston, Beacon Press.
Merquior, J.G. (1980), *Rousseau and Weber: two studies in the theory of legitimacy*, London, Routledge & Kegan Paul.
Merton, Robert K. (1968), *Social Theory and Social Structure* (enl. ed.), New York, The Free Press.
Michels, Robert (1927), *Bedeutende Männer: charakterologische Studien*, Leipzig, Quelle & Meyer.
Michels, Robert (1934), *Politica ed Economia*, Turin, Unione Tipografico-Editrice Torinese.
Michels, Robert (1949), *First Lectures in Political Sociology*, Minneapolis, University of Minnesota Press.
Mill, John Stuart (1929), *Principles of Political Economy*, New York, Longmans Green.
Mitchison, Naomi (1982), 'Aldous Huxley on war and intellectual survival,' *Times Literary Supplement*, 11 June, p. 635.
Mitzman, Arthur (1973), *Sociology and Estrangement: three sociologists of Imperial Germany*, New York, Alfred A. Knopf.

Moehling, Karl A. (1972), 'Martin Heidegger and the Nazi Party: an examination,' Ph D diss., Dekalb, Ill., Northern Illinois University.

Moehling, Karl A. (1977), 'Heidegger and the Nazis,' *Heidegger, The Man and the Thinker, Listening: Journal of Religion and Culture*, vol. 12, pp. 92-105.

Mommsen, Theodor (1952), 'Last wishes,' *Past and Present*, vol. 1, p. 71.

Mommsen, Wolfgang J. (1959), *Max Weber und die deutsche Politik, 1890-1920*, Tübingen, Mohr.

Mommsen, Wolfgang J. (1963), 'Zum Begriff der "plebiszitären Führerdemokratie" bei Max Weber,' *Kölner Zeitschrift für Soziologie und Sozialpsychologie*, vol. 15, pp. 295-322.

Mommsen, Wolfgang J. (1965), 'Universalgeschichtliches und politisches Denken bei Max Weber,' *Historische Zeitschrift*, vol. 201, pp. 557-612.

Mommsen, Wolfgang J. (1974a), *The Age of Bureaucracy: perspectives on the political sociology of Max Weber*, New York, Harper & Row.

Mommsen, Wolfgang J. (1974b), *Max Weber und die deutsche Politik, 1890-1920* (2d ed., rev. and enl.), Tübingen, Mohr.

Morgenthau, Hans J. (1946), *Scientific Man vs. Power Politics*, Chicago, University of Chicago Press.

Morgenthau, Hans J. (1962), *Politics in the Twentieth Century*, 3 vols, Chicago, University of Chicago Press, vol. 1, *The Decline of Democratic Politics*; vol. 3, *The Restoration of American Politics*.

Morgenthau, Hans J. (1974), 'Justice and power,' *Social Research*, vol. 41, pp. 163-75.

Morgenthau, Hans J. (1977), 'Fragment of an intellectual autobiography: 1904-1932,' in Thompson and Myers (1977), pp. 1-17.

Morgenthau, Hans J. (1978), *Politics among Nations: the struggle for power and peace* (5th ed., rev.), New York, Alfred A. Knopf.

Mosse, George L. (1964), *The Crisis of German Ideology: intellectual origins of the Third Reich*, New York, Grosset & Dunlap.

Nagel, Ernest (1961), *The Structure of Science: problems in the logic of scientific explanation*, New York, Harcourt, Brace & World.

Neumann, Franz (1942), *Behemoth: the structure and practice of National Socialism, 1933-1944*, New York, Oxford University Press.

Neumann, Franz (1953), 'The Social Sciences,' in Neumann et al. (1953), pp. 4-26.

Neumann, Franz; Peyre, Henri; Panofsky, Erwin; Köhler, Wolfgang; and Tillich, Paul (1953), *The Cultural Migration: the European scholar in America*, Philadelphia, University of Pennsylvania Press.

Neurath, Otto (1936), 'Encyclopédie comme "modèle,"' *Revue de Synthèse*, vol. 12, pp. 187-201.

Neurath, Otto (1959), 'Sociology and physicalism,' in Ayer (1959), pp. 282-317.

Neurath, Otto; Carnap, Rudolf; and Morris, Charles (1970), *Foundations of the Unity of Sciences: toward an international encyclopedia of unified science*, vol. II, Chicago, University of Chicago Press.

Nietzsche, Friedrich Wilhelm (1924), *The Will to Power: an attempted transvaluation of all values*, New York, Macmillan.

Nolte, Ernst (1963), 'Max Weber vor dem Fascismus,' *Der Staat*, vol. 2, pp. 1-24.
Nozick, Robert (1974), *Anarchy, State, and Utopia*, New York, Basic Books.
Nyíri, J.C. (1982), 'Wittgenstein's later work in relation to conservatism,' in McGuinness (1982), pp. 44-68.
Oakes, Guy (1982), 'Methodological ambivalence: the case of Max Weber', *Social Research*, vol. 49, pp. 589-615.
Oakeshott, Michael (1962), *Rationalism in Politics, and Other Essays*, London, Methuen & Co.
Oakeshott, Michael (1974), *Human Conduct*, New York, Oxford University Press.
Ogburn, William F. (1930), 'The folkways of a scientific sociology,' 1929 presidential address, *American Sociological Society*, vol. 24, pp. 1-11.
Ouchi, William (1981), *Theory Z: how American business can meet the Japanese challenge*, Reading, Mass., Addison-Wesley.
Pachter, Henry (1976), 'Heidegger and Hitler: the incompatibility of *Geist* and politics,' *Boston University Journal,* vol. 24, pp. 47-55.
Parsons, Talcott (1968), *The Structure of Social Action*, New York, The Free Press.
Pinson, Koppel (1966) *Modern Germany* (2d ed.), New York, Macmillan.
Poggi, Gianfranco (1978), *The Development of the Modern State: a sociological introduction*, Stanford, Stanford University Press.
Pois, Robert (1972), *Friedrich Meinecke and German Politics in the Twentieth Century*, Berkeley and Los Angeles, University of California Press.
Polanyi, Michael (1966), *The Tacit Dimension*, Garden City, NY, Doubleday.
Popper, K.R. (1966), *The Open Society and Its Enemies*, 2 vols, London, Routledge & Kegan Paul, vol. 2, *The High Tide of Prophecy: Hegel, Marx and the aftermath.*
Pound, Roscoe (1927), Commencement Address, reprinted in *American Association of University Professors Bulletin*, vol. 13, pp. 569-74.
Purcell, Edward A., Jr (1973), *The Crisis of Democratic Theory: scientific naturalism and the problem of value*, Lexington, The University Press of Kentucky.
Putnam, Hilary (1981), *Reason, Truth and History*, Cambridge, University Press.
Radbruch, Gustav (1913), *Einführung in die Rechtswissenschaft* (2d ed.), Leipzig, Quelle & Meyer.
Radbruch, Gustav (1936), 'Anglo-American jurisprudence through Continental eyes,' *Law Quarterly Review*, vol. 208, pp. 530-45.
Radbruch, Gustav (1950), 'Legal philosophy,' in Wilk (1950), pp. 43-224.
Radbruch, Gustav (1951), *Der Innere Weg: Aufriss meines Lebens*, Stuttgart, K.F. Koehler.
Rauschning, Hermann (1939), *The Revolution of Nihilism: warning to the West*, New York, Longmans, Green.
Rawls, John (1971), *A Theory of Justice*, Cambridge, Mass., Harvard University Press (Belknap Press).

Reichenbach, Hans (1951), *The Rise of Scientific Philosophy*, Berkeley, University of California Press.

Remmling, Gunter W. (1975), *The Sociology of Karl Mannheim*, London, Routledge & Kegan Paul.

Rickert, Heinrich (1926), 'Max Weber und seine Stellung zur Wissenschaft,' *Logos*, vol. 15, pp. 222-37.

Rieff, Philip (1972), *Fellow Teachers*, New York, Harper & Row.

Ringer, Fritz K. (1969), *The Decline of the German Mandarins: the German academic community, 1880-1933*, Cambridge, Mass., Harvard University Press.

Röhrich, Wilfried (1972), *Robert Michels: vom sozialistisch-syndikalistischen zum faschisten Credo*, Berlin, Duncker & Humblot.

Rorty, Richard (1979), *Philosophy and the Mirror of Nature*, Princeton, Princeton University Press.

Rorty, Richard (1980), 'Pragmatism, relativism, and irrationalism,' presidential address of the American Philosophical Association, *Proceedings and Addresses of the American Philosophical Association* (August), pp. 719-38.

Rosen, Stanley (1969), *Nihilism: a philosophical essay*, New Haven, Yale University Press.

Rosen, Stanley (1980), *The Limits of Analysis*, New York, Basic Books.

Rosenberg, Arthur (1965), *A History of the German Republic*, New York, Russell & Russell.

Ross, Ronald J. (1979), 'Critic of the Bismarckian Constitution: Ludwig Windthorst and the relationship between Church and State in Imperial Germany,' *Journal of Church and State*, vol. 21, pp. 483-506.

Roth, Guenther (1963), *The Social Democrats in Imperial Germany: a study in working-class isolation and national integration*, Totowa, NJ, Bedminster Press.

Roth, Guenther (1965), 'Political Critiques of Max Weber: some implications for political sociology,' *American Sociological Review*, vol. 30, pp. 213-23.

Roth, Guenther (1971a), 'Political critiques,' in Bendix and Roth (1971), pp. 55-69.

Roth, Guenther (1971b), '"Value-neutrality" in Germany and the United States,' in Bendix and Roth (1971), pp. 34-54.

Roth, Guenther (1976), 'Religion and revolutionary beliefs: sociological and historical dimensions in Max Weber's work,' *Social Forces*, vol. 55, pp. 257-72.

Roth, Guenther and Schluchter, Wolfgang (1979), *Max Weber's Vision of History: ethics and methods*, Berkeley and Los Angeles, University of California Press.

Rudner, Richard (1969), 'No science can be value-free,' in Krimerman (1969), pp. 754-8.

Russell, Bertrand (1938), *Power: a new social analysis*, London, Allen & Unwin.

Salz, Arthur (1921), *Für die Wissenschaft: gegen die Gebildeten unter ihren Verächtern*, Munich, Drei Masken.

Samuel, R.H. and Hinton Thomas, R. (1949), *Education and Society in*

Modern Germany, London, Routledge & Kegan Paul.

Scaff, Lawrence A. (1973), 'Max Weber's politics and political education,' *American Political Science Review*, vol. 67, pp. 128-41.

Scaff, Lawrence A. (1981), 'Max Weber and Robert Michels,' *American Journal of Sociology*, vol. 86, pp. 1269-86.

Schaaf, Julius Jacob (1946), *Geschichte und Begriff: eine kritische Studie zur Geschichtsmethodologie von Ernst Troeltsch und Max Weber*, Tübingen, Mohr.

Scheele, Godfrey (1946), *The Weimar Republic: overture to the Third Reich*, London, Faber & Faber.

Scheler, Max (1960a), *Gesammelte Werke*, vol. 6, Berne, Francke Verlag.

Scheler, Max (1960b), *On the Eternal in Man*, London, Student Christian Movement Press.

Scheler, Max (1961), *Man's Place in Nature*, New York, Noonday Press.

Scheler, Max (1963), *Schriften zur Soziologie und Weltanschauungslehre*, ed. Maria Scheler (2d exp. ed.), Berne and Munich, Francke Verlag.

Schelting, Alexander von (1934), *Max Webers Wissenschaftslehre: das logische Problem der historischen Kulturerkenntnis, die Grenzen der Soziologie des Wissens*, Tübingen, Mohr.

Schilpp, P.A. (ed.) (1957), *The Philosophy of Karl Jaspers*, New York, Tudor.

Schilpp, P.A. (ed.) (1963), *The Philosophy of Rudolf Carnap*, LaSalle, Ill., Open Court Press.

Schlick, Moritz (1962), *Problems of Ethics*, New York, Dover. Originally published as *Fragen der Ethik* (1930), Vienna, J. Springer.

Schluchter, Wolfgang (1979a), 'The paradox of rationalization: on the relation of ethics and world,' in Roth and Schluchter (1979), pp. 11-64.

Schluchter, Wolfgang (1979b), 'Value-Neutrality and the ethic of responsibility,' in Roth and Schluchter (1979), pp. 65-116.

Schluchter, Wolfgang (1981), *The Rise of Western Rationalism: Max Weber's developmental history*, Berkeley and Los Angeles, University of California Press.

Schmidt, Gustav (1964), *Deutscher Historismus und der Übergang zur parlamentarischen Demokratie: Untersuchungen zu den politischen Gedanken von Meinecke, Troeltsch, Max Weber*, Lübeck, Mathiesen.

Schmitt, Carl (1931), *The Necessity of Politics: an essay on the representative idea of the Church in modern Europe*, London, Sheed & Ward.

Schmitt, Carl (1932), *Legalität und Legitimität*, Munich and Leipzig, Duncker & Humblot.

Schmitt, Carl (1940), *Positionen und Begriffe: im Kampf mit Weimar-Genf-Versailles, 1923-1939*, Hamburg, Hanseatische Verlagsantalt.

Schmitt, Carl (1976), *The Concept of the Political*, New Brunswick, NJ, Rutgers University Press.

Schmölz, Franz-Martin (1962), 'Das Dilemma der politischen Ethik bei Max Weber,' in Dempf et al. (1962), pp. 476-96.

Scholz, Heinrich (1915), *Politik und Moral*, Gotha, Perthes.

Schorske, Carl E. (1955), *German Social Democracy, 1905-1917: the development of the Great Schism*, Cambridge, Mass., Harvard University Press.

Schroeter, Gerd (1980), 'Max Weber as outsider: his nominal influence on German sociology in the twenties,' *Journal of the History of the Behavioral Sciences*, vol. 16, pp. 317-32.

Schroeter, Gerd (1982), 'Weber and Weimar: a response to Factor and Turner,' *Journal of the History of the Behavioral Sciences*, vol. 18, pp. 157-62.

Schumpeter, Joseph A. (1950), *Capitalism, Socialism, and Democracy*, New York, Harper & Row.

Schumpeter, Joseph A. (1954), *History of Economic Analysis*, London, Oxford University Press.

Schutz, Alfred (1957), 'Max Scheler's epistemology and ethics,' *Review of Metaphysics*: II, vol. 11, pp. 486-501.

Schwabe, Klaus, (1961), 'Zur politischen Haltung der deutschen Professoren im Ersten Weltkrieg,' *Historische Zeitschrift*, vol. 193, pp. 601-34.

Shapere, Dudley (1969), 'Notes toward a post-positivistic interpretation of science,' in Achinstein and Barker (1969), pp. 115-60.

Sheehan, James J. (1966), *The Career of Lujo Brentano*, Chicago, University of Chicago Press.

Shils, Edward A. (1981a), 'Some academics, mainly in Chicago,' *The American Scholar*, vol. 50, pp. 179-96.

Shils, Edward A. (1981b), *Tradition*, Chicago, University of Chicago Press.

Sidgwick, Henry (1874), *The Methods of Ethics*, London, Macmillan.

Simey, T.S. (1966), 'Max Weber: man of affairs or theoretical sociologist?' *Sociological Review*, vol. 14, pp. 303-27.

Slater, Phil (1977), *Origin and Significance of the Frankfurt School: a Marxist perspective*, London, Routledge & Kegan Paul.

Smith, Datus (1937), 'A plea for unprincipled education,' *American Scholar*, vol. 6, pp. 411-20.

Smith, Woodruff D. (1978), *The German Colonial Empire*, Chapel Hill, University of North Carolina Press.

Sombart, Werner (1936), *Soziologie: was sie ist und was sie sein sollte*, Berlin, Akademie der Wissenschaften.

Spengler, Oswald (1934), *The Hour of Decision, Part One: Germany and world-historical evolution*, New York, Alfred A. Knopf.

Spiegelberg, Herbert (1971), *The Phenomenological Movement*, The Hague, Martinus Nijhoff.

Spranger, Eduard (1925), *Der gegenwärtige Stand der Geisteswissenschaften und die Schule* (2d exp. ed.), Leipzig and Berlin, B.G. Tuebner.

Spranger, Eduard (1925), *Der gegenwärtige Stand der Geisteswissen-Geisteswissenschaften*, Berlin, Akademie der Wissenschaften.

Stammer, Otto (ed.) (1972), *Max Weber and Sociology Today*, New York, Harper Torchbooks.

Stark, Gary D. (1981), *Entrepreneurs of Ideology: neoconservative publishers in Germany, 1890-1933*, Chapel Hill, University of North Carolina Press.

Stark, Werner (1958), *The Sociology of Knowledge*, Chicago, The Free Press.

Staude, John Raphael (1967), *Max Scheler, 1874-1928: an intellectual portrait*, New York, The Free Press.

Steding, Christoph (1932), *Politik und Wissenschaft bei Max Weber*, Breslau, Wilh. Gottl. Korn.

Stevenson, C.L. (1937), 'The emotive meaning of ethical terms,' *Mind*, n.s. vol. 46, pp. 14-31.

Stolper, Gustav (1942), *This Age of Fable: the political and economic world we live in*, New York, Reynal & Hitchcock.

Storing, Herbert J. (ed.) (1962), *Essays on the Scientific Study of Politics*, New York, Holt, Rinehart & Winston.

Strasser, Gregor (1978), 'Thoughts about the tasks of the future,' in Lane and Rupp (1978), pp. 88-94.

Strauss, Leo (1953), *Natural Right and History*, Chicago, University of Chicago Press.

Strauss, Leo (1957), 'What is political philosophy?' *Journal of Politics*, vol. 19, pp. 343-68.

Strauss, Leo (1962), 'An epilogue,' in Storing (1962), pp. 305-27.

Strauss, Leo (1969), *Thoughts on Machiavelli*, Seattle, University of Washington Press.

Strauss, Leo (1972a), 'Philosophy as rigorous science and political philosophy,' *Interpretation*, vol. 2, pp. 1-9.

Strauss, Leo (1972b), 'Political philosophy and the crisis of our time,' in Graham and Carey (1972), pp. 217-42.

Strauss, Leo (1973), *Persecution and the Art of Writing*, Westport, Conn., Greenwood Press.

Strauss, Leo (1975), *Political Philosophy: six essays by Leo Strauss*, Indianapolis, Pegasus.

Strauss, Leo (1978), 'An unspoken prologue to a public lecture at St. John's,' *Interpretation*, vol. 7, pp. 1-3.

Stritch, Thomas (1978), 'After forty years: Notre Dame and "The Review of Politics",' *Review of Politics*, vol. 40, pp. 437-46.

Struve, Walter (1973), *Elites against Democracy: leadership ideals in bourgeois political thought in Germany*, Princeton, Princeton University Press.

Stumme, John R. (1977), 'Introduction,' in Tillich (1977), pp. ix-xxvi.

Thielicke, Helmut (1969), *Nihilism: its origin and nature – with a Christian answer*, New York, Schocken Books.

Thompson, Kenneth and Myers, Robert (eds) (1977), *Truth and Tragedy: a tribute to Hans Morgenthau*, Washington, DC, New Republic Book Co.

Tillich, Paul (1952), 'Autobiographical reflections,' in Kegley and Bretall (1952), pp. 3-21.

Tillich, Paul (1957), *The Protestant Era* (abr. ed.), Chicago, University of Chicago Press.

Tillich, Paul (1966), *On the Boundary: an autobiographical sketch*, New York, Charles Scribner's Sons.

Tillich, Paul (1977), *The Socialist Decision*, New York, Harper & Row.

Tirpitz, Grand Admiral von (1919), *My Memoirs*, vol. 1, New York, Dodd, Mead.

Töpner, Kurt (1970), *Gelehrte Politiker und politisierende Gelehrte: die Revolution von 1918 im Urteil deutscher Hochschullehrer*, Göttingen, Musterschmidt.

Torrance, John (1974), 'Max Weber: methods and the man,' *Archives Européennes de Sociologie*, vol. 15, pp. 127-65.

Treitschke, Heinrich von (1897), *Politik*, vol. 1, Leipzig, S. Hirzel.

Tribe, Keith (1979), 'Introduction to Weber,' *Economy and Society*, vol. 8, pp. 172-6.

Trigg, Roger (1973), *Reason and Commitment*, Cambridge, Cambridge University Press.

Troeltsch, Ernst (1921), 'Die Revolution in der Wissenschaft,' *Schmollers Jahrbuch für Gesetzgebung, Verwaltung und Volkswirtschaft im deutschen Reich*, vol. 45, pp. 65-94.

Turner, Bryan S. (1981), *For Weber: essays on the sociology of fate*, London and Boston, Routledge & Kegan Paul.

Turner, Stephen P. (1982), 'Bunyan's cage and Weber's casing,' *Sociological Inquiry*, vol. 52, pp. 84-7.

Van Heijenoort, J. (ed.) (1970), *Frege and Gödel: two fundamental texts in mathematical logic*, Cambridge, Mass., Harvard University Press.

Vermeil, E. (1955), 'The origin, nature, and development of German nationalist ideology in the 19th and 20th centuries,' in Baumont et al. (1955), pp. 3-111.

Voegelin, Eric (1930), 'Max Weber,' *Kölner Vierteljahrsschrift für Soziologie*, vol. 9, pp. 1-16.

Voegelin, Eric (1948), 'The origins of scientism,' *Social Research*, vol. 15, pp. 462-94.

Voegelin, Eric (1952), *The New Science of Politics*, Chicago, University of Chicago Press.

Voegelin, Eric (1978), *Anamnesis*, Notre Dame, Ind., University of Notre Dame Press.

Warner, R. Stephen (1970), 'The role of religious ideas and the use of models in Max Weber's comparative studies of non-capitalist societies,' *Journal of Economic History*, vol. 30, pp. 74-99.

Watnick, Morris (1962), 'Relativism and class consciousness: Georg Lukács,' in Labedz (1962), pp. 142-65.

Weber, Alfred (1977), *Farewell to European History*, Westport, Conn., Greenwood Press.

Weber, Marianne (1975), *Max Weber: a biography*, New York, Wiley.

Weber, Max (1946), *From Max Weber: essays in sociology*, ed. H.H. Gerth and C. Wright Mills, New York, Oxford University Press.

Weber, Max (1949), *The Methodology of the Social Sciences*, ed. Edward A. Shils and Henry A. Finch, New York, The Free Press.

Weber, Max (1954), *Le savant et le politique*, Paris, Plon.

Weber, Max (1956), 'Max Weber on Bureaucratization in 1909', in Mayer (1956), pp. 125-31.

Weber, Max (1958), *The Protestant Ethic and the Spirit of Capitalism*, New York, Charles Scribner's Sons.

Weber, Max (1971), *Gesammelte politische Schriften*, ed. Johannes Winckelmann, (3d ed., rev.), Tübingen, Mohr.

Weber, Max (1973), *Wissenschaftslehre*, Tübingen, Mohr.

Weber, Max (1974), *On Universities: the power of the State and the dignity of the academic calling in Imperial Germany*, Chicago, University of Chicago Press.

Weber, Max (1976), *Wirtschaft und Gesellschaft: grundriss der verstehenden Soziologie* (5th ed., rev.), vol. 1, Tübingen, Mohr.

Weber, Max (1978a), *Economy and Society: an outline of interpretive sociology*, ed. Guenther Roth and Claus Wittich, 3 vols, Berkeley and Los Angeles, University of California Press.

Weber, Max (1978b), *Max Weber: selections in translation*, ed. W.G. Runciman, Cambridge, Cambridge University Press.

Weber, Max (1980), 'The national state and economic policy (Freiburg address),' *Economy and Society*, vol. 9, pp. 428-49.

Wegener, Walther (1962), *Die Quellen der Wissenschaftsauffassung Max Webers und die Problematik der Werturteilsfreiheit der Nationalökonomie: ein wissenschaftssoziologischer Beitrag*, Berlin, Duncker & Humblot.

Wehler, Hans-Ulrich (1968), *Bismarck und der Imperialismus*, Cologne, Kiepenheuer & Witsch.

Weyembergh, Maurice (1972), *Le voluntarisme rationnel de Max Weber*, Brussels, Palais des Académies.

Wilbrandt, Robert (1928), 'Max Weber, ein deutsches Vermächtnis,' *Die neue Rundschau*, vol. 39, pp. 449-64.

Wilk, Kurt (ed.) (1950), *The Legal Philosophies of Lask, Radbruch, and Dabin*, Twentieth Century Legal Philosophy, vol. 4, Cambridge, Mass., Harvard University Press.

Wilson, Bryan (ed.) (1970), *Rationality*, New York, Harper & Row.

Winch, Peter (1958), *The Idea of a Social Science and Its Relation to Philosophy*, London, Routledge & Kegan Paul.

Winch, Peter (1970), 'Understanding a primitive society,' in Wilson (1970), pp. 78-111.

Winckelmann, Johannes F. (1952), *Legitimität und Legalität in Max Webers Herrschaftssoziologie*, Tübingen, Mohr.

Winston, Richard and Winston, Clara (eds) (1975), *An Exceptional Friendship: the correspondence of Thomas Mann and Erich Kahler*, Ithaca, Cornell University Press.

Wittfogel, Karl A. (1924), *Geschichte der bürgerlichen Gesellschaft von ihren Anfängen bis zur Schwelle der grossen Revolution*, Vienna, Malik-Verlag.

Wittfogel, Karl A. (1931), *Wirtschaft und Gesellschaft Chinas: Versuch der wissenschaftlichen Analyse einer grossen asiatischen Agrargesellschaft*, Leipzig, C.L. Hirschfeld.

Wittgenstein, Ludwig (1980), *Culture and Value*, ed. G.H. von Wright, Chicago, University of Chicago Press.

Wrong, Dennis (ed.) (1970), *Max Weber*, Englewood Cliffs, NJ, Prentice-Hall.

Wurgaft, Lewis D. (1977), *The Activists: Kurt Hiller and the politics of action on the German Left, 1914-1933*, Transactions of the American Philosophical Society, vol. 67, pt 8, Philadelphia, American Philo-

sophical Society.
Zweig, Stefan (1964), *The World of Yesterday: an autobiography*, Lincoln, University of Nebraska Press.

Index

Routledge Social Science Series

Routledge & Kegan Paul
London, Boston, Melbourne and Henley

39 Store Street, London WC1E 7DD
9 Park Street, Boston, Mass 02108
296 Beaconsfield Parade, Middle Park,
Melbourne, 3206 Australia
Broadway House, Newtown Road,
Henley-on-Thames, Oxon RG9 1EN

Contents

Authors wishing to submit manuscripts for any series in this catalogue should send them to the Social Science Editor, Routledge & Kegan Paul plc, 39 Store Street, London WC1E 7DD.

● *Books so marked are available in paperback also.*
○ *Books so marked are available in paperback only.*
All books are in metric Demy 8vo format (216 × 138mm approx.) unless otherwise stated.

International Library of Sociology
General Editor John Rex

GENERAL SOCIOLOGY

Alexander, J. Theoretical Logic in Sociology.
Volume 1: Positivism, Presuppositions and Current Controversies. *234 pp.*
Volume 2: The Antinomies of Classical Thought: *Marx and Durkheim.*
Volume 3: The Classical Attempt at Theoretical Synthesis: *Max Weber.*
Volume 4: The Modern Reconstruction of Classical Thought: *Talcott Parsons.*
Barnsley, J. H. The Social Reality of Ethics. *464 pp.*
Brown, Robert. Explanation in Social Science. *208 pp.*
● Rules and Laws in Sociology. *192 pp.*
Bruford, W. H. Chekhov and His Russia. *A Sociological Study. 244 pp.*
Burton, F. and **Carlen, P.** Official Discourse. *On Discourse Analysis, Government Publications, Ideology. 160 pp.*
Cain, Maureen E. Society and the Policeman's Role. *326 pp.*
● **Fletcher, Colin.** Beneath the Surface. *An Account of Three Styles of Sociological Research. 221 pp.*
Gibson, Quentin. The Logic of Social Enquiry. *240 pp.*
Glassner, B. Essential Interactionism. *208 pp.*
Glucksmann, M. Structuralist Analysis in Contemporary Social Thought. *212 pp.*
Gurvitch, Georges. Sociology of Law. *Foreword by Roscoe Pound. 264 pp.*
Hinkle, R. Founding Theory of American Sociology 1881–1913. *376 pp.*
Homans, George C. Sentiments and Activities. *336 pp.*
Johnson, Harry M. Sociology: *A Systematic Introduction. Foreword by Robert K. Merton. 710 pp.*
● **Keat, Russell** and **Urry, John.** Social Theory as Science. *Second Edition. 278 pp.*
Mannheim, Karl. Essays on Sociology and Social Psychology. *Edited by Paul Keckskemeti. With Editorial Note by Adolph Lowe. 344 pp.*
Martindale, Don. The Nature and Types of Sociological Theory. *292 pp.*
● **Maus, Heinz.** A Short History of Sociology. *234 pp.*
Merquior, J. G. Rousseau and Weber. *A Study in the Theory of Legitimacy. 240 pp.*
Myrdal, Gunnar. Value in Social Theory: *A Collection of Essays on Methodology. Edited by Paul Streeten. 332 pp.*
Ogburn, William F. and **Nimkoff, Meyer F.** A Handbook of Sociology. *Preface by Karl Mannheim. 656 pp. 46 figures. 35 tables.*
Parsons, Talcott and **Smelser, Neil J.** Economy and Society: *A Study in the Integration of Economic and Social Theory. 362 pp.*
Payne, G., Dingwall, R., Payne, J. and **Carter, M.** Sociology and Social Research. *336 pp.*
Podgórecki, A. Practical Social Sciences. *144 pp.*
Podgórecki, A. and **Łos, M.** Multidimensional Sociology. *268 pp.*
Raffel, S. Matters of Fact. *A Sociological Inquiry. 152 pp.*
● **Rex, John.** Key Problems of Sociological Theory. *220 pp.*
Sociology and the Demystification of the Modern World. *282 pp.*
● **Rex, John.** (Ed.) Approaches to Sociology. *Contributions by Peter Abell, Frank Bechhofer, Basil Bernstein, Ronald Fletcher, David Frisby, Miriam Glucksmann, Peter Lassman, Herminio Martins, John Rex, Roland Robertson, John Westergaard and Jock Young. 302 pp.*
Rigby, A. Alternative Realities. *352 pp.*
Roche, M. Phenomenology, Language and the Social Sciences. *374 pp.*
Sahay, A. Sociological Analysis. *220 pp.*
Strasser, Hermann. The Normative Structure of Sociology. *Conservative and Emancipatory Themes in Social Thought. 286 pp.*

Strong, P. Ceremonial Order of the Clinic. *267 pp.*
Urry, J. Reference Groups and the Theory of Revolution. *244 pp.*
Weinberg, E. Development of Sociology in the Soviet Union. *173 pp.*

FOREIGN CLASSICS OF SOCIOLOGY

● **Gerth, H. H.** and **Mills, C. Wright.** From Max Weber: *Essays in Sociology. 502 pp.*
● **Tönnies, Ferdinand.** Community and Association (*Gemeinschaft und Gesellschaft*). *Translated and Supplemented by Charles P. Loomis. Foreword by Pitirim A. Sorokin. 334 pp.*

SOCIAL STRUCTURE

Andreski, Stanislav. Military Organization and Society. *Foreword by Professor A. R. Radcliffe-Brown. 226 pp. 1 folder.*
Bozzoli, B. The Political Nature of a Ruling Class. *Capital and Ideology in South Africa 1890–1939. 396 pp.*
Bauman, Z. Memories of Class. *The Prehistory and After life of Class. 240 pp.*
Broom, L., Lancaster Jones, F., McDonnell, P. and **Williams, T.** The Inheritance of Inequality. *208 pp.*
Carlton, Eric. Ideology and Social Order. *Foreword by Professor Philip Abrahams. 326 pp.*
Clegg, S. and **Dunkerley, D.** Organization, Class and Control. *614 pp.*
Coontz, Sydney H. Population Theories and the Economic Interpretation. *202 pp.*
Coser, Lewis. The Functions of Social Conflict. *204 pp.*
Crook, I. and **D.** The First Years of the Yangyi Commune. *304 pp., illustrated.*
Dickie-Clark, H. F. Marginal Situation: *A Sociological Study of a Coloured Group. 240 pp. 11 tables.*
Fidler, J. The British Business Elite. *Its Attitudes to Class, Status and Power. 332 pp.*
Giner, S. and **Archer, M. S.** (Eds) Contemporary Europe: *Social Structures and Cultural Patterns. 336 pp.*
● **Glaser, Barney** and **Strauss, Anselm L.** Status Passage: *A Formal Theory. 212 pp.*
Glass, D. V. (Ed.) Social Mobility in Britain. *Contributions by J. Berent, T. Bottomore, R. C. Chambers, J. Floud, D. V. Glass, J. R. Hall, H. T. Himmelweit, R. K. Kelsall, F. M. Martin, C. A. Moser, R. Mukherjee and W. Ziegel. 420 pp.*
Kelsall, R. K. Higher Civil Servants in Britain: *From 1870 to the Present Day. 268 pp. 31 tables.*
● **Lawton, Denis.** Social Class, Language and Education. *192 pp.*
McLeish, John. The Theory of Social Change. *Four Views Considered. 128 pp.*
● **Marsh, David C.** The Changing Social Structure of England and Wales, 1871–1961. *Revised edition. 288 pp.*
Menzies, Ken. Talcott Parsons and the Social Image of Man. *206 pp.*
● **Mouzelis, Nicos.** Organization and Bureaucracy. *An Analysis of Modern Theories. 240 pp.*
● **Ossowski, Stanislaw.** Class Structure in the Social Consciousness. *210 pp.*
● **Podgórecki, Adam.** Law and Society. *302 pp.*
Ratcliffe, P. Racism and Reaction. *A Profile of Handsworth. 388 pp.*
Renner, Karl. Institutions of Private Law and Their Social Functions. *Edited, with an Introduction and Notes, by O. Kahn-Freud. Translated by Agnes Schwarzschild. 316 pp.*
Rex, J. and **Tomlinson, S.** Colonial Immigrants in a British City. *A Class Analysis. 368 pp.*
Smooha, S. Israel. *Pluralism and Conflict. 472 pp.*
Strasser, H. and **Randall, S. C.** An Introduction to Theories of Social Change. *300 pp.*

Wesolowski, W. Class, Strata and Power. *Trans. and with Introduction by G. Kolankiewicz. 160 pp.*
Zureik, E. Palestinians in Israel. *A Study in Internal Colonialism. 264 pp.*

SOCIOLOGY AND POLITICS

Acton, T. A. Gypsy Politics and Social Change. *316 pp.*
Burton, F. Politics of Legitimacy. *Struggles in a Belfast Community. 250 pp.*
Crook, I. and **D.** Revolution in a Chinese Village. *Ten Mile Inn. 216 pp., illustrated.*
de Silva, S. B. D. The Political Economy of Underdevelopment. *640 pp.*
Etzioni-Halevy, E. Political Manipulation and Administrative Power. *A Comparative Study. 228 pp.*
Fielding, N. The National Front. *260 pp.*
● **Hechter, Michael.** Internal Colonialism. *The Celtic Fringe in British National Development, 1536–1966. 380 pp.*
Levy, N. The Foundations of the South African Cheap Labour System. *367 pp.*
Kornhauser, William. The Politics of Mass Society. *272 pp. 20 tables.*
● **Korpi, W.** The Working Class in Welfare Capitalism. *Work, Unions and Politics in Sweden. 472 pp.*
Kroes, R. Soldiers and Students. *A Study of Right- and Left-wing Students. 174 pp.*
Martin, Roderick. Sociology of Power. *214 pp.*
Merquior, J. G. Rousseau and Weber. *A Study in the Theory of Legitimacy. 286 pp.*
Myrdal, Gunnar. The Political Element in the Development of Economic Theory. *Translated from the German by Paul Streeten. 282 pp.*
Preston, P. W. Theories of Development. *296 pp.*
Varma, B. N. The Sociology and Politics of Development. *A Theoretical Study. 236 pp.*
Wong, S.-L. Sociology and Socialism in Contemporary China. *160 pp.*
Wootton, Graham. Workers, Unions and the State. *188 pp.*

CRIMINOLOGY

Ancel, Marc. Social Defence: *A Modern Approach to Criminal Problems. Foreword by Leon Radzinowicz. 240 pp.*
Athens, L. Violent Criminal Acts and Actors. *104 pp.*
Cain, Maureen E. Society and the Policeman's Role. *326 pp.*
Cloward, Richard A. and **Ohlin, Lloyd E.** Delinquency and Opportunity: *A Theory of Delinquent Gangs. 248 pp.*
Downes, David M. The Delinquent Solution. *A Study in Subcultural Theory. 296 pp.*
Friedlander, Kate. The Psycho-Analytical Approach to Juvenile Delinquency: *Theory, Case Studies, Treatment. 320 pp.*
Gleuck, Sheldon and **Eleanor.** Family Environment and Delinquency. *With the statistical assistance of Rose W. Kneznek. 340 pp.*
Lopez-Rey, Manuel. Crime. *An Analytical Appraisal. 288 pp.*
Mannheim, Hermann. Comparative Criminology: *A Text Book. Two volumes. 442 pp. and 380 pp.*
Morris, Terence. The Criminal Area: *A Study in Social Ecology. Foreword by Hermann Mannheim. 232 pp. 25 tables. 4 maps.*
Rock, Paul. Making People Pay. *338 pp.*
● **Taylor, Ian, Walton, Paul** and **Young, Jock.** The New Criminology. *For a Social Theory of Deviance. 325 pp.*
● **Taylor, Ian, Walton, Paul** and **Young, Jock.** (Eds) Critical Criminology. *268 pp.*

SOCIAL PSYCHOLOGY

Bagley, Christopher. The Social Psychology of the Epileptic Child. *320 pp.*
Brittan, Arthur. Meanings and Situations. *224 pp.*
Carroll, J. Break-Out from the Crystal Palace. *200 pp.*
● **Fleming, C. M.** Adolescence: Its Social Psychology. *With an Introduction to recent findings from the fields of Anthropology, Physiology, Medicine, Psychometrics and Sociometry. 288 pp.*
● The Social Psychology of Education: *An Introduction and Guide to Its Study. 136 pp.*
Linton, Ralph. The Cultural Background of Personality. *132 pp.*
● **Mayo, Elton.** The Social Problems of an Industrial Civilization. *With an Appendix on the Political Problem. 180 pp.*
Ottaway, A. K. C. Learning Through Group Experience. *176 pp.*
Plummer, Ken. Sexual Stigma. *An Interactionist Account. 254 pp.*
● **Rose, Arnold M.** (Ed.) Human Behaviour and Social Processes: *an Interactionist Approach. Contributions by Arnold M. Rose, Ralph H. Turner, Anselm Strauss, Everett C. Hughes, E. Franklin Frazier, Howard S. Becker et al. 696 pp.*
Smelser, Neil J. Theory of Collective Behaviour. *448 pp.*
Stephenson, Geoffrey M. The Development of Conscience. *128 pp.*
Young, Kimball. Handbook of Social Psychology. *658 pp. 16 figures. 10 tables.*

SOCIOLOGY OF THE FAMILY

Bell, Colin R. Middle Class Families: *Social and Geographical Mobility. 224 pp.*
Burton, Lindy. Vulnerable Children. *272 pp.*
Gavron, Hannah. The Captive Wife: *Conflicts of Household Mothers. 190 pp.*
George, Victor and **Wilding, Paul.** Motherless Families. *248 pp.*
Klein, Josephine. Samples from English Cultures.
1. Three Preliminary Studies and Aspects of Adult Life in England. *447 pp.*
2. Child-Rearing Practices and Index. *247 pp.*

Klein, Viola. The Feminine Character. *History of an Ideology. 244 pp.*
McWhinnie, Alexina M. Adopted Children. *How They Grow Up. 304 pp.*
● **Morgan, D. H. J.** Social Theory and the Family. *188 pp.*
● **Myrdal, Alva** and **Klein, Viola.** Women's Two Roles: *Home and Work. 238 pp. 27 tables.*
Parsons, Talcott and **Bales, Robert F.** Family: Socialization and Interaction Process. *In collaboration with James Olds, Morris Zelditch and Philip E. Slater. 456 pp. 50 figures and tables.*

SOCIAL SERVICES

Bastide, Roger. The Sociology of Mental Disorder. *Translated from the French by Jean McNeil. 260 pp.*
Carlebach, Julius. Caring for Children in Trouble. *266 pp.*
George, Victor. Foster Care. *Theory and Practice. 234 pp.*
Social Security: *Beveridge and After. 258 pp.*
George, V. and **Wilding, P.** Motherless Families. *248 pp.*
● **Goetschius, George W.** Working with Community Groups. *256 pp.*
Goetschius, George W. and **Tash, Joan.** Working with Unattached Youth. *416 pp.*
Heywood, Jean S. Children in Care. *The Development of the Service for the Deprived Child. Third revised edition. 284 pp.*
King, Roy D., Ranes, Norma V. and **Tizard, Jack.** Patterns of Residential Care. *356 pp.*
Leigh, John. Young People and Leisure. *256 pp.*
● **Mays, John.** (Ed.) Penelope Hall's Social Services of England and Wales. *368 pp.*

Morris Mary. Voluntary Work and the Welfare State. *300 pp.*
Nokes. P. L. The Professional Task in Welfare Practice. *152 pp.*
Timms, Noel. Psychiatric Social Work in Great Britain (1939–1962). *280 pp.*
● Social Casework: *Principles and Practice. 256 pp.*

SOCIOLOGY OF EDUCATION

Banks, Olive. Parity and Prestige in English Secondary Education: a Study in Educational Sociology. *272 pp.*
● **Blyth, W. A. L.** English Primary Education. *A Sociological Description.* 2. Background. *168 pp.*
Collier, K. G. The Social Purposes of Education: *Personal and Social Values in Education. 268 pp.*
Evans, K. M. Sociometry and Education. *158 pp.*
● **Ford, Julienne.** Social Class and the Comprehensive School. *192 pp.*
Foster, P. J. Education and Social Change in Ghana. *336 pp. 3 maps.*
Fraser, W. R. Education and Society in Modern France. *150 pp.*
Grace, Gerald R. Role Conflict and the Teacher. *150 pp.*
Hans, Nicholas. New Trends in Education in the Eighteenth Century. *278 pp. 19 tables.*
● Comparative Education: *A Study of Educational Factors and Traditions. 360 pp.*
● **Hargreaves, David.** Interpersonal Relations and Education. *432 pp.*
● Social Relations in a Secondary School. *240 pp.*
School Organization and Pupil Involvement. *A Study of Secondary Schools.*
● **Mannheim, Karl** and **Stewart, W. A. C.** An Introduction to the Sociology of Education. *206 pp.*
● **Musgrove, F.** Youth and the Social Order. *176 pp.*
● **Ottaway, A. K. C.** Education and Society: An Introduction to the Sociology of Education. *With an Introduction by W. O. Lester Smith. 212 pp.*
Peers, Robert. Adult Education: *A Comparative Study. Revised edition. 398 pp.*
Stratta, Erica. The Education of Borstal Boys. *A Study of their Educational Experiences prior to, and during, Borstal Training. 256 pp.*
● **Taylor, P. H., Reid, W. A.** and **Holley, B. J.** The English Sixth Form. *A Case Study in Curriculum Research. 198 pp.*

SOCIOLOGY OF CULTURE

● **Eppel, E. M.** and **M.** Adolescents and Morality: *A Study of some Moral Values and Dilemmas of Working Adolescents in the Context of a changing Climate of Opinion. Foreword by W. J. H. Sprott. 268 pp. 39 tables.*
● **Fromm, Erich.** The Fear of Freedom. *286 pp.*
● The Sane Society. *400 pp.*
Johnson, L. The Cultural Critics. *From Matthew Arnold to Raymond Williams. 233 pp.*
Mannheim, Karl. Essays on the Sociology of Culture. *Edited by Ernst Mannheim in co-operation with Paul Kecskemeti. Editorial Note by Adolph Lowe. 280 pp.*
Structures of Thinking. *Edited by David Kettler, Volker Meja and Nico Stehr. 304 pp.*
Merquior, J. G. The Veil and the Mask. *Essays on Culture and Ideology. Foreword by Ernest Gellner. 140 pp.*
Zijderfeld, A. C. On Clichés. *The Supersedure of Meaning by Function in Modernity. 150 pp.*
Reality in a Looking Glass. *Rationality through an Analysis of Traditional Folly. 208 pp.*

SOCIOLOGY OF RELIGION

Argyle, Michael and **Beit-Hallahmi, Benjamin.** The Social Psychology of Religion. *256 pp.*
Glasner, Peter E. The Sociology of Secularisation. *A Critique of a Concept. 146 pp.*
Hall, J. R. The Ways Out. *Utopian Communal Groups in an Age of Babylon. 280 pp.*
Ranson, S., Hinings, B. and **Bryman, A.** Clergy, Ministers and Priests. *216 pp.*
Stark, Werner. The Sociology of Religion. *A Study of Christendom.*
Volume II. *Sectarian Religion. 368 pp.*
Volume III. *The Universal Church. 464 pp.*
Volume IV. *Types of Religious Man. 352 pp.*
Volume V. *Types of Religious Culture. 464 pp.*
Turner, B. S. Weber and Islam. *216 pp.*
Watt, W. Montgomery. Islam and the Integration of Society. 230 pp.
Pomian-Srzednicki, M. Religious Change in Contemporary Poland. *Sociology and Secularization. 280 pp.*

SOCIOLOGY OF ART AND LITERATURE

Jarvie, Ian C. Towards a Sociology of the Cinema. *A Comparative Essay on the Structure and Functioning of a Major Entertainment Industry. 405 pp.*
Rust, Frances S. Dance in Society. *An Analysis of the Relationships between the Social Dance and Society in England from the Middle Ages to the Present Day. 256 pp. 8 pp. of plates.*
Schücking, L. L. The Sociology of Literary Taste. *112 pp.*
Wolff, Janet. Hermeneutic Philosophy and the Sociology of Art. *150 pp.*

SOCIOLOGY OF KNOWLEDGE

Diesing, P. Patterns of Discovery in the Social Sciences. *262 pp.*
● **Douglas, J. D.** (Ed.) Understanding Everyday Life. *270 pp.*
● **Hamilton, P.** Knowledge and Social Structure. *174 pp.*
Jarvie, I. C. Concepts and Society. *232 pp.*
Mannheim, Karl. Essays on the Sociology of Knowledge. *Edited by Paul Kecskemeti. Editorial Note by Adolph Lowe. 353 pp.*
Remmling, Gunter W. The Sociology of Karl Mannheim. *With a Bibliographical Guide to the Sociology of Knowledge, Ideological Analysis, and Social Planning. 255 pp.*
Remmling, Gunter W. (Ed.) Towards the Sociology of Knowledge. *Origin and Development of a Sociological Thought Style. 463 pp.*
Scheler, M. Problems of a Sociology of Knowledge. *Trans. by M. S. Frings. Edited and with an Introduction by K. Stikkers. 232 pp.*

URBAN SOCIOLOGY

Aldridge, M. The British New Towns. *A Programme Without a Policy. 232 pp.*
Ashworth, William. The Genesis of Modern British Town Planning: *A Study in Economic and Social History of the Nineteenth and Twentieth Centuries. 288 pp.*
Brittan, A. The Privatised World. *196 pp.*
Cullingworth, J. B. Housing Needs and Planning Policy: *a Restatement of the Problems of Housing Need and 'Overspill' in England and Wales. 232 pp. 44 tables. 8 maps.*
Dickinson, Robert E. City and Region: *A Geographical Interpretation. 608 pp. 125 figures.*
The West European City: *A Geographical Interpretation. 600 pp. 129 maps. 29 plates.*

Humphreys, Alexander J. New Dubliners: *Urbanization and the Irish Family. Foreword by George C. Homans. 304 pp.*

Jackson, Brian. Working Class Community: *Some General Notions raised by a Series of Studies in Northern England. 192 pp.*

● **Mann, P. H.** An Approach to Urban Sociology. *240 pp.*

Mellor, J. R. Urban Sociology in an Urbanized Society. *326 pp.*

Morris, R. N. and **Mogey, J.** The Sociology of Housing. *Studies at Berinsfield. 232 pp. 4 pp. plates.*

Mullan, R. Stevenage Ltd. *438 pp.*

Rex, J. and **Tomlinson, S.** Colonial Immigrants in a British City. *A Class Analysis. 368 pp.*

Rosser, C. and **Harris, C.** The Family and Social Change. *A Study of Family and Kinship in a South Wales Town. 352 pp. 8 maps.*

● **Stacey, Margaret, Batsone, Eric, Bell, Colin** and **Thurcott, Anne.** Power, Persistence and Change. *A Second Study of Banbury. 196 pp.*

RURAL SOCIOLOGY

● **Mayer, Adrian C.** Peasants in the Pacific. *A Study of Fiji Indian Rural Society. 248 pp. 20 plates.*

Williams, W. M. The Sociology of an English Village: *Gosforth. 272 pp. 12 figures. 13 tables.*

SOCIOLOGY OF INDUSTRY AND DISTRIBUTION

Dunkerley, David. The Foreman. *Aspects of Task and Structure. 192 pp.*

Eldridge, J. E. T. *Industrial Disputes. Essays in the Sociology of Industrial Relations. 288 pp.*

Hollowell, Peter G. The Lorry Driver. *272 pp.*

● **Oxaal, I., Barnett, T.** and **Booth, D.** (Eds) Beyond the Sociology of Development. *Economy and Society in Latin America and Africa. 295 pp.*

Smelser, Neil J. Social Change in the Industrial Revolution: *An Application of Theory to the Lancashire Cotton Industry, 1770–1840. 468 pp. 12 figures. 14 tables.*

Watson, T. J. The Personnel Managers. *A Study in the Sociology of Work and Employment, 262 pp.*

ANTHROPOLOGY

Brandel-Syrier, Mia. Reeftown Elite. *A Study of Social Mobility in a Modern African Community on the Reef. 376 pp.*

Dickie-Clark, H. F. The Marginal Situation. *A Sociological Study of a Coloured Group. 236 pp.*

Dube, S. C. Indian Village. *Foreword by Morris Edward Opler. 276 pp. 4 plates.*

India's Changing Villages: *Human Factors in Community Development. 260 pp. 8 plates. 1 map.*

Fei, H.-T. Peasant Life in China. *A Field Study of Country Life in the Yangtze Valley. With a foreword by Bronislaw Malinowski. 328 pp. 16 pp. plates.*

Firth, Raymond. Malay Fishermen. *Their Peasant Economy. 420 pp. 17 pp. plates.*

Gulliver, P. H. Social Control in an African Society: a Study of the Arusha, Agricultural Masai of Northern Tanganykia. *320 pp. 8 plates. 10 figures.*

Family Herds. *288 pp.*

Jarvie, Ian C. The Revolution in Anthropology. *268 pp.*

Little, Kenneth L. Mende of Sierra Leone. *308 pp. and folder.*

Negroes in Britain. *With a New Introduction and Contemporary Study by Leonard Bloom. 320 pp.*

Tambs-Lyche, H. London Patidars. *168 pp.*
Madan, G. R. Western Sociologists on Indian Society. *Marx, Spencer, Weber, Durkheim, Pareto. 384 pp.*
Mayer, A. C. Peasants in the Pacific. *A Study of Fiji Indian Rural Society. 248 pp.*
Meer, Fatima. Race and Suicide in South Africa. *325 pp.*
Smith, Raymond T. The Negro Family in British Guiana: *Family Structure and Social Status in the Villages. With a Foreword by Meyer Fortes. 314 pp. 8 plates. 1 figure. 4 maps.*

SOCIOLOGY AND PHILOSOPHY

● **Adriaansens, H.** Talcott Parsons and the Conceptual Dilemma. *200 pp.*
Barnsley, John H. The Social Reality of Ethics. *A Comparative Analysis of Moral Codes. 448 pp.*
Diesing, Paul. Patterns of Discovery in the Social Sciences. *362 pp.*
● **Douglas, Jack D.** (Ed.) Understanding Everyday Life. *Toward the Reconstruction of Sociological Knowledge. Contributions by Alan F. Blum, Aaron W. Cicourel, Norman K. Denzin, Jack D. Douglas, John Heeren, Peter McHugh, Peter K. Manning, Melvin Power, Matthew Speier, Roy Turner, D. Lawrence Wieder, Thomas P. Wilson and Don H. Zimmerman. 370 pp.*
Gorman, Robert A. The Dual Vision. *Alfred Schutz and the Myth of Phenomenological Social Science. 240 pp.*
Jarvie, Ian C. Concepts and Society. *216 pp.*
Kilminster, R. Praxis and Method. *A Sociological Dialogue with Lukács, Gramsci and the Early Frankfurt School. 334 pp.*
Outhwaite, W. Concept Formation in Social Science. *255 pp.*
● **Pelz, Werner.** The Scope of Understanding in Sociology. *Towards a More Radical Reorientation in the Social Humanistic Sciences. 283 pp.*
Roche, Maurice, Phenomenology, Language and the Social Sciences. *371 pp.*
Sahay, Arun. Sociological Analysis. *212 pp.*
● **Slater, P.** Origin and Significance of the Frankfurt School. *A Marxist Perspective. 185 pp.*
Spurling, L. Phenomenology and the Social World. *The Philosophy of Merleau-Ponty and its Relation to the Social Sciences. 222 pp.*
Wilson, H. T. The American Ideology. *Science, Technology and Organization as Modes of Rationality. 368 pp.*

International Library of Anthropology
General Editor Adam Kuper

● **Ahmed, A. S.** Millennium and Charisma Among Pathans. *A Critical Essay in Social Anthropology. 192 pp.*
Pukhtun Economy and Society. *Traditional Structure and Economic Development. 422 pp.*
Barth, F. Selected Essays. *Volume 1. 256 pp.* Selected Essays. *Volume II. 200 pp.*
Brown, Paula. The Chimbu. *A Study of Change in the New Guinea Highlands. 151 pp.*
Duller, H. J. Development Technology. *192 pp.*
Foner, N. Jamaica Farewell. *200 pp.*
Gudeman, Stephen. Relationships, Residence and the Individual. *A Rural Panamanian Community. 288 pp. 11 plates, 5 figures, 2 maps, 10 tables.*
The Demise of a Rural Economy. *From Subsistence to Capitalism in a Latin American Village. 160 pp.*

Hamnett, Ian. Chieftainship and Legitimacy. *An Anthropological Study of Executive Law in Lesotho. 163 pp.*
Hanson, F. Allan. Meaning in Culture. *127 pp.*
Hazan, H. The Limbo People. *A Study of the Constitution of the Time Universe Among the Aged. 208 pp.*
Humphreys, S. C. Anthropology and the Greeks. *288 pp.*
Karp, I. Fields of Change Among the Iteso of Kenya. *140 pp.*
Kuper, A. Wives for Cattle. *Bridewealth in Southern Africa. 224 pp.*
Lloyd, P. C. Power and Independence. *Urban Africans' Perception of Social Inequality. 264 pp.*
Malinowski, B. and **de la Fuente, J.** Malinowski in Mexico. *The Economics of a Mexican Market System. Edited and Introduced by Susan Drucker-Brown. About 240 pp.*
Parry, J. P. Caste and Kinship in Kangra. *352 pp. Illustrated.*
Pettigrew, Joyce. Robber Noblemen. *A Study of the Political System of the Sikh Jats. 284 pp.*
Street, Brian V. The Savage in Literature. *Representations of 'Primitive' Society in English Fiction, 1858–1920. 207 pp.*
Van Den Berghe, Pierre L. Power and Privilege at an African University. *278 pp.*

International Library of Phenomenology and Moral Sciences
General Editor John O'Neill

Adorno, T. W. Aesthetic Theory. Translated by C. Lenhardt.
Apel, K.-O. Towards a Transformation of Philosophy. *308 pp.*
Bologh, R. W. Dialectical Phenomenology. *Marx's Method. 287 pp.*
Fekete, J. The Critical Twilight. *Explorations in the Ideology of Anglo-American Literary Theory from Eliot to McLuhan. 300 pp.*
Green, B. S. Knowing the Poor. *A Case Study in Textual Reality Construction. 200 pp.*
McHoul, A. W. How Texts Talk. *Essays on Reading and Ethnomethodology. 163 pp.*
Medina, A. Reflection, Time and the Novel. *Towards a Communicative Theory of Literature. 143 pp.*
O'Neill, J. Essaying Montaigne. *A Study of the Renaissance Institution of Writing and Reading. 244 pp.*
Schutz. A. Life Forms and Meaning Structure. *Translated, Introduced and Annotated by Helmut Wagner. 207 pp.*

International Library of Social Policy
General Editor Kathleen Jones

Bayley, M. Mental Handicap and Community Care. *426 pp.*
Bottoms, A. E. and **McClean, J. D.** Defendants in the Criminal Process. *284 pp.*
Bradshaw, J. The Family Fund. *An Initiative in Social Policy. 248 pp.*
Butler, J. R. Family Doctors and Public Policy. *208 pp.*
Davies, Martin. Prisoners of Society. *Attitudes and Aftercare. 204 pp.*
Gittus, Elizabeth. Flats, Families and the Under-Fives. *285 pp.*
Holman, Robert. Trading in Children. *A Study of Private Fostering. 355 pp.*
Jeffs, A. Young People and the Youth Service. *160 pp.*
Jones, Howard and **Cornes, Paul.** Open Prisons. *288 pp.*
Jones, Kathleen. History of the Mental Health Service. *428 pp.*

Jones, Kathleen with **Brown, John, Cunningham, W. J., Roberts, Julian** and **Williams, Peter.** Opening the Door. *A Study of New Policies for the Mentally Handicapped. 278 pp.*

Karn, Valerie. Retiring to the Seaside. *400 pp. 2 maps. Numerous tables.*

King, R. D. and **Elliot, K. W.** Albany: Birth of a Prison—End of an Era. *294 pp.*

Thomas, J. E. The English Prison Officer since 1850. *258 pp.*

Walton, R. G. Women in Social Work. *303 pp.*

● **Woodward, J.** To Do the Sick No Harm. *A Study of the British Voluntary Hospital System to 1875. 234 pp.*

International Library of Welfare and Philosophy

General Editors Noel Timms and David Watson

○ **Campbell, J.** The Left and Rights. *A Conceptual Analysis of the Idea of Socialist Rights. About 296 pp.*

● **McDermott, F. E.** (Ed.) Self-Determination in Social Work. *A Collection of Essays on Self-determination and Related Concepts by Philosophers and Social Work Theorists. Contributors: F. P. Biestek, S. Bernstein, A. Keith-Lucas, D. Sayer, H. H. Perelman, C. Whittington, R. F. Stalley, F. E. McDermott, I. Berlin, H. J. McCloskey, H. L. A. Hart, J. Wilson, A. I. Melden, S. I. Benn. 254 pp.*

● **Plant, Raymond.** Community and Ideology. *104 pp.*

● **Plant, Raymond, Lesser, Harry** and **Taylor-Gooby, Peter.** Political Philosophy and Social Welfare. *Essays on the Normative Basis of Welfare Provision. 276 pp.*

Ragg, N. M. People Not Cases. *A Philosophical Approach to Social Work. 168 pp.*

Timms, Noel (Ed.) Social Welfare. *Why and How? 316 pp. 7 figures.*

● **Timms, Noel** and **Watson, David** (Eds) Talking About Welfare. *Readings in Philosophy and Social Policy. Contributors: T. H. Marshall, R. B. Brandt, G. H. von Wright, K. Nielsen, M. Cranston, R. M. Titmuss, R. S. Downie, E. Telfer, D. Donnison, J. Benson, P. Leonard. A. Keith-Lucas, D. Walsh, I. T. Ramsey. 230 pp.*

● Philosophy in Social Work. *250 pp.*

● **Weale, A.** Equality and Social Policy. *164 pp.*

Library of Social Work

General Editor Noel Timms

● **Baldock, Peter.** Community Work and Social Work. *140 pp.*

○ **Beedell, Christopher.** Residential Life with Children. *210 pp. Crown 8vo.*

● **Berry, Juliet.** Daily Experience in Residential Life. *A Study of Children and their Care-givers. 202 pp.*

○ Social Work with Children. *190 pp. Crown 8vo.*

● **Brearley, C. Paul.** Residential Work with the Elderly. *116 pp.*

● Social Work, Ageing and Society. *126 pp.*

● **Cheetham, Juliet.** Social Work with Immigrants. *240 pp. Crown 8vo.*

● **Cross, Crispin P.** (Ed.) Interviewing and Communication in Social Work. *Contributions by C. P. Cross, D. Laurenson, B. Strutt, S. Raven. 192 pp. Crown 8vo.*

● **Curnock, Kathleen** and **Hardiker, Pauline.** Towards Practice Theory. *Skills and Methods in Social Assessments. 208 pp.*

● **Davies, Bernard.** The Use of Groups in Social Work Practice. *158 pp.*

Davies, Bleddyn and **Knapp, M.** Old People's Homes and the Production of Welfare. *264 pp.*

● **Davies, Martin.** Support Systems in Social Work. *144 pp.*

Ellis, June. (Ed.) West African Families in Britain. *A Meeting of Two Cultures. Contributions by Pat Stapleton, Vivien Biggs. 150 pp. 1 map.*

○ **Ford, J.** Human Behaviour. *Towards a Practical Understanding. About 160 pp.*

● **Hart, John.** Social Work and Sexual Conduct. *230 pp.*

Heraud, Brian. Training for Uncertainty. *A Sociological Approach to Social Work Education. 138 pp.*

Holder, D. and **Wardle, M.** Teamwork and the Development of a Unitary Approach. *212 pp.*

● **Hutten, Joan M.** Short-Term Contracts in Social Work. *Contributions by Stella M. Hall, Elsie Osborne, Mannie Sher, Eva Sternberg, Elizabeth Tuters. 134 pp.*

Jackson, Michael P. and **Valencia, B. Michael.** Financial Aid Through Social Work. *140 pp.*

● **Jones, Howard.** The Residential Community. *A Setting for Social Work. 150 pp.*

● (Ed.) Towards a New Social Work. *Contributions by Howard Jones, D. A. Fowler, J. R. Cypher, R. G. Walton, Geoffrey Mungham, Philip Priestley, Ian Shaw, M. Bartley, R. Deacon, Irwin Epstein, Geoffrey Pearson. 184 pp.*

Jones, Ray and **Pritchard, Colin.** (Eds) Social Work With Adolescents. *Contributions by Ray Jones, Colin Pritchard, Jack Dunham, Florence Rossetti, Andrew Kerslake, John Burns, William Gregory, Graham Templeman, Kenneth E. Reid, Audrey Taylor.*

○ **Jordon, William.** The Social Worker in Family Situations. *160 pp. Crown 8vo.*

● **Laycock, A. L.** Adolescents and Social Work. *128 pp. Crown 8vo.*

● **Lees, Ray.** Politics and Social Work. *128 pp. Crown 8vo.*

● Research Strategies for Social Welfare. *112 pp. Tables.*

○ **McCullough, M. K.** and **Ely, Peter J.** Social Work with Groups. *127 pp. Crown 8vo.*

● **Moffett, Jonathan.** Concepts in Casework Treatment. *128 pp. Crown 8vo.*

Parsloe, Phyllida. Juvenile Justice in Britain and the United States. *The Balance of Needs and Rights. 336 pp.*

● **Plant, Raymond.** Social and Moral Theory in Casework. *112 pp. Crown 8vo.*

Priestley, Philip, Fears, Denise and **Fuller, Roger.** Justice for Juveniles. *The 1969 Children and Young Persons Act: A Case for Reform? 128 pp.*

● **Pritchard, Colin** and **Taylor, Richard.** Social Work: Reform or Revolution? *170 pp.*

○ **Pugh, Elisabeth.** Social Work in Child Care. *128 pp. Crown 8vo.*

● **Robinson, Margaret.** Schools and Social Work. *282 pp.*

○ **Ruddock, Ralph.** Roles and Relationships. *128 pp. Crown 8vo.*

● **Sainsbury, Eric.** Social Diagnosis in Casework. *118 pp. Crown 8vo.*

● **Sainsbury, Eric, Phillips, David** and **Nixon, Stephen.** Social Work in Focus. *Clients' and Social Workers' Perceptions in Long-Term Social Work. 220 pp.*

● Social Work with Families. *Perceptions of Social Casework among Clients of a Family Service. 188pp.*

Seed, Philip. The Expansion of Social Work in Britain. *128 pp. Crown 8vo.*

● **Shaw, John.** The Self in Social Work. *124 pp.*

Smale, Gerald G. Prophecy, Behaviour and Change. *An Examination of Self-fulfilling Prophecies in Helping Relationships. 116 pp. Crown 8vo.*

Smith, Gilbert. Social Need. *Policy, Practice and Research. 155 pp.*

● Social Work and the Sociology of Organisations. *124 pp. Revised edition.*

● **Sutton, Carole.** Psychology for Social Workers and Counsellors. *An Introduction. 248 pp.*

● **Timms, Noel.** Language of Social Casework. *122 pp. Crown 8vo.*

● Recording in Social Work. *124 pp. Crown 8vo.*
● **Todd, F. Joan.** Social Work with the Mentally Subnormal. *96 pp. Crown 8vo.*
● **Walrond-Skinner, Sue.** Family Therapy. *The Treatment of Natural Systems. 172 pp.*
● **Warham, Joyce.** An Introduction to Administration for Social Workers. *Revised edition. 112 pp.*
● An Open Case. *The Organisational Context of Social Work. 172 pp.*
○ **Wittenberg, Isca Salzberger.** Psycho-Analytic Insight and Relationships. *A Kleinian Approach. 196 pp. Crown 8vo.*

Primary Socialization, Language and Education
General Editor Basil Bernstein

Adlam, Diana S., *with the assistance of Geoffrey Turner and Lesley Lineker.* Code in Context. *272 pp.*
Bernstein, Basil. Class, Codes and Control. *3 volumes.*
● 1. *Theoretical Studies Towards a Sociology of Language. 254 pp.*
2. *Applied Studies Towards a Sociology of Language. 377 pp.*
● 3. *Towards a Theory of Educational Transmission. 167 pp.*
Brandis, Walter and **Henderson, Dorothy.** Social Class, Language and Communication. *288 pp.*
Cook-Gumperz, Jenny. Social Control and Socialization. *A Study of Class Differences in the Language of Maternal Control. 290 pp.*
● **Gahagan, D. M.** and **G. A.** Talk Reform. *Exploration in Language for Infant School Children. 160 pp.*
Hawkins, P. R. Social Class, the Nominal Group and Verbal Strategies. *About 220 pp.*
Robinson, W. P. and **Rakstraw, Susan D. A.** A Question of Answers. *2 volumes. 192 pp. and 180 pp.*
Turner, Geoffrey J. and **Mohan, Bernard A.** A Linguistic Description and Computer Programme for Children's Speech. *208 pp.*

Reports of the Institute of Community Studies

Baker, J. The Neighbourhood Advice Centre. A Community Project in Camden. *320 pp.*
● **Cartwright, Ann.** Patients and their Doctors. *A Study of General Practice. 304 pp.*
Dench, Geoff. Maltese in London. *A Case-study in the Erosion of Ethnic Consciousness. 302 pp.*
Jackson, Brian and **Marsden, Dennis.** Education and the Working Class: *Some General Themes Raised by a Study of 88 Working-class Children in a Northern Industrial City. 268 pp. 2 folders.*
Madge, C. and **Willmott, P.** Inner City Poverty in Paris and London. *144 pp.*
Marris, Peter. The Experience of Higher Education. *232 pp. 27 tables.*
● Loss and Change. *192 pp.*
Marris, Peter and **Rein, Martin.** Dilemmas of Social Reform. *Poverty and Community Action in the United States. 256 pp.*
Marris, Peter and **Somerset, Anthony.** African Businessmen. *A Study of Entrepreneurship and Development in Kenya. 256 pp.*
Mills, Richard. Young Outsiders: *a Study in Alternative Communities. 216 pp.*
Runciman, W. G. Relative Deprivation and Social Justice. *A Study of Attitudes to Social Inequality in Twentieth-Century England. 352 pp.*

Willmott, Peter. Adolescent Boys in East London. *230 pp.*

Willmott, Peter and **Young, Michael.** Family and Class in a London Suburb. *202 pp. 47 tables.*

Young, Michael and **McGeeney, Patrick.** Learning Begins at Home. *A Study of a Junior School and its Parents. 128 pp.*

Young, Michael and **Willmott, Peter.** Family and Kinship in East London. *Foreword by Richard M. Titmuss. 252 pp. 39 tables.*

The Symmetrical Family. *410 pp.*

Reports of the Institute for Social Studies in Medical Care

Cartwright, Ann, Hockey, Lisbeth and **Anderson, John J.** Life Before Death. *310 pp.*

Dunnell, Karen and **Cartwright, Ann.** Medicine Takers, Prescribers and Hoarders. *190 pp.*

Farrell, C. My Mother Said. . . *A Study of the Way Young People Learned About Sex and Birth Control. 288 pp.*

Medicine, Illness and Society
General Editor W. M. Williams

Hall, David J. Social Relations & Innovation. *Changing the State of Play in Hospitals. 232 pp.*

Hall, David J. and **Stacey M.** (Eds) Beyond Separation. *234 pp.*

Robinson, David. The Process of Becoming Ill. *142 pp.*

Stacey, Margaret *et al.* Hospitals, Children and Their Families. *The Report of a Pilot Study. 202 pp.*

Stimson, G. V. and **Webb, B.** Going to See the Doctor. *The Consultation Process in General Practice. 155 pp.*

Monographs in Social Theory
General Editor Arthur Brittan

● **Barnes, B.** Scientific Knowledge and Sociological Theory. *192 pp.*

Bauman, Zygmunt. Culture as Praxis. *204 pp.*

● **Dixon, Keith.** Sociological Theory. *Pretence and Possibility. 142 pp.*

The Sociology of Belief. *Fallacy and Foundation. 144 pp.*

Goff, T. W. Marx and Mead. *Contributions to a Sociology of Knowledge. 176 pp.*

Meltzer, B. N., Petras, J. W. and **Reynolds, L. T.** Symbolic Interactionism. *Genesis, Varieties and Criticisms. 144 pp.*

● **Smith, Anthony D.** The Concept of Social Change. *A Critique of the Functionalist Theory of Social Change. 208 pp.*

● **Tudor, Andrew.** Beyond Empiricism. *Philosophy of Science in Sociology. 224 pp.*

Routledge Social Science Journals

The British Journal of Sociology. *Editor – Angus Stewart; Associate Editor – Leslie Sklair. Vol. 1, No. 1 – March 1950 and Quarterly. Roy. 8vo. All back issues available. An international journal publishing original papers in the field of sociology and related areas.*

Community Work. *Edited by David Jones and Majorie Mayo. 1973. Published annually.*

Economy and Society. *Vol. 1, No. 1. February 1972 and Quarterly. Metric Roy. 8vo. A journal for all social scientists covering sociology, philosophy, anthropology, economics and history. All back numbers available.*

Ethnic and Racial Studies. *Editor – John Stone. Vol. 1 – 1978. Published quarterly.*

Religion. Journal of Religion and Religions. *Chairman of Editorial Board, Ninian Smart. Vol. 1, No. 1, Spring 1971. A journal with an inter-disciplinary approach to the study of the phenomena of religion. All back numbers available.*

Sociological Review. *Chairman of Editorial Board, S. J. Eggleston. New Series. August 1982, Vol. 30, No. 1. Published quarterly.*

Sociology of Health and Illness. *A Journal of Medical Sociology. Editor – Alan Davies; Associate Editor – Ray Jobling. Vol. 1, Spring 1979. Published 3 times per annum.*

Year Book of Social Policy in Britain. *Edited by Kathleen Jones. 1971. Published annually.*

Social and Psychological Aspects of Medical Practice

Editor Trevor Silverstone

Lader, Malcolm. Psychophysiology of Mental Illness. *280 pp.*

● **Silverstone, Trevor** and **Turner, Paul.** Drug Treatment in Psychiatry. *Third edition. 256 pp.*

Whiteley, J. S. and **Gordon, J.** Group Approaches in Psychiatry. *240 pp.*